The Representation of Place

Historical Urban Studies

Series editors: *Jean-Luc Pinol* and *Richard Rodger*

Titles in the series include:

Printed Matters: Printing, Publishing and Urban Culture in Europe in the Modern Period
Malcolm Gee and Tom Kirk (eds)

Identities in Space: Contested Terrains in the Western City since 1850
Simon Gunn and Robert J. Morris (eds)

Body and City: Histories of Urban Public Health
Sally Sheard and Helen Power (eds)

Urban Fortunes: Property and Inheritance in the Town, 1700–1900
Jon Stobart and Alastair Owens (eds)

Advertising and the European City: Historical Perspectives
Clemens Wischermann and Elliott Shore (eds)

Urban Governance: Britain and Beyond since 1750
Robert J. Morris and Richard H. Trainor (eds)

The Artisan and the European Town, 1500–1900
Geoffrey Crossick (ed.)

Cathedrals of Urban Modernity: The First Museums of Contemporary Art, 1800–1930
J. Pedro Lorente

Capital Cities and their Hinterlands in Early Modern Europe
Peter Clark and Bernard Lepetit (eds)

The Representation of Place

Urban planning and protest in France and Great Britain, 1950–1980

Michael James Miller

With a foreword by José-Maria Ballester, Director of Culture and Cultural and Natural Heritage, Council of Europe

ASHGATE

Published by
Ashgate Publishing Limited
Gower House
Croft Road
Aldershot
Hants GU11 3HR
England

Ashgate Publishing Company
Suite 420
101 Cherry Street
Burlington, VT 05401-4405
USA

Ashgate website: http://www.ashgate.com

British Library Cataloguing in Publication Data
Miller, Michael James
The representation of place : urban planning and protest in France and Great Britain, 1950-1980. - (Historical urban studies)
1. City planning - Great Britain - History - 20th century 2. City planning - France - History - 20th century 3. City planning - Citizen participation 4. Social movements - Great Britain - History - 20th century 5. Social movements - France - History - 20th century
I. Title
307.1'16'0941'09045

Library of Congress Cataloging-in-Publication Data
Miller, Michael, 1967-
The representation of place : urban planning and protest in France and Great Britain, 1950-1980 / Michael Miller.
p. cm. -- (Historical urban studies series)
Includes bibliographical references (p.).
ISBN 0-7546-0653-8
1. Urban renewal--France--Roubaix--Citizen participation--Case studies. 2. Spatial behavior-- France--Roubaix--Case studies. 3. Protest movements--France--Roubaix--History--20th century. 4. Urban renewal--Scotland--Glasgow--Citizen participation--Case studies. 5. Spatial behavior--Scotland--Glasgow--Case studies. 6. Protest movements--Scotland--Glasgow--History--20th century. I. Title. II. Historical urban studies.

HT178.F7 R685 2002
307.3'416'09414409045--dc21

2002016496

ISBN 0 7546 0653 8

Printed and bound in Great Britain by MPG Books Ltd, Bodmin, Cornwall

Contents

General Editors' Preface

Density and proximity of buildings and people are two of the defining characteristics of the urban dimension. It is these which identify a place as uniquely urban, though the threshold for such pressure points varies from place to place. What is considered an important cluster in one context – a few hundred inhabitants or buildings on the margins of Europe – may not be considered as urban elsewhere. A third defining characteristic is functionality – the commercial or strategic position of a town or city which conveys an advantage. Over time, these functional advantages may diminish, or the balance of advantage may change within a hierarchy of towns. To understand how the relative importance of towns shifts over time and space is to grasp a set of relationships which is fundamental to the study of urban history.

Towns and cities are products of history, yet have themselves helped to shape history. As the proportion of urban dwellers has increased, so the urban dimension has proved a legitimate unit of analysis through which to understand the spectrum of human experience and to explore the cumulative memory of past generations. Though obscured by layers of economic, social and political change, the study of the urban milieu provides insights into the functioning of human relationships and, if urban historians themselves are not directly concerned with current policy studies, few contemporary concerns can be understood without reference to the historical development of towns and cities.

This longer historical perspective is essential to an understanding of social processes. Crime, housing conditions and property values, health and education, discrimination and deviance, and the formulation of regulations and social policies to deal with them were, and remain, amongst the perennial preoccupations of towns and cities – no historical period has a monopoly of these concerns, They recur in successive generations, albeit in varying mixtures and strengths; the details may differ but the central forces of class, power and authority in the city remain. If this was the case for different periods, so it was for different geographical entities and cultures. Both scientific knowledge and technical information were available across Europe and showed little respect for frontiers. Yet despite common concerns and access to broadly similar knowledge, different solutions to urban problems were proposed and adopted by towns and cities in different parts of Europe. This comparative dimension informs urban historians as to which were systematic factors and which were of a purely local nature: general and particular forces can be distinguished.

These analytical frameworks, considered in a comparative context, inform the books in this series.

Jean-Luc Pinol, *Universitié de Tours*
Richard Rodger, *University of Leicester*
2003

List of Figures

List of Tables

List of Abbreviations

Alma-Gare case study

ADN	*Archives Départementales du Nord*
AGIR	*Association de Gestion, d'Information et de Recherche*
AIR	*Association Inter-quartiers de Roubaix*
ANE	*Archives de Nord Éclair*
APF	*Association Populaire Familiale*
APU	*Atelier Populaire de l'Urbanisme*
ARC	*Association pour la Résorption des Courées*
CFDT	*Confédération Française Démocratique du Travail*
CFTC	*Confédération Française des Travailleurs Chrétiens*
CGT	*Confédération Général du Travail*
CGTU	*Confédération Général du Travail Unitaire*
CIAM	*Congrès Internationaux d'Architecture Moderne*
CIL	*Comité Interprofessionnel du Logement*
COS	*coefficient d'occupation des sols*
CSCV	*Confédération Syndicale du Cadre de Vie*
CUDL	*Communauté Urbaine de Lille*
EOPAG	*Equipe Opérationnelle Permanente pour Alma-Gare*
HBM	*habitations à bon marché*
HLM	*habitations à loyer modéré*
MRP	*Mouvement Républicain Populaire*
MRU	*Ministère de la Reconstrucion et de l'Urbanisme*
OPAH	*opération programmée d'amélioration de l'habitat*
ORSUCOMN	*Organisme Régional pour la Suppression des Courées de la Métropole Nord*
PACT	*Propagande et Action Contre les Taudis*
POS	*plan d'occupation des sols*
PRI	*programmes de relogement de l'habitat insalubre*
PSU	*Parti Socialiste Unifé*
RHI	*résorption de l'habitat insalubre*
RPF	*Rassemblement du Peuple Français*
RU	*rénovation urbaine*
SACOMUL	*Société d'Aménagement de la Communauté Urbaine de Lille*

SAEN	*Société d'Aménagement et d'Equipement du Nord*
SAR	*Société d'Aménagement de Roubaix*
SARR	*Société d'Aménagement de la Région de Roubaix*
SART	*Société d'Aménagement de la Région de Roubaix-Tourcoing*
SDAU	*schéma directeur d'aménagement et d'urbanisme*
SEM	*société économie mixte*
SPT	*Syndicat Patronal du Textile*
UNR	*Union pour la Nouvelle République*
ZAC	*zone d'aménagement concerté*
ZUP	*zone á urbaniser par priorité*

Gorbals Case Study

CCG	Corporation of the City of Glasgow
CDA	Comprehensive Development Area
GDC	Glasgow District Council
GEAR	Glasgow Eastern Area Redevelopment
GI	Gorbals Initiative
HTA	Hutchesontown Tenants' Association
LTA	Lauriston Tenants' Association
ML	Mitchell Library (Glasgow)
NBA	National Building Agency
SSHA	Scottish Special Housing Association

Foreword

José-Maria Ballester
Director of Culture and Cultural and Natural Heritage, Council of Europe

The city is perhaps one of Europe's most complex cultural artefacts, and consequently one in which the Council of Europe's Cultural and Natural Heritage Department has a particular interest. Through the Technical Co-operation and Consultancy Programme this Department provides expertise and support to ensure the sensitive and sustainable development of historic towns and cities throughout Europe. In this we have always sought integrated and comprehensive solutions that go beyond the mere protection of historic areas to address the urban environment as a whole and to promote the social inclusion that is the right of every citizen. This philosophy has increasingly led our experts to take the architectural and historical value of the urban environment as a starting point for addressing a wide range of issues that concern the social and economic infrastructure of cities: social facilities, infrastructure, environment, economic development, transport networks, tourism and so on.

It is essential that the dynamics generated in this process are not to the detriment of the most disadvantaged citizens. And nowhere is this more appropriate than in the field of housing provision. Historic neighbourhoods emptied of their inhabitants are also emptied of their meaning and become little more than showcases for restoration techniques.

One of the best examples of the sustainable approach to regeneration acknowledged by the Council was initiated in Lisbon in the early 1990s. Following technical cooperation with the city, the Council of Europe implemented the 'Lisbon Debate on the rehabilitation of housing in ancient centres as a factor of economic development and social cohesion'. This forum for innovative methods considers how the living conditions of the citizens of these areas can be improved without altering the social structure of their neighbourhoods.

The aim of the Debate is easily stated, but the elements that inform it are complex, and none more so than the cultural processes involved. For this reason, I welcome the publication of *The Representation of Place*. As this book makes clear, our cities are also made up of a myriad memories, identities and histories and, as a consequence, socioeconomic data, as essential as they are, only paint a partial picture. It is absolutely essential to reach an understanding of this cultural dimension of 'place' if we are to derive a comprehensive vision of our cities and understand how they are experienced by their inhabitants.

The Representation of Place does not pretend to be a manual for those working in the field of urban regeneration. It does, however, offer a valuable introduction to one of the most elusive aspects of the city. It draws attention to the importance of interpreting the cultural fabric that binds communities and offers informative case studies for anyone wishing to unravel the complexities of the neighbourhoods that make up our cities. It illustrates that if a development is not in keeping with local expectations, or with the memories invested in that area, then it is unlikely to find cultural resonance amongst the inhabitants and thus risks becoming yet another well-intentioned but ill-fated project. It also highlights the massive potential of locally organized groups to draw upon locally rooted beliefs and to express their views of the past, present and future with passion, eloquence, determination and energy. By tapping into this energy and promoting regenerating strategies that are sympathetic to 'places' as they are understood by their inhabitants, we take an important step towards achieving our ultimate goal of social inclusion in Europe's cities and towns.

Strasbourg, France

Acknowledgements

I would like to express my thanks to René Leboutte for his advice and support, and to Bo Stråth for his enthusiasm, vision and constructive criticism. I am also extremely grateful to all those who took the time to read my work and offer valuable comments including Michael Keating, Doreen Massey, Richard Rodger, Stefaan De Rynck and Christian Topalov. I am particularly indebted to the late Bernard Lepetit, whose ideas provided the foundation for this work.

In the course of this research, I plied many libraries and archives. I am especially grateful to the staff of the Mitchell Library in Glasgow and to the staff of the *biblioteca* at the European University Institute in Florence.

This book would not have been possible without the support of the *Association Inter-Quartiers* in Roubaix and, in particular, of Roger Leman, who allowed me access to his private collection of material from the days of the *Atelier Populaire d'Urbanisme*.

Finally, thanks to the Department of Culture and Cultural and Natural Heritage at the Council of Europe for taking an interest in this publication.

Michael James Miller
Florence

History is not then
The devastating bulldozer that they say.
It leaves underground passageways, crypts, holes
and hiding places. There are those who survive.

Eugenio Montale,
From 'La storia', *Satura*.

Frontispiece A bulldozer clearing *courées* in Roubaix
Reproduced from back cover of 'Trois autres quartiers changent de visage', Roubaix, *Périodique d'information municipale* (August 1974).

CHAPTER ONE

Introduction

Context and aims

In Marco Ferreri's film of 1974, *Non toccare la donna bianca*,[1] an arrogant and vainglorious General George Custer, played by Marcello Mastroianni, trots the United States 7th Cavalry into oblivion at the hands of the united Indian nations led by Sitting Bull, at the Battle of Little Big Horn. What is noteworthy about Ferreri's film, in the context of this book, is that the action does not take place in the wilderness of Montana in 1876, but in 1970s Paris. And not even Paris, Texas. This is most definitely Paris, France, and it is most definitely Parisians who look on curiously as Mastroianni, in full period cavalry uniform, petulantly stamps his foot, only to bring his perfectly polished riding boot down on that notorious canine adornment of Parisian pavements.

Most of Ferreri's film was shot in and around les Halles, which at that time was a huge gap site in the centre of the city. In the early 1970s, after a highly contentious planning battle, the old central market at les Halles was razed to the ground to be replaced by the subterranean shopping centre and labyrinthine *métro*/RER station we know today. The film's metaphor is clear: the government wants the land for the railroad, and the displaced Indian tribes, consisting of long-haired young men and women, are herded off to the reservations – no doubt located in Paris's peripheral *grands ensembles*. Yet these tribes wish to go 'home' to their old lands, and it is precisely to prevent this reappropriation of the centre that Custer's cavalry is dispatched.[2] Meanwhile the shaman counsels the tribes that their one hope of defeating the might of the US army is to abandon the arrogance of the individual warrior and the divisiveness of tribal

---

[1] *Non toccare la donna bianca/Touche pas la femme blanche*, (released in English as *Don't Touch the White Woman!*) directed by Marco Ferreri, with Catherine Deneuve, Marcello Mastroianni, Michel Piccoli, Ugo Tognazzi and Philippe Noiret. 102 mins, colour, Italy/France, 1974.

[2] The scenario is not historically accurate. The catalyst for Custer's Last Stand was the presence of gold and other minerals in the Black Hills, which lay within the reservation area granted to the Sioux and Cheyenne by the US government. Finding their land invaded by prospectors, these tribes moved off the reservation in the winter of 1875–76 to return to their traditional hunting grounds in Montana and the Dakotas. The 7th Cavalry was dispatched to ensure that they returned to the reservation.

loyalties. It is only by presenting a united front that they can hope to achieve victory. And this is precisely what they do, in a hail of arrows and spears, as bulldozers continue their clearance, and cranes glitter on the skyline.

Ferreri's satirical reinterpretation of the Battle of Little Big Horn is thinly disguised Marxist urban sociology (or a satirical reinterpretation of Marxist sociology, perhaps). From the late 1960s until at least the mid-1970s, many European cities witnessed a resurgence in territorially-based protest activities. This, in turn, stimulated research into the phenomenon and provided an important impetus for the renaissance of urban sociology in the 1970s. But while Ferreri's film represents the spatialization of the class struggle – and the transplanting of the Battle of Little Big Horn to the centre of Paris seems to confirm the applicability of this model across both time and space – it is impossible to ignore the specificity of the setting. Indeed, it is the juxtaposition of 1870s Mid-West and 1970s Paris that highlights the specificity of these places. Paris contains its own histories, associations and myths, with the result that Ferreri's decision to set his film in the French capital taps into themes such as the Paris *Commune* (almost contemporary with Custer's Last Stand), and the Spring of 1968; with the difference that under Ferreri's paving stones – *sous les pavées* – lay the prairie, not *la plage*. The Parisian 'Indians' wanted to return to a place that was 'theirs' just as, 100 years before, the Sioux and Cheyenne, having seen their sacred Black Hills invaded by prospectors, had chosen to return to their traditional hunting grounds outside the reservations.

As these examples suggest, and as this book will seek to show, we cannot escape the power of these specific sociocultural products called 'places', for they exert a strong influence on how we conceive of ourselves and our world. And yet, until recently, the concept of place as a theme of academic investigation in general, and as a means of examining conflictual processes in the city in particular, has been largely overlooked. Instead, research into urban protest has been driven by themes that were put into play in the early 1970s as a result of the paradigm established by Marxist structuralist sociology. A key work in this context was Henri Lefebvre's *La Production de l'Espace* of 1974.[3] In Lefebvrian terms, Marco Ferreri was depicting the production of space by a privileged centre of capitalist wealth and power (the railroad interests supported by the US government) which 'endeavours to mould the spaces it dominates (i.e. peripheral spaces), and ... seeks, often by violent means, to reduce the obstacles and resistance it encounters here'.[4] In *Non toccare la donna bianca*, we are shown a rare example of successful resistance to this capitalist space, yet we have the benefit of historical knowledge and we know

[3] This only appeared in English translation seven years later, under the title *The Production of Space* (Oxford: Blackwell, 1991). See also H. Lefebvre, *La Révolution Urbaine* (Paris: Gallimard, 1970).

[4] Lefebvre, *The Production of Space*, p. 49.

that the resistance of the American Indians at Little Big Horn is an exceptional moment, for they are destined to be swept away.

One of the most significant aspects of the work of Lefebvre and of others, such as David Harvey,[5] is the importance they have assigned to space.[6] Space, in their sense, is not a static grid upon which society is constructed. From Lefebvre's perspective, capitalism produces abstract space – that is, space that is both a product and, simultaneously, a means of production. In this sense, space cannot be separated from other productive sources, from the social division of labour that shapes it, or from the state and the superstructures of society.[7] It was this insight into spatial theory that paved the way for the emergence of the urban social movement as a key concept for understanding the resurgence and dynamics of protest activity in the city.

Manuel Castells made a key contribution to the idea of the urban social movement in his book entitled *Luttes Urbaines* from 1975. In this work, Castells argued that a new form of urban politics was emerging, based on territorial interests and provoked by changing conditions of collective consumption. In short, stakes such as the provision of housing and amenities were seen to provoke popular opposition to the policies of the state or, indeed, to broader economic restructuring promoted by governments in the interests of capital. Castells' work, with its rather rigid emphasis on structural relationships, was to prove highly influential, and provided a cornerstone for the influential school of neo-Marxist thought on urban protest.[8] Then in 1983, Castells published *The City and the Grassroots – A Cross-Cultural Theory of Urban Social Movements*. In this work, which aimed at locating the urban-based protest movements in a historical context, Castells presented collective

---

[5] Harvey's early work, including *Social Justice and the City* (London: Edward Arnold, 1973).

[6] To different degrees – Lefebvre was criticized both by Castells in *The Urban Question* (London: Edward Arnold, 1977) and by Harvey in *Social Justice and the City* for assigning urban space too central a position in his early work.

[7] Lefebvre, *The Production of Space*, p. 85.

[8] See, for example, D. Mehl, 'Les luttes des résidents dans les grands ensembles', *Sociologie du Travail*, no. 3 (1975); Lojkine, 'Stratégies des grandes entreprises, politiques urbaines et mouvements sociaux urbains', *Sociologie du Travail*, no. 1 (1975); and the special issue of *Autrement* from September 1976, featuring contributions from: E. Cherki and D. Mehl, 'Les luttes urbaines, facteurs de changement?'; *idem*, 'Quelles luttes? quels acteurs? quels résultats?'; G. Lamarche-Vadel and A. Cotlenko, 'Alma-Gare – le singulier et le politique'; M. Marcelloni, 'L'Italie: un modèle?'; J. Granlo Pires, 'A Lisbonne: "Casa sim, barracas nao!"'; C. Pierre, 'Intégrer ces luttes dans le combat politique'; L. Caul-Futy, 'L'efficacité d'un syndicalisme du cadre de vie'; R. de Caumont, 'Les GAM: une stratégie, des techniques pour changer le quotidien'; N. Duc Nhuân, 'Pièges et ambiguïtés de l'action militante'; and M. Castells, 'Mouvements urbains et voie démocratique vers le socialisme', *Autrement*, no. 6 (September 1976).

consumption as a source of inequalities distinct from those of the workplace, and emphasized the plurality of the class composition of these initiatives. The 'urban social movements' identified by Castells seemingly offered a new form of political expression in what left-wing thinkers and political activists were coming to regard as increasingly moribund national political systems, and where neo-liberal policies were beginning to erode the power of the trade unions, as in the United Kingdom and the United States. Despite the general enthusiasm with which the concept of the 'urban social movement' was picked up, both in academia and beyond, and although many of the movements identified had a clear geographical locus, little attention was paid to the influence of place on their form and direction. At best, researchers gave a passing nod to the structure of local politics, but place was generally regarded as little more than a container for sociopolitical processes.[9] The lack of attention accorded to the concept of place was largely due to the theoretical origins of the 'urban social movement'.[10] According to Marxist theorists, 'place' was a reactionary concept, since it seemed to play little or no part in the modernist

[9] The 'urban social movement' was to have an enduring influence in the field of political science, where it became increasingly elaborated and refined by 'radical' and 'liberal' scholars alike: see, for example, P. Dunleavy, *Urban Political Analysis* (London: Macmillan Press, 1980); S.S. Fainstein and N.I. Fainstein, 'Economic Restructuring and the Rise of Urban Social Movements', *Urban Affairs Quarterly*, 21:2 (1985); and C.M. Reintges, 'Urban Movements in South African Black Townships: A Case Study', *International Journal of Urban and Regional Research*, 14:1 (1990). By the 1980s, according to Pickvance, there was a feeling that urban social movements were in decline: see C. Pickvance, 'The Rise and Fall of Urban Movements and the Role of Comparative Analysis', *Environment and Planning D: Society and Space*, 3 (1985), p. 33. Mullins also pointed to their decline in both number and significance, while asserting that they remain an integral part of urban development: Mullins, 'Community and Urban Movements', *Sociological Review*, 35:2 (1987), p. 347. In 1987, Richard Harris argued that, 'In today's world there are no 'urban social movements', only social movements which have found their clearest expression in urban politics': R. Harris, 'The Social Movement in Urban Politics: A Reinterpretation of Urban Reform in Canada', *International Journal of Urban and Regional Research*, 11:3 (1987), p. 377. More recently, from a political science perspective, the theme has been incorporated into the broader concept of social movements, including the anti-nuclear movement, environmental movement, peace movement and, most recently, the alliance of interests formed around the opposition to GATT that exploded on the streets of Seattle in November 1999 and that has come to be associated with the anti-globalization movement.

[10] In the field in geography, the apparently paradoxical reluctance of geographers to consider the issue of place also stemmed from their struggle in the late 1960s to establish geography as a scientific discipline. To achieve this, they purged geography of its idiographic tradition, turning their backs on the exceptional and the local, and embracing universal laws which located causality at an abstract, global level.

ideal of progress and history.[11] This has proved to be a resilient point of view, and Harvey continues to argue that places are being 'eroded' by the impact of capitalist development: 'The viability of actual places has been powerfully threatened through changing material practices of production, consumption, information flow and communication, coupled with the radical reorganization of space relations and of time horizons within capitalist development.'[12] The result, from Harvey's perspective, is that locally-based challenges to rapidly globalizing economic systems have little hope of establishing an alternative conception of time and space to that produced by capitalism.[13] Even in its more post-structural manifestations, such as Soja's *Postmodern Geographies*, spatial theory has tended to revert to relations of production as the core of relations of power.[14]

All the same, by the late 1980s 'place' was creeping back onto the agenda, and it has now become established as an important concept in social theory. We do not need to look far for the reasons for this resurgence of interest. If we pick up any newspaper we are confronted by a catalogue of place-based issues, ranging from the local to the global. In particular, the collapse of the Soviet Union initiated a process of fragmentation throughout Central and Eastern Europe and Central Asia, as groups that felt united by common national identities strove to give physical form to their nationalist aspirations, while those who did not belong all too often became the victims of what has been dubbed 'ethnic cleansing'. At the same time, in Central and Western Europe, the European Union, regarded by some as a dire threat to national sovereignty, has been busy creating a new place-based identity: the European citizen is born to the strains of Beethoven's *Ninth*. But, paradoxically, a unified Europe

[11] John Agnew has pointed to the inherent contradiction in the rejection of 'place' in Marxist, structuralist thought. 'At the "deepest" level, so to speak, the intellectual devaluation of place in Marxist political economy is a product of an analysis that *accepts*, indeed welcomes, the logic of liberal capitalism and its associated features of individual atomism and commodification of people and places': J.A. Agnew, 'The Devaluation of Place in Social Science', in J.A. Agnew and J.S. Duncan (eds), *The Power of Place: Bringing Together Geographical and Sociological Imaginations* (Boston: Unwin Hyman), p. 22.

[12] D. Harvey, 'From Space to Place and Back Again: Reflections on the Condition of Postmodernity', in J. Bird et al. (eds), *Mapping the Futures: Local Cultures, Global Changes* (London and New York: Routledge, 1993), p. 25.

[13] Ibid.

[14] Soja argues for the revalorization of space, for a materialist interpretation of geography intertwined with a materialist interpretation of history, in such a way that neither one takes precedence over the other. The result is a spatio-temporal structuring of social life, making concrete social action and social relations, including class relations. Soja attempts to set up a dialectic whereby space is both that which is produced by, and that which produces, social life. See E. Soja, *Postmodern Geographies: The Reassertion of Space in Critical Social Theory* (London: Verso, 1989).

does not automatically mean uniformity, and many euros' worth of funding go to encourage regional developments, community initiatives and cultural programmes. Meanwhile, on a local level, newspapers inform us that 'places' are constantly under threat – from planners and architects, from insensitive developers, from 'foreigners' or, quite simply, from 'modern life'. Indeed, Agnew argues that capitalism (and the resistance to it) creates a new pressure for place to provide a structuring role.[15] Perhaps there has also been, as Cosgrove suggests, a 'need' to rediscover a human dimension in the science of space: 'Place as an organising concept owes its popularity in contemporary human geography to its incorporation of human meaning into otherwise abstract and mathematical spatial concepts.'[16]

The concept of 'place', as this book will show, lends itself to new modes of thought that encourage a multiplicity of views based on gender, race, ethnicity, class, culture and other categories by which people identify themselves and are identified,[17] and on which society is organized.[18] Indeed, the re-evaluation of 'place' has also been promoted by a parallel growth of interest in 'identity' as a key concept in the social sciences. In the post-1989 context in particular, national and regional identities have come to receive considerable attention, as has, from a historical perspective, the process of nation-building in the nineteenth century.[19] Of course, this is scarcely surprising, since many of these

---

[15] Agnew, borrowing heavily from Giddens, argues that labour power is a distinct form of commodity because it resists being treated as other commodities for the reason that it has certain requirements which tie it to a particular locale. Labour therefore cannot be globalized in the sense of the commodities it produces and 'class relations are thus structured through the *place-based* exigencies of commodification *and* resistance': Agnew, 'The Devaluation of Space in Social Science', p. 23.

[16] Cosgrove, 'Power and Place in the Venetian Territories' in Agnew and Duncan, *The Power of Place*, p. 104.

[17] With specific reference to the city, a good example of this approach is found in R. Fincher and J.M. Jacobs (eds), *Cities of Difference* (New York and London: The Guifford Press, 1998).

[18] Significantly, an important contribution to the 'rediscovery' of place has come from gender theory. In particular, feminist theorists have attacked traditional views which associate 'place' with 'home', and so with ideas of rest, seclusion and peace, while in fact, for many women, 'home' is neither restful nor peaceful. Related to the 'place–home' perspective is the romantic image of place as that which does not change, cherished by all those who leave. But this view of the unchanging place of origin implies the ability to leave in the first instance, a privilege which has been traditionally masculine (historians of migration would rightly dispute this point, but certainly to *choose* to leave or to *choose* to return implies a degree of power which is often denied to women). Looking still deeper into the idea of place, gender theorists have argued that place as home and place as origin are in fact characterizations of 'mother' or 'woman', the constant reference at the centre of life.

[19] For a discussion of the rise of identity as an academic concept, see B. Stråth, 'Introduction. Myth, Memory and History in the Construction of Community' in *idem*

identity claims are partially informed by particular constructions of place, be it the 'homeland', the symbolic cultural landscape, the capital city, the frontier, the home or some other place-derived metonym for national or regional communities.

It is this new interest in 'place' that provides the inspiration for, and forms the basis of, this book. In the pages that follow, I will seek to build upon the idea of place and place-based identities and to elaborate their temporal dimension and historical roots – that is, to examine how 'places' are constructed as, simultaneously, past, present and future. This framework is then employed in order to consider examples of public protest against urban planning projects from a historical perspective (without reifying these examples, *a priori*, as urban social movements).[20] The two cases examined in detail here are both examples of place-based protest dating from the 1970s – one in northern France and the other in Scotland. Through these studies I will explore how local groups construct their own identity and, in turn, attempt to have this identity recognized and accepted by other actors. In other words, this book looks at how place and place-based identities are employed by various groups at a local (rather than a national) level. In this way, the analysis of political structures, actors and interests that form the basis of political science thought is not ignored, but is, rather, enriched by concepts such as myths, memories and the construction of community. Of course, this approach also inevitably raises questions over the nature of the interaction of local and global forces. Here I would argue that it is only from a historical point of view that these themes can be satisfactorily understood, for without such a perspective we find ourselves 'inside' the constructions we seek to examine. In the two cases analysed in this book, the specific historical context is the crisis of the modernist paradigm in urban planning in Western Europe in the 1970s.

The approach adopted here also offers a means to 'listen' to the polyphonic voices of the city and so escape the tyranny of dominant discourses promoted by elite groups in the urban realm. A key element here is the examination of the relationship between places and words, for it is in the naming and categorizing of places that they are granted or denied existence. In particular, this book examines how identities founded upon the idea of 'slum' were challenged, either by the discovery of 'community', or by the charging of a particular word – in this case the French term '*quartier*' (neighbourhood) with new meaning.

(ed.), *Myth, Memory and History in the Construction of Community* (Brussels: PIE-Peter Lang, 2000), pp. 20–4. For a critical view of the development of 'the feeling of identity', see L. Niethammer, 'Maurice Halbwachs: Memory and the Feeling of Identity', in ibid., pp. 75–93.

[20] I use the term 'urban planning' as a generic term. The thesis considers France and Great Britain, and both these countries have their specific terminology – respectively '*urbanisme*' and 'town planning'.

This brings me to a final point concerning the broad aims of this book: the project of investigating and setting down these case studies is, in and of itself, justification enough for this research, for each not only offers a fascinating insight into the way groups interact, negotiate and compete in issues around urban planning in general and housing provision in particular, but also provides an enticing subject for historical curiosity. In short, they both tell good stories about human determination and commitment.

To sum up, and to return to the example of Marco Ferreri's film, the aim of this book is not to consider urban conflicts in terms of militant resistance to the production of capitalist space, as the United Indian Nations sought to resist the progress of the railroad. Rather, it is to consider how the various groups involved – the native Americans, Mastroianni's cavalry, the railroad company and the US government – conceived of the place over which they were fighting, and how these different conceptions informed their self-perception, their convictions, their actions and their visions of the future.

The opacity of place[21]

The idea of 'place' is pervasive.[22] In *The Oxford English Dictionary*, the entry for 'place' (and this is only the noun) occupies more than three and a half pages, bearing testimony to its many uses in the English language.[23] The word's origins lie in the Greek *platea*, meaning broad way, which was later incorporated into Latin where its meaning expanded to refer also to an open space. Under one of its general definitions in the dictionary, that of 'a material

---

[21] Thanks to Doreen Massey of the Open University for valuable comments on earlier drafts of this section.

[22] The discussion of 'place' in this section consciously echoes both Mary Douglas's ideas on institutions in *How Institutions Think* (Syracuse: Syracuse University Press, 1986), and Michel Foucault's ideas on 'discourse'. For Foucault, discourses were underpinned by power and desire. Discourse provides the means to put knowledge to work in society, controlling its valorization, distribution and attribution. Foucault argued, for example, that it was because Mendel did not obey the rules of the dominant discourse that biologists of the nineteenth century failed to see that what he was saying was 'true'. 'Mendel disait vrai, mais il n'était pas "dans le vrai" du discours biologique de son époque': Foucault, *L'ordre du discours* (Paris: Editions Gallimard, 1971), pp. 36–7. Such systems of exclusion, Foucault argued, were founded upon institutional support, which was simultaneously renewed and reinforced by a 'thickness' of practices such as teaching and the production of books (ibid., p. 19). He also argued that there are certain procedures which enable the control of discourses. The first is to master the powers which the discourse contains, the second is to control the emergence of the discourse, and the third is to impose a certain number of rules upon those who carry the discourse, restricting it to 'initiates'.

[23] *The Oxford English Dictionary*, pp. 937–41.

space', we read that place may be 'a particular part of space, of defined or undefined extent, but of definite situation'. It is also 'the portion of space actually occupied by a person or thing; the position of a body in space, or with reference to other bodies; locality; situation'. In addition, it is 'a portion of space in which people dwell together; a general designation for a city, town, village, hamlet, etc'. Pushing on through the definitions, it becomes apparent that place need not have a physical identity. It can simply be a 'position or situation with reference to its occupation or occupant', and thus 'a proper, appropriate, or natural place (for the person or thing in question to be in or occupy); sometimes in an ideal or imaginary region'. The key element in these definitions seems to be that place possesses a characteristic that identifies it in undifferentiated space and, moreover, that it somehow falls naturally into the order of things, in the sense of 'a place for everything and everything in its place'. But these definitions, which inform our common-sense view of place, beg certain important questions. Where does the idea of place as 'natural' come from? Who decides on the appropriate 'place for everything'? And how and why should a particular spatial area receive the designation of 'place' as if it demonstrates some inherent characteristic of 'placeness'?

If place is considered to be a distinct part of space, this implies an act of distinguishing. To distinguish is to see and identify something as different, and seeing and identifying are social constructions. As Cosgrove has pointed out with respect to landscape, it '... is not merely the world we see, it is a construction, a composition of that world. Landscape is a way of seeing the world'.[24] Potential places in undifferentiated space only become 'real' places when they are identified as such. Can we, for example, meaningfully talk about places on a distant star until that star enters our field of knowledge, either through astronomical observation or scientific exploration? The sociocultural dimension of place becomes even clearer when one considers places that have no physical form – those that are imagined or designed and those that exist in computer programs, religious visions or dreams. In these cases it is even harder to assert that the social meaning of places is natural and, thus, uncontentious.[25]

The position adopted in this book is that it is social actors who enjoy hegemony in the exercise of power relations who are best positioned to ascribe to, promote and maintain their construction of place, and, from there, to present

---

[24] D.E. Cosgrove, *Social Formations and Symbolic Landscapes* (London: Croom Helm, 1984), p. 13.

[25] Moreover, Massey has pointed out the cultural specificity of our idea of place, juxtaposing our perception of place as bounded and distinct with that of nomadic tribes or Australian Aborigines who do not make these bounded divisions: D. Massey, 'The Conceptualization of Place', in D. Massey and P. Jess (eds), *A Place in the World? Places, Culture and Globalisation* (Oxford: The Open University and Oxford University Press, 1995), p. 51.

it as 'common sense'.[26] As Harvey argues, if place is a social construction, 'there is, then, a politics to place construction ranging dialectically across material, representational and symbolic activities which find their hallmark in the way in which individuals invest in places and thereby empower themselves collectively by virtue of that investment.'[27] In appearing to be one thing or another, a place obscures the elements of its construction and, shaping our thoughts through this construction, represses or marginalizes any attempts to have it portrayed as another. Place, in this sense, is an opaque construction that squeezes ideas into a common shape founded upon a seemingly essential rightness that is inherent in its nature. More than this, these constructions must, in order to be successful, assign a 'sameness' to the elements that form a particular place, suppressing any variation that does not correspond to the identity it has assumed. Alan Mayne makes this point forcefully with respect to the 'slum':

> The term *slum*, encoded with the meanings of a dominant bourgeois culture, in fact obscured and distorted the varied spatial forms and social conditions to which it was applied. Universal in its application, it subsumed the innermost working-class districts of every city – notwithstanding their diversity of occupations, incomes, ethnic backgrounds, and household arrangements; and the variation in age, size and labour and housing markets amongst cities – into one all-embracing concept of an outcast society.[28]

It is the apparent neutrality of place and its 'fit' with nature that makes the control of its meaning such a valuable stake. Constructions such as these have the power to include and exclude, for the nature of a place creates certain expectations concerning those who should belong to it, and establishes the dichotomy of insider and outsider, of 'us and them'. This is the power that allows certain groups to draw boundaries and impose binary oppositions in the form of *x*/not-*x*, and from there to say who belongs and who does not belong.[29]

---

[26] In this respect, although postmodern thought concerning identity and location tends to emphasize ambiguity and multiplicity, cities are not, as Pratt points out, 'blurred, chaotic, borderless places', for behind these representations of urban space, there are 'hierachized grids of difference'. Pratt, 'Grids of Difference: Place and Identity Formation', in Fincher and Jacobs, *Cities of Difference*, p. 44.

[27] Harvey, 'From Space to Place and Back Again', p. 24.

[28] A. Mayne, *The Imagined Slum. Newspaper Representation in Three Cities 1870–1914* (Leicester University Press, 1993), p. 2.

[29] This process of 'othering' – that is, of setting up a dichotomic relation through which a particular group establishes its own identity by attributing different and often negative identities and characteristics to other groups and the places they occupy – is a product of the establishment of insider and outsider. An urban historical example of the phenomenon is found in J.M. Merriman, *The Margins of City Life. Explorations on the French Urban Frontier, 1815–1851* (Oxford and New York: Oxford University Press, 1991), Merriman argues that in the nineteenth century, fear came to dominate

And more than this, it is this same hegemony in power relations that allows actors to identify places *as* places.[30] The actions of identifying, categorizing and mapping represent the power to assign an existence to certain places while denying it to others, like medieval maps which declared of uncharted areas that 'here there be monsters'.[31] Indeed, King, in his investigation of mapping and power, emphasizes the importance of maps in creating our social reality:

> Cultural mappings play a central role in establishing the territories we inhabit and experience as real, whatever their ontological status. The power to draw or redraw the map is a considerable one, involving as it does the power to define ... what is or is not real. When a sharp distinction is made between map and territory a particular construction of reality is reified. A map that serves specific interests appears to be an objective representation of exterior reality. The mapped reality appears to be inviolate, existing on the territory itself rather than being the outcome of particular institutional and representative practices.[32]

The apparent naturalness of place derives in part from its opacity, which assigns it a quality of 'innocence', and in part from its historical 'rightness'. For place to function as a construction, it must be able to demonstrate a historical rootedness, for to speak of a place is not only to give something meaning in the present, it is also to activate meanings about its past, as well as expectations for its future. In a process of feedback, place simultaneously legitimates, and is legitimated by, a self-fulfilling reading of history. This historical narrative extends, in a linear fashion, from a mythical origin to the present. And the singularity of this trajectory confirms the 'fit' of both the present and the origin. Indeed, foundation myths are employed time and time again to promote a

---

the bourgeois discourse – fear of prostitutes, beggars and other 'outcasts' and fear of workers who almost came to be seen as 'dangerous' by definition. Both these groups were associated with the periphery of the city, the *faubourg*.

[30] D. Massey, 'Places and Their Pasts', *History Workshop Journal*, no. 39 (1995), p. 190. For an example of this point, see Christine Lamarre, 'La ville des géographes français de l'époque moderne, XVIIe–XVIIIe siècles', *Genèses*, no. 33 (1998), pp. 4–27. Lamarre discusses the statistical classification of the French urban system, and how elements of this system evaded classification. Classification is also a theme taken up by Christian Topalov who, considering Charles Booth's statistical inquiry into living conditions in London at the turn of the nineteenth century, notes that 'objective' statistics and the mapping of social categories was a development that responded to new, reformist perspectives on social problems in the city and their treatment. 'Si on classe autrement les populations et leurs espaces, c'est pour pouvoir les réformer par les nouveaux moyens': C. Topalov, 'La ville "Terre Inconnue". L'enquête de Charles Booth et le peuple de Londres, 1886–1891' *Genèses*, no. 5 (1991), p. 34.

[31] Of course, the choice of scale, both geographical and historical, also has a bearing on what is assigned existence and what is not. See B. Lepetit, 'Architecture, géographie, histoire: usages de l'échelle', *Genèses*, no. 13 (1993), pp. 118–38.

[32] G. King, *Mapping Reality. An Explanation of Cultural cartographies* (New York: St Martin's Press, 1996), p. 16.

particular sociocultural construction of place. Wolfgang Kaschuba offers the example of the Battle of Blackbird Field for the idea of Serbian nationhood and the role of this myth in justifying Serbian oppression of the ethnic Albanians in Kosovo during 1998 and 1999.[33] As Kaschuba points out, foundation myths were a key element in the nineteenth century and first half of the twentieth century as identity was constructed on the basis of national community. After the Second World War a more 'unmythical' perception of the world emerged but, by the 1990s, the foundation myth was being resurrected. Again, this was in the name of the nation although this time, Kaschuba argues (echoing David Harvey's point), the purpose is to protect the idea of the nation from global processes rather than to construct it from the local level.

If dominant constructions of place employ linear readings of history, then they also give shape to, and are shaped by, the collective memory of the social actors who operate in and around these places. In this way, 'place' can be regarded as similar to 'institutions' in the theoretical framework developed by Mary Douglas who argues that institutions, by which she means 'legitimised social groupings',[34] squeeze the ideas of their members in such a way that 'an answer is only seen to be a right one if it sustains the institutional thinking that is already in the minds of individuals as they try to decide'.[35] According to Douglas, memories that correspond to the nature of the institution are preserved, while others that are incompatible are forgotten. In this way, self-knowledge is filtered through the institutions to which groups adhere.

> Institutions systematically direct individual memory and channel our perceptions into forms compatible with the relations they authorise. They fix processes that are essentially dynamic, they hide their influence, and they rouse our emotions to a standardised pitch on standardized issues. Add to all this that they endow themselves with rightness and send their mutual corroboration cascading through all the levels of our information system. No wonder that they easily recruit us into joining their narcissistic self-contemplation.[36]

Place and memory likewise enjoy a 'mutual corroboration', whereby collective memories of social actors that are inconsistent with the dominant construction of place become marginalized or buried. In all this, what we might call

---

[33] In 1389, the Serbs lost the battle of the Blackbird Field (*Kosovopolje*) against the Turks, but this moment also saw the birth of the Serbian myth of national and ethnic community, and the Blackbird Field legend came to represent the Serbs' heroic struggle in the name of Christianity and civilization. See W. Kaschuba, 'The Emergence and Transformation of Foundation Myths', in Stråth, *Myth and Memory*, pp. 217–26.

[34] Douglas, *How Institutions Think*, p. 46. Douglas excludes from her idea of institution, 'any purely instrumental or provisional practical arrangement that is recognised as such': ibid., p. 46.

[35] Ibid., p. 4.

[36] Ibid., p. 92.

'institutionalized' place, in recognition of Douglas's observations, remains opaque, hiding the power architecture of its construction and veiling ideology behind the innocence of its definition as 'a particular part of space, of defined or undefined extent, but of definite situation'. For if the elements of its construction were to become clear and unambiguous, its power would be compromised.

Clearly, therefore, to think about places requires not only that we understand that they are neither natural nor neutral, but also that we have at our disposal an alternative analytical framework that allows us to break free from the grip of their 'narcissistic self-contemplation'.

Places past and future

One of the most innovative exponents of 'place' as an analytical concept is the geographer Doreen Massey. Massey proposes that we should think of space as 'stretched out social relations',[37] in such a way that place 'may be seen as the location of particular sets of intersecting social relations, intersecting activity spaces, both local ones and those that stretch more widely, even internationally. And every place is, in this way, a unique mixture of the relations which configure social space.'[38] Massey's approach has reinvested 'place' with a significance that structuralist analyses had long denied it. Moreover, it offers a new perspective from which to view locally-based situations of conflict.[39]

In contrast to the 'institutionalized' construction of place founded upon ideas of internal coherence and boundedness, Massey's conception of place as a location of unique sets of intersecting social relations relies on ideas of connections, of movement and of inter- and intrarelations. Every place consists of social networks of links, activities, connections and locations that lead to and from it, and each set of new links to a place brings new elements which, according to their influence, mould, and are moulded by, the existing characteristics of the place. In this conception, place escapes identification with eternal, natural truth. It allows us to think of place as open and interlinked, and it is this openness that gives it its uniqueness.[40] From this perspective, the very characteristics on which 'institutionalized' constructions of place are founded

---

[37] Massey, 'The Conceptualization of Place', p. 53.

[38] Ibid., p. 61. By activity spaces, Massey means the network of connections and locations within which an agent operates.

[39] See D. Massey and P. Jess, 'Places and Cultures in an Uneven World', in Massey and Jess, *A Place in the World?*, pp. 215–39.

[40] For an approach to urban life as a tension between movement and settlement, where cities are conceived of as open, occupying places within a wider network of connections, see J. Allen, D. Massey and M. Pryke (eds), *Unsettling Cities. Movement/Settlement* (London and New York: Routledge).

are, in fact, a product of wider contacts with the world beyond the place itself. In this way, Massey's approach directly opposes Harvey's view that 'local' places are being eroded by 'global' forces, arguing instead that the 'global' and the 'local' are in a constant process of interaction.

Places and histories

The specific combinations of social relations that form places in Massey's approach do not only exist in the present, but also exist over time in what she terms an 'envelope of space–time'.[41] That is to say, these combinations are not fixed, and the nature and geography of their interconnections change over time.[42] The space–time envelope involves the idea of continuity through change and thus offers yet another challenge to essentialist claims for the 'real' character of a place, for if we think of places as space–time envelopes of intersecting social relations, then constructions which pretend to contain the essence of a place necessarily lose their validity. There can be no single identity for a place, since various social groups will be differently located in relation to the overall complexity of social relations.[43] These groups will read these relations in different ways and so promote different interpretations according to their sociogeographical positions.[44]

Groups that enjoy hegemony in the exercise of power relations are best positioned to promote their interpretations of place. These groups construct their linear histories in the form of a relentless narrative that, starting from some specified origin, eventually arrives, blazing self-justifying glory, in the present. But this linear chronology is a delusion since, as Bernard Lepetit has argued, it establishes a double fiction: that of the positive evolution of humanity and that of an objectivized development which is not the product of a particular point of view.[45] In Lepetit's conception, historical perspective and timescale feed into a multiple view of history which is, as he puts it, 'the process by which time transforms a single present into a multiplicity of possible pasts'.[46] In other words, this multiplicity of pasts do not explode from their individual origins, but from a unique present. To illustrate this point, Lepetit considers the case

---

[41] P. Jess and D. Massey, 'The Contestation of Place', in Massey and Jess, *A Place in the World?*, p. 134.

[42] Massey, 'The Conceptualization of Place', p. 63.

[43] D. Massey, *Space, Place and Gender* (Cambridge: Polity Press), p. 121.

[44] Massey, 'Places and their Pasts', p. 185.

[45] B. Lepetit, 'Le présent de l'histoire', in *idem* (ed.), *Les Formes de l'expérience* (Paris: Albin Michel, 1995), pp. 295–6.

[46] '... le processus par lequel le temps transforme un présent unique en une multiplicité de passés possibles': B. Lepetit, 'Passé, présent et avenir des modèles urbains d'auto-organisation', in B. Lepetit and D. Pumain (eds), *Temperalités Urbaines* (Paris: Anthropos, 1993), p. 122.

of a specific type of place – the city. The city exists in a social sense and has a physical manifestation of social and cultural practices. Its activities, its institutions and its urban form are all historically rooted, but all these elements do not necessarily have the same rhythms or the same age. From Lepetit's perspective:

> ... the city ... is never synchronous with itself: the urban fabric, the behaviour of the citizens, the policies of urban, economic or social planning unfurl according to different chronologies. But, at the same time, the city is completely in the present. Or rather, it is completely located in the present by the social actors who shoulder all the temporal responsibility.[47]

The city thus consists of elements that are at one and the same time part of earlier ages and part of the present time. The unifying principle for all these elements, according to Lepetit, is provided by the social practices of the moment:[48] '... the objects, institutions and rules only exist in as much as they are put in use, and they do not provide a simple setting for action but configure the resources, changed by practice, which the actors have at their disposal.'[49] The past is distinguished from the present, and this distinction takes place in the present and leads, through either appropriation or denial of pertinence, to the past being assigned new meaning. This appropriation or denial of pertinence is a selection process whereby a group, located in the present, sifts through the past, identifying elements which can lend support to its social practices, while suppressing other elements which are not consistent with these practices. As Jean-Michel Chaplain puts it in his study of the weaving industry in Louviers, a good example of historical research based on this theoretical foundation, 'At every instant, the most immediate relation with our environment is already a historical interrogation'.[50]

---

[47] '... la ville ... n'est jamais synchrone avec elle-même: le tissu urbain, le comportement des citadins, les politiques d'aménagement urbanistique, économique ou social se déploient selon des chronologies différentes. Mais, en même temps, la ville est toute entière au présent. Ou plutôt, elle est tout entière mise au présent par des acteurs sociaux sur qui repose toute la charge temporelle': B. Lepetit, 'Une herméneutique urbaine est-elle possible?' in Lepetit and Pumain, *Temperalités Urbaines*, p. 293.

[48] Lepetit, 'Le présent de l'histoire', p. 293.

[49] '... les objets, les institutions et les règles n'existent que pour autant qu'ils sont mis en usage, et que, de l'autre, ils ne dessinent pas un simple cadre pour l'action mais configurent les ressources, changées par la pratique, dont les acteurs disposent': ibid., p. 297.

[50] '... à chaque instant, le rapport le plus immédiat avec notre cadre de vie est déjà une interrogation historique': J-M. Chaplain, *La Chambre des Tisseurs. Louviers: Cité Drapière, 1680–1840* (Seyssel: Champ Vallon, 1984), p. 13. Another excellent empirical example, and this time particularly relevant for the present work, is Coing's study of the impact of an urban renewal project upon the population of a Parisian neighbourhood in the mid-1960s. See H. Coing, *Rénovation Urbaine et Changement Social: L'îlot no. 4 (Paris 13e)* (Paris: Les Editions Ouvrières, 1966).

Lepetit's example of *la ville* can be read in two senses: it is a metaphor of history as a city and, simultaneously, a metaphor of the city as history – a guide for those in fields such as urban history, who seek to understand the city and its social practices as an object of historical research. Specifically, this idea of different rhythms, different ages, different observers and different observation points[51] allows us to conceptualize history in ways that open up the possibility of polyphonic histories and simultaneously undermine any presumption to prioritize a single voice.

Places and memories

I have already touched on the potential of memory to enter into a mutually reinforcing relation with particular constructions of place, but memory also has the subversive potential to undermine such constructions. By memory I mean 'collective memory', in the sense developed by Maurice Halbwachs. In this context, 'collective memory' is memory perpetuated by a group, and founded on shared data and shared conceptions.[52] For Halbwachs, collective memory differs from history in at least two ways. First, collective memory, unlike history, represents 'a current of continuous thought whose continuity is not at all artificial', in the sense that it retains from the past only those elements which continue to live, or are capable of living in the consciousness of the group which keeps the memory alive.[53] Second, collective memory is distinguished from history because there are many collective memories, while history, clearly demarcated and bounded, is unitary.[54] However, the division between history and memory becomes blurred from a perspective such as the one advocated here, where histories are multiple and constructed in the present. At one extreme, history is, as Pierre Nora states, 'the reconstruction, always problematic and incomplete, of that which is no more ... a representation of the past'[55] – echoing Halbwachs' references to the artificiality and incomplete nature of history – but, at the other, history merges with memory. This interface between history and memory becomes even clearer in Halbwachs' assertion that remembrance is anchored in the present: 'As I have said many times, a remembrance is in very large measure a reconstruction of the past achieved with data borrowed from the present, a reconstruction prepared, furthermore, by reconstructions of

---

[51] See, for example, Lepetit and Pumain, *Temporalités Urbaines*.

[52] M. Halbwachs, *The Collective Memory*, trans. F.J. Ditter and V.Y. Ditter (New York: Harper Colophon Books, 1980), p. 31.

[53] Ibid., p. 80.

[54] Ibid., p. 83.

[55] '... la reconstruction toujours problématique et incomplète de ce qui n'est plus ... une représentation du passé', P. Nora (ed.), *Les Lieux de Mémoire I: La République* (Paris: Gallimard, 1984), p. xix.

earlier periods wherein past images have already been altered.'[56] Halbwachs emphasizes that the past does not conserve itself but, rather, at each stage of its development, society recasts its memories in such a way as to put them in accordance with the conditions of the present, in a process of permanent reshaping and perpetual reconstruction.[57] Memory expresses the past starting from the present and, as collective memory, it serves the group to which it belongs, contributing to this group's self-definition and transforming itself as the group evolves.

In Halbwachs' conception of collective memory he establishes a dialectic relationship between spatial settings and memory. Collective memory draws upon spatial images and, at the same time, in creating physical traces, social groups define their spatial setting and insert their memories there.[58] Places therefore contain elements that are only intelligible to a certain group, for these elements correspond to the life of their society, through the attachment to habits, customs and the familiar scene: 'when a group has lived a long time in a place adapted to its habits, its thoughts as well as its movements are in turn ordered by the succession of images from these external objects.'[59] For this reason, as Coing points out in his study of a Parisian 'working-class' district undergoing renewal, *quartiers* or neighbourhoods are not interchangeable in the eyes of those who live in them: 'Culture takes form there [the neighbourhood] in an original amalgam of stones and people, slowly fashioned by time.'[60] But if the bonds that attach a group to a particular place are almost invisible in day-to-day life, then these same bonds assume extreme clarity 'in the very moment of their destruction'.[61] For this reason, moments of crisis and conflict are particularly important if one wishes to study constructions of place, for it is in these moments that such constructions are most clearly put in evidence.

Places and myths

If memory interfaces with history, then it also interfaces with myth. Myths are the building blocks of identities where collective memories do not reach. There are no witnesses to myth (at least none that can be interrogated), and therein lies

[56] Halbwachs, *The Collective Memory*, p. 69.

[57] This idea emerges as a theme in Halbwachs' early work. See, for example, *La topographie légendaire des évangiles en terre sainte*, 2nd edn (Paris: Presses Universitaires de France, 1971), p. 150.

[58] B. Lepetit, 'Une herméneutique urbaine est-elle possible?', in Lepetit and Pumain, *Temporalités Urbaines*, p. 295.

[59] Halbwachs, *The Collective Memory*, p. 133.

[60] 'La culture s'y est incarnée en un amalgame original de pierres et d'hommes, lentement façonné par le temps': Coing, *Rénovation Urbaine et Changement Social*, p. 83.

[61] Halbwachs, *The Collective Memory*, p. 131.

its power: we cannot call up a memory to confirm or refute a myth. Nor do myths stand up to scientific inquiry but, then again, we do not expect them to. As Kaschuba states, myths demand to be used, not to be questioned: 'They represent extremely highly condensed cultural codifications that tell us, "quote me, use me, believe me, but don't ask me!", because myths discard their concrete temporal and spatial references and try to assume *universal* meaning.'[62]

My use of the term 'myth' in this book is less rigid, more relative and certainly less precise than the structural, anthropological sense assigned to it by Claude Lévi-Strauss. All the same, I would echo Lévi-Strauss in saying that, 'myths get through in man unbeknownst to him',[63] in the sense that they are internalized and we are not always aware of their power. Moreover, to pick up on Kaschuba's point, Lévi-Strauss argued that '[myth] gives man, very importantly, the illusion that he can understand the universe and that he *does* understand the universe. It is, of course, only an illusion.'[64] When I use the term 'myth' in this work, I refer to something that is commonly understood to be scientifically unfounded, bounding on the untrue, but never explicitly false. As White puts it, 'The term "myth" has come to stand for any discourse deemed to be ahistorical, unscientific, illogical, and irrational; in a word, everything conceived to be "uncivilised". Indeed, in modernist discourses, myth cannot be dissociated from the "primitive".'[65] But myths never enter the realm of the untrue because, paradoxically, they contain their own truths. As Stråth argues, 'Myths assume the dimensions of reality in the sense, and to the extent, that people believe in them. From this perspective, they cannot be separated or distinguished from reality and truth, but rather they constitute this reality and truth through language.'[66]

Particular constructions of places may be empowered by myths – nation-states have their founding myths, as do many cities (the wanderings of Aeneas after the fall of Troy, leading eventually to the foundation of Rome, for example). These offer a justification, beyond historical time, for the existence of these places. But founding myths are particular cases. Other myths create and perpetuate certain values, such as self-sacrifice, corruption, hospitality or treachery, and myths of this kind may form the basis of a community's self-understanding, or may equally be imposed by one group upon another.[67] In this

---

[62] Kaschuba, 'The Emergence and Transformation of Foundation Myths', p. 218.

[63] C. Lévi-Strauss, *Myth and Meaning* (London and Henley: Routledge and Kegan Paul, 1978), p. 3.

[64] Ibid., p. 17.

[65] H. White, 'Catastrophe, Communal Memory and Mythic Discourse: The Uses of Myth in the Reconstruction of Society', in Stråth, *Myth and Memory*, p. 49.

[66] Stråth, 'Introduction. Myth, Memory and History in the Construction of Community', p. 25.

[67] The mythical attributes of place are like Doreen Massey's essentialist places – that is, places that appear to have distinct and definite characteristics and that are both

sense, myths represent another level of homogenization and the denial of multiplicity, and they become yet another justification for an 'us' and a 'them', for an 'our place' and a 'their place'. In this way they form plots in which collective memories are inserted, and these plots help to give form to memories, confirming their rightness and their fit. As Stråth puts it:

> The plots constitute tropes in which legitimacy and historical meaning are sought and confirmed by emphasising specific values or characteristics .... History takes on primordial proportions, yet a myth does not evolve from the 'nature' of a thing, and it is never eternal, rather, it has a specific historical foundation.[68]

If myths are not inherent in the 'nature' of things, then, like history, and like memory, they must draw their life from the present. And it is their influence on the present, and their continued mobilization, that ensures their perpetuation in future presents.

Places and their futures

The idea of history, memory and myth presented here is one that emphasizes the continuity between these categories, all of which exist in the present and inform our vision of the past. When we bring the past to bear, when history, memory and myth are applied with the aim of understanding, changing, resolving or challenging, then this action gives the past an active dimension that carries it into the realm of experience. As Koselleck puts it:

> Experience is present past, whose events have been incorporated and can be remembered. Within experience a rational reworking is included, together with unconscious modes of conduct which do not have to be present in awareness. There is also an element of alien experience conveyed by generations or institutions.[69]

---

unchanging and bounded. Such a view presumes a specific relationship between the assumed identity of a place and its history, and uses tradition as a vehicle for this relationship. See Massey, *Space, Place and Gender*. Essentialist places claim authenticity and create a tension between their truth, in as much as we believe them and act upon them, and their falsity – for what is 'the real Africa' or even 'the real English village'? Myth is like the homogeniszing adjective applied to the urban category, which seems to hold true over time and space, but which, on closer inspection, only obscures a myriad other meanings – '*le quartier chaud*', 'the slum', 'the university town', 'the City of Light'.

[68] Stråth, 'Introduction. Myth, Memory and History in the Construction of Community', p. 20.

[69] R. Kosselleck, *Futures Past. On the Semantics of Historical Time* (Cambridge, MA: MIT Press, 1985), p. 272.

Experience, in turn, cannot be had without expectation (and vice versa). To continue Koselleck's line of argument:

> At once person-specific and interpersonal, expectation also takes place in the today; it is the future made present; it directs itself to the not-yet, to the nonexperienced, to that which is to be revealed. Hope and fear, wishes and desires, cares and rational analysis, receptive display and curiosity: all enter into expectation and constitute it.[70]

Koselleck highlights the difference between the two concepts by employing a different spatial metaphor for each; the 'space of experience' and the 'horizon of expectation'.

> It makes sense to say that experience based on the past is spatial since it is assembled into a totality, within which many layers of earlier times are simultaneously present, without, however, providing any experience of the before and after .... Chronologically, all experience leaps over time; experience does not create continuity in the sense of an additive preparation of the past. To borrow an image ... it is like the glass front of a washing machine, beyond which various bits of wash appear now and then, but are all contained within the drum.[71]

As for expectation, Koselleck states:

> By contrast, it is more precise to make use of the metaphor of an expectation horizon instead of a space of expectation. The horizon is the line beyond which a new space of experience will open, but which cannot yet be seen. The legibility of the future, despite possible prognoses, confronts an absolute limit, for it cannot be experienced.[72]

Applying these concepts to our discussion of place, the present of a place is never understood without simultaneously bringing into play experiences of the past or expectations for the future. In other words, expectation is the infinity of futures mediated by a sociocultural position in the present and conditioned by an experience of the past. As such, expectations are never a free choice, but are regulated by what is 'appropriate' and what is 'possible'. A potential future may become an impossibility when the historical narrative for a place changes or when certain collective memories are reactivated or, alternatively, consigned to oblivion. These changes take place in the present, but involve a backwards revision, adjusting the space of experience accordingly. At the same moment, this opens certain horizons of expectation while closing others. In considering processes of construction and reconstruction in the city, particular futures become concretized in the form of carefully structured planning documents (which often include a short historical sketch of the social and physical history of the area in question) and finely coloured maps. The production of these

[70] Ibid.
[71] Ibid., p. 273.
[72] Ibid.

documents creates the expectation that this experts' vision of the future will be realized for the good of the town as a whole. At the same time, with their rational, technical discourse and slick graphics, these documents make all other possible futures look unfeasible or fanciful.

It is this stake in the conception of the future that makes the control of the institutionalized construction of a place in the present and, by extension, the control of that place's past, such an important issue for social actors, and gives rise to conflict over places and their meanings.

Place-based conflicts

Rethinking places, their pasts and their futures in this way enables us to take a fresh look at conflicts that employ a territorial reference. These disputes may be national as, for example, in Umberto Bossi's attempts to establish his Republic of Padania in the north of Italy, or local, as in the countless disagreements over the location or character of new developments which, it is claimed, will alter the nature of a particular place. And, in turn, all these disputes are not simply about government, frontiers, shopping centres or modernist architecture; they are about people – the people who belong and the people who do not, those who are and those who are not, those who have and those who have not.

Conflicts arise over claims for the nature of Massey's space–time envelope. Groups adhere to particular readings of a place's past (readings founded on the collective memories that sustain these groups) which confirm and legitimate their understanding of it in the present, and in turn creates a certain horizon of expectation for the future nature of that place and their role in it. In the context of this book, the future for an area understood as a 'slum' of some form or another is very different to the future of the same area if it is identified as a 'community'. Those with the power to establish the definition of a place ensure that this definition serves their ends and provides the 'right answers' from their own perspective; they legitimate this definition by attempting to give it a historical validity and they maintain it through their influence in power relations. As Depaule and Topalov point out, '... the words of the city appear to reveal relations of strength, of which they are at one moment the instruments, at another the stakes'.[73] Not that these groups – and this is an important point – are free to construct places how and as they would. When a meaning for an area is constructed, this meaning is never entirely new. The material for this construction is found lying around amongst the debris of the old, and the

[73] '... les mots de la ville apparaissent comme révélateurs de rapports de force dont ils sont tantôt des instruments tantôt des enjeux': J-C. Depaule and C. Topalov, 'Les mots de la ville', *Genèses*, no. 33 (1998), p. 3.

innovation lies in the way in which this material is combined.[74] In this sense, construction represents the assemblage of parts in the present in order to recount a particular history, refilling the space of experience which expands towards a horizon of expectation. But this construction must find a sociocultural resonance. The construction may arise from new readings of old historical materials, it may involve the denial of certain memories or their consignment to oblivion or, again, it may ask for the reworking of myths in a new context but, for it to be successful, for it to find resonance, it cannot be an unconditional construction *ex nihilo*.

Dominant groups may lose their power or they may identify new priorities which require new meaning to be assigned to a place. New social alliances may be formed, and new discourses and representations employed to establish a new construction or to promote one of the myriad alternative social constructions, constantly shifting, melting, interacting and reforming behind the opacity of place. It is hardly surprising that these processes are rarely without conflict or resistance. At every stage there is a possibility, albeit small, of breaking the domination of the institutionalized meaning of place and establishing a new identity.

It is the recognition of the social, political and economic influence at stake that makes the battle over the interpretation of place so important.[75] In the 1990s Bossi sought to legitimate the idea of Padania in the minds of Italians because this legitimation would have been the grounds for a separate state of relatively affluent northern Italians who would have been free from the obligation of paying taxes to support the relatively poor areas of the south. Bossi's choice of Padania as the name for his new republic was an attempt to establish a link between his longed-for state and the long recognized (and economically prosperous) area of Pianura Padana (which lies between Turin and Milan), although the boundaries of the two areas show no geographical correspondence. Moreover, when Bossi assembled a band of his followers at the head of a little valley in the Italian Alps in the summer of 1996 to witness him draw water from the source of the River Po and then take this water to Venice, one might suggest that he was attempting to legitimate his claims on two counts. The first count was geographical, since the Po is the unifying

---

[74] This point is made by White: 'The word "construction" derives from Latin "construire", which indicates an activity of building by "piling up" a number of pre-existing things, each being used as "parts". In other words, the concept of "construction" presupposes a "de-struction" of something else, a fragmentation of a structure, the remains of which can be used to "construct" another one. In this way, it is not the elements of the constructed entity that will be new, but only their specific combination.' See White, 'Catastrophe, Communal Memory and Mythic Discourse', p. 49.

[75] Massey argues that boundaries and identities are attempts to stabilize the meaning of particular space–time envelopes and that these attempts at stabilization are constantly the site of social contest. See Massey, *Space, Place and Gender*, p. 5.

element in northern Italy. It flows from the west of the country, through the flat land of Pianura Padana, and reaches the Adriatic at a point just south of Venice. Bossi had selected Venice to be his new capital and the surrounding Veneto was, and continues to be, the core area of his support. Second, there was a historical legitimation, because the Po is traditionally a symbol of fertility and productivity, and its mighty waterway offers a seemingly unchanging feature, linking Bossi's separatist claims in the present to Italy's pre-unification past.

This chapter opened with a short discussion of why, for a long time, academic theorists preferred the concept of 'space' over 'place' and, consequently, tended to marginalize place-based disputes. David Harvey, for example, has argued that globalization has reduced place to a mere commodity and that inhabitants of places will sometimes attempt to resist this commodification on the basis of political action which establishes a link between place and social identity.[76] For Harvey, however, such movements are inevitably founded on feelings of rootlessness, nostalgia and tradition and are therefore reactionary rather than radical. Moreover, these oppositional movements are generally better at organizing in, and dominating, place than they are at commanding space, where the power of capital to coordinate accumulation ensures that these organizations can be leap-frogged or marginalized by capitalist dynamics. Consequently, in Harvey's view, this form of politics is doomed to failure.[77] But while Harvey sees the phenomenon in terms of a hopeless adhesion to the characteristics of the 'local' in the face of the 'global', the approach adopted here is to see these disputes as being about the very definitions of the characteristics of place – about, as Jess and Massey put it, 'a different set of relations to place and to the power relations which construct social space'.[78] This model allows not only for the global to influence the local, but also for the local to spill out into the global. Bossi, for example, was motivated not by a fear that global forces would erode the local identity of northern Italy so much as by locally inspired economic opportunism to capitalize on political and economic global links. Moreover, this global–local interaction is not new, as histories of trade and invasion testify. The novelty of the situation perceived by Harvey lies, perhaps, in the intensity of the process. The speed of change required by international capital and the revision and rediscovery of geo-histories happens at an ever-increasing rate. As

[76] Harvey, *The Condition of Postmodernity: An Enquiry into the Origins of Cultural Change* (Oxford: Basil Blackwell, 1989), p. 302.

[77] Harvey, 'From Space to Place and Back Again', p. 25. For Harvey, more radical and potentially more successful social movements would search to liberate space and time from its current thrall to capitalism, striving for an alternative society which would understand time and value in different ways. They would, however, in attempting to establish their own organization of space and time, open themselves up to the dissolving power of money and the definitions of time and space which are the result of capital accumulation. See Harvey, *The Condition of Postmodernity*, p. 238.

[78] Jess and Massey, 'The Contestation of Place', p. 150.

a result, memory, experience and history may cease to be fully synchronized, and it is this which contributes to Harvey's sense of rootlessness, to this search for 'belonging'.

Of course, many groups in locally-based protests *do* consider that the places they identify with are under siege, but the threat does not derive directly from global forces. Certainly the global has its part to play, but it is the mediation between global and local factors that produces the uniqueness of situations. One such situation may arise in a housing or planning dispute, when a group is faced with a traumatic event that shakes or challenges its relationship with the place it occupies. In these circumstances, according to Halbwachs:

> It resists with all the force of its traditions, which have effect. It searches out and partially succeeds in recovering its former equilibrium amid novel circumstances. It endeavours to hold firm or reshape itself in a district or on a street that is no longer ready-made for it but was once its own.[79]

The section that follows outlines the methodology employed in this book in order to examine this form of resistance.

Methodology and sources

This research presented in this book is based on two case studies. The specific reasons for selecting these two examples are discussed below, as are the methodological implications of adopting a comparative framework of analysis. Here, let it suffice to say that one case study examines the initiative of a locally-based organization – the *Atelier Populaire d'Urbanisme* – to take charge of the replanning and rebuilding of a district of nineteenth-century workers' housing called Alma-Gare, in the town of Roubaix in Northern France. The second case examines the efforts of the Anti-Dampness Campaign in the area of Gorbals, in Glasgow, Scotland, to seek recognition of, and compensation for, the damp conditions in the public housing development in which they lived. Both examples reached their climax in the course of the 1970s. In the pages that follow, I consider how the main protagonists in each example sought to promote their particular construction of place in a process marked by both conflict and negotiation. In the two cases, the material is organized in such a way as to permit an examination not only of the elements underpinning the institutional view of place, but also of those informing the challenge to that construction from a locally-based group. I give particular consideration to how the protest groups involved in each example represented themselves, their area and the population that lived there. The cases also examine how some form of

[79] Halbwachs, *The Collective Memory*, p. 134.

resolution was reached in these conflictual relations (without pretending that these resolutions were in any way definitive).

As far as possible, I identify the values and interests of the main groups involved (concentrating principally on the local activists and the local authorities). Having said this, it is important not to view these groups as homogeneous. Local councils, residents of neighbourhoods and local protest groups alike are marked by a whole range of internal divisions and interests that pull in different directions. For this reason, I avoid making categorical statements about interests and stakes, but instead try to incorporate the idea that stakes evolve and that interests may not always be unambiguous, or even apparent, to the actors themselves.

It should be clear from the discussion thus far that the purpose of this book is not to present a historical analysis in the Rankian sense of 'how it really was' – *wie es eigentlich gewesen* – but to consider how histories, memories and myths inform competing 'realities'. As Coing observes from his research on residents' recollections of their *quartier*, there can be no pretence to objectivity when dealing with memories:

> The image is ... founded upon, at one and the same time, what remains of the old neighbourhood, and the memories (and nostalgia) of the inhabitants. We therefore have to take into account the element of deformation inherent in memory; the past played an important role in the stories, confusing willy-nilly the various periods, juxtaposing contemporary facts and events prior to the 1914 war. Rather than dating the facts and separating the plans – an impossible task – we set ourselves to drawing out the significance of these recollections of the past.[80]

Moreover, as Pierre-Yves Saunier points out, if we are interested in the construction of a place – and he takes the example of a *quartier* or neighbourhood – it is not enough to compile anecdotes, descriptions and memories simply to give colour to descriptions based on a more 'serious' foundation. Instead, we must be aware of how actors are informed by these images:

> ... there is more to glean from the analysis of the genesis of these images of neighbourhoods, considering them as social representations that furnish models of that which is real to actors in the definition of their behaviour, and therefore as facts that it is permissible to deconstruct.[81]

---

[80] 'L'image est ... fondée à la fois sur ce qui subsiste du quartier ancien, et sur les souvenirs (et les nostalgies) des habitants; il nous faut alors compter avec la part de déformation inhérente à la mémoire; le passé joua un grand rôle dans les récits, confondant pêle-mêle toutes les époques, juxtaposant des faits contemporains et des événements d'avant la guerre de 1914. Plutôt qu'à dater les faits et à dissocier les plans, tâche impossible, nous nous sommes attaché à dégager la signification de ces rappels du passé.' Coing, *Rénovation Urbaine et Changement Social*, p. 23.

[81] 'On peut penser qu'il y a plus à glaner de l'analyse de la genèse de ces images de quartiers, en considérant celles-ci comme des représentations sociales qui fournissent

The approach I adopt in these pages assigns considerable importance to verbal representations of places as a means to understand the elements of their construction for, as Cosgrove and Daniels state on the opening page of *The Iconography of Landscape*:

> the meanings of verbal, visual and built landscapes have a complex interwoven history. One cannot understand a built environment without understanding the written and verbal representation of it. This is not as an 'illustration', *but as constituent images of its meaning or meanings.*[82]

Of course, this type of approach has provoked considerable tension between its supporters, 'the post-structural, linguistic left', and its opponent in the 'traditional left'.[83] This tension, however, seems to stem in large part from vested interests and deliberate provocation from both sides and there seems to be little reason why these approaches should not be mutually enriching rather than mutually antagonistic. Having said this, I would point out that it is deeply ironic that so many postmodern texts, apparently concerned with otherness, marginality, 'giving voice' and so on, employ a language that is so impenetrable that it allows access only to select initiates. In their obfuscation they perpetuate, or replicate, the elitism they purport to challenge.

My intention is by no means to present the city only as text. Rather, it is to employ sources – some of which involve textual representation – to seek to understand how myths, memories and beliefs contribute to the construction and maintenance of a particular sociopolitical 'reality', and how this dominant 'reality', which informs elite attitudes and assumptions, may be modified, challenged or even overturned. In order to understand the origin and the impact of these constructions, it is essential to understand the object to which they are applied. This book seeks to demonstrate how, for example, poverty, poor living conditions, damp housing, modern architecture and so on are mediated by, and incorporated in, cultural constructions, through the words used to categorize them. In this way, social history escapes marginalization and remains a central element of research.

---

des modèles du réel aux acteurs dans la définition de leur conduite, et donc comme des faits qu'il est loisible de déconstruire.' P-Y. Saunier, 'La ville en quartiers: découpages de la ville en histoire urbaine', *Genèses*, no. 15 (1994), p. 113.

[82] D.E. Cosgrove and S. Daniels (eds), *The Iconography of Landscape: Essays on the Symbolic Representation, Design and Use of Past Environments* (Cambridge: Cambridge University Press, 1988), p. 1.

[83] An excellent example of this tension is provided by the exchanges between Alan Mayne, author of *The Imagined Slum*, and David Englander who reviewed this book in *Urban History*, 21:2 (1994), pp. 309–11. There then followed Mayne's reply in 'A Barefoot Childhood: So What? Imagining Slums and Reading Neighbourhoods', *Urban History*, 22:3 (1995), pp. 380–9, and Englander's 'Urban History or Urban Historicism: Which? A response to Alan Mayne', *Urban History*, 22:3 (1995), pp. 390–91.

In *The Imagined Slum*, Alan Mayne makes the point that to discuss 'slums' as if they were a given, already existing 'somewhere out there', is to reify a social construction rather than question it (and the same argument may be applied to 'urban social movements' for example).[84] But if Mayne claims that 'slums are myths' (in so doing, provoking the wrath of David Englander[85]) he qualifies this, arguing that:

> This is not to say, for example, that Chicago's turn-of-the century poverty belt did not exist, or to downplay the shocking disequilibrium between it and Millionaires' Row. Nor is it to dispute the miserable living conditions that, by the late nineteenth century, had become the entrenched norm among the multi-storey tenements of Scottish cities. The deplorable life choices available to inner-city residents were real in material and absolute senses which do not extend to slums. I do not mean that slums were not real. They were, after all, a universal feature of big cities. Their reality, however, lay in the constructions of common-sense conviction, and in the certainties of public knowledge which common-sense undertakings sustained, rather than the material conditions of everyday living.[86]

I argue that it is essential to consider representation because situations, conditions and objects can be assigned different, often contradictory meanings. Indeed, as this book shows, a 'slum' may be transformed into a 'neighbourhood' or '*quartier*' without any substantial change in its material conditions.[87]

---

[84] My intention in this book is not to trace the emergence of the concept of 'slum', and anyone interested in this theme would do well to start with Mayne's monograph. All the same, a fascinating glimpse at late nineteenth-century philanthropy and the construction of the category of 'slum' is provided by the article, 'Flashes from the Slums: Pictures Taken in Dark Places by the Lightning Process. Some of the Results of a Journey through the City with an Instantaneous Camera – the Poor, the Idle, and the Vicious', from *The Sun* (New York), 12 February 1888, and reprinted in B. Newhall (ed.), *Photography: Essays and Images* (New York: Museum of Modern Art). The article discusses the photographic work of Jacob A. Riis (1849–1914), who used his camera to represent the slums of New York's Lower East Side. Although the title, 'Pictures taken from Dark Places' refers to the flash photography technique employed by Riis for night-time shots, it clearly also has social and moral undertones.

[85] 'Call me old-fashioned. I don't mind, Call me a sentimental Leftie. I don't mind that either. I do mind, though, when I am told in a book-length study that claims to be a serious work of history that its focus is upon urban society and its manifestations as a text rather than a state of affairs.' Englander, 'Urban History or Urban Historicism: Which? A response to Alan Mayne', p. 390.

[86] Mayne, *The Imagined Slum*, p. 1.

[87] As Depaule and Topalov argue, words effectively structure urban space: 'des catégories de l'urbaine sont à l'œuvre dans les termes génériques (village, ville, bourg), comme dans les divisions larges ou fines de la ville (quartier/faubourg, *extra muros*/ *intra muros*) ou, entre spatial et social, dans les jeux de la stigmatisation urbaine, plus généralement dans le façon dont les identités s'inscrivent dans des territoires, parfois aussi s'effacent.' Depaule and Topalov, 'Les mots de la ville', p. 2.

Here, we are in the world of historical construction, and the meaning assigned to an area is anything but neutral. As Topalov explains:

> The representation of certain aspects of reality as a 'social problem' is a historical construction. For all that, it is not arbitrary, because it is mobilized in practical projects which play a role in a society's structural problems. In other terms, a social problem only exists insofar as it is designated by concrete social groups as the object of possible action.[88]

Undoubtedly, the use of particular words has an important part to play in the representation of places, but these constructions are also promoted by language in the wider sense – through symbolic actions and protest tactics, for example – and substantial parts of the chapters that follow concentrate on how locally organized groups in each case under examination attempted to breathe life into their vision of their district through such initiatives. With the aim of drawing these themes together for both case studies, I also identify a small number of 'key events'. These were events that were, indisputably, assigned importance by the campaigners themselves, although their 'key' identification in these pages is because they succinctly draw together the main themes that run through each of the studies.

Comparison

If, as I have argued in the preceding sections, history is constructed in the present, then historical comparison can hardly escape the same conclusion. Comparisons, with their identified salient differences and similarities are not founded on eternal truths, but are constructions of the present. For this reason, every explanation of difference or similarity is contingent on our contemporary world-view. In this sense, we may argue that *all* history is comparative, for it involves the assessment of the past in the context of the present, or more exactly, the confrontation of our perception of the present with our perception of the past, as it is located in the present.[89]

If our endeavour is to explode historical givens and common-sense explanations and to find multivocal discourses where once there was only the single voice, then comparison offers a valuable tool by which to approach this

---

[88] 'la représentation des certains aspects de la réalité comme "problème social" est une construction historique. Elle n'est pas pour autant arbitraire, car elle est mobilisée dans des projets pratiques qui jouent un rôle dans les conflits structurels d'une société. En d'autres termes, un problème social n'existe que dans la mesure ou il est désigné par des groupes sociaux concrets comme objet d'action possible.' C. Topalov, 'La ville "congestionnée". Acteurs et langage de la reforme urbaine à New York au début du XXe siècle', *Genèses*, no. 1 (1990), p. 109.

[89] J. Kaye, 'Comparison, A Contingent Juxtaposition of Austria and Sweden', discussion paper presented at the European University Institute, Florence, 8 November 1999, p. 1.

goal. An explicitly comparative approach, such as the one adopted in this work, has the potential to liberate our thinking from the dominance of the monodimensional study, to identify patterns in larger themes and to make us aware of absent elements in one case through the identification of these elements in the other.[90]

In employing comparison, my intention is to establish a form of dialogue between the two cases selected for study. Either of these examples would, in and of itself, stand as an example of public protest against urban planning projects and, in this way, offer interesting historical insights into the processes that shape the urban realm, but together they create a holistic interaction which is greater than their simple sum. While accepting that any differences or similarities identified are not essential, these may still be organized and interpreted in such a way as to take us beyond the specificity of one or other of the cases. If part of the aim of comparison is to identify more generally applicable issues from a pair of historical events, this is not the same as striving to derive universal laws. Rather, the case studies are enriched in a mutual 'question and answer' process, and their 'truths' emerge in this relative context, instead of being measured against an external, objective, scientific model.

The analysis of both case studies has been nuanced by the identification of 'crisis moments'. There are two reasons for this approach. First, as suggested earlier in this chapter, it is in the moment that something – be it an identity, a building, a lifestyle or an animal species – is perceived to be at risk or threatened that the values, beliefs and ideas invested in that thing are made explicit. So long as there is no suggestion of change, no perception of threat, then beliefs tend to remain implicit and unexpressed. Indeed, there may even be no conscious awareness that such beliefs exist. Therefore it is, to echo Halbachs' point, in the very moment that groups find their local environment under threat of change that they give voice to their beliefs and make explicit that which had, until then, been only implicit. Crises provoke a revision or a

[90] Comparative history is often the subject of ambitious statements and yet its application is little more than patchy. Heinz-Gerhard Haupt, commenting on the difficulties of comparative history, with particular reference to Germany, Great Britain and France, has pointed out, first, the difficulty of acquiring detailed knowledge of primary sources in different countries, secondly, the refusal of a historiography that constructs theoretically its own object, gives it boundaries through definitions and takes up the aim of being able to pronounce upon social processes, structures and mentalities, and, finally, the institutional logic of national university systems that remain prisoners of the supremacy of national histories. He also points out specific national features that have impeded this development – Germany's particular links with its own historical past, the lack of a form of sociology that privileges comparison in Great Britain (cf. Weber in Germany and Durkheim in France), and a scepticism with regard to a more systematically connected and structured form of historical research in France. See H-G. Haupt, 'La Storia Comparata', *Passato e Presente*, 11:28 (1993), p. 19.

reinforcing of beliefs, the past is no longer taken for granted and the future is up for grabs.[91] The second reason for employing the concept of crisis is a more pragmatic one. That is, it helps to impose a common framework upon the two case studies, pinning each of them down to a pivotal moment. In both cases, an initial phase of apparent consensus has been identified, which is then followed by a crisis moment – a moment when, as the French activists put it, everyone caught fire. There then ensued a period when the various groups involved struggled over the meaning of these places, attempting to impose their respective visions of the future. Using this framework it becomes easier to understand the successive phases of the events in Alma-Gare and the Gorbals, and to locate them in a comparative context.

This crisis model is also mirrored in the more general discussion of French and British attitudes towards the city and its problems in Chapter Two. The modernist paradigm of urban planning experienced a growing crisis from the late 1960s onwards. This paradigm had been founded on the construction of certainty: the certainty of progress, that what came after was better than that which proceeded it; the certainty of growth optimism, that economic divergences in national populations were unproblematic because the dynamic of economic growth would make the redistribution of wealth unnecessary; and the technological certainty that the solutions to all ills were within the grasp of science. It was in the moment that these certainties began to crumble that doubts emerged over the direction that societies were taking, and it is this context that forms the background to the case studies.

The case studies

The two case studies examined in this book – Alma-Gare and the Gorbals – deal with locally-based protest actions that were directed at influencing the urban

---

[91] Dunleavy has used the example of the Breckton protest in London which followed the infamous collapse of the Ronan Point tower block due to a gas explosion in one of the flats on 17 May 1968, to illustrate this point from a political science perspective. The collapse shifted the normal power relationship between the local authority and the residents whom they were trying to rehouse. The event unexpectedly tipped the balance in favour of these residents who took the opportunity to organize a protest action against the renewal process. Dunleavy concludes that this example provides objective evidence that, 'in the absence of the normal coercive power relationships between the public housing apparatus and "slum" residents, the latter would have chosen a different housing future, most basically one controlled by them. Thus mass-protest on mass housing issues should be understood as the product of continued domination, politically as well as ideologically, the reflection of a powerless situation constantly reproduced by the routine exercise of power by the public housing apparatus.' Dunleavy, 'Protest and Quiescence in Urban Politics: A Critique of Some Urban and Structuralist Myths', *International Journal of Urban and Regional Research*, no. 1 (1977), p. 215.

environment in a limited geographical area and that provoked situations of tension and conflict with the structures of local government. The urban environment in question was not a privileged 'historical' one where local interest groups might have easily agreed on the need to protect or conserve what they regarded as a valuable piece of historical heritage. On the contrary, these are examples of cases where attitudes to the urban environment were much more ambiguous and contradictory, and where issues did not simply crystallize around an elitist definition of cultural heritage or architectural interest. These studies therefore offer the possibility of posing questions such as: 'How do populations react when their homes are officially recognized as 'slums' and earmarked for demolition?', 'What happens when groups with little power, and no political voice, identify valuable elements in their environment – elements that may not be reflected in "objective" cultural assessments of heritage?' and 'What possibilities do these groups have when this environment comes under threat?'

Both Alma-Gare and the Gorbals were widely recognized as areas of poor-quality housing associated with the nineteenth-century industrial era of their city's past. While Roubaix's nineteenth-century prosperity had been based on textile production, Glasgow's was derived from a range of heavy industry, including shipbuilding and locomotive construction. Either way, the demand for cheap labour in the nineteenth century meant that both districts came to house a population that was marginalized in social, economic and political terms, even if, geographically, they were located close to the administrative centres of their respective towns. Each area was also characterized by a distinct urban morphology, be this the *courées* in Alma-Gare (see Chapter Three), or the tenements in the Gorbals (see Chapter Five). These morphologies generally came to be associated with poverty and urban decline, and the *courées* and the tenements came to epitomize the very worst housing conditions, not just locally, but also on a national level. It was hardly surprising, then, that these areas should have become the ideal targets for the ambitious urban renewal programmes of the post-war period. The consensus identified in each case was based on the general understanding that these areas – Alma-Gare and Gorbals – were slums of one kind or another. The crisis, when it came, was accompanied by the 'discovery' of 'new' attributes of the two areas – attributes founded on social solidarity and creativity that lent themselves to the idea of 'community'.

More specifically, the French case considers the conflict between, on the one hand, the *Atelier Populaire d'Urbanisme* (APU), an unofficial planning workshop established in the area of Alma-Gare in the town of Roubaix in Northern France and, on the other, the 'official' participants in the planning process, including the *Municipalité de Roubaix* and various construction and rehousing organizations. The *Atelier* claimed to represent the population of Alma-Gare. This population, they argued, had a right to decide on their own collective future, not only in terms of housing provision, architectural design and the use and layout of public space, but also with respect to the management of the local economy.[92] The *Atelier* was eventually successful in achieving its aims, winning the right to contribute substantially to the restructuring process in Alma-Gare.

The second case considers the conflicts that emerged between Glasgow District Council and a group of its tenants over the living conditions in the modern public housing developments provided in the area of the Gorbals in Glasgow, Scotland. In particular, it concentrates on the issue of dampness in the development called Hutchesontown 'E' and the emergence of the Gorbals Anti-Dampness Campaign. This Campaign, on behalf of the tenants of this new development, waged a long battle to have the problem of dampness first recognized and then acted upon.

In both cases, the historical period of interest lies between 1950 and 1980, although these chronological boundaries are merely intended to act as general guidelines. In Alma-Gare and the Gorbals alike, the majority of the campaigning took place during the 1970s, but to understand the historical context of these initiatives it is necessary to examine the early post-war period, marked as it was by the desire of national governments in Western Europe to take charge of the restructuring of their cities in general and the provision of housing in particular (see Chapter Two). The year 1980 serves as an arbitrary and flexible end-point. By this time, both Alma-Gare and the Gorbals were embarking on new phases in their urban histories and the issues promoted by the protest groups had largely been played through. This is not to suggest that the events considered here have no bearing on the perceptions and identities of these areas today – far from it – but by the 1980s new priorities were emerging in both towns. Space and time, in the most mundane sense, prevent these developments from being discussed here.

Although as briefly discussed in Chapter Two there are differences in the organization of political structures in France and Great Britain, the principal actor in the process of renewal, and therefore the main target for expressions of discontent in both cases, was the local authority – the *Municipalité de Roubaix* and the Corporation of the City of Glasgow (which became Glasgow District Council in 1973). As is apparent from the discussion in Chapters Three and Five, post-war local politics in both towns had been dominated by forces from the political left. The respective administrations were, therefore, particularly susceptible to arguments concerning the housing conditions of the 'working class'. By the 1970s these administrations were also concerned about the

[92] What Douglass and Friedmann term, 'counter-planning by the heretofore excluded sectors of civil society'. M. Douglass and J. Friedmann, editors' introduction to *Cities for Citizens: Planning and the Rise of Civil Society in a Global Age* (Chichester: John Wiley and Sons, 1998), p. 4.

economic future of their towns, both of which were facing serious difficulties in the wake of the decline of their traditional economic bases.

While the two cases are marked by many similarities, from the perspective of this research there is a key difference that distinguishes them; in Alma-Gare, the local protests began *prior* to the demolition of the area and many of the subsequent actions were aimed at determining the nature of this demolition and the form of the new construction. In the Gorbals, however, for reasons discussed in Chapter Five, wholesale demolition took place, and local discontent only began to find a voice *after* tenants had been moved into their new flats. Applying Charles Tilly's distinction between different forms of 'collective action', Alma-Gare represents a *proactive* collective action – that is, an action that 'asserts group claims that have not previously been exercised'.[93] The Gorbals, on the other hand, represented a *reactive* collective action; these, according to Tilly, 'consist of group efforts to reassert established claims when someone else challenges or violates them'.[94] This difference inevitably had a bearing on how each group viewed its past, present and future and negotiated elements of its collective memory. It is therefore a theme that is developed throughout the chapters that follow.

Finally, one clearly cannot disregard the different national settings for these studies. The national level inevitably has an impact on the two examples, and some of the most pertinent distinctions that emerge as a result are discussed in the final chapter. All the same, the intention of this book is not to compare France and Great Britain, and the subsequent chapters show that the significance of the two cases emerges as much *despite* national differences as *because* of them. Clearly, if the aim was simply to demonstrate that there are differences between France and Great Britain then it would scarcely be necessary to embark upon a voyage through urban planning and public protest in the 1970s. The approach adopted here is that, without denying national specificities,[95] each country provides a very similar context for this form of study – a context defined by modernist preoccupations with economic efficiency, urban rationality, functionalism and the panacea seemingly offered by technology and industrial production techniques, and, by the 1970s, a growing crisis in this position.

Sources

In an ideal world, historical comparisons would make use of fully compatible sources for each case study investigated. Inevitably, such a luxury is rarely, if

---

[93] C. Tilly, 'Major Forms of Collective Action in Western Europe 1500–1975', *Theory and Society*, 3:(1976), p. 368.

[94] Ibid., p. 367.

[95] Which would, in any case, be paradoxical given the discussion of the significance of place in this chapter.

ever, offered, especially if the comparison happens to operate across national boundaries. In this study, the combined set of French and British sources is skewed in various ways. And yet this should not be disheartening: if, as suggested above, comparison is a dialogue, then this dialogue may well be richer if the two voices are not of the same pitch and timbre. Indeed, 'imperfect' cases such as these give the historian licence to go beyond the pretence of objectivity and rationality and to take a chance on historical intuition and instinct.

For Alma-Gare, the material came from several different sources. First, there were official planning documents from the period leading up to and including the events in question. These took the form of both written texts and maps. Technical in nature, they offer an 'official' vision of the future of Alma-Gare and indicate how this district was to dovetail with the rest of the town. Most of these documents were located in the Archives de la Mairie de Roubaix, while others were provided directly by municipal officials in the Direction Générale de l'Aménagement et de l'Urbanisme and the Service d'Aménagement du Territoire. A mountain of official correspondence was also located in the Archives Départementales du Nord in Lille (indicated as ADN in the notes on the text, accompanied by the identification number for each *dossier*).

Second, there was a range of documentation held by the Association Inter-Quartiers de Roubaix (identified as AIR in the text) More precisely, this was the private collection of Monsieur Roger Leman, a founder member of the *Atelier Populaire d'Urbanisme*. Eclectic and unsorted, these documents included *tracts* or pamphlets for distribution to the population of Alma-Gare, newspaper cuttings, typed notes for meetings, collective reflections on the progress of the APU's campaign, correspondence with various organizations including the town hall, the *office d'HLM* (the office for public housing) and various construction and rehousing agencies, notes from APU working groups, and a copy of the *carte-affiche*, the alternative planning document for Alma-Gare drawn up by the APU in 1977. These documents were to provide the core of the Alma-Gare research, for they permitted an invaluable view of the language and tactics employed by the activists, as well as an insight into the everyday operation of the *Atelier*.

In the course of the 1970s, members of the APU were responsible for several publications, normally in left-wing or progressive Catholic journals.[96] In 1980

---

[96] For example, R. Leman, 'L'Alma Gare n'est pas encore Rasé', *Cadres CFDT*, nos 338–39 (1989), pp. 56–58 and *idem*, 'Roubaix: lier le social et l'économique', *Parole et Société*, nos 3–4 (1982), pp. 204–209. See also R. Leman and M-A. Leman, 'L'urbanisme, la rénovation des vieux quartiers ne sont pas des fatalités' *Sauvegarde de l'enfance*, no. 2 (1980), pp. 293–99. In 1976, Lamarche-Vadel and Cotlenko contributed an article on Alma-Gare to a special edition of *Autrement* on 'Luttes Urbaines': G. Lamarche-Vadel and A. Cottlenko, 'Alma-Gare – le singulier et le politique',

Eric Verbrackel, a participant in the APU, produced a thesis at the University of Lille entitled, 'L'Atelier populaire d'urbanisme de l'Alma-Gare à Roubaix'.[97] Then, in 1982, the APU contributed, along with the *Municipalité* and various architects who had worked on the project, to a collective text entitled *Roubaix Alma-Gare. Lutte Urbaine et Architecture*.[98] This book was intended to record the story of Alma-Gare and to celebrate its success rather than provide an academic analysis. These various texts were all employed as primary sources, on the basis that they represented the public position that the APU wished to promote.

Finally, use was also made of newspaper reports. Local newspapers – *Nord Matin*, *Nord Eclair* and *Voix du Nord* – frequently ran stories on protest actions in Alma-Gare or outlined new planning proposals. Many of these stories were held as press cuttings held in the archives of *Nord Eclair* (ANE in the notes on the text). Moreover, the events in Alma-Gare even made it to the pages of *Le Monde*.[99] The reader should note that all extracts from documents and newspaper reports are provided in English translation, with elements of the French original included only in cases where words or phrases are particularly significant, unusual or, indeed, ambiguous. English translations are also provided for quotations from monographs, collected works and academic articles published in French; however, in this case the original text is included in full in the notes.

This array of sources offers a perfect illustration of Lepetit's city located entirely in the present, but consisting of different ages and different rhythms. They capture the evanescence of stories concerning the town of Roubaix and its *courées* at a national level, their constant 'bubbling' at the level of the local press (with an occasional eruption into headline news), the workaday administration surrounding the development of Alma-Gare (and the greater attention paid by political representatives as local elections came around), the technical expertise and objectivity that resonates in the periodic planning documents, the intense moments of protest, and the day-to-day work involved in the *Atelier*'s campaign to win a voice in the planning process.

If the exact counterparts of these sources could not be found for Glasgow it is my hope, in any case, that the outcome, in the sense of Lepetit's model, is the same.

Autrement, no. 6 (1976), pp. 62–69. Other contributors included Cherki and Mehl, and Castells.

[97] E. Verbrackel, 'Atelier Populaire d'Urbanisme de l'Alma Gare à Roubaix', unpublished thesis, University of Lille, 1980.

[98] APU-CSCV, 'La démarche au quotidien', in P. Prouvest, *Roubaix Alma-Gare. Lutte Urbaine et Architecture*(Bruxelles: Editions de Atelier d'Art Urbain, 1982), pp. 17–38.

[99] Other papers and journals ran stories on the topic at various moments, and these are cited in the text.

On the whole, the material for the Scottish case study was more centralized, and the majority of research was carried out in the city's Mitchell Library (identified as ML in the notes), which also includes the Strathclyde Regional Archives. Glasgow Corporation/District Council material was housed in the Mitchell Library's Glasgow Collection. This included a wide range of documents and plans, with their supporting surveys, in draft as well as final form. The availability of this material was such that local plans for the Gorbals could easily be consulted alongside city plans.

These official documents were complemented by the Mitchell Library's complete catalogue of *The Gorbals View* (latterly *The View*), from its first edition in April 1967, until January 1979. *The Gorbals View* was a monthly publication which could lay claim to being Scotland's first community newspaper. The impetus for its foundation came from a nucleus that was to form the editorial group of this monthly publication, several of whom were church ministers concerned at the living conditions in the old tenements. Indeed, the early editions of the paper are full of calls for the demolition process to be speeded up, along with local news and features, pages from Gorbals churches and clubs, and features on economic cooking and cheap fashion tips. As various tenants groups emerged, these undertook to produce an article for the paper every month. As a result, one is able to gain a good idea of the main preoccupations of these organizations. I paid particular attention to the Hutchesontown Tenants' Association and the Gorbals Anti-Dampness Campaign, both of which made a regular contribution to the paper. As tensions began to develop over the redevelopment of the Gorbals (Chapter Six), *The View* became increasingly critical of Glasgow's councillors. Local meetings and protest activities were well publicized, as well as amply reported.

Like the *Atelier Populaire d'Urbanisme*, the Anti-Dampness Campaign eventually became the subject of a publication. In 1979 the Scottish Council of Social Services published *The Dampness Monster: A Report of the Gorbals Anti-Dampness Campaign.*[100] This text informed tenants of their housing rights and suggested ways of influencing intransigent local councils, based on the experience of the Anti-Dampness Campaign. Written with the cooperation of campaign members, and resisting the temptation to glamorize the events in the Gorbals, this text was a useful source for understanding the day-to-day working of the campaign. More recent documentation on the Gorbals was provided by the Gorbals Initiative (Indicated by GI in the notes).

These sources were augmented by a close examination of the city press. Particular attention was given to *The Glasgow Herald*, a 'quality' broadsheet, and its more 'popular' sister paper, *The Evening Times*. The press provided

[100] R. Bryant, *The Dampness Monster: A Report of the Gorbals Anti-Dampness Campaign* (Edinburgh: Scottish Council of Social Services, 1979).

accounts of conditions in the Gorbals 'slums', descriptions of the new projects, reports on council meetings and, once they had gained a certain profile, coverage of the actions of the Hutchesontown Tenants' Association and the Gorbals Anti-Dampness Campaign. The *Herald* also provided an account of Glasgow District Council's financial trials and tribulations during the 1970s and 1980s.

Structure

The pages that follow are divided into six chapters. Chapter Two offers a brief comparative introduction to the development of planning theory and legislation in France and Great Britain, with particular emphasis on the evolution of attitudes towards the older parts of the city and the definition and treatment of 'slum' areas of one form or another.

Chapter Three introduces the Alma-Gare case study. It provides a political, economic and social setting for the protest activities that developed in the 1970s. In particular, it considers the characteristics of the *courées* and discusses the meanings constructed around this form of architecture. It also examines the elements that contributed to the construction of the consensus over the requirement to demolish the housing stock in this area of Roubaix.

Chapter Four considers the breakdown of this consensus. It traces the key events in the struggle between the local activists and Roubaix's municipal council, including the formation of the *Atelier Populaire de l'Urbanisme*. It examines the tactics employed by these groups and suggests how each activated different historical arguments in order to justify their particular vision of the future.

Chapter Five introduces the second case study, that of the Gorbals in Glasgow. As in Chapter Three, a political, economic and social context is provided. The chapter then goes on to discuss the different meanings assigned to the 'old' and 'new' Gorbals, and concludes with the construction of a consensus over the 'miracle' of transformation.

Chapter Six opens by considering the breakdown of consensus over the meaning of the 'new' Gorbals, a breakdown based on flaws in the physical structure and spatial arrangement of the modern housing. The issue of dampness in the Hutchesontown 'E' development and the formation of the Gorbals Anti-Dampness Campaign is given particular attention. The chapter then analyses how different elements in the identity of the Gorbals were activated and reactivated in the discourse and tactics of the Anti-Dampness Campaign and the city council in the struggle that ensued.

To conclude, Chapter Seven draws together the two case studies in a comparative context. It examines the significance of their similarities and differences and the issues raised therein. It also considers the relations between global forces and local initiatives in terms of shaping locally-based identities.

Finally, it picks up and develops Lepetit's metaphor of the city as history, history as the city, in the light of the approach adopted and the findings derived from the two studies.

CHAPTER TWO

Changing attitudes to the built environment: urban planning in France and Great Britain

This chapter outlines official attitudes towards the built environment in France and Britain in the twentieth century, with particular emphasis on the changing perceptions of areas of older housing. The aims of this chapter are threefold: first, to provide an administrative and legislative context for the chapters which follow; second, to illustrate the subjective and contextual nature of the definition of 'slum' housing; and third, to examine the general shift in planning philosophy from the late 1960s on, whereby planning ceased to conceive of a definite goal, a 'utopian' end-point which supposedly reflected a broad consensus on the 'common good', and shifted its emphasis towards social issues and local concerns. This went hand-in-hand with the 'rediscovery' of existing communities rather than their construction *ex nuovo*. Indeed, such is the lure of the concept of community that it has now become the panacea for all urban ills.[1]

In many respects, the history of planning in the twentieth century is the history of how national governments took control of the production of the built environment. This development was accompanied by the emergence of a profession of planning experts who were 'qualified' to make decisions about the future form of the city. In the post-war period, on which this chapter concentrates, this process took place in the context of the development of the modern welfare state, and ideas of affluence and social functionalism.[2] These

---

[1] A recent American publication on 'historic communities' and 'urban sprawl' provides a good example of how 'community' has become idealized. Community is defined as 'a place (not a marketplace) for co-operation more than competition, a home where people of disparate views can speak face-to-face, stand accountable to one another, reconcile their differences, and reach agreements on action to be taken by all.' R. Moe and G. Wilkie, *Changing Places: Rebuilding Community in the Age of Sprawl* (New York: Henry Holt & Co., 1997), p. 74. The case studies that follow illustrate that, while this may be a reality promoted by community groups, it covers over internal tensions, divisions and conflicts.

[2] By welfare state, I refer to the general concept of government intervention in consumption and life-cycle issues such as unemployment payments, health provision, pensions and housing.

ideas, in turn, were underpinned by the modernist project and the construction of certainty, clarity and stability through the ideas of rational political and economic planning. It was only with the public protests and economic crisis of the late 1960s and early 1970s that the illusory nature of this certainty became apparent.

Planning activities are legitimated by a particular reading of place. Some places, such as national parks or historic town centres, apparently quintessential and unchanging, seem to provide their own 'right answers' in planning terms, generally based on the idea that their defining characteristics should be protected or enhanced. Other places, however, have more ambiguous identities, and in these cases planning represents the outcome of a process of conflict and negotiation amongst groups with more or less power – government departments, local authorities, residents, developers, pressure groups and so on. The planning policy adopted is based on a particular construction of place and generally reflects the interests of those actors who wield most power in social relations.

Of particular interest for this study is the concept of 'slum' and the identification of certain areas as '*insalubre*' or 'unfit for human habitation'. The term 'slum' first came into use in the English language in the first half of the nineteenth century. Derived from the verb 'slumber', it entered London slang or cant and was initially used to designate a room, but by 1824 had been used to refer to a courtyard or street inhabited by the poor.[3] The French equivalent of 'slum' is '*taudis*'. While the contemporary meaning of '*taudis*' is ill-maintained, poor or sub-standard housing, its origin is middle French, '*se tauder*', meaning 'to put under shelter', '*taudis*' being the shelter provided for workers engaged in preparing earthworks during a military siege.[4] As Rodger points out, in the nineteenth century, a term such as 'slum' bore distinct moral implications,[5] while, as we shall see, many of the developments in planning

---

[3] *Oxford English Dictionary*. See also A. Mayne, *The Imagined Slum. Newspaper Representations in Three Cities, 1870–1914* (Leicester: Leicester University Press, 1993), pp. 127–28. Mayne states that the use of the term as a noun can be traced to J.H. Vaux's *Flash Dictionary* of 1812. The meaning of the term subsequently broadened to the extent that, by the second quarter of the nineteenth century the expression 'back slum' was used to describe whole districts of London. By the second half of the century the term was being simplified to 'slum'.

[4] *Grand Larousse de la Langue Française*. Earlier still, *un taud* was a cover erected over the deck of a boat at anchor to protect it from the rain. This in turn came from the Norse term *tjald*, meaning tent.

[5] Nineteenth-century explanations for 'defective housing conditions' ranged from 'intemperance, idleness and injudicious expenditure' on the part of those who lived in the housing, to more liberal interpretations, which considered such behaviour as, 'understandable, though unacceptable, forms of escapism from oppressive housing'. R. Rodger, *Housing in Urban Britain 1780–1914: Class. Capitalism and Construction* (Basingstoke and London: Macmillan, 1989), p. 2. From the British perspective,

during the twentieth century were aimed at producing a scientifically objective, neutral and quantifiable measure for housing conditions. This in turn created a certain expectation for the treatment of these areas – their surgical removal and replacement by a functionally efficient piece of urban infrastructure. All the same, as argued in Chapters Five and Six in particular, the moral aspects of 'slum life' were never far from the surface, even in the latter part of the twentieth century.

French and British urban organization and structure

Before proceeding, it is worth outlining the basic characteristics of the French and British urban structures and the organization of the governmental structures which administer them.

The urban structures of France and Great Britain are markedly different; Paris dominates its urban hierarchy to a much greater extent than London, and only three other French conurbations – Lille, Lyon and Marseille – have populations of over 1 million. The French urban hierarchy continues to be dominated by the structure established under the *Ancien Régime* which, beyond the national capital, favoured regional centres such as Bordeaux, Rouen, Lyon and Marseille.[6] In the second half of the nineteenth century France experienced urban growth as a result of industrialization, particularly in the Loire, the Lorraine region and in the north around Lille, Roubaix and Tourcoing. Nonetheless, the earlier hierarchy was largely maintained; as Roncayolo states, 'the city in France is a structure of much greater duration and strength than that of industry'.[7] It was only in the post-war period that the country experienced a major drive towards urbanization. This was largely as a result of a rising birthrate, which had remained low right up to the Second World War, but which began to increase from 1945, in part encouraged by government subsidies such

---

political and economic factors saw to it that social characteristics received the blame for poor housing and not vice versa; 'character deficiencies were responsible for the slums and so moral regeneration offered a solution to the housing problem ... reform emphasised moral rather than environmental improvement, a stance which dovetailed with ideological stands such as Christian teaching regarding family life and sobriety, the sanctity of property rights, prevailing *laissez-faire* orthodoxy in economic and social affairs, and ratepayers' insistence on economism in government.' Ibid., p. 44.

[6] For a detailed discussion of the French urban structure prior to the major phase of industrialization see B. Lepetit, *Les Villes dans la France Moderne (1740–1840)* (Paris: Albin Michel, 1988).

[7] 'la ville est en France une structure de durée et de force bien supérieures à celles de l'industrie'. Marcel Roncayolo cited in H-G. Haupt, *Histoire Sociale de la France depuis 1789* (Paris: Editions de la Maison des Sciences de L'Homme, 1993), pp. 91–92.

as family allowances.[8] This high birthrate continued through the 1950s and much of the 1960s, a decade when many British cities were already beginning to experience urban decline.[9]

The French local government system has three tiers: 22 *régions*, created in 1955 as economic planning regions; 96 *départements*, which originate from the end of the eighteenth century to provide a nationwide framework for law and administration; and 36 750 *communes*, dating back to the French Revolution. While differing markedly in terms of size and resources, all *communes* have powers to control planning activity and, to some extent, infrastructure development. Historically branches of central government – state field services – have delivered local services on behalf of the *communes*.[10] Indeed, from 1944 and the formation of the Ministère de la reconstruction et de l'urbanisme[11] until 1981, with the new movement towards decentralization, the urban planning process fell almost exclusively into the realm of central government technocrats. In services other than the field services, central government has been represented at the local level by the *préfecture*. When considering the structure of French local government it is important to note the close interdependence between the political and administrative spheres. In particular, the mayor is an important figure commanding a combination of both political and administrative powers.[12]

In addition to this three-tiered structure of local government, there are various mechanisms which have evolved to overcome the administrative divisions in this system. For the present study, the most important of these is the *communauté urbaine*, established under the law of 31 December 1966, since this marked a transfer of key services from the *communes* – notably, in the realms of planning, property management, public services and real estate – and represented an attempt to overcome the difficulty of coordinating and carrying out planning at the level of the *communes* in major urban areas. The first four *communautés urbaines* were created in Bordeaux, Lyon, Strasbourg and the Lille–Roubaix–Tourcoing *métropole*. The *Communauté Urbaine de Lille* (CUDL) incorporates 87 *communes* and covers an area of 61 212 hectares.

---

[8] J. Blondel, *Contemporary France: Politics, Society and Institutions* (London: Methuen, 1974), p. 9.

[9] Paris and its region achieved a rate of growth of around 8 per cent between 1962 and 1968, and many provincial cities achieved even higher rates. Ibid., p. 13.

[10] P. Le Galès and J. Mawson, *Management Innovations in Urban Policy: Lessons from France*, Working Paper (Luton: Local Government Management Board, 1994), p. 5.

[11] The ministry of reconstruction and town planning. In French, town planning is generally translated as *urbanisme*, a neologism derived from the Latin *urbs*, the city. The creation of the term is attributed to Ildefonso Cerdá, a Catalan architect and engineer who first used it in 1867 in his *Teoria general de l'urbanización*.

[12] Le Galès and Mawson, *Management Innovations in Urban Policy*, p. 5.

The British urban system still exhibits certain characteristics founded upon trade, market networks, defence and regional centres developed prior to the Industrial Revolution, but it also owes much to the socioeconomic developments of the last 250 years. London, of course, has long been the largest city, but many of the other major cities – such as Birmingham, Glasgow, Manchester, Liverpool and Newcastle – came to prominence in the course of the eighteenth and nineteenth centuries through their activities in trade and industry. Unlike French towns and cities, which have traditionally formed part of a nationwide centralized network managed by the national government, British towns have largely been managed from the local level and have thus enjoyed a degree of autonomy from central government.

While Scotland has a national capital – Edinburgh – it cannot be claimed that it has an urban network distinct from that of the rest of Britain. It does, however, have a local government structure separate from that of England and Wales. Until the Local Government (Scotland) Act, 1973, Scottish local government consisted of four city administrations, 21 large burghs, 176 small burghs, 33 counties and 196 districts. The Wheatley Commission of 1969 on local government recommended a two-tier system of government for Scotland. This was introduced under the 1973 Act and gave rise to nine regional councils, 53 district councils and the three island authorities of Orkney, Shetland and the Western Isles, where the two-tier system was not applied. Six of the nine regions divided planning powers between the regional and district authorities, while in the other three less densely populated regions, the districts had no planning powers. Essentially, the regions dealt with strategic issues such as roads, education, water supply and treatment and social services, while the districts were concerned with housing, refuse collection and leisure and tourism, as well as local land use planning.[13] Local government reorganization, implemented in mainland Scotland in April 1996, has done away with the regions and replaced them with 30 single-tier, all-purpose authorities.

There are two other differences between Scotland and England worth noting here. First, Scottish urban housing has traditionally been in the form of flats, and the tenement was the standard model of working-class accommodation in the nineteenth-century city (for more on tenement form, see Chapter Five), whereas the English model was that of the terraced house or back-to-back. As Rodger explains;

> The reasons for the distinctive housing form were an amalgam of higher Scottish building costs, a unique tenurial system, known a feuing, which increased land costs and ground burdens, a method of building finance

[13] For a full discussion of these changes see, for example, A. Midwinter, 'Shaping Scotland's New Local Authorities: Arguments, Options, Issues', *Local Government Studies*, 19:3 (1993), pp. 351–67.

> for small builders based on the technicalities of feuing which intensified building industry instability, and average real wages approximately 20–30 per cent below comparable English trades in the 1850s.[14]

The second important difference is that Scotland had, and continues to have, a much higher proportion of public housing in its stock than England. Between 1919 and 1941, as much as 70 per cent of Scottish housing was provided by local authorities, while in England virtually the same proportion (72.2 per cent) was built by the private sector.[15] As for the post-war period, of the 1 million houses constructed in Scotland between 1945 and 1984, over 76 per cent were provided by public sector agencies.[16]

Targeting the 'slums'

France

In France, the earliest legal measures against *logements insalubres* were contained in the law of 13 April 1850, which could require an owner to undertake whatever work was necessary to bring a property to a 'reasonable standard' or, alternatively, could forbid habitation should conditions be found to be irredeemable. This law, together with other legislative texts such as the *décret-loi*[17] of 25 March 1852, which introduced building regulations, the law of 5 April 1884, which imposed a general plan of street levelling and alignment upon *communes*, and the public health law of 1902, represented the genesis of planning as a public activity in France. The 1902 law gave *préfets* and mayors the right to declare a building *insalubre*, and gave *communes* the right, within certain limits, to purchase unfit housing by compulsory order. This law defined

---

[14] Rodger, *Housing in Urban Britain 1780–1914*, p. 36.

[15] R. Rodger and H. Al-Qaddo, 'The Scottish Special Housing Association and the Implementation of Housing Policy, 1937–87', in R. Rodger (ed.), *Scottish Housing in the Twentieth Century* (Leicester: Leicester University Press, 1989), p. 185.

[16] A. Gibb, 'Policy and Politics in Scottish Housing since 1945', in Rodger, *Scottish Housing in the Twentieth Century*, p. 157. In his introduction to this book, Rodger ('Introduction', p. 12) points out that the high proportion of public housing in Scotland has contributed to a particular sensitivity amongst Scottish electors to administrative performance and tenant politics. Gibb explains that this concentration has also been a catalyst for, and a product of, Labour Party pre-eminence in Scottish politics: 'The long tradition of Labour domination of Scottish politics at all levels was reinforced by the huge public sector housing programme, and the equally long tradition of Labour involvement with housing issues as a part of their socialist programmes developed into a powerful political weapon.' Gibb, 'Policy and Politics in Scottish Housing since 1945', p. 166.

[17] A *décret-loi* is a statutory order.

a *logement insalubre* as one which was 'dangerous for the health of occupants or of neighbours, either in and of itself, or due to the way it is inhabited'.[18] This was clearly a relative concept, but it is significant as an expression of the will of central government that private housing should, to some extent, come under the supervision of the *communes*. It is also interesting to note that, according to this definition, a building *per se* was not *insalubre*, but rather this label resulted from human presence in or around it.

The first law pertaining directly to urban planning was the *loi Cornudet* of 1919,[19] which had been discussed as early as 1912, but had been delayed by the outbreak of the First World War. This law introduced autonomous powers for urban planning for both the largest *communes* and for those experiencing rapid change. However, the process of drawing up plans which the law entailed, and their subsequent approval by means of a public inquiry, was both complex and laborious. The first plans only received final approval on the eve of the Second World War – too late to prevent much of the housing development that the law had been intended to control, particularly around Paris. The *loi Loucher* of 1928 introduced the concept of public housing provision with the aim of encouraging the construction of affordable housing (*habitations à bon marché*, HBM). The inter-war period also saw the development of regional planning, first with the law of 1932 which introduced the *projet d'aménagement de la région parisienne*, and later with the *décret-loi* of 1935, which extended the concept of regional plans across the country.

The single most important French planning law for the immediate post-war period was the *loi d'urbanisme* of 15 June 1943, which was deliberately intended to shift the balance of planning powers away from the *régions* and *communes* and towards central government. With the law of 1943, the basis of the centralized post-war planning system in France was established, a structure that would survive right up to the measures for decentralization introduced in 1983. A distinguishing feature of the 1943 system was the conviction that it was possible to derive a planning blueprint for the future based on the information available and circumstances prevailing at the time of a plan's formulation. The practical result of this planning methodology was a tendency to produce plans which were not only predominantly physical in nature, but also inflexible in character.

Another indication of the will of central government to assume responsibility for directing France's urban growth and developing its infrastructure and industry was the creation of the *Ministère de la Reconstruction et de*

---

[18] '... dangereux pour la santé des occupants ou des voisins, soit par lui-même, soit par les conditions dans lesquelles il est habité.'

[19] French laws often receive the name of their promoter – Cornudet was responsible for the law's introduction in the Chamber of Deputies.

l'Urbanisme (MRU) in November 1944.[20] This was the first time in France that a single administrative organization had existed to deal specifically with urban issues. For the first five years of its existence, the MRU assigned priority to rebuilding the nation's infrastructure and industry, while doing little to ameliorate the condition of the housing stock. The French government, however, did not have the financial means to match its urban ambitions and was compelled to assign part of the task of rebuilding to the private sector. In fact, the role of the private sector has long been important in urban France; for example, certain infrastructure services, such as the provision of water, have been undertaken by private companies since the nineteenth century. In the post-war period this participation has extended to include the construction and management of urban projects. The *sociétés économie mixte* (SEMs) have been one of the principal means by which the financing of various forms of development, including house building and urban renewal, has been carried out.[21] While the local authority maintains the majority share in the enterprise (normally something between 50 and 80 per cent), private sector partners are also invited to participate. The SEM is therefore a limited company in which, as majority shareholders, the local *collectivités* assume both overall control of the operation and the financial risk involved.

The new post-war system worked well for the period of reconstruction, but by the 1950s problems were appearing, which demanded a new approach. First and foremost, the housing crisis could no longer be overlooked. The Second World War had seen some 450 000 houses totally destroyed and another 850 000 left uninhabitable.[22] However, the crisis was not only precipitated by war damage, but also by the growth of the urban industrial population fuelled by rural–urban migration (particularly in the Paris region) and a hiatus in house building and maintenance during the war years. In 1850 there had been 8.5 million people living in towns with a population of more than 2000, a figure which represented 24 per cent of the total French population at the time. By 1950 there were 22 million: 54 per cent of the population.[23] While much of the growth was concentrated in the Paris area, from around 1950 many provincial French towns also began to boom, and Lyon, Marseille and the Lille conurbation all passed the 1 million mark. The plight of the homeless and inadequately housed, which became particularly acute during the harsh winters

---

[20] Ministry of Reconstruction and Planning. See D. Voldman (ed.), *Images, Discours et Enjeux de la Reconstruction des Villes Françaises après 1945*, Cahiers de l'Insitut d'histoire du temps présent, no. 5 (Paris: Centre national de la recherche scientifique, 1987), p. 6.

[21] E. Chaperon-Davidovitch, *Les Instruments de Planification Urbaine* (Paris: La Documentation Française, 1976), p. 11.

[22] The major cities which suffered from war damage were Le Havre, Rouen, Caen, Brest, Lorient, Saint-Nazaire, Strasbourg, Mulhouse, Marseille and Toulon.

[23] Cited in Chaperon-Davidovitch, *Les Instruments de Planification Urbaine*, p. 8.

of 1953 and 1954, was championed by *abbé* Pierre, a priest whose activities did much to make the general public more aware of the housing shortage, and housing conditions became a favourite theme for the media at this time. Demographic trends also began to provoke concerns over housing provision, as marriage rates and, subsequently, birthrates began to rise. Brun and Roncayolo have interpreted these demographic trends as an expression of the *idéologie de croissance* – growth ideology – that marked the post-war period.[24]

In 1950 the massive government housing effort got under way. This year was marked by the setting up of treasury loans at very favourable rates for the construction of *habitations à loyer modéré* (HLM)[25] – that is, housing constructed for rent at the initiative of local government and intended for low-income households. It also saw the establishment of the *Crédit Foncier de France* to provide loans to fund construction, and the introduction of legislation to make participation in the *Comité Interprofessionel du Logement* (CIL) compulsory for all private sector firms with a workforce of more than ten employees. (CIL had originally been set up by textile factory owners in Roubaix in 1929 as a paternalistic organization which contributed 1 per cent of the value of salaries towards workers' housing.) Yet it was not simply the housing crisis that provoked the government to encourage construction. As Vayssière points out, from the Second World War until 1957, the aim behind the reconstruction of French cities was the fast and efficient imposition of the 'technical policies of the state',[26] founded on a vision of effective transport systems, the flexibility of architectural units, the mobility of manual workers, and a better adjustment of the industrial potential of each *département*. Thus the restructuring of the run-down districts of French cities and the creation of new zones of housing in peripheral areas had a clear strategic economic aim.

Eugène Claudius-Petit, Minister of Reconstruction and Planning from September 1948 to January 1953, announced a target of 20 000 housing units to be constructed in France per month. This was a major undertaking which could only be achieved by the rationalization of building methods and the use of new techniques of industrial construction such as the *système Castor*. These systems used prefabricated parts assembled on-site according to a basic formula which

---

[24] J. Brun and M. Roncayolo, 'Production de la ville et du bâti', in G. Duby (ed.), *Histoire de la France Urbaine*, Vol. 5, ed. M. Roncayolo (Paris: Senil, 1985), p. 290. They also note that it was in this atmosphere of growth that investors began to invest in housing construction. As construction costs fell in relation to the level of rents, this option became even more attractive. Government at all levels was enthusiastic to encourage these investors: 'c'est l'époque où il devient nécessaire pour un maire d'avoir l'image d'un bâtisseur'. Ibid., p. 289.

[25] 'housing at moderate rent'. This replaced the HBM.

[26] 'politiques techniques d'Etat'. B. Vayssière, 'La Reconstruction en France', in J. Dethier and A. Guiheux (eds), *La Ville: Art et Architecture en Europe* (Paris: Editions du Centre Pompidou, 1994), p. 412.

offered flexibility as to the number of housing units constructed. Building sites could thus be organized around mechanization and the repetition of building elements. Drawing upon the economies of scale, these 'system building' techniques provided a much cheaper means of construction housing than traditional methods. As a result of this combination of political will and technical ability, the annual housing construction rate rose rapidly. In 1938, a total of 56 000 houses had been constructed in France.[27] By 1954, the year *abbé* Pierre introduced his *cités d'urgence* – emergency shelters – the figure had risen to 240 000 units per year, and by 1956 the construction rate had surpassed 300 000 units, partly through a greater budgetary commitment to public construction and an increase in grants to the private sector, but also partly as a result of a reduction in housing unit floorspace.[28]

Despite these figures, President De Gaulle called for an even greater effort. At a press conference on 24 July 1958, he emphasized the necessity of a system of centralized planning in order to ensure that construction programmes benefited France as a whole:

> The housing problem is of such dimensions that one can only envisage a solution by means of extremely extensive phases which challenge all sorts of subjects and all sorts of interests. We must not only construct wherever necessary, under whatever conditions are necessary, but also distribute these developments throughout the country in a way that will suit the whole of France.[29]

From 1954 to 1967, construction rates in the public sector were irregular, but overall the trend was upwards: in 1953, 18 000 HLMs for rent were started; by 1967 this figure had risen to 129 000.[30] HLMs also grew as a proportion of the overall housing output in these years: by 1964, despite a dip between 1960 and 1964, 28 per cent of housing authorized was public or para-public, and by 1968 this figure had risen to 36 per cent.[31]

---

[27] As compared with 360 000 in Great Britain and 400 000 in Germany for the same year. See Randet et al., *Trente-cinq ans d'urbanisme* (Paris: Centre de Recherche et de Recontres d'Urbanisme, 1981), p. 11.

[28] Ibid., p. 17. The maximum level of annual production (550 000) was reached in 1972 after stagnation in the mid-1960s. Brun and Roncayolo, 'Production de la ville et du bâti', p. 289.

[29] 'Le problème du logement est d'une telle dimension qu'il ne peut être envisagé de solution par étapes extrêmement étendues et qui mettent en cause toute espèce de sujets et toute espèce d'intérêts. Il s'agit non seulement de construire où il faut, dans les conditions qu'il faut, et de les répartir sur le territoire d'une manière qui convienne au développement de la France tout entière.' Cited in G. Garin and J.P. Muret, 'Chronologie: 1958–1967', in Randet et al., *Trente-cinq ans d'urbanisme*, p. 103.

[30] C. Topalov, *Le Logement en France. Histoire d'une marchandise impossible* (Paris: Presses de la Fondation nationale des sciences politiques, 1990), p. 244.

[31] Ibid., p. 237.

From around 1955 onwards, the centralized housing drive began to produce the *grands ensembles* – massive developments of apartment blocks and collective infrastructure. These developments were often badly constructed from poor-quality, prefabricated industrial materials which could be assembled both quickly and cheaply and were, moreover, generally located on the urban periphery, where land was cheapest. The *grands ensembles* contained a wide range of housing categories which, depending on one's political perspective, were intended either to match the requirements of different socioeconomic divisions of the population, or to impose divisions within the working class.[32] In an attempt to impose greater control over the development of the *grands ensembles* and to extend its own role as constructor, the government introduced the *zone à urbaniser par priorité* (ZUP) on 31 December 1958. The ZUP – the first of a bewildering array of French zonal planning tools – had to cover an area at least large enough to contain 5000 housing units plus the necessary ancillary equipment and infrastructure. Between 1960 and 1970, more than 200 ZUPs were created in France, representing some 1 million housing units.[33] The legislative tools associated with the ZUP enabled a higher rate of construction than had previously been possible, and while the ZUP ultimately produced *grands ensembles* on an even bigger scale, these were less bereft of services and facilities than the earlier examples. Such ambitious projects inevitably involved the movement of a large number of people but, in contrast to the situation in

[32] The *grands ensembles* in fact contained a wide range of housing categories; *logements économiques normalisés* (1952), *logements populaires et familiaux* (1954), *logements des cités de transition* (1960), *immeubles à loyer normal* (1961), *programmes sociales de relogement* (1961), *immeubles à loyer modéré* (1968), *programmes à loyer réduit* (1968). These were intended to house different socioeconomic divisions of the population. One perspective argues that these different categories responded to ideas of social justice, aiming to reduce the resource gap between different categories of the population in the field of housing. An alternative view, which derives from a Marxist perspective, held that the state multiplied its housing categories in order to produce divisions within the working class by introducing a system of relative privilege. However, Mehl, arguing from a Marxist perspective, concludes that the position of different social classes in the housing structure does not precisely correspond to their position in the structure of employment. See Mehl, 'La lutte des résidents dans les grandes ensembles', *Sociologie du Travail*, no. 3 (1975), pp. 351–71. Brun and Roncayolo suggest that the state was not clear as to whether social segregation or social mixing best served its needs and that, in any case, the allocation of housing was more decentralized than is normally recognized, being the task of CILs, *collectivités locales* and SEMs. Brun and Roncayolo, 'Production de la ville et du bâti', p. 298.

[33] J-C. Marquis, *L'Aménagement du Territoire et Urbanisme* (Hellemes: Ester, 1991), p. 78. The *zone à urbaniser par priorité* was replaced by the *zone d'aménagement concerté* (ZAC) in 1967. The ZAC was essentially an extension of the concept of the ZUP and represented a more flexible and versatile planning tool which was intended to facilitate and coordinate planning projects between *collectivités publiques* and private developers.

Britain where local authorities often had difficulty in persuading neighbouring authorities to accept overspill populations (Glasgow being a case in point), in France, the fact that central government and not the local *communes* played the key role in these operations made the movement of populations from clearance areas across administrative boundaries to peripheral *grands ensembles* relatively unproblematic.

The architectural form of French public housing in this period was derived from the modernist style. Indeed, modernism was invoked even when its principles were manipulated. The high-quality materials, facilities, open space provision and sheer good design found in the projects of Le Corbusier or the Bauhaus architects were frequently dispensed with in order to reduce costs. In practice, the *grands ensembles* which sprang up on the periphery of French cities were distorted versions of the modernist vision, twisted to meet political and financial requirements.[34] This form of housing was finally brought to an end by the *circulaire Guichard* in 1973, which forbade the construction of *ensembles d'habitation* of more than 2000 houses and blocked those projects already under way. However, it is important to remember that at the time of their construction, the *grands ensembles*, like the equivalent developments in Britain, were widely welcomed as providing the solution to the housing issue. They offered larger, better-equipped apartments to those who had spent years on housing waiting lists living in run-down, insanitary conditions, and they presented both local and central government with a means to construct quickly and cheaply at a time when this was a pressing social and political requirement.

As for areas of older, run-down housing, central government introduced two successive forms of planning tools aimed at restructuring existing areas of cities; *rénovation urbaine* (RU) and *résorption de l'habitat insalubre* (RHI). The process of *rénovation urbaine* was instigated in 1958 under the Third Plan (1958–61). This initiated what Levy has described as the most important restructuring of French urban centres since Haussman's restructuring of Paris under Napoleon III.[35] It was this law that permitted the huge renewal operations of the 1960s – particularly in the Parisian region, where there were more than 100 operations, covering over 600 hectares and involving the demolition of

---

[34] Playing devil's advocate, Jacques Brun reminds us of the 'modernist' ideal in the 1950s which saw housing as a product for consumption which would be renewed, according to taste and technical developments, within a period of some 20 years. On this basis, we should not be shocked by the ephemerality of so much of the post-war public housing stock. J. Brun, 'Nouvelles approches', in Duby, *Histoire de la France*, Vol. 5, p. 325.

[35] J-P. Levy, 'Les quartiers anciens, une histoire qui finit bien?', in J-P. Levy (ed.), *La Réhabilitation des quartiers anciens et de l'habitat existant: Acteurs, procédures, effets at conséquences sociales* (Toulouse: Presses Universitaires du Mirail, 1990), p. 11.

more than 50 000 houses and the construction of some 85 000.[36] In fact, like the English term 'renewal', '*rénovation*' is rather misleading since it refers in fact to a process of complete demolition followed by entirely new construction. The target for this *rénovation* was areas of housing classified as *zones de rénovation urbaine*. In these *zones* the majority of buildings had been designated *insalubre* – that is, they were considered to provide a level of hygiene below the accepted norm. The criteria employed in this judgement included the geological situation, the narrowness of the street, the proximity of industry, the quality of construction, the presence of damp, the condition of the stairs and the general state of each property.[37]

The initial stages of the process of *rénovation* were carried out by public sector planning agencies and involved the acquisition of the buildings and land within the *zone de rénovation urbaine*, by compulsory purchase if necessary. The population within the perimeter of the *zone* was rehoused and the buildings were demolished. Meanwhile, an operational plan for the area was drawn up. Once cleared, the land was prepared for construction and put in the hands of builders, who constructed housing, and the *commune*, which provided the necessary infrastructure. If *rénovation* was generally presented as the act of removing substandard housing to replace it with new, it was also a means of making more efficient use of high-value urban ground space and an attempt to modernize the fabric – and, indeed, the demographic structure – of the city in response to contemporary requirements.

The *rénovation* procedure was very costly, both for the public agencies involved and for local government, since they were required to split the deficit of any operation equally. In part, deficits were large because of the scale of the *rénovation* operations, but also because the public sector was burdened by the costs of clearance and infrastructure provision, while the principal beneficiary of the operation was the private sector.[38] The high cost of *rénovation urbaine* to the public sector finally led to its replacement by *résorption de l'habitat insalubre* under the hastily prepared *loi Vivien* of 10 July 1970 and its subsequent *décrets d'application* in 1971. The RHI procedure was derived from the *loi Debré* of 14 December 1964,[39] which was originally intended to

[37] P. Merlin and F. Choay, *Dictionnaire de l'Urbanisme et de l'Aménagement* (Paris: Presses Universitaires de France, 1988), p. 579.

[37] Coing, *Rénovation Urbaine et Changement Social: L'îlot no. 4 (Paris 13e)* (Paris: Les Editions Ouvrières, 1966), p. 33.

[38] In this, Roubaix, was an exception in that the operations had a distinctly 'social' character, but this only contributed to the size of the deficit.

[39] The *loi Debré* allowed for the compulsory purchase of 'land upon which are employed, for the purpose of habitation, premises or installations which are unsuited to this use for reasons of hygiene, security or salubrity'. Translation of citation from the *loi Debré* in Descamps, 'La résorption des courées de la Métropole Nord', unpublished thesis, University of Lille (1976), p. 4.

facilitate the expropriation of land in *bidonvilles* or shanty towns, but was later extended to include other problem areas including the *courées* of towns such as Roubaix and Tourcoing in the north.[40]

Like *rénovation urbaine*, *résorption de l'habitat insalubre* involved identifying an area of housing as *insalubre*, evacuating the population of the designated area, clearing the land and, finally, constructing new housing. Unlike *rénovation*, however, this last phase had to be public – that is, either HLM housing or collective infrastructure. A special financial procedure known as *programmes de relogement de l'habitat insalubre* (PRI) was introduced for families coming from areas designated *insalubre*. PRI ensured that priority in the allocation of funds was accorded to the construction of housing, the precise number of units being fixed as a function of the number of families whose homes were targeted for demolition in the RHI process. For example, construction programmes in Roubaix between 1970 and 1973 saw 1807 houses demolished and 2194 new houses built in their place and, of this new housing, almost all was assigned for the *programme de relogement de l'habitat insalubre*.[41] RHI also provided a much more highly developed element of social support or *action sociale* for an area undergoing renewal than had been available under *rénovation*, and for this reason the social services had an important role to play. Programmes of social education were provided in order both to facilitate the process of evacuation (and to discourage resistance) and to 'stabilize' residents in their new homes and encourage them towards 'good habits'. Paradoxically, the conditions of access to public housing via PRI were quite rigorous: those who were automatically excluded from the process included the economically inactive (the elderly, the unemployed or the long-term ill for example), single people, and families with four or more children. This resulted in public housing allocated for PRI often laying empty for many months because of the difficulty of finding suitable tenants from the population of 'slum' areas.

The RHI procedure was more flexible than that of *rénovation*, and more efficient in terms of the procedures of compulsory purchase and the rapid evacuation of the inhabitants of the area. Moreover, the discourse on *insalubrité* under RHI was both more developed and more technical than under *rénovation*: an *îlot insalubre* was defined as one in which the *conseil départemental d'hygiène* assessed 80 per cent of the buildings in the block to be in a condition liable to be injurious to health. A *circulaire* of 27 August 1971 laid out a method intended to objectivize the measurement of *insalubrité*. This involved a list

[40] The characteristics of the *courées* will be discussed in detail in Chapter Three. They were assimilated with the *bidonvilles* after the decision of the *Conseil d'Etat* in 1969–70. This had little impact, since the *loi Vivien* was voted in shortly afterwards.

[41] D. Cornuel and B. Duriez, *Le mirage urbain: histoire de logement à Roubaix* (Paris: Editions Anthropos, 1983), p. 191.

of 12 essential criteria and 10 secondary criteria, all to be assessed as ‘good’, ‘mediocre’ or ‘poor’. The 12 essential criteria were:

1. Surroundings and servicing [*desserte*]
2. Prospect and illumination
3. The general provision of the *plan d’occupation des sols* and the density of construction
4. The general layout of the housing; volumes and habitable surfaces
5. The general nature of construction and the materials employed
6. Presence of humidity due to rising damp
7. Presence of humidity due to water penetration, inadequate waterproofing, poor ventilation or poor insulation
8. Quality of ventilation
9. Heating facilities and number and quality of flues
10. Number and quality of WCs and quality of wastewater plumbing
11. State of common facilities, courtyards, stairs, passages and so on
12. State of general upkeep and possibility of deterioration

On the basis of this complex system of scoring, a building was identified as either habitable or *insalubre*. Of those buildings classified *insalubre*, the scoring also indicated whether their condition was remediable or irremediable.

In short, in comparison with the earlier legislation, RHI reduced the cost of renewal, made the procedure less laborious and speeded the eviction process. However, in a sense, RU and RHI represented the same process, regardless of judicial definitions – that is, they involved the identification of areas of unfit housing through the ‘objective’ application of a technical definition which left no scope for other identifications, such as ‘home’ or ‘community’. The dysfunctional old housing was replaced by functional new housing founded on the modernist paradigm, and just as there was a reconstruction of the housing stock, so too was there a rationalization of the population of the old housing, not all of whom were entitled to an apartment in the new developments.

Great Britain

The origins of statutory town planning in Great Britain lie in nineteenth-century reactions to the unplanned urban areas which emerged in the wake of the Industrial Revolution.[42] The earliest measures were not strictly to do with

[42] There were, of course, exceptions to the general pattern of uncontrolled development – notably the workers’ housing at Port Sunlight, started in 1888 by William Hersketh Lever close to the site of his new factory, and George Cadbury’s model village started in 1894 next to his factory in Birmingham. An earlier example was that of Robert Owen’s New Lanark in central Scotland which marked a visionary, if unsuccessful,

planning, but were founded on sanitary and public health initiatives and measures to combat smog.[43] Thus, for example, the Public Health Act of 1848 granted sanitary powers to local boards of health, while the Public Health Act of 1875 attempted to impose sanitary regulations on the areas of poor-quality housing which were being thrown up to cater for the rapidly expanding industrial workforce. The first general powers which enabled municipalities to undertake positive planning emerged with the Town and Country Planning Act of 1909 and the Housing, Town Planning etc. Act of 1919, which established a system of rigid, zone-based extension planning for the layout of new streets and the provision of piped water, sewerage and gas.

The legacy of poor-quality nineteenth-century housing was not only much greater in Britain than in France, but also much greater in Scotland than in England. According to Rodger and Al-Qaddo, 'Urban Scots were five times more overcrowded than their English counterparts in 1911'. This persuaded government statisticians to amend the Scottish criterion for overcrowding so that it appeared less unfavourable.[44]

By the end of the First World War, Britain was facing a serious housing crisis; house building had ceased during the war and the existing stock had continued to decline unchecked. Furthermore, rent control measures introduced in 1915 had exacerbated the problem by making the construction of housing for rent unattractive to the private sector.[45] To counter this trend, the 1919 Act made it a statutory requirement that local authorities should provide housing with

---

attempt to establish an alternative social and economic system. See A. Sutcliffe, *Towards The Planned City* (Oxford: Basil Blackwell, 1981), pp. 57 & 64.

[43] Urban poverty became a pressing issue in nineteenth-century Britain. This concern reflected the development of paternalism and philanthropy amongst the middle classes, the perceived threat to social stability engendered in the rapid changes brought about by industrial development, the 'destabilizing' effect of migrant workers and the growth of self-awareness amongst the working classes. Some of the most famous nineteenth-century surveys of living conditions of the urban poor are provided by Chadwick's *Report on the Sanitary Conditions of the Labouring Population of Great Britain* (1842), ed. and intro. M.W. Flinn (Edinburgh: Edinburgh University Press, *c.*1965, originally published London: Poor Law Commission, 1842), Friedrich Engels, *The Condition of the Working Class in England from Personal Observation and Authentic Sources* (London: Laurence and Wishart, 1984; originally published 1845; English edn 1892), Charles Booth, with his *Descriptive Map of London Poverty*, Publication no. 130 (London: London Topographical Society, 1889; repr. 1984), and Joseph Rowntree's 1901 survey of poverty in York.

[44] Rodger and Al-Qaddo, 'The Scottish Special Housing Association and the Implementation of Housing Policy, 1937–87', p. 184. Reasons for the higher levels of overcrowding in Scotland included lower average wage rates than in England, and a narrow economic base (textiles, iron and steel, heavy industry) that was prone to both structural and cyclical problems in the inter-war period. Ibid., pp. 184–5.

[45] M.S. Gibson and M.J. Langstaff, *An Introduction to Urban Renewal* (London: Hutchison, 1982), p. 22.

the support of an Exchequer subsidy, and it was this measure which marked the genesis of the British council estate. Despite further legislation, such as the Town and Country Planning Act 1932, much of the initial impetus of the 1909 and 1919 Acts was dissipated in the course of the inter-war period. As in France, the legislation proved to be complicated, and it failed to provide authorities with sufficient powers in the face of private suburban housing development.

As for slum clearance, little demolition was undertaken during the 1920s since, in the face of a general housing shortage, slum areas fulfilled a need, albeit inefficiently. By the end of this decade however, the scale of the problem had become apparent and clearance became an important political issue. Under the 1929–31 Labour government, Arthur Greenwood introduced the Housing and Slum Clearance Act 1930 with the aim of easing demographic pressure in the most congested cities by shifting population to council estates and so permitting the replanning of the dense urban centres. The act gave local authorities powers for area clearance and compulsory purchase, and from this point on slum clearance gained momentum, reaching an inter-war peak in 1939.[46]

It would be misleading to identify the Second World War as marking a clean break in the philosophy of town planning. Rather, as Cherry argues, many of the ideas underpinning post-war planning practice developed from inter-war planning thought.[47] Particularly influential was the inter-war report of the Barlow Commission which was set up prior to the outbreak of war in order to review and reassess the planning system.[48] This report, submitted in 1940, was to form the basis of post-war planning philosophy. It called for the redevelopment of congested areas and the dispersal of both population and industry from these areas. This eventually resulted in the ambitious New Town Act of 1946.[49] The new towns were intended to give direction to the movement of population out of the cities, since the expansion of existing urban centres was constrained by green belts – bands of undeveloped land around cities

---

[46] In England and Wales, according to Gibson and Langstaff, *An Introduction to Urban Renewal*, p. 24. Cullingworth quotes a demolition rate of 90 000 per year in 1938. See J.B. Cullingworth, *Town and Country Planning in Britain*, 10th edn (London: Unwin Hyman, 1988), p. 270.

[47] G.E. Cherry, *Urban Change and Planning: A History of Urban Development in Britain since 1750* (Henley-on-Thames: G.T. Foulis & Co, 1972), p. 156.

[48] Set up as the Royal Commission on the Distribution of the Industrial Population under Sir Montague Barlow.

[49] Since this date some 25 new towns have been designated, with another three which might more accurately be termed town extension schemes. The first New Town Act was passed in 1946 and the second in 1959. For a discussion of the New Town phenomenon in Great Britain see F. Shaffer, *The New Town Story* (London: Palladin, 1970).

upon which development was prevented by law.[50] The Barlow Report also recommended setting up a central planning agency, and this resulted in the establishment of the Ministry of Town and Country Planning in 1943.

As in France, the British government in the post-war period was keen to influence industrial location, and the Distribution of Industry Act was introduced in 1945 with the aim of promoting regional balance. However, the single most important piece of legislation was the Labour government's Town and Country Planning Act 1947, under which all pre-war enactments were repealed and a new era in comprehensive land planning was initiated. With the 1947 Act, virtually all development was brought under government control by making it subject to planning permission. County councils and county borough councils were required to prepare and submit development plans for their areas to the appropriate government minister. These plans indicated proposals for land use and the physical aspects of the environment, including sectors for residential, industrial and business purposes, schools, shopping areas and principal traffic routes. Like the equivalent legislation in France, this represented the philosophy of inflexible 'blueprint' planning – that is, the identification of an ultimate *goal*, while tending to overlook the *process* by which this goal might be achieved. The 1947 Act also gave local authorities the power to declare Comprehensive Development Areas (CDAs): within areas characterized by obsolete housing (that is, areas where housing was found to be in a poor structural and sanitary condition) and by bad layout (that is, an inefficient road system and mixed land uses) local authorities had the right to rehouse the population, take ownership of property by compulsory purchase if necessary, demolish the existing buildings and reconstruct, employing the functional separation of housing, industry, roads and so on. This operation was carried out with subsidies from the Exchequer. In practice, CDAs were restricted almost exclusively to city centre redevelopments incorporating offices and commerce and therefore had little impact on the housing problem. Glasgow, as discussed in Chapters Five and Six, was an exception to this rule.

The system of town and country planning set up in Britain after the Second World War was an ambitious one which bore the mark of Victorian utopian thinking. Sutcliffe argues that after the war, the general expectation of social progress and an extension of democracy towards socialism contributed to a widely held assumption that planning powers would be strengthened.[51] As Ravetz puts it, the conditions in post-war Britain created a very particular atmosphere: 'In the 1940s the effort, sacrifice, hope and euphoria of planning

---

[50] In Britain the green belts produced a characteristic molecular urban form distinct from the more tentacular form found in most of Europe. See A. Sutcliffe, 'La Reconstruction en Grande-Bretagne', in Dethier and Guiheux, *La Ville*.

[51] Ibid., p. 410.

were at such a pitch that people very naturally thought the magnificent phoenix of town planning, emerging from the ashes of war, was the authentic golden bird.'[52]

The planning system created in this period was characterized by a sense of confidence which united an elite group of 'experts' and social reformers who together strove to create a 'utopia on the ground'.[53] The 1947 Act incorporated no legal requirement that the public should have an opportunity to become involved in the process of plan development. The requirements of the community were decided by its political representatives and communicated to the 'technical elite' of planners who produced the plan. This system rested on the conviction that a 'best' or 'optimal' solution existed. This in turn implied that planning was somehow neutral and that the planner was an apolitical actor whose task was simply to apply their technical expertise to the objective maximization of the 'public good'.

After the Second World War slum clearance was suspended as attention was directed once more towards combating the general housing shortage.[54] In the course of the War, 200 000 houses had been destroyed, with a further 250 000 damaged to the extent of being uninhabitable.[55] Even bombing was not free of social bias; since industrial areas were the principal targets, it was the surrounding working-class housing which bore the brunt of bomb damage. The 'housing drive' began in 1946 under the new Labour government, with local authorities, supported by government subsidies, as the principal builders.[56] At this time, Britain's construction record and planning system was regarded as a model for other countries, including France.[57] Between 1945 and 1950, Britain constructed five to six times more housing than France. Not only was the sheer amount of construction impressive, so too was the legislation, the new town policy, the operation of local government and the overarching organizational

[52] A. Ravetz, *Remaking Cities* (London: Croom Helm, 1980), pp. 57–58.

[53] Ibid., p. 40.

[54] For efforts to repair Britain's housing stock in the immediate post-war period, see J. Yelling, 'Public Policy, Urban Renewal and Property Ownership, 1945–55', *Urban History*, 22 (1995), pp. 48–62. Within a short time it was felt that clearance, rather than repair, offered the best way ahead.

[55] D.V. Donnison (1967), *The Government of Housing*, p. 163. Cited in Gibson and Langstaff, *An Introduction to Urban Renewal*, p. 26.

[56] One of the best and most comprehensive accounts of the urgency and dynamism of the housing drive in post-war Scotland, England, Northern Ireland and Wales is provided by M. Glendinning and S. Muthesius, *Tower Block: Modern Public Housing in England, Scotland, Wales and Northern Ireland* (New Haven and London: Yale University Press/ Paul Mellon Centre for Studies in British Art, 1994). This work succeeds in locating the efforts of individual councils, and indeed, individual councillors, in the wider social, economic, political and intellectual context of the period.

[57] France also looked to the USA and, due to the quality of its architecture, Sweden.

system.[58] However, after a positive start, Labour's housing campaign began to lose its momentum, and the Conservatives' undertaking to build 300 000 houses per year was a significant element in their election victory of 1951. By 1953 the Conservatives had fulfilled their housing target, partly as a result of improvements in the general economic situation and partly due to a relaxation of the building standards laid down for the construction of new council dwellings. By 1954 they had introduced a housing policy which encouraged the role of the private sector in housing provision. They also increased levels of housing improvement grants.[59] From the 1950s the private housing sector began to expand, while subsidies for local authority construction were eroded and, after 1959, building for the private sector became the dominant element in the construction market.

On the initiative of Harold Macmillan, at that time Conservative Minister of Housing and Local Government, slum clearance was finally resumed in 1954, partly prompted by the findings of the 1951 census, which had revealed the extent of unfit housing. Labour too, recognizing the importance of clearance for the housing issue, gave the project its wholehearted support. As Ravetz has pointed out, and indeed, as is borne out by the events analysed in Chapters Five and Six, this opened a field of potential conflict between Labour administrations and local community groups when opposition to clearance began to grow.

In 1957 the Housing Act for England and Wales was introduced, which defined the stages involved in clearance, including the definition of the area, the acquisition of property and the issue of financial compensation for residents. The procedure was defined by central government, and local authority discretion only came into operation at the stage of rehousing the displaced population.[60] This act included a set of criteria to define an 'unfit' dwelling, based on the provision of facilities for the storage and preparation of food, ventilation, lighting and the structural stability of the building. The 1957 Act states in section 4(1):

> in determining ... whether a house is unfit for human habitation, regard shall be had to its condition in respect to the following matters, that is to say:
> a) repair
> b) stability
> c) freedom from damp
> d) natural lighting
> e) ventilation

---

[58] Morel, 'Reconstruire, dirent-ils. Discours et doctrines de l'urbanisme', in Voldman, *Images, Discours et Enjeux*, p. 39.

[59] Gibson and Langstaff, *An Introduction to Urban Renewal*, p. 27.

[60] Ibid., p. 32.

> f) water supply
> g) drainage and sanitary conveniences
> h) facilities for storage, preparation and cooking of food and for the disposal of waste water
> and the house shall be deemed unfit for human habitation if and only if it is so far defective in one or more of the said matters that it is not reasonably suited for occupation in that condition.[61]

The 1957 Act represented an attempt to provide an objective set of criteria to assess the condition of a house but, in practice, each of these measures was subjectively judged by a medical officer or environmental health officer. In addition, under the 1957 Act, any back-to-back dwellings were automatically designated 'unfit'.[62] The act also provided powers which enabled areas of housing to be condemned *en bloc*, and an area identified for clearance might also include sound houses if it was considered that the area as a whole suffered from 'bad arrangement' or that the properties in question prevented the complete redevelopment of the area.[63] A local authority was not required by law to demonstrate that such demolition was absolutely *necessary*, but simply that it was *reasonable*.

Until the introduction of the Housing (Scotland) Act of 1969, Scottish legislation regarding clearance and redevelopment closely mirrored that of England and Wales. However, on the recommendation of the 1967 Scottish Advisory Committee's report on the condition of the nation's older housing stock,[64] the 1969 Act introduced the concept of 'tolerable' rather than 'unfit' housing in an attempt to obtain a greater degree of objectivity in the assessment of housing conditions. Cullingworth lists the factors that contribute to make a house 'tolerable': it must be structurally stable and substantially free from damp; it must have satisfactory provision for natural and artificial lighting, ventilation and heating; and there should be adequate piped water, a sink providing both hot and cold water, and a WC located in the house or building for

[61] Section 4 (1) of Housing Act, 1957. Cited in D.A. Kirby, *Slum Housing and Residential Renewal: The Case in Urban Britain* (London: Longman, 1979), p. 14. This definition was to remain virtually unchanged, although under the 1969 Housing Act the list was amended to include 'satisfactory internal arrangement', while the term 'storage' was deleted.

[62] 'Back-to-backs' were a distinct form of nineteenth-century working-class housing found in England and Wales. They were generally terraced, two-storey brick-built buildings. They were arranged in such a way that two terraces, back to back, shared a common wall. With only one external wall for windows and a door, efficient ventilation was impossible.

[63] A. Ravetz, *The Government of Space: Town Planning in Modern Society* (London: Faber & Faber, 1986), p. 75.

[64] Scottish Housing Advisory Committee, *Scotland's Older Houses* (London: HMSO, 1967).

the exclusive use of its occupants. The house must also provide for the drainage and disposal of foul and surface water, have satisfactory facilities for cooking food and satisfactory access to all external doors and outbuildings. While this set of criteria did not remove the element of subjective judgement, the advantage of this system over its English counterpart was that a house was automatically below the acceptable standard if it failed on *any one* of these criteria, whereas the English and Welsh equivalent required local authorities to make an *overall assessment* of the property's condition.[65] In Scotland, the tenement building has been the principal target for demolition, with some 300 000 demolished since the Second World War. Many of these were in a particularly bad condition and their internal construction would have made upgrading both difficult and costly. Added to this was the issue of multiple ownership since, with several property owners under the same roof, repair and upgrading were further complicated.[66]

In the 1960s, planning increasingly became a means of controlling, directing and encouraging growth. This period was marked by the optimistic belief that social justice could be achieved by the creation of more wealth rather than through a more just distribution of existing resources. At heart, the solution was technical; consumption was the watchword of the affluent society and progress was to be achieved through technology. It was an era encapsulated by Harold Wilson's image at the 1963 Labour Party Conference of a new Britain 'forged in the white-heat of a technological revolution'.[67] In this atmosphere, issues of energy and environment were given little consideration. For example, the Parker Morris Report of 1961 provided a new set of housing standards which barely touched upon the economics of heating and fuel.[68] The functional separation of urban land uses – housing, industry, road systems, shopping and so on – became a key element in the rational, scientific planning methods which represented the paradigm in this period.

Massive demolition programmes demanded a complementary programme of house construction, and in the prevailing political and social climate tower blocks were hailed as the solution. Their rise was due in part to government subsidies, in part to architectural fashion and in part to an inconclusive debate on the need to protect land from urban sprawl in order to maintain it for agricultural purposes. Large and politically influential construction companies

---

[65] Cullingworth, *Town and Country Planning in Britain*, 10th edn, pp. 272–73.

[66] Thus, under the 1974 Act local authorities have the power to require the compulsory improvement of whole tenement blocks or closes, since improvement must be carried out collectively.

[67] Cited in S.V. Ward, *Planning and Urban Change* (London: Paul Chapman Publishing, 1994), p. 121.

[68] Central Housing Advisory Committee, *Homes for Today and Tomorrow* [Parker Morris Report] (London: HMSO, 1961).

were keen to employ the new high-rise 'system building' techniques which allowed them to construct tower blocks as mass-produced objects. Here, for example, is an advertising feature by Wimpey Construction from *The Glasgow Herald* in June 1964:

> The essence of any economic system of mass production is continuity. That holds good whether they are motor cars, canned peas, guitars, or houses that are being produced.
> Once the necessary plant and equipment have been purchased and installed they must be kept going in order to pay their way. Tower cranes, concrete mixers, or skips standing idle are wasting somebody's money ...[69]

It is interesting to note the positive emphasis given to efficient mass production and the parallel between 'canned peas' and houses in this text – a parallel entirely consistent with the belief that technology and progress went hand-in-hand.

Market pressure, heavy advertising and efficient lobbying on the part of these large construction firms contributed to the huge shift towards mass-produced housing which marked the 1950s and 1960s. Between 1950 and 1970, almost 1.5 million people were rehoused from slum dwellings and waiting lists into high-rise flats.[70] Each construction system was patented and both off-site prefabrication and on-site assembly required specialized equipment and involved considerable economies of scale beyond the capabilities of small firms. As a result, over 75 per cent of industrialized high-rise flats were built by the largest seven construction firms; by contrast, these same firms accounted for only around 6 per cent of the nation's total construction output.[71]

System building had been first employed on mainland Europe, where it had proved both cheaper and more efficient than it ever was in Britain.[72] In architectural terms, the developments undertaken in this period can be divided into three basic types, each of which was derived from ideas of the International Movement in architecture. The first was the tower or point block which, according to Ward, was derived from precedents on mainland Europe, including inter-war schemes in France and post-war schemes in Sweden. The second form was the slab block, which can be traced back to Le Corbusier and his theoretical work for *la ville radieuse* and the applied form of the *unité d'habitation* as constructed in Marseilles (1946–52). The third type was the deck-access block, a horizontal form linking flats by elevated 'streets' which also owed its origins to Le Corbusier.[73]

---

[69] 'Speed and Saving in Wimpey Building: Equipment Kept in Continuous Use', *The Glasgow Herald* (16 June, 1964), p. 14.

[70] P. Dunleavy, *Urban Political Analysis* (London: Macmillan Press, 1980), p. 122.

[71] Ibid., pp. 122–23.

[72] Ravetz, *The Government of Space*, p. 83.

[73] Ward, *Planning and Urban Change*, p. 157.

In Britain, assembly techniques and the materials employed were often inadequate and, in many cases, system-built blocks proved unsuitable for the climate: dampness and condensation were to plague the residents of numerous developments throughout the country. At the time, however, system building was seen as a panacea. It enabled local authorities to purchase complete housing packages from a single construction firm, and the firms involved were willing to offer substantial financial incentives to councils who were able to provide a constant supply of fresh sites, thus ensuring that expensive plant did not lie unused for any length of time and that transportation costs between sites were minimized. This alliance was further encouraged by central government, which preferred local authorities to stick to a single system.[74] Construction companies were therefore well placed to exert sales pressure on local authorities and, as Dunleavy has pointed out, cities which achieved very close relations with specific contractors through public housing schemes also undertook substantial urban motorway or ring-road programmes with the same firms.[75] The sales pressure was such that, in certain cases, it even went as far as corruption.[76]

Between 1956 and 1967, central government gave ever larger subsidies to councils willing to build increasingly high blocks of flats, to the extent that the rising real costs of these flats were offset. Ward quotes figures for England and Wales indicating that the proportion of flats of all kinds approved for the public sector rose from 23 per cent in 1953 to 55 per cent in 1964, while, of that total, the number of flats in high blocks (over five stories) rose from below 7 per cent between 1953 and 1959, to just under 26 per cent in 1964, before falling to below 10 per cent in 1970. The number of very high blocks (over 15 storeys) showed a similar pattern, reaching a peak of over 10 per cent in 1965 and 1966.[77]

Nevertheless, it is worth adding that slum clearance operations, system building and high flats, whether in Britain or France, were not only to do with financial expediency and the will of central government; they also represented, for city councils, a very striking means of expressing civic pride. They offered a clear visual statement of a city committed to the modernist ideal of progress and of a city government concerned with the lives of its citizens.

---

[74] Ibid., p. 158.

[75] Birmingham, Glasgow and Leeds for example. See Dunleavy, *Urban Political Analysis*, p. 123.

[76] Perhaps the most celebrated case was that of T. Dan Smith, Labour leader of Newcastle City Council in the 1960s. Smith represented the new breed of dynamic local councillor, at one stage chartering a private jet to assess candidates for the post of city planner. He was later jailed for illegal dealings with construction companies.

[77] Ward, *Planning and Urban Change*, p. 156.

Discovering the social dimension

France

During the 1960s it became increasingly clear that the planning system in the form established in 1943 was essentially too complex and too unwieldy to work efficiently. The utopian end-point increasingly came to be understood as a mirage on a distant horizon. Moreover, the task of producing these blueprint-type plans had been assigned to a class of 'experts' whose training was in architecture, and this had tended not only to result in plans of a predominantly physical nature which overlooked social aspects, but also to create administrative imprecision and judicial uncertainty with respect to the application of building permits.[78]

Moreover, as already noted, French society was undergoing a profound transformation, with a huge drive towards urbanization as the nation was transformed from one founded largely on agriculture to one where industry played an increasingly important role. These factors demanded greater responsiveness in the planning system, and the *loi d'orientation foncière* (also known as the *loi Pisani*) was passed on 30 December 1967, with the aim of making the process of plan development more flexible. The *loi Pisani* introduced two new plans to replace those established under the 1943 Act.[79] The first of these was the *schéma directeur d'aménagement et d'urbanisme* (SDAU), a document with a strategic perspective and no direct legal implications, outlining general planning policies at an *intercommunale* level (although the *commune* of Paris warranted its own SDAU). The second new planning document was the *plan d'occupation des sols* (POS), which was devised to operate at the level of individual *communes* or districts within the framework provided by the SDAU (where one existed). The purpose of the POS was to outline all aspects of construction parcel by parcel, and it dealt with a time horizon of five to ten years.

While these legislative changes were significant, some of the most far-reaching influences on French planning at this time were external to the system. The growing importance of the social sciences, combined with developments such as the human rights movement, opposition to the war in Vietnam and the events of 1968 (which slowed the application of laws) challenged the very basis of expertise and certainty upon which post-war planning had been constructed and helped to shape the view that society was not a homogeneous entity.

[78] J-P. Lacaze, *Les Méthodes de l'Urbanisme* (Paris: Presses Universitaires de France, 1990), p. 108.

[79] The switch from the *plan directeur d'urbanisme* and the *plan d'urbanisme de détail* was not immediate since these plans were not required to be replaced before 1 January 1978.

Planning, which had previously considered where and how to build, increasingly addressed social issues. These developments were further encouraged by the economic changes of the 1970s; in 1973, OPEC imposed a fourfold increase in the price of oil, bringing an end to the optimism which had characterized the 1960s.

Indicative of these changes was the launch of *Plan Construction* in 1971, identified as a priority action under the Sixth Plan (1971–75). *Plan Construction* was essentially a research programme intended to coordinate studies which would unite modern construction techniques (and thus lower construction costs) with socioeconomic 'managerial' innovations in order to produce a habitat better adapted to the requirements of society as they were perceived at the time. Through *Plan Construction* working groups were established and research and development contracts for experimental work were drawn up. Particular emphasis was given to social themes – for example, one of the first working groups established under *Plan Construction* dealt with information and teaching methods for the lived environment.[80] Although the influence of *Plan Construction* was limited, its formation represented a significant change in approach to housing provision, and it would have a key role to play in Alma-Gare.

Meanwhile, the output of public sector housing began to decline: 1966 saw a reform of HLM financing, and loan conditions became more severe.[81] Further financial changes were made in 1970, 1975 and again in 1977. As a result, public housing rents rose, it became more difficult to fill new HLM flats and, from 1974, tenants' protests gathered momentum.[82] By 1976 the share of public and para-public housing in the total housing authorized in that year stood at 23 per cent. Stagnation followed and then collapse, so much so that by 1980 the proportion of public housing authorized had fallen to 17 per cent.[83] In addition, soaring energy prices and rising inflation in the 1970s ensured that the government's enthusiasm for large construction projects began to wane. The giant projects of the 1960s were called into question, particularly as demographic growth slowed; in 1962, demographic projections for France had suggested a population of 100 million by the year 2000, but by 1973 this had been revised downwards to 60 million.[84] Moreover, the *grands ensembles* had

---

[80] 'information et pédagogie de l'habitat'. See Garin and Muret, 'Chronologie: 1968–1980', p. 197.

[81] Until 1966, HLM loans had been financed directly by the Treasury. In this year, however, the financing mechanism was changed and the *Caisse des dépôts* assumed the role of lender to the *Caisse des prêts HLM*.

[82] Topalov, *Le Logement en France*, p. 244.

[83] Ibid., p. 237.

[84] D. Rousseau and G. Vauzeilles, *L'Aménagement Urbain* (Paris: Presses Universitaires de France, 1992), p. 40.

begun to produce their own problems: communities isolated on the peripheries of cities; deteriorating physical fabric; poor levels of services and amenities;[85] underdeveloped transport links; over-large scale; monotonous design; and the segregation of France's growing population of unemployed and immigrants on low incomes.[86] The media reinforced public opinion against the massive housing schemes, and one of the last to be completed, at Sarcelles (where construction ran from 1957 to 1974), gave rise to the neologism '*sarcellite*', with its implied criticism of the dormitory function of these developments. In response to these changes, collective facilities were abandoned in favour of smaller elements of infrastructure designed to serve local neighbourhoods. Similarly, renewal procedures, whether RU or RHI, were proving to be both expensive and financially inefficient, and they came to be seen as disruptive to both the social and physical urban tissue. Politicians responded to this reaction against quantity construction by shifting to a discourse founded on 'quality of life' and quality of construction. Thus a new vocabulary appeared which included terms such as '*action social*', '*mètres carrés sociaux*' and '*animation sociale*'.[87] The *loi Galley* of December 1975, which definitively repealed the ZUP procedure, the key to the *grands ensembles*, also drew attention to the need for the general public to be kept informed regarding planning projects and for those directly affected by a project to have the right to express their opinion, in this way influencing the planning process, albeit in a small way.

In this new economic context, the sharing of the cost of major urban projects between the government, public bodies and specialist economic organizations began to give way to an increased willingness to accept private initiatives in the urban realm, and the property and housing markets began to play a more important role in directing the focus of planning activity. Moreover, concepts of urban management – the organization of cities or areas within their pre-existing

[85] The French term *équipements collectifs* refers to all facilities installed on a particular site, including road and service networks, buildings to serve the resident population, and the necessary collective services. Subdivisions of this term are *équipements d'infrastructure* which include roads, car parks, transport and communications, water and drainage and collective spaces, and *équipements de superstructure* which are mostly buildings for collective use, such as administration, education, health, sanitation, culture, sport and commerce. The use of these buildings, while not necessarily free, is open to all. See Merlin and Choay, *Dictionnaire de l'Urbanisme et de l'Aménagement*, p. 265.

[86] Subsequently attempts have been made to improve the *grands ensembles*. Employment poles have been created, but these are often business parks or technology parks and therefore fail to match the employment needs of most of the residents of the *grands ensembles*. Substantial improvements have been made in the provision of *équipements* – social facilities, but more particularly commercial facilities. See Brun, 'Nouvelles approches', p. 346.

[87] 'action directed towards social ends', 'square metres allocated for social purposes', 'promotion of social life'. See Randet et al., *Trente-cinq ans d'urbanisme*, p. 64.

fabric – and rehabilitation began to replace the idea of renewal as the solution for areas of older housing. A law of 3 January 1977 switched the emphasis of government loans from large projects to individuals and their properties – from *aides à la pierre* to *aides à la personne*[88] – in an attempt to encourage populations to remain in their local areas and so preserve social networks. A *circulaire* of 1 June 1977 marked another important step in this direction, introducing the *opération programmée d'amélioration de l'habitat* (OPAH). This was a three-way agreement between a *commune*, central government and home owners which aimed at improving the housing environment while preserving both the characteristics of the urban fabric and the social structure of the rehabilitated housing by ensuring that residents on modest incomes were not forced to move out of the area. These operations were generally limited in their extent to between 100 and 150 houses. Housing rehabilitation was accompanied by social measures, and a team was established to oversee each operation and to ensure communication between the various groups involved, including the residents, the technicians and the politicians. The success of an OPAH relied on the ability of the public sector to mobilize the interest of the private property owners. Ultimately the process could be as costly as *rénovation* and, without the appropriate measures, could still result in the replacement of a low-income population by a wealthier one. In 1980, a new concept emerged, that of *insalubrité remediable*, which allowed for the rehabilitation of unfit housing and permitted a gradual process that was more responsive to the requirements of the older sections of French cities.

If all this pointed to a new attitude on the part of central government, then this was confirmed by significant changes in the early 1980s when laws were introduced with the aim of decentralizing administrative activity. These laws did little to alter the form of the basic planning tools, but were significant for shifting responsibility for their development to the *communes*.

Great Britain

By the early 1960s the planning system, unresponsive and overloaded, was facing a crisis. May 1964 saw the setting up of the Planning Advisory Group with the aim of reviewing the general structure of the planning system. The proposals of this group eventually led to the Town and Country Planning Act 1968 for England and Wales and the 1969 Act for Scotland. These acts created a two-tier hierarchy of plans: the structure plan which operated at a strategic level (like the SDAU in France) and the local plan which was intended to give a more detailed picture at the local scale (equivalent to the POS). The rigid structure of

---

[88] From subsidies directed at buildings to subsidies directed at the inhabitants of these buildings.

the development plan introduced in 1947, with its optimum solution drawn up according to circumstances prevailing at one particular moment and the precise expectations this created, was replaced by a flexible system of guidelines. In Scotland, as in England and Wales, the new arrangements placed more emphasis on the 'pseudo-organic' *process* of change rather than on the ultimate urban form defined by the static 'blueprint' plan.[89] Each phase of development was no longer dependent on additional growth towards an ultimate goal, but could function efficiently in its own right and permit scope for subsequent revision. In addition, these new laws made public participation, albeit in a limited form, a statutory requirement in the preparation of structure and local plans.

As in France, the problems were not only internal to the system, and by the late 1960s there was a growing recognition of the pluralist nature of society on the part of the public and politicians alike. Consequently, in a society composed of a mosaic of interest groups whose goals did not necessarily coincide, and which were even mutually exclusive, planning could hardly claim to equate to the imposition of the higher good:

> The utilitarian notion that in a society such as ours was said to be there could be such a thing as the public interest, the notion that a profession called town-planning could in these circumstances be trained up to and could claim to interpret it – all this was rejected. Planners were now seen as looking after no interest but their own.[90]

These changes were accompanied by a general decline in public confidence in the planning profession. Its performance came under scrutiny and what had once been lauded as its post-war 'achievements' began to be perceived as post-war 'failures'.

The strong alliance of interests around system-built flats, which included central and local governments, large construction firms, planners and architects,[91] was eventually challenged by growing criticism directed at mass housing from sociologists, the media and the general public. On a financial level, the subsidies for high-rise flats began to appear inappropriate in the face of the rising real cost of constructing tower blocks, and in 1967 the building subsidy system was changed to discourage their construction. Moreover, the

---

[89] 'Pseudo-organic' is used to refer to a process which, to some extent, reproduces the gradual evolution and growth through accretion which we associate with the medieval town. There is thus a contrast between the mechanical 'blueprint' paradigm and the biological, 'pseudo-organic' paradigm.

[90] L. Esher, *A Broken Wave: The Rebuilding of England 1940–1980* (London: Allen Lane, 1981), p. 77.

[91] This was true in as much as high-rise flats and the like reflected the preferences of the modern movement, although system building in itself removed the need for architectural input.

physical fabric of the system-built blocks became a source of concern.[92] Things fell apart. The Ronan Point disaster in May 1968, when a gas explosion caused the progressive collapse of one corner of a 22-storey system-built tower block in London, resulting in four fatalities, is often pointed to as the symbolic end of high-rise flats.[93] The deck-access system survived a few years longer and seemed to offer a means of overcoming the social isolation associated with high-rises, but here, too, design problems became apparent and projects such as Hulme V in Manchester and Hutchesontown 'E' in Glasgow ('the Dampies') entered the national consciousness as symbols of the failure of this form of building. By this time, public housing had, to a large extent, become synonymous with system building, with the result that the discourse on the 'failure' of industrial construction techniques in the media and in the political and public sphere contributed to an acute crisis of legitimacy in the public provision of housing in general.[94]

Even before the reappraisal of system building, and as early as 1960, there were indications that the slum clearance programme was not operating as efficiently as had been hoped. J.B. Cullingworth produced a book entitled *Housing Needs and Planning Policy* in which he suggested that the emergence of 'slums' was an ongoing process and argued for a policy of subsidized rehabilitation.[95] The Dennington Committee, appointed by the government in 1965 to consider the relative efficiency of slum clearance and housing repair, recommended that careful consideration be given to a more efficient allocation of resources between replacement and repair of houses.[96] The slum clearance programme had received massive government backing yet, according to reports from local medical officers of health, the volume of unfit housing was not diminishing.[97] By the late 1960s these themes were being incorporated into government policy, and a more sympathetic attitude towards the rehabilitation of old properties began to emerge.

---

[92] Gibb provides a colourful and detailed catalogue of the physical shortcomings of system-built flats in 'Policy and Politics in Scottish Housing since 1945', p. 168.

[93] With no internal structural frame, the failure of one wall in a point block would start a chain reaction of collapse.

[94] Dunleavy, *Urban Political Analysis*, p. 94.

[95] J.B. Cullingworth, *Housing Needs and Planning Policy. A Restatement of the Problem of Housing Need and 'Overspill' in England and Wales* (London: Routledge & Kegan Paul, 1960). See also, Kirby, *Slum Housing and Residential Renewal*, p. 72.

[96] Ibid., p. 73.

[97] Despite the massive efforts of the post-war period, 'slums' turned out to be a moving target. In Scotland in the late 1970s, 160 000 houses failed to meet the minimum tolerable standard and another 250 000 (representing 14 per cent of Scotland's total housing stock) sheltered households classified as living in 'unsatisfactory conditions'. Figures cited in Gibb, 'Policy and Politics in Scottish Housing since 1945', p. 172.

But changing attitudes towards Britain's areas of old housing were not only informed by financial expediency. Slum clearance, originally seen as the solution to the problems of the inner city was increasingly seen as a destructive activity tearing apart the close-knit communities which Young and Willmott had studied in the 1950s.[98] Furthermore, in the late 1950s and early 1960s there was a massive emphasis on the concept of 'community' in American sociology, which inevitably had an impact on British thinking.[99] The year of 1961 saw the publication of Jane Jacob's influential *The Death and Life of Great American Cities*, with its emphasis on the values of the old urban fabric, human scale, social interaction and mixed land use – anathema to the functional division of space associated with modernist planning principles. By the late 1960s sociology and urban planning were becoming estranged; sociologists were sceptical that architects possessed the tools to design new communities, while architects criticized sociologists for describing only what existed.[100] In any case, the new developments designed to replace the slums seemed unable to recreate this elusive concept of 'community' and, as a result, lost communities came to be idealized, while legislation was introduced to discourage the destruction of those that had survived. The 1969 Housing Act facilitated the allocation of home improvement grants and introduced the concept of General Improvement Areas which incorporated special measures to upgrade both old houses and the general environment. The Scottish version of the 1969 Act introduced Housing Treatment Areas, defined as areas within which over 50 per cent of housing fell below tolerable standard. In fact, this act represented one of the first indications that the rehabilitation of the existing tenement stock in Scottish cities was a feasible proposition.[101] The legislation involved in housing treatment areas was more flexible than that available in England and Wales since it offered three clear possibilities to local authorities: blanket demolition of all housing in an area, blanket improvement to meet the tolerable standard, or a combination of the two. In Scotland, just as in England and Wales, the impact

---

[98] See M. Young and P. Willmott, *Family and Kinship in North London* (London: Routledge & Kegan Paul, 1957).

[99] Glendinning and Muthesius, *Tower Block*, p. 101. The authors also offer a summary of the evolution of the concept of 'community' in planning terms: 'Before the 1940s, the term "community" was rarely used in English planning and architectural discussions. It was first taken up chiefly by town planners, who thought of it in terms of the unity of parts of towns, which, in practice, entailed large areas of public green between groups of houses, as well as between blocks of flats. From the later fifties ... the architectural designer's search for a kind of space, or area, which had qualities of enclosure, usually characterized as "urban"; the earlier kind of openness now began to be despised. By the sixties, "community" was chiefly understood as the association of small groups in narrowly confined areas.' Ibid., p. 96.

[100] Ibid., p. 102.

[101] Gibb, 'Policy and Politics in Scottish Housing since 1945', p. 170.

of these new measures tended to be socially skewed since government grants to individuals did not cover the full cost of improvements and so were generally taken up only by the wealthier owner-occupiers. There was also little incentive for landlords to apply for these grants since they would not themselves benefit from the improvements, nor were they likely to recoup their cost through rent. All the same, the 1969 Acts indicated that the government was beginning to shift its attention from individual houses to whole areas. Another significant development was the establishment of the Urban Programme through the Local Government Grants (Social Need) Act 1969, which provided a special source of government funding for approximately 100 local authorities to help alleviate poverty and foster communities. Initiatives funded under the Programme included training centres, youth projects, nursery school provision and regeneration programmes.

With the oil crisis and the collapse of the property boom in the early 1970s, the promise of unlimited growth vanished, economic forecasts began to look gloomy, concern grew about structural weaknesses in the economy and the government imposed cuts in public expenditure. As in France, the demographic as well as the economic situation was changing; population projections were revised downwards in the wake of the 1960s baby boom. In this atmosphere of uncertainty, economic priorities began to hold sway over political interests in the planning process and, in this context, Farnell has gone as far as to say that, if a plan did not facilitate the pursuit of economic interests, the likelihood of it being completed and implemented was minimal.[102] The 'inner city' became a concern and, in 1977, the influential government White Paper, *Policy for the Inner Cities* was published, linking issues of economic decline, racial discrimination and environmental problems.[103]

All these changes required that planning assumptions be reassessed, and the predominantly physical approach to housing improvement increasingly gave way to, or at least incorporated, social factors.[104] The Housing Act of 1974 introduced Housing Action Areas which were not only defined by physical criteria – that is, the condition of the housing – but also by social criteria such as overcrowding and the presence of a disproportionate number of elderly persons or young families. Then, in 1975, the Department of the Environment issued its famous circular stating that:

> ... except in a few cities the programme of large-scale slum clearance should be drawing to a close. Where authorities have been seeking to clear

[102] R. Farnell, *Local Planning in Four English Cities* (Aldershot: Gower, 1983), p. 17.

[103] *Policy for the Inner Cities*, published by HMSO in June 1977.

[104] At the local level, however, authorities were still structured to advance the cause of slum clearance and, indeed, into the 1970s government subsidies still tended to favour the slum clearance option.

> housing, especially dwellings which are fit or owner-occupied, it has proved much less easy to demonstrate that redevelopment is the best course, and the resistance to such action has been increasing from residents of all kinds.[105]

We may add to these reasons others suggested by Ravetz, notably the huge expense which redevelopment programmes incurred and the problems associated with housing large immigrant communities in council estates.[106]

Conclusions

What becomes apparent in considering the development and form of British and French planning from a comparative perspective is that, despite differences in details, many of the general themes are the same.

Much of twentieth-century urban planning in Great Britain and France has been characterized by a distinct paradigm which emerged in the course of the nineteenth century.[107] Choay has called this the 'progressive' model of planning, which aimed at advancement and productivity, and placed emphasis on scientific application, hygiene, space and light.[108] It was epitomized by Garnier's 1901 plans for a *cité industrielle* and by the work of the *Congrès internationaux d'architecture moderne* (CIAM) founded in 1928. CIAM conceived of cities organized according to functionalist and geometric order – functionalism being one of the grand themes to have emerged in spatial thinking over the last two centuries. Functionalism is intricately bound to the idea of progress – the belief that that which is done today surpasses that which was done yesterday. The functionalist paradigm thus bears the mark of evolutionism and upholds the superiority of adaptation. The concept drew inspiration from new technical developments – in the field of architecture these included new materials such as concrete, iron and later, steel – and also from the contribution of new disciplines such as engineering. Of course, the roots

---

105 Department of Environment Circular 13/75, *Renewal Strategies*, 1975. Cited in Cullingworth, *Town and Country Planning in Britain*, 10th edn, p. 276.

106 Ravetz, *The Government of Space*, p. 92. Immigrant families were reluctant to take council housing partly because they preferred to rent privately or buy property close to others of the same background, and partly through their fear of isolation and racism on council estates. Certain council tenants exhibited resentment towards immigrant groups who they perceived as unnecessarily privileged given their status as 'outsiders' or 'newcomers'.

107 For an analysis of the development of planning thought in Germany, Great Britain, France and the USA in the nineteenth and early twentieth centuries, the emergence of ideas and their cross-fertilization, see Sutcliffe, *Towards the Planned City*.

108 See F. Choay, 'La règne de l'urbain et la morte de la ville', in Dethier and Guiheux, *La Ville*, esp. pp. 27–30.

of Choay's progressive model of planning go much deeper – to the vision of a rationally ordered society that emerged during the seventeenth century and which, with respect to modernist design in the twentieth century, found its expression in the combination of what Glendinning and Muthesius have described as the combination of 'the thinking of generally Fordist economics with that of Classical science'.[109]

The principles of 'progressive' planning were widely adopted in the post-war period. France and Britain emerged from the Second World War facing not only the pressing issue of reconstruction, but also a major housing crisis founded on a general scarcity of housing and the poor condition of the existing stock. In both cases central government showed itself willing to take charge of the built environment, and new sets of laws were formulated accordingly.[110] In both countries, the post-war legislation was based on utopian principles. Planning was essentially a physical activity which strove to define an ideal state. The end-state 'blueprint' plans which were produced represented the functionalist doctrine in planning, a normative activity which incorporated a hierarchical list of needs spatially distributed according to function.[111] These plans, both in France and Britain, represented the belief that, in Koselleck's terms, it was possible to apply a rational reworking of experience to the extent that the 'space of experience' reached the 'horizon of expectation', thus drawing the future into the present and making the non-experienced already subject to control.[112] Utopia was a fixed point on this horizon, and it existed because, for a short time at least, everyone believed it existed.

Ultimately, the post-war legislation in both countries was to prove to be too rigid and was unable to respond effectively to the demands made upon it. By the late 1960s new sets of plans had been introduced in both countries in an attempt to escape the constraints of the 'blueprint'. By this time, not only had the social sciences exploded the myth of apolitical planning,[113] but public participation had also become a much more important issue, and consequently the new legislation allowed for a degree of influence from outside the system. On the whole, participation referred to the act of consulting residents as to their views on a plan and providing an educational dimension for them. It did not generally

---

[109] Glendinning and Muthesius, *Tower Block*, p. 10.

[110] Moreover, the logic of rationality also applied to those responsible for producing the built environment, and volunteers and philanthropists were replaced by professionals, technicians and local government administrators. See, for example, H. Meller, 'Urban Renewal and Citizenship: The Quality of Life in British Cities, 1890–1990', *Urban History*, 22:1 (1995), pp. 63–84.

[111] Lacaze, *Les Méthodes de l'Urbanisme*, p. 56.

[112] R. Koselleck, *Futures Past. On the Semantics of Historical Time* (Cambridge, MA: MIT Press, 1985), p. 272.

[113] G.E. Cherry, 'The Development of Planning Thought', in M.J. Bruton (ed.), *The Spirit of Purpose and Planning* (London: Hutchison & Co., 1974), p. 79.

extend to the process of drawing up plans, nor to the ultimate decision-making. Participation therefore took place within an agenda that had been predefined by planners and politicians with the consequence that, despite the new measures, these groups continued to control the overall process thanks to their technical expertise and mastery of the planning discourse. The concessions made to the public were therefore always of limited scope.

Another reason for the promotion of public participation was perhaps to be found in the perceived 'failures' of the respective planning systems, such as mass housing projects, urban motorways and inner city decline, and the need to strengthen public confidence in the planning process. As Cullingworth points out, 'whether, or to what extent, these were "failures" and, if so, the degree to which "planning" was to blame are questions which are seldom raised, let alone answered in their historical context'.[114] We can go further and say that these 'failures' were undoubtedly also constructed in the context of major socioeconomic transformations experienced in France and Britain in the late 1960s and 1970s. The 'progressive' model responded to a set of concerns and beliefs which underwent a profound reassessment in this period. The certainty that had been invested in the post-war welfare state society crumbled. Fragmentation and uncertainty gradually replaced growth, optimism and a belief in technology, and planning activity was readjusted accordingly. Certainty found its refuge in the market, and consequently the role of planners became much more concerned with flexibility, responsiveness and facilitation rather than control.

If the general trends in planning in Britain and France showed distinct parallels, then so too did the evolution of attitudes towards slum clearance programmes and large-scale housing projects. Pseudo-objective measures were developed to assess the extent of 'slum' housing, and the response to the identified housing crisis was to demolish and rebuild in a modernist style, using industrial construction techniques. Excess population from overcrowded inner city areas were decanted to peripheral estates, *grands ensembles* or the new towns. The bulldozer became a symbol for the destruction of the old and the herald of the new. But renewal schemes proved to be costly, the legislation unwieldy, and the procedure slow. Equally, the social cost was high: large urban areas were left blighted, communities were broken up and the new housing – the tangible symbol of progress – proved to be inadequate, both socially and in terms of its physical fabric. Moreover, the energy crisis and rising inflation made the high-rises and *barres* economically unfeasible. By the late 1960s renovation and repair were receiving increasing support from both governments and, by the 1970s, with a greater sensitivity towards the 'local'

[114] Cullingworth, *Town and Country Planning in Britain*, 10th edn, p. 385.

and the rediscovery of 'community', areas of old housing in French and British cities began to take on positive dimensions.

Inevitably, the two countries also exhibit certain differences. In France, planning, like all other activities, was highly centralized right up to the reforms of the early 1980s, and central government tended to play a much more direct role in the planning process. In Britain the opposite was the case, with local authorities enjoying considerable discretion in the planning system, at least until their powers began to be eroded from 1979 onwards under the Thatcher administration. In Britain, post-war planning was considered to be value-free, an activity undertaken by experts in an apolitical environment within the broad programme of social reconstruction and modernization, and imposed from above on the population. On the other hand, the link between politics and administration had always been much more readily accepted in France, where the planner was unambiguously a state technocrat with a political agenda. Indeed, the static vision of the modern city which sprang from a convergence between this functionalist doctrine in planning and the bureaucratic normalization and codification of infrastructure by government organizations was particularly marked in France with its traditional emphasis on centralism.[115] Also France has tended to rely far more heavily on zonal-based planning tools, while the British system has tended to work at the level of individual land parcels: it was only at the end of the 1960s, with the General Improvement Areas, Housing Treatment Areas and so on, that a clearer emphasis on areas began to emerge.

Finally, we may conclude that there is no longer a conception of a fixed ideal state which may be achieved through planning, and the management of existing resources is now as essential an element of planning as construction *ex nihilo*. The form of planning represented by the 1943 Act in France and the 1947 Act in Britain was only made possible by a consensus within government and the planning profession as to the problems to be tackled – problems principally concerned with reconstruction, modernization and the need to redistribute population and employment – and the means by which a solution might be achieved. When consensus over these issues began to dissolve, so utopia, understood as a single fixed point on the horizon, also vanished into a myriad potential futures. It is to the conflict and negotiation around these futures that we turn in the chapters that follow.

---

[115] Lacaze, *Les Méthodes de l'Urbanisme*, pp. 56–7.

CHAPTER THREE

The *courées* of Roubaix: constructing a consensus

This chapter introduces the first case study, which deals with the area of Alma-Gare in Roubaix, France. Alma-Gare lies to the north-west of the town centre, on the main road route between Roubaix and the neighbouring town of Tourcoing (see Figure 3.1). It takes its name from its proximity to Roubaix's railway station and from the commercial street, rue de l'Alma, which crosses the area (Alma, in turn, from the Battle of the Alma in 1854, during the Crimean War). The area is also sometimes referred to as Gare Alma, particularly in popular discourse, but both names refer to the same spatial entity. Within the area of Alma-Gare is located La Redoute, one of the largest and best-known French mail order firms. This section of the town, like other popular areas of Roubaix such as Pile and Cul de Four, demonstrates the characteristics of an urban village – that is, it is relatively self-contained and has considerable shopping facilities, particularly along rue de l'Alma and rue Blanchemaille.

While it is almost always easier to identify the centre of an area rather than its boundaries, it seems that, for the period of this study, the physical extent of Alma-Gare was a generally recognized as being defined by a number of distinct features.[1] To the west, the area was more or less circumscribed by a railway track which represented a distinct physical boundary, particularly since this track could only be crossed at the extreme points of the area. Another substantial boundary lay to the north, in the form of the canal, while to the north-east was the Rue de Tourcoing, which marked the division between Alma-Gare and the neighbouring *quartier* of Cul de Four. The southern limit of the area was the least clearly defined, lying somewhere between the predominantly industrial area of La Fosse aux Chênes and the rue de l'Alma.

The first part of this chapter provides an analysis of the historical development of Roubaix, with particular emphasis on its evolution as a mono-industrial textile town and the emergence of a particular form of workers' housing – the *courées*. The second section of the chapter charts shifting attitudes towards these *courées* in the context of political and economic

[1] The description of the area is intended to reflect what was broadly understood by the actors at the time as the spatial extent of Alma-Gare.

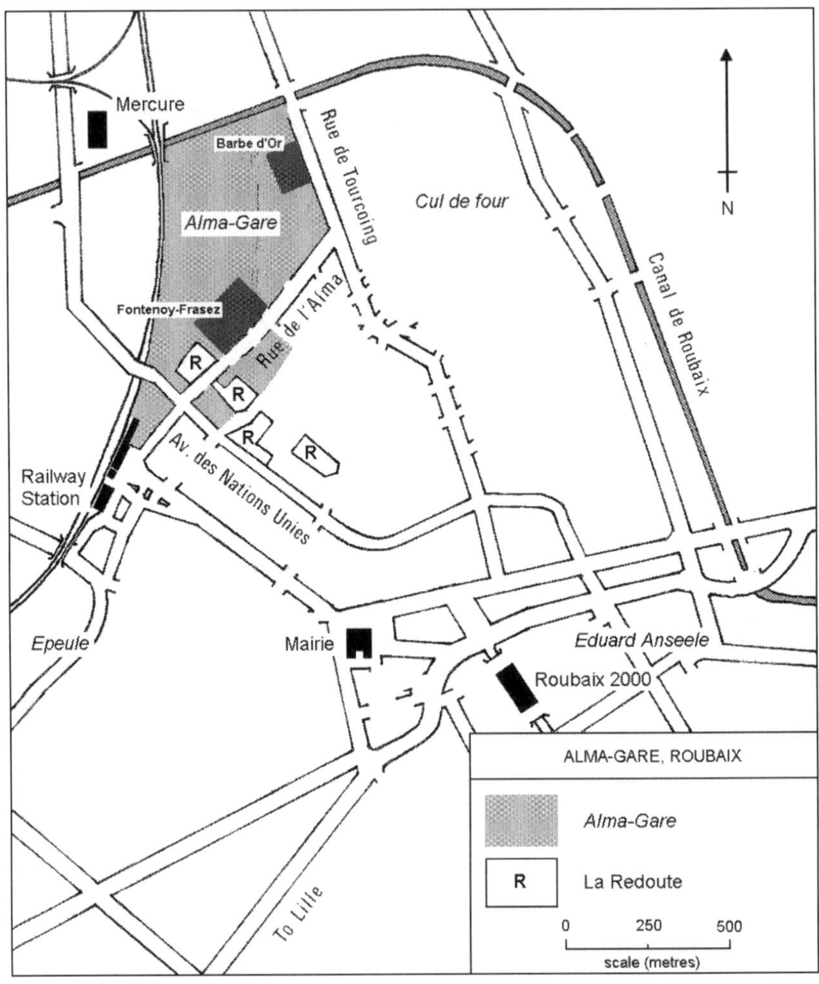

3.1 Location map of Alma-Gare

changes in the town and the emergence of a broad consensus over the demolition of this form of housing. The final section looks specifically at Alma-Gare and how the *Municipalité de Roubaix* presented its demolition as both an economic and a moral imperative.

Roubaix: the social, political and economic contexts

At the beginning of the nineteenth century, Roubaix was little more than a large market town. In 1801 it had a population of 8151, but by 1896 this figure had risen to 124 661, representing the highest rate of population growth of any French town in that period (see Table 3.1, p. 80).[2] Along with the neighbouring town of Tourcoing, Roubaix came to represent the largest concentration of textile employment in France.

From the sixteenth century, Roubaix had been the centre of a significant rural wool-spinning and weaving industry, but until the end of the *Ancien Régime* the town was stifled by legal restrictions imposed upon it by neighbouring Lille. Specifically, Roubaix was forbidden to dye the cloth it produced and, instead, the dyeing process had to be carried out in Lille. In this way, the larger city was able to control Roubaix's textile output.[3] Roubaix received a huge boost to its economic fortunes following the authorization of free work in the countryside in 1762. An additional impetus came from the treaty of commerce with Great Britain signed in 1786, and then from the abolition of corporations in 1791.[4]

Until the nineteenth century, textile workers worked at home and were also partially engaged in agricultural activity. They worked for merchants from whom they bought raw materials and to whom they sold their finished products.[5] Technical developments – principally the introduction of mechanized techniques developed in Britain – combined with the need for more efficient production, brought home work to an end.[6] Workshops or factories were established and workers travelled daily to their place of employment. Prior to

[2] P. Bruyelle, 'Roubaix face aux grandes mutations récentes', in Y-M. Hilaire (ed.), *Histoire de Roubaix* (Dunkerque: Editions des Beffrois, 1984), p. 316.

[3] As Chaplain points out, this was not an unusual practice in the large textile centres. See J-M. Chaplain, *La chambre des tisseurs: Louviers: Cité Drapière: 1680–1840* (Seyssel: Champ Vallon, 1984), p. 68.

[4] Ibid., p. 30.

[5] D. Cornuel and B. Duriez, 'L'Evolution de la propriété immobilière à Roubaix: 1884–1974', *Revue du Nord*, 58:229 (April–June 1976), p. 248.

[6] Spinning jennies were introduced in France around 1771, and by 1789 there were 15 in Roubaix, each with 50 or 60 spindles. But spinning jennies did not preclude home work and so did not profoundly affect the geography of the textile industry. Rather it was the water-frame and the mule-jenny which directed the manufacturing process into the factories. See Chaplain, *La chambre des tisseurs*, p. 75.

this first phase of industrialization Roubaix and its agricultural hinterland had specialized in wool products, but with early industrialization the town saw a huge growth in its product base, which came to be dominated by the production of nankeen – a cotton fabric, normally buff or yellow in colour. The town persisted with cotton production until around 1830, when there was a resurgence of wool products, encouraged by modifications in the production process.[7]

As was often the case in France, the initial impetus for industrialization came from modest capital investments by agriculturists, merchants or families who were long established in the area. While machinery was important, much of the strength of Roubaix's industry – and much of the profits – came from speculation in raw materials rather than technical innovation. Mechanization had the effect of introducing interurban specialization: originally spinning and weaving had been carried out in the same establishments, but with mechanization there developed specialist spinning workshops which sold their thread for weaving. Some towns produced more thread than they consumed, whilst others which specialized in weaving purchased thread from elsewhere. By 1808, the development of such specialist roles was obvious in the division between Roubaix as a centre for weaving and neighbouring Tourcoing as a centre for spinning.[8] Chaplain points out that such specialization was not linked to local sources of energy (and, in fact, both these towns lacked hydraulic power), but was rather to do with inherited social and employment structures, since the textile industry was generally more reliant on these factors than upon natural resources.[9] Thus, Roubaix's industrial dynamic was perpetuated by the presence of a core of trained workers which acted as a magnet to textile activities and, in turn, this concentration of activities served to attract a community of purchasers.

Roubaix's textile factories were generally medium-sized operations, within which the division of labour was relatively limited. They were run on a family basis, which meant that operations in the factory were normally overseen by the

[7] Ibid., p. 31.

[8] According to Chaplain, in 1808 Tourcoing had only 508 looms as opposed to 23 778 spindles, Lille had 595 looms and 43 846 spindles, while Roubaix had 5500 looms and 38 948 spindles. Roubaix had 19 mill-owners who employed 188 workers at mule-jennies to produce thread, but as many as 173 textile manufacturers who, together, employed 5500 weavers and 18 500 other workers. Collectively the three *communes* of Lille, Roubaix and Tourcoing produced 450 000kg of thread annually in this period, but Roubaix consumed 1 152 000kg and was forced to buy supplies from other parts of the *département*. In the year IX (1798), Roubaix wove 92 per cent of the 84 100 pieces of cotton produced in the *département*. All figures from Chaplain, *La chambre des tisseurs*, p. 159.

[9] Ibid., p. 148.

owner himself or by members of his family, and there were few intermediaries in this hierarchy.[10] Until around 1830, the workforce consisted mainly of young workers from the nearby *communes*, but as the textile industry grew and employment demand increased, workers were drawn from further afield.[11] Belgian Flanders represented an important nearby reserve of manual workers for Roubaix's factories, since the development of Belgium's own textile industry was hampered because Belgian products could not easily enter the valuable French market. Moreover, the decline of rural craft work had forced the Flemish workforce to look further afield for employment and, although some travelled as far as the mining basin in Northern France to work, many preferred to find jobs in Roubaix and Tourcoing in order to remain closer to their homes. An additional attraction for this workforce was the strength of the French franc against the Belgian currency, particularly at the end of the nineteenth century.[12]

Initially, many workers arrived at the factories by foot. Railways appeared in 1842 and horse-drawn trams in 1882, with electric tramways arriving some 12 years later. These transport innovations made travel easier for Roubaix's workforce, but the provision of housing close to the factories was to prove to be a more satisfactory solution for workers and employers alike. For the workers, housing around the factories did away with the inconvenience and fatigue of travel when the working day was already long – 15 hours up to 1848, and 12 hours thereafter, with a one and a half hour meal break at midday.[13] Proximity to the workplace also meant that whole families could find employment there (textile work was open to both women and men) and, moreover, workers were within earshot of the factory bell and could more easily avoid the fines imposed for arriving late at work. As for the employers, housing close to the factory not only facilitated the surveillance of the workforce, but also helped guarantee its stability in a period when it was still highly mobile. Moreover, housing around the factory removed the workforce from the rhythm of agricultural production and freed them from the vagaries of the northern French climate which might otherwise have impeded their arrival at the workplace.[14]

---

[10] B. Duriez and D. Cornuel, 'La naissance de la politique urbaine: le cas de Roubaix', *Les annales de la recherche urbaine – recherches et débats*, no. 4 (July 1979), p. 26.

[11] M. Le Blan, 'Notes sur une étape dans la genèse d'un espace industriel: la construction des "forts" roubaisiens dans la première moitie du XIXe siècle', *Revue du Nord*, 63:248 (March 1981), p. 68.

[12] M. Battiau, 'Raisons et effets de la concentration spatiale de nombreux textiles dans l'agglomeration Roubaix–Tourcoing', *Hommes et Terres du Nord*, 2 (1984), p. 74.

[13] J. Prouvost, 'Les courées à Roubaix', *Revue du Nord*, 51:201 (June 1969), p. 312.

[14] Cornuel and Duriez, 'L'Evolution de la propriété immobilière à Roubaix: 1884–1974', p. 249.

Table 3.1 Population figures for Roubaix, 1801–1926

Year	Population	Average change per year
1801	8151	–
1850	34 456	+536.8
1896	124 661	+1961.0
1911	122 723	-129.2
1926	117 209	-367.6

Source: P. Bruyelle, 'Roubaix face aux grandes mutations récentes', in Y-V. Hilaire, *Histoire de Roubaix* (Dunkerque: Editions des Beffrois, 1984), p. 316.

The growing textile workforce and the provision of workers' housing inevitably had a profound effect on Roubaix's population profile. As noted, the population figures for the commune of Roubaix in the nineteenth century demonstrate rates of growth unequalled by any other French town in this period.

Table 3.1 illustrates that between 1801 and 1850 the population of Roubaix quadrupled. The main driving force behind this massive increase was immigration as a result of employment in the textile industry. The period from 1850 to 1896, when Roubaix's population reached its maximum, saw a similar rate of increase and, according to Prouvost, it was only from 1873 that natural increase become the primary motor of population growth in the town.[15]

The physical development of Roubaix which accompanied this demographic explosion consisted almost exclusively of textile factories and workers' housing. Indeed, given the town's massive population growth it is hardly surprising that many of those who were not employed in the textile industry were builders or bricklayers. The new housing tended to form distinct neighbourhoods or *quartiers*: for example, in the north of the town were the *quartiers* of Alma-Gare and of Cul de Four, in the south-western part there was Epeule, while in the south-east lay the *quartiers* associated with rue des Longues Haies and rue Jules Guesde. Only in the southern part of Roubaix was workers' housing not constructed, this area being developed for large houses for the wealthiest residents of the town in the early years of the twentieth century.

The peculiar nature of Roubaix's urban development is demonstrated by the lack of a clearly defined, fully developed town centre. Housing was constructed around factories rather than around an urban core. For example, the housing in Longues Haies – perhaps the most celebrated of all the *quartiers* in Roubaix due to a combination of industrial militancy, desperately poor living conditions

[15] Figures taken from Gaston Motte, *Etude de la progression de la population à Roubaix au cours du XIXe siècle*. Cited in Prouvost, 'Les courées à Roubaix', p. 312.

and a healthy dose of literary nostalgia provided by the novels of Maxence Van der Meersch[16] – was constructed specifically to serve the factories which had located alongside Roubaix's canal. This multi-nuclear form was reinforced since shops to serve the working population tended to appear along streets in each *quartier* rather than in the centre of the town. The result was that Roubaix developed more as a cluster of small industrial 'villages' than as a 'conventional' town with a distinct central area, spatially and functionally defined.

Other factors also contributed to ensure that Roubaix's urban functions remained tied to the textile industry and, on a commercial level, did not develop beyond the provision of basic retail services. For example, neighbouring Lille not only fulfilled the administrative functions for the region, it was also the dominant retail centre, particularly for luxury goods, and this acted as a break on Roubaix's development. In addition, the Belgian frontier workers employed in Roubaix's factories preferred to spend their wages in Belgium where they could take advantage of the relative strength of the French franc.[17] Thus Roubaix's commercial characteristics remained limited, and even to this day the town's lack of a fully developed commercial and service sector consistent with its size remains an important political and planning issue. A final observation with respect to Roubaix's physical layout concerns the presence of textile factories 'embedded' in the urban fabric. The town's morphology offered a closely woven fabric of workers' housing and textile factories. These factories, like the housing surrounding it, were brick-built, and often featured towers and crenellations, elements borrowed from the vocabulary of castle architecture. In Lyon (which specialized in the production of silk), and even in Lille (which was always regarded as the rival of the complementary pairing of Roubaix and Tourcoing), the tendency in the nineteenth century was for industry to move away from the centre of the town, leaving behind finishing operations and tertiary activities such as commercial services. This decentralizing tendency, however, did not appear in Roubaix and Tourcoing until as late as the 1950s.[18] This was partly a consequence of Lille's regional dominance in terms of administration and commercial activity, but was also partly a result of the geopolitical position of these towns: the possibilities for expansion were restricted to the north, east and west by the Franco-Belgian border, while to the south lay Lille.

Nineteenth-century Roubaix was not only notable for its general layout, but also for the specific form of its housing for the textile workers. In examining

---

[16] Maxence Van der Meersch (1907–51). His novels include *Quand les sirènes se taisent* (Paris: Albin Michel, 1951) and *Gens du Nord* (Paris: Presses de la Cité, 1993).

[17] Battiau, 'Raisons et effets de la concentration spatiale de nombreux textiles dans l'agglomeration Roubaix-Tourcoing', p. 75.

[18] Ibid., p. 73.

this housing, we are confronted by a number of specific terms, the best known of which, and certainly the most culturally resonant, is '*courée*', the local diminutive of *cour*, the term for a court or yard.[19] Generally, the *courées* consisted of anything from two to 20 dwellings – with the average number being around 12 – set around a narrow court which most often ran perpendicular to the street. These dwellings were narrow, brick-built houses (3.5m by 4 or 5m on average) of no more than two floors. Each house, while sharing walls with its immediate neighbours, was an individual unit accessed by its own front door. In the courtyard were located the shared WCs and a tap or hand pump – the communal water supply (see Figure 3.2). The most frequently cited description of the *courée* form was provided by Jacques Prouvost in 1969:

> A *courée* is a collection of small houses, each one joined to its neighbours, which face on to a narrow passage. One enters through a dark corridor. At the far end of the courtyard, the communal WCs (the *communs* in the local dialect) are located in a hut. Near to the street there is a tap for drinking water and sometimes, right up to the present day, a water pump. In general the houses in the *courée* consisted of only two rooms and had neither outbuildings nor corridor; one entered directly into the only room on the ground floor, which served at one and the same time as the dining room, the kitchen, the bathroom and sometimes even became the bedroom for the children at night. A very steep staircase linked this single room directly to a bedroom which often had an extremely low ceiling.[20]

The early *courée* developments in the nineteenth century were quite large and allowed for a small garden in front of the houses, but the garden was soon dispensed with, and a report in 1869 recorded the narrowest *courée* as having a breadth of only 2.10m. It contained 22 dwellings and housed a population of 123. The widest was 11m and contained 36 houses and 164 inhabitants.[21] In addition, the housing in the first *courées* had the benefit of proper foundations, but this was done away with in subsequent construction in order to satisfy the requirements of cheap and fast construction.

---

[19] Prouvost, 'Les courées à Roubaix', p. 308. While in Roubaix the *courée* was specifically intended for workers, its inhabitants in other parts of the *région du Nord* included a broader section of society.

[20] 'Une courée est un ensemble de petites maisons accolées les unes aux autres, se faisant face sur un étroit passage. On y entre par un corridor sombre. Au fond de la cour, une baraque abrite les W.-C. collectifs (en patois, les communs). Près de la rue, un robinet d'eau potable et, quelquefois encore de nos jours, une pompe. L'habitation en courée ne possède en général que deux pièces, pas de dépendance, ni de couloir; on pénètre directement dans l'unique pièce du rez-de-chaussée qui sert à la fois de salle à manger, de cuisine, de cabinet de toilette et se transforme parfois la nuit en chambre d'enfants. L'escalier très raide part de cette unique pièce pour aboutir à une chambre à coucher, souvent très basse de plafond.' Prouvost, 'Les courées à Roubaix', p. 307.

[21] Ibid., p. 316.

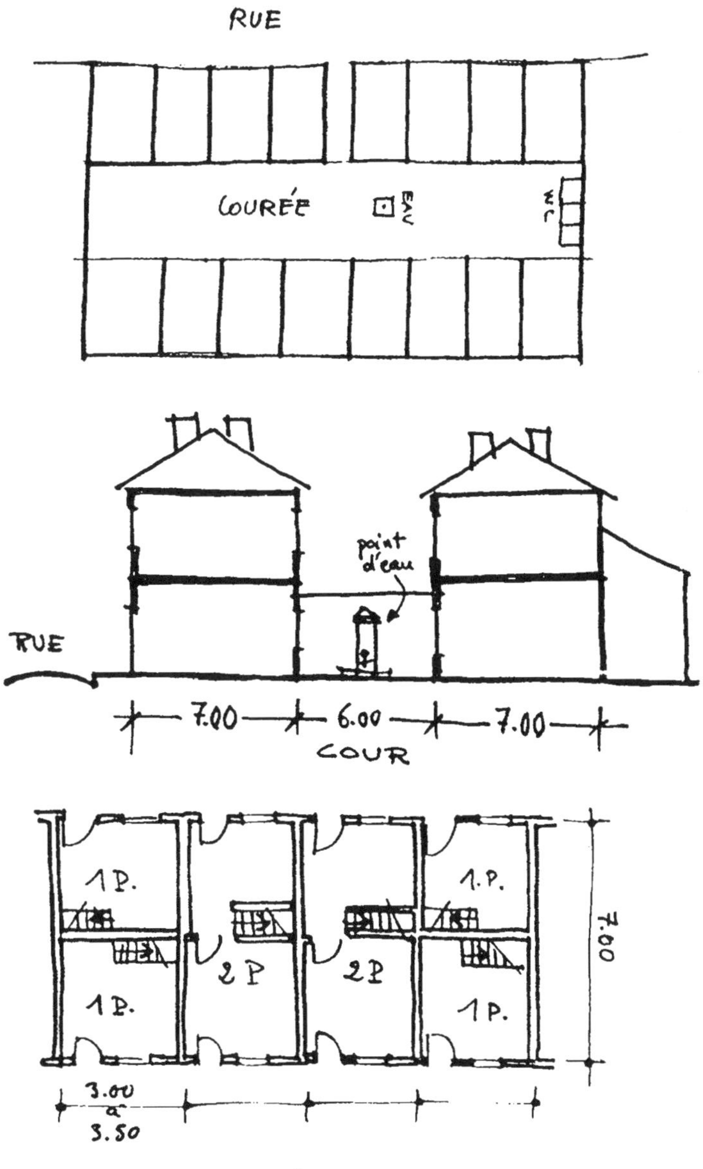

3.2 Plan and elevation of a typical *courée*
Reproduced from 'Roubaix: L'APU 2. Stratégie du capital et stratégie populaire', *Place*, no. 6 (Winter 1977), p. 17.

As for the other terms referring to the form and arrangement of workers' housing, a *cour* was the name often given to a large courtyard surrounded by anything between 20 and 60 houses. Similarly, the term *fort* referred to a dense group of houses with some form of courtyard space in the centre.[22] The first *forts* were constructed in Roubaix between 1818 and 1820, and ranged in size from 40 dwellings for the smallest to 100 dwellings for the largest – Fort Frasez – which was built in 1838.[23] Like the *courées*, the *cours* and *forts* consisted of terraced houses and incorporated a communal water pump and latrines, and an open-air water course for waste water. *Forts*, *cours* and *courées* often included a grocery shop, a tavern, a bistro, or a combination of the three. These were important meeting places for residents, particularly given the restricted living space in the houses. Normally the shop or bistro was located in the largest house of the development – the one that occupied the street frontage and through which one entered the courtyard behind. It is clear that the various terms associated with Roubaix's morphology incorporate a high degree of overlap, and in practice they were often employed interchangeably. Moreover, one often finds that the term *courée* is applied without distinction to all housing built for textile workers.[24] In this book, *courée* is used to refer generically to the whole 'family' of nineteenth- and early twentieth-century housing provided for workers in Roubaix, unless a specific distinction is made.[25]

Surprisingly perhaps, it was generally not Roubaix's industrialists who provided housing for their workers. Rather this role was assumed by shopkeepers, traders, mill-owners, artisans, *rentiers* and farmers who had a small amount of capital which they wished to invest for a secure and profitable return (*courées* often took the name of their owners or, otherwise, the name of a saint). Cornuel and Duriez carried out a study of the owners of properties in the *courées* in three different *quartiers* of Roubaix.[26] They found that, in 1884, the most important category of owners was made up of artisans (self-employed

[22] According to Prouvost, the word *fort* may have derived from the Napoleonic campaigns, 'car le souvenir des mots militaires était resté vivace'. Ibid., p. 308. Despite the connotations of the term, the houses did not necessarily form a square. During the Second Empire (1852–70) the term *fort* was temporarily replaced by *cité*.

[23] Their size was such that they were normally constructed at the edge of the town, on agricultural land.

[24] For example, despite its name, the *Organisation pour la Suppression des Courées de la Métropole Nord* (ORSUCOMN), created in 1969, had as its aim the clearance of *all* forms of outmoded workers' housing, not just the eponymous *courées*.

[25] For notes on the historical precedents for the *courées*, see Cornuel and Duriez, 'L'Evolution de la propriété immobilière à Roubaix: 1884–1974', p. 248; Le Blan, 'Notes sur une étape dans la genèse d'un espace industriel', p. 67; Prouvost, 'Les courées à Roubaix', p. 311; and J. Vincentini and M-C. Vilment, 'L'Evolution du cadre de vie à Roubaix de 1945 à 1977', unpublished thesis, University of Lille (1977), p. 44.

[26] Cornuel and Duriez, 'L'Evolution de la propriété immobilière à Roubaix: 1884–1974'.

craftsmen) and shopkeepers. The second largest category of owners was the *rentiers*, some of whom effectively regarded ownership as a 'profession'. Many of these investors were of rural origin and their capital came from real estate amassed in previous generations. Otherwise, it came from profits made more recently as a result of Roubaix's burgeoning economy. Investment did not require large reserves of capital; as noted, houses in *courée* form were small and the construction material poor, so they were generally cheap to construct. Moreover, in the three areas selected by Cornuel and Duriez, most *propriétaires* only owned between five and eight houses.[27]

In the context of housing provision, the factory owners and the *propriétaires rentiers* enjoyed a symbiotic relationship. The demand for housing generated by industrial expansion satisfied the desire on the part of the latter for investment opportunity, while the presence of the *propriétaires rentiers* freed the industrialists from the requirement of investing in housing. Factory owners, who had larger reserves of capital than the *propriétaires rentiers*, preferred to invest this capital in the construction of factories, in exploiting technical developments or in speculation in raw materials. Having said this, there was a small amount of factory housing constructed at the initiative of Roubaix's industrialists, most of which was provided with the aim of attracting specific kinds of workers – that is, workers with special qualifications or those capable of training the workforce in new techniques.

The construction of the *courées* was not governed by an overall plan,[28] but each element tended to be the work of a single developer and so benefited from some sort of localized scheme, however perfunctory this may have been. This scheme tended to be dictated by a combination of three factors. The first of these was land values, as the desire to maximize investment required that houses were built at the highest density possible: '... the construction of houses in courts was the response to a logic which could be simply stated thus: to construct the maximum number of houses possible on the smallest area of land, at the least cost.'[29] Moreover, the price of land was substantially higher along street frontages than for land lying behind these frontages. A second factor was the *contribution des portes et fenêtres*, a tax levied on all houses facing onto the street, although a *décret* of 14 July 1848 introduced an exemption for housing intended for workers.[30] The third factor was building legislation, which

[27] Ibid., p. 251.

[28] That is, a plan at the municipal level.

[29] '... la construction de maisons en cours répond à une logique qui peut s'exprimer simplement ainsi: construire le plus de maisons possible sur le plus petit terrain, au moindre coût.' Cornuel and Duriez, 'L'Evolution de la propriété immobilière à Roubaix: 1884–1974', p. 252.

[30] J. Descamps, 'La résorption des courées de la Métropole Nord', unpublished thesis, University of Lille (1976), p. 27.

Table 3.2 The construction of workers' housing in Roubaix, 1851–1938

Year	Housing units	Households	Population	Number of *cours, courées, forts, impasses, cités*
1851	6202	7157	34 456	33
1856	7293	11 825	39 180	81
1861	8794	9879	49 274	156
1866	11 838	13 512	64 706	119
1869	–	–	–	381
1896	24 829	36 879	124 661	690
1901	26 476	35 173	124 365	997
1906	27 242	36 773	121 017	1270
1911	29 217	36 966	122 723	–
1912	–	–	–	1324
1936	33 988	38 917	107 105	–
1938	–	–	–	1133

Source: Prouvost, 'Les courées à Roubaix', *Revue du Nord*, 51:201 (1969), p. 311. Drawn from the *Dénombrement à Roubaix* and the *Rapports du maire*.

generally only applied to buildings on the street. It thus made economic sense that, in order to avoid high purchase costs, taxes and restrictive building codes, developers should purchase land in long, thin strips, perpendicular to the street. In order to maximize the construction potential of these narrow land parcels a double row of houses was built along its longest length. These houses would be accessed by the narrow passage from the street which, as noted, generally passed through the larger, street-front property.[31] Since the street-front property occupied the most expensive land and almost always contained a small business, it could generate a much higher level of rent than the buildings behind.

Table 3.2 traces the evolution of Roubaix's housing stock from 1851 to 1938. The maximum number of *courées* – 1324 – was achieved in 1912, some 16 years after Roubaix's demographic peak. This represented approximately 50 per cent of the town's housing stock at the time.

From the start, the *courées* were crowded and, indeed, some developments which had originally been intended to house only single men became home to whole families. The interest of the builders and investors to squeeze the maximum number of houses into a given area produced high population

[31] The narrower this passage was, the better, in order to maximize the ground space for construction.

densities,[32] and this, combined with population pressure and the poor standard of construction, soon caused living conditions to deteriorate. Even in the nineteenth century there were protests against conditions in the *courées*. This form of architecture, which restricted both natural light and ventilation, was considered to be a major factor contributing to ill-health, particularly in the wake of the cholera epidemic of 1865–66 which left more than 2000 dead in Roubaix. The *courées* were also considered by some to represent a moral danger as a result of the concentration of 'foreigners' which they sheltered.[33] A number of *commissions des logements insalubres* were set up under the law of 13 April 1850 in order to investigate housing conditions, but these had little impact and the building rate continued to rise, particularly between 1866 and the end of the century.

Roubaix's industrialists tended to live beside their workforce since, like their employees, their houses were close to their textile factories, or even above the factory offices. This proximity ensured a high degree of interaction between the two groups. In particular, the owners were able to undertake personally the supervision and surveillance of their workforce. Moreover, this spatial proximity also permitted them to move into the private sphere of their employees with relative ease. For example, the factory-owner or his wife would visit the homes of workers on the occasion of important family events such as births, marriages, illness or death, and the children of employers and employees would mix until the former went to study and the latter entered the factory.[34] But if the spatial distance between the homes of the industrialists and the workers was small, the social distance always remained large.

While the arrangement of space in the *courées* served the interests of the factory-owners, facilitating supervision and enabling a large population of workers to be regulated by the rhythms of factory life, the same spatial arrangement also encouraged close bonds amongst the residents of the *courées*. These bonds developed both through contact in the workplace and through social links in the domestic sphere. As noted, the houses in the *courées* were in

---

[32] The *coefficient d'occupation des sols* (COS) is a measure of building density given as the proportion of built floorspace to the total area of the land parcel. This measure was introduced in 1967 under the *loi d'orientation foncière* as a measure for the *plan d'occupation des sols*. A COS of 0.5 might refer to 250m^2 floorspace in an area of 500m^2, for example. Applying this measure retrospectively, the COS for the *courées* was often over 1.5, which is high, particularly for housing which is not in apartment form. See Cornuel and Duriez, 'L'Evolution de la propriété immobilière à Roubaix: 1884–1974', p. 252. Despite this, Cornuel and Duriez suggest that, with respect to the social norms of the period, the *courées* were seen as satisfactory.

[33] B. Duriez and D. Cornuel, *Transformations économiques, évolution des rapports politiques et restructuration urbaine: Roubaix 1960–1975* (Villeneuve d'Ascq: Centre d'Analyse du Développement, 1975), p. 22.

[34] Duriez and Cornuel, 'La naissance de la politique urbaine: le cas de Roubaix', p. 28.

the form of individual units, but in many respects the independence of each house was illusory given the high degree of collective living which the *courées* required of their inhabitants. Lack of living space necessitated the use of the shared semi-public space of the courtyards on to which the *courée* houses faced – as a clothes-drying area, for example, or as a space in which children could play. Moreover, these courtyards were often so narrow that houses facing each other looked directly into one another's rooms. Added to this was the social interaction required by the use of the communal WCs and water pump or, later, water tap, and the use of the local shop or bistro. All these factors contributed to a high degree of social interaction amongst households in the *courées*.

Relations between the factory-owners and the workforce were not only characterized by spatial proximity, but also by a strong degree of paternalism on the part of the former towards the latter, manifest in a tradition of 'good works'. For example, factory-owners sought to pre-empt industrial unrest by providing certain bonuses to their employees, notably financial support in times of illness and *allocations familiales*.[35] This paternalism emerged as a voluntarist practice in the nineteenth century, but the arrangements of the various factories were formalized when a local system of family support was set up after the First World War by factories belonging to the *Consortium de l'Industrie Textile*. All factories which participated in this organization made a contribution, equivalent to 2 per cent of the wages paid, to an interfactory compensation fund. Such a fund linked workers and their families to the factories which took part in it and so ensured the stability of the workforce. This was also a means of controlling the morality of the workforce since there were conditions attached to access to these funds – conditions which were not simply to do with the situation of the family, but also to do with the attitude of the family members towards their employers.[36]

Although this tradition of paternalism clearly had an instrumental dimension, it was also underpinned by a strong religious commitment. Indeed, religion was omnipresent, and employers and their workforce alike participated in the same Catholic model of religious life.[37] Often there was a factory church, the construction of which was financed by the factory-owner. Hiring was frequently conditional on the production of a certificate of baptism, mass for the workers was held on factory holidays, schooling had a strong religious content, there was a flourishing religious press, and workers and their families were provided with welfare by members of church organizations.[38]

---

[35] Financial support for families with children.

[36] D. Cornuel and B. Duriez, *Le mirage urbain: histoire de logement à Roubaix* (Paris: Editions Anthropes, 1983), p. 29.

[37] Duriez and Cornuel, 'La naissance de la politique urbaine: le cas de Roubaix', p. 39.

[38] Cornuel and Duriez, *Le mirage urbain: histoire de logement à Roubaix*, p. 18.

Towards the close of the nineteenth century, factory-owners began to give up their proximity to the factory and move away from the industrial areas of Roubaix, constructing new, large houses in the south of the town, especially along the Rue de Paris.[39] In escaping the shadow of the factory, they were establishing a spatial distance between themselves and their workers that matched the social distance which already separated them. They were also abandoning one of the keystones of their control over the textile workforce but, despite this change, the paternalist attitude of Roubaix's industrialists persisted into the twentieth century.

There were also other important changes taking place around this time, not least the gradual development of workers' organizations. The strikes of May and June 1880 marked the renaissance of the workers' movement in France after the crushing of the Paris Commune in 1871, and the solidarity which developed amongst the strikers contributed towards the emergence of cooperative and mutual societies. Roubaix's first cooperative, *l'Avenir du Parti Ouvrier*, was set up by Henri Carette and his supporters in Rue Vallon in Alma-Gare. Carette went on to be elected Roubaix's first Socialist mayor in 1892. Despite this early initiative and, indeed, despite Roubaix's mono-industrial profile, the town's textile workers were slow to organize. This was due to a number of factors. First, the structure of the textile industry tended to inhibit unionization; there were many small to medium-sized factories, which discouraged communication between different workforces. Second, in 1887, factory-owners gave their support to a mixed industrial union – the *syndicat mixte de l'industrie roubaisienne* – in an attempt to pre-empt the development of workers' unions, to which they were strongly opposed. This *syndicat*, which lasted until 1919, brought together workers and employers in factory councils in which, not surprisingly, the employers had the stronger hand. Third, the textile workers were marked by internal divisions – principally between those who lived in Roubaix and those who travelled to work each day, and between those who were French and those who were Belgian. There were also divisions between the unions when these organizations finally emerged, with the CGTU[40] having a 'revolutionary' profile, the CGT[41] being 'reformist' and the CFTC[42] being linked to the factory-owners through their religious dimension and their corporatist perspective.[43]

The factory-owners maintained an autocratic attitude in the face of unionization and, on the whole, refused to negotiate with workers' organizations,

[39] Duriez and Cornuel, 'La naissance de la politique urbaine: le cas de Roubaix', p. 28.
[40] Confédération Générale du Travail Unitaire, founded in 1922.
[41] Confédération Générale du Travail, founded in 1895.
[42] Confédération Française des Travailleurs Chrétiens, founded in 1919.
[43] Duriez and Cornuel, 'La naissance de la politique urbaine: le cas de Roubaix', p. 31.

particularly the radical CGTU. Gradually, the intransigence of the bosses forced the unions together, and the inter-war period was marked by a string of bitter industrial conflicts. There were major strikes in 1921 (the general textile strike, August to October 1921), 1924 to 1925 (known as the *grève glorieuse*), 1926 (the *grèves du tapis*), 1928 to 1929 (the strike of the *dix sous*), 1931 and 1936. During periods of industrial strife, the morphology of the *courées* assumed a tactical significance. Their physical layout was labyrinthine, which facilitated covert communication between their inhabitants and avoided the need to take to the main streets. Equally, the warren of lanes, courts and passageways presented severe problems for the forces of order, who, during certain periods of industrial unrest, had to be issued with maps in order to orientate themselves.[44] Most famous of all perhaps was the attempt by the mounted police to enter the *quartier* of Longues Haies during the strikes of 1921 – the cavalry charge was thwarted by a combination of the narrowness of the passageways and their confusing geography.

In the face of growing worker organization, the significance of religion and paternalism in the workplace began to decline. The traditional relations between the workers and their employers also changed as central government started to play a more important role in industrial relations – a development which was not welcomed by Roubaix's factory-owners. In particular, they disapproved of the national extension of the benefits which they had developed for their own workers since, in this way, these benefits became a right rather than a useful lever in industrial relations.

But it was not only in the area of industrial relations that Roubaix's factory-owners were facing problems. The town's textile industry reached its peak at the end of the nineteenth century, entered a phase of stagnation and then, from around 1910, began to decline. This decline was initially due to the First World War and then as a result of the depression of the 1930s. Throughout the inter-war period there was little investment in the industry's infrastructure, partly because the economic climate restricted investment in capital equipment and partly because such investment had traditionally never been a priority for the factory-owners. With the decline of the textile industry in this period, and the population loss which this entailed for Roubaix (see Table 3.1), so the construction of the *courées* slowed. Moreover, from 1920, developments in the transport system enabled daily commuting from the mining area in the north

[44] As noted, some *courées* were named after their owners, while others were given the names of saints, but their designation was confusing, and an *arrêté* from the mayor on 20 December 1869 required owners to put up name plaques at the mouth of the *courées* to avoid confusion concerning addresses, voting lists and the collection of census material. See Prouvost, 'Les courées à Roubaix', p. 314.

(which had also become a labour pool for the textile industry) and from across the Belgian border, which reduced the demand for housing. In addition to these factors, a law had been passed in 1914 to freeze the level of domestic rents. While this measure favoured employers (low rents allowed employers to keep wages down, something which the government considered essential if France was to be competitive in the post-war period), it was clearly not in the interests of landlords, and it resulted in the neglect of properties and a slowing of construction rates. The situation for landlords was exacerbated by inflation, so much so that they could no longer rely on revenue from their properties as their sole income. The last *courée* in Roubaix, the *cité* Duretête frères in rue de Leers, consisting of 19 houses, was constructed in 1934.[45]

In 1943, at the initiative of Albert Prouvost, who ran the Lainière factory in Roubaix, the textile factory-owners of Roubaix and Tourcoing established the *Comité Interprofessionnelle du Logement* (CIL) as a mechanism by which the textile interests could encourage and direct housing provision for the working population in the two towns. The CIL's operation was achieved through a financial contribution equivalent to 1 per cent of salaries paid by each firm to a central fund.[46] Although the CIL originated as an initiative of the textile sector, the industry wanted to extend the initiative to employers throughout the Roubaix–Tourcoing agglomeration and, given the influence of the textile industry, it was not difficult to persuade others to adopt the formula. From 1944, 90 per cent of employers in the agglomeration were making a 1 per cent contribution to the CIL.[47] In assuming the responsibility for housing, the town's industrialists were effectively denying this initiative to Roubaix's *Municipalité* and establishing their own authority in the field of housing provision. Of course, the CIL also echoed the paternalistic tradition which had emerged in the nineteenth century, and certainly served the interests of good labour relations by encouraging the cooperation of the workforce. In 1953 the French government made the 1 per cent contribution obligatory on a nationwide basis and, in institutionalizing this contribution, effectively reduced the degree of influence which the industrialists of Roubaix–Tourcoing had initially obtained from their initiative. By 1970 there were 136 CILs in France, of which four were in the *métropole du Nord* (that is, in Lille, Roubaix, Tourcoing and the surrounding *communes*).

---

[45] Ibid., p. 312.

[46] In certain years this contribution even reached 2 per cent in Roubaix and Tourcoing. The idea of an employers' contribution towards the social requirements of their workers was not a new one; we have seen that the 1 per cent or 2 per cent mechanism had already been employed by the *consortium de l'industrie textile* to finance the system of *allocation familiales* after the First World War.

[47] Cornuel and Duriez, *Le mirage urbain: histoire de logement à Roubaix*, p. 68.

Strictly speaking, the CIL was not a constructor but a financing organization, responsible for the collection and distribution of the 1 per cent contribution. The contribution was assigned to the *sociétés HLM* – public housing agencies – which, in theory, remained legally independent of the CIL, although in practice this was not always the case. By means of the 1 per cent contribution and a system of complementary funding from central government, the CIL came to have considerable influence over housing activities in Roubaix. It was the CIL that took the initiative after the Second World War to introduce the most modern prefabrication techniques in order to build more cheaply, so initiating a new phase of construction in Roubaix: between 1947 and 1962, the organization was responsible for promoting the construction of 4000 housing units in and around the city.[48] In this way, the CIL began to have a meaning in Roubaix's popular discourse more akin to a house as a physical entity than to an organization. As such, the population distinguished it from that other 'house', the HLM – 'a CIL's better than an HLM'.[49] In addition to favouring new construction, one of the CIL's founding aims had been to promote the demolition of housing identified as *insalubre*; despite this intention, however, the CIL demolished only 406 dwellings in the *cours* and *courées* of the *métropole du Nord* between 1945 and 1968.

The post-war period: crisis and fragmentation

Roubaix emerged from the Second World War with little damage and, together with neighbouring Tourcoing, it continued to maintain its position as the largest concentration of textile employment in France. However, the lack of investment in the industry throughout the inter-war years was beginning to take its toll, and the town's industrial structure was becoming increasingly obsolete. Moreover, the system exhibited such a degree of over-specialization that it was highly susceptible to any external influences which might unbalance it. The early years of the post-war period were characterized by increased competition from abroad, rising wage levels at home and innovations in the field of synthetic fibres. These developments not only precipitated the textile crisis of 1951, but also visited more profound and long-term effects on the industry.

Textile firms responded to the post-war crisis by implementing restructuring programmes. This restructuring saw them abandon the traditional pursuit of profits through speculation in raw materials and seek instead to gain a return on their capital through investment in the production process, and particularly through the introduction of faster machines, automated techniques and new

[48] Bruyelle, 'Roubaix face aux grandes mutations récentes', p. 328.

[49] '... un CIL c'est mieux qu'un HLM'. Cited in Cornuel and Duriez, *Le mirage urbain: histoire de logement à Roubaix*, p. 81.

materials. The financial commitment which this modernization involved was beyond the means of many of the Roubaix's smaller enterprises. Some of these were forced to close as increased competition weeded out the weaker firms, while others were taken over by the survivors, which in turn grew larger. The position of Roubaix's smaller firms became even more uncertain with the creation of the EEC in 1957 and the consequent removal of trade barriers, and with the development of competition from countries in South-east Asia and the Far East. The early post-war period therefore marked a transition as Roubaix's textile industry came to be dominated by larger groups with regional, national or even international interests.

With the post-war crisis there was also evidence of a clear fragmentation of interests within the textile industry. The drive towards efficiency in this period of economic difficulty provoked two different responses. First, there were companies which embarked upon the vertical integration of all the production and retail operations associated with the textile industry. These companies tended to remain in the hands of powerful local businessmen, and their interests were represented by the *Syndicat Patronal du Textile* (SPT). Second, there were companies which were horizontally integrated into large corporations with diverse product bases, such as the *Groupe Prouvost* or *Agache-Willot*. For the first group of companies, still founded on family ties and local capital, textile production remained of paramount importance, and this production remained tied to a specific location. It was therefore in the interest of this group to maintain a relatively stable population of textile workers in Roubaix. For the second group, however, textiles represented only one element in their product base, and Roubaix represented only one of many possible locations within a global space. When proximity to raw materials or cheap wages required it, these corporations would relocate elsewhere, even overseas.

The crisis in the textile sector and the consequent attempts at restructuring also reduced employment possibilities for the town's population and, moreover, changed the characteristics of the industry's workforce. First, automation meant a dequalification of jobs and thus a reduced demand for skilled workers. This was by no means compensated for by a small increase in employees capable of training workers in the new production techniques and in others qualified to ensure the maintenance of the new machinery. One of the consequences of this development was to reinforce the division of interests between the skilled and unskilled elements of the textile industry's workforce. The second implication of the post-war restructuring was a reduction in the proportion of women in the workforce of the textile sector. This was partly because of the heavier nature of the work required by the new machinery, and partly because of the introduction of teamwork which permitted more efficient levels of production and enabled machinery to be operated 24 hours a day, thus facilitating the recovery of capital equipment costs. The gender shift was further exacerbated by changes in employment in other areas, particularly by the decline of the mining industry, which tended to push men towards employment in the textile sector.[50]

The third major implication of the changes undergone by the industry was that working conditions deteriorated, and this, combined with the decline in jobs for skilled workers, pushed qualified manual workers to leave the textile industry. They were replaced in turn by unskilled workers, often immigrants, who were employed by the industry at low wages. Immigration, as we have seen, has always been an important element in Roubaix's development. Roubaix's nineteenth century migration had been sustained almost exclusively by Belgians seeking work in the textile industry, and in 1949 there were still 25 000 in the agglomeration.[51] By 1962, however, there were only 4 300 Belgians employed in Roubaix, 60 per cent of whom were employed in the textile industry. This decline can be attributed to the exchange rate moving against the French franc, the difficulties experienced by the textile industry and the expansion of Belgium's own industrial base. The Belgian immigrant population was replaced by other nationalities. After the Second World War the first wave of migrants arrived from Italy, Poland, Spain and Portugal to be followed by migrants from North Africa – Tunisia, Morocco and Algeria.

The arrival of these economically disadvantaged groups also had the effect of accentuating the socioeconomic disparities which were emerging between recession-hit Roubaix and the rest of the region. By 1968, non-French accounted for 14 per cent of Roubaix's population of 114 547,[52] and this proportion continued to grow through the 1970s, reaching 22.5 per cent in 1975, after which the growth began to slow. By early 1981, the proportion of immigrants had begun to decline, and by 1982 the percentage of non-French stood at 20.8 per cent.[53] In this year, Italians accounted for some 75 per cent of Roubaix's non-French population from within the EEC, but in the same year, 83 per cent of the non-French came from outside the EEC. The non-EEC figure at that time included Portuguese and Spanish who together accounted for 28.5 per cent of the non-French population.[54]

The right to vote did not extend to the non-French population, which meant that its political influence was small and its ability to represent its own interests (which were, in any case, diverse) was limited.[55] Frequently they have acted as

---

[50] Ibid., p. 58.

[51] Bruyelle, 'Roubaix face aux grandes mutations récentes', p. 310.

[52] Ibid., p. 316.

[53] Ibid., p. 320. These are official figures and do not take into account the unseen dimension of illegal immigration.

[54] All figures cited in ibid.

[55] The issues of ethnicity, race and racism are hugely complex and go beyond the scope of this research. It is clear, for example, that to speak generally of 'North Africans' is already a simplification which not only glosses over both national and ethnic identities, but also ignores intergenerational differences and the subtleties of 'origin', 'birth',

scapegoats for Roubaix's socioeconomic problems, including the city's poor public image, the dilapidated housing stock, the erosion of the voting base, the poorly developed consumer sector and rising crime levels (this is particularly the case for the North African population). Roubaix's socioeconomic difficulties combined with this large and visible immigrant population also contributed to a bedrock of support for the extreme right. Le Pen's list obtained 19.1 per cent of the vote in Roubaix in the European elections of June 1984, as compared to a national average of 11 per cent. More recently, the rise of 'Islamic fundamentalist' activity in France has provided yet another platform from which to attack the North African population.[56]

The attempts at restructuring Roubaix's textile industry did little to slow its decline. Between 1950 and 1970, the number of firms belonging to the *Syndicat Patronal du Textile* diminished by 53 per cent, and this in turn had an impact on the town's ancillary services. This figure reflects both the process of de-industrialization which occurred throughout the period, and the attempts on the part of the textile industry to make itself leaner and fitter. The economic crisis of the 1970s, and particularly after 1974, sent more shock waves through the textile industry. The rate of factory closures increased and, according to an inquiry undertaken by the *Chambre de Commerce et d'Industrie*, between 1972 and 1978, 16 per cent of industrial land (35.2ha) disappeared in Roubaix.[57] If Roubaix is considered along with Tourcoing, the figures become even bleaker, with a total of 40 000 textile jobs lost in the Roubaix–Tourcoing agglomeration between 1960 and 1982.[58]

This turbulent post-war history was played out against a political landscape which remained remarkably constant for most of this period.[59] Prior to the Second World War the *Municipalité de Roubaix* had a relatively minor role to play in the town due to the power and influence of the textile industrialists. However, town hall politics came to be more influential after 1945 as the *Municipalité* attempted to establish a degree of influence in urban affairs, in a move that mirrored central government's concern about urban issues on a national scale. Ideas of social functionalism, welfare and technological expertise began to inform the local level, just as they did the national.

'descent' and 'attachment'. The aim of this limited discussion is simply to establish that there existed, and continues to exist, in Roubaix a substantial proportion of the population who are systematically disadvantaged because of their non-French origin.

[56] See, for example, the discussion in both the local and national press provoked by the events of 29 March 1996 which culminated in a police siege at 59, Rue Carette, Roubaix. Four North African men died when RAID special forces stormed the house.

[57] Bruyelle, 'Roubaix face aux grandes mutations récentes', p. 310.

[58] Battiau, 'Raisons et effets de la concentration spatiale de nombreux textiles dans l'agglomération Roubaix-Tourcoing', p. 75.

[59] For a more detailed discussion of party politics in Roubaix, see the two chapters by F.P. Codaccioni (pp. 259–304) in Hilaire, *Histoire de Roubaix*.

From the end of the war until the mid-1970s, municipal power was held by a socialist–centrist coalition headed by a Socialist mayor whose deputies were drawn not only from the Socialist Party, but also from the *Rassemblement du Peuple Français* (RPF) and the *Mouvement Républicain Populaire* (MRP). The Socialists enjoyed widespread support, drawing votes from the middle classes as well as the working classes, although Roubaix demonstrated different voting patterns in national elections.[60] The existence of a socialist–centrist alliance suggests that the parties involved were prepared to overlook partisan politics in order to combat the economic decline of the town. The inception of the alliance also demonstrated a degree of political pragmatism on the part of the Socialist Party. The Socialists had been in control of the town hall throughout the German occupation. As a result, they found themselves in a precarious position after the Liberation and, in the first post-war municipal elections, held in 1945, the MRP made a significant impact upon the Socialists' support base. This was in part because some of the members of the Socialist Party had adopted a neutral or even *pétainiste* stance during the war and in part because there was a feeling that the Socialist members of the *Municipalité* represented the 'old guard' – traditionalists who were ill-equipped to lead the party in the post-war atmosphere.[61] Given the difficulties faced by the Socialist Party, a political alliance with centrist parties was a useful means by which to shore up its support base.[62] Over and above these considerations, the long-term success of this coalition owed much to the personality of Victor Provo, who held the office of mayor for 35 years, from 1942 to 1977. Many of Roubaix's population felt a particular affection for Provo, who wielded a high degree of moral authority.[63]

---

[60] On the national level, Roubaix gave solid support to De Gaulle from 1958 to 1969. From the mid- to late 1960s, however, the political equilibrium in Roubaix began to shift gradually towards the left. This shift was temporarily halted by the events of spring 1968, and in the general elections of June of that year the Gaullists held Roubaix. However, in April 1969 Roubaix rejected De Gaulle's proposals for regional reorganization and reform of the senate. From this point, support for the left grew: the Socialists won the legislative elections of March 1973 and Mitterand easily secured a local majority over Giscard d'Estaing in the presidential elections of May 1974. Victory also fell to the left in the legislative elections of March 1978, the presidential elections of April and May 1981, and again in the legislative elections of June 1981.

[61] Codaccioni, 'La vie politique à Roubaix sous l'administration de Victor Provo (1942–77)' in Hilaire, *Histoire de Roubaix*, p. 260.

[62] From this point on, the MRP's grip on the electorate began to slacken. A new Gaullist party emerged in 1947 at the initiative of the General himself. This was the RPF, the *Rassemblement du Peuple Français*, and in the municipal elections of October 1947 the RPF won a majority of 17 000 over the MRP. The MRP was finally dissolved in 1967, and the Gaullist UNR (*Union pour la nouvelle république*, founded in 1958) became increasingly powerful, both nationally and in Roubaix.

[63] Provo was also president of the CUDL from 1967 to 1971, elected *député du Nord* in 1952, and re-elected in 1956 until 1958.

The *Municipalité de Roubaix* recognized the CIL's potential to regenerate Roubaix's housing stock – a task for which the town hall was not yet equipped. Of course, in adopting this pragmatic attitude, the *Municipalité* chose to overlook the ideological tensions which marked an alliance between an employers' organization and a workers' party – tensions which in any case were moderated by the presence of a minority of centrist councillors in the municipal government. Until the introduction of effective renewal legislation, the CIL, with its efficient financing mechanism, was considered to be in the best position to offer a solution to Roubaix's housing problems. Since housing and the physical renewal of the town was an important issue, and the provision of housing for the working population was, of course, in keeping with Socialist ideology, the *Municipalité* accepted this situation.

Those who would not accept the socialist–centrist compromise, most notably the Communist Party, found themselves excluded from town hall politics. The Communists in Roubaix had started the post-war period with a groundswell of support that was largely due to the involvement of young party workers in the Resistance during the Occupation. Generally, the Communist Party found significant support in the older areas of Roubaix, both in the pre-war public housing projects and in the *courées*, and particularly in Alma-Gare. Its members refused to join the Socialist Party in an alliance with the MRP because of the latter's Christian links and, as they saw it, reactionary position. The Socialists and Communists were therefore at loggerheads throughout much of the post-war period, and Codaccioni suggests that the impact of this disunity on the political left, and the effect it had upon the electorate, was yet another factor which facilitated relations between the Socialists and the more centrist political factions.[64] The Communist Party also opposed the CIL's influence in the town, viewing the textile bosses as its enemy and holding them directly responsible for the construction and perpetuation of the *courées*.

The municipal elections of March 1977 marked a turning point in Roubaix's local politics. Provo had retired, and his socialist–centrist alliance was replaced by a union of the left – the *Union de Forces de Gauche* – under Pierre Prouvost, formerly Provo's deputy mayor. Prouvost's list, which faced a centre–right alliance, consisted of Socialists, the *Parti Socialiste Unifié* (PSU), the Communists (who had been excluded from power since 1959), and the radical left, under the slogan 'the Future of Roubaix'.[65] This shift to the left reflected changes in the *Parti Socialiste* at the national level: from the early 1970s it had begun to enjoy a renaissance in France and, at the same time, the Communist Party had begun to move closer to it. Prouvost's list won the 1977 elections, meaning that Roubaix not only had a Socialist mayor, but also all its deputies

64 Codaccioni, 'La vie politique à Roubaix sous l'administration de Victor Provo (1942–1977)', in Hilaire, *History de Roubaix*, p. 265.

65 'l'Avenir de Roubaix'.

were drawn from the left. The left's control of Roubaix lasted for six years. In the municipal elections of March 1983, the Socialists, who had held power in the town hall since 1912, were defeated by André Diligent and his unified list of opposition dominated by the *Centre Démocrates Sociaux*.[66]

Paradoxically, the social and economic fragmentation which marked Roubaix in the post-war period contributed to the development of a consensus, albeit one marked by clear tensions, amongst the locally-based textile firms represented by the SPT, local interests associated with the town's commercial and service sectors, and the *Municipalité de Roubaix*. This consensus was founded on a belief in the urgent need to develop a viable and prosperous tertiary sector in the town. In 1970, the president of the SPT expressed his wish to see 50 per cent of employment taken up by the tertiary sector by 1985.[67] While it may appear strange that the textile industry should have supported the development of Roubaix's service sector, tertiary activities offered certain clear benefits. First, tertiarization allowed the industry to expand and diversify its economic interests in the face of the continuing economic crisis. Some textile concerns invested in commercial functions such as Flunch, Libre Service Bricolage and Auchan,[68] and also began to develop mail order services, most notably La Redoute, Trois Suisses and Damart. Second, they considered that developing the tertiary sector offered a means of attracting a more stable workforce to Roubaix. This movement was also encouraged by the operation of the CIL, since the provision of the appropriate housing (and the appropriate exclusion mechanisms) was an important means by which the SPT could attract and maintain this workforce. In the difficult post-1974 economic climate, factory-owners made an even greater effort to rid themselves of what they considered the most unstable elements in the foreign workforce, principally North Africans and single male immigrants (often one and the same). At the same time, they improved working conditions in order to tempt back French workers and those elements of the foreign workforce they considered most stable.[69] Finally, the issue of tertiary development was closely connected to a desire to reshape the widely held image of Roubaix as a dreary, recession-bitten textile town.[70] For the textile industry, the improvement of the town's *image*

---

[66] The list also included the *Centre National des Indépendants*, *Rassemblement pour la République* (RPR), *Républicains*, *indépendants* and *sans étiquette*. Diligent had also led the list against the *Union de Forces de Gauch* in 1977, under the slogan 'Sauver Roubaix' – 'Save Roubaix'.

[67] Cornuel and Duriez, *Le mirage urbain: histoire de logement à Roubaix*, p. 160.

[68] Respectively a self-service restaurant chain, a DIY store and a hypermarket.

[69] ABAC-Paris and APU-Roubaix, 'Roubaix: le quartier de l'Alma-Gare', in J.L. Flamand et al., *La Question du logement et le mouvement ouvrier français* (Paris: Editions de la Villette, 1981), p. 179.

[70] In one sense, this can be seen as a precursor of the post-industrial phenomenon that was to become familiar in the 1980s, as the market increasingly came to be regarded

de marque[71] was important because it was a means by which to break what was regarded as a vicious circle, whereby immigrant workers contributed to the poor image of the textile industry, which in turn made it difficult to employ French workers.

The development of Roubaix's tertiary sector was also promoted by the *Chambre de Commerce et d'Industrie* on behalf of local commercial interests and those already involved in the service sector.[72] From the perspective of these groups, the development of the tertiary sector was a means of transforming Roubaix following the departure of the textile industry and of establishing a new, wealthier population and thus a new consumer base. This group resented the presence of the immigrant population because of their limited spending power and their contribution to the commercially damaging image of Roubaix as a mono-industrial textile town. In the context of the *image de marque* it is interesting to note the distress caused, particularly amongst retailers, at the decision to designate the Motte-Bossut factory as a historical monument.[73] This building was located in the very centre of the town and was constructed in the crenellated *château-fort* style which was so evocative of Roubaix's industrial past. For commercial interests in the area, this designation, and the legal protection it afforded, institutionalized precisely the image they hoped to erase.

The third important promoter of the tertiary drive was the *Municipalité de Roubaix*. Faced with the decline of the textile sector and the movement of skilled workers out of the town, the *Municipalité* was experiencing a reduction in fiscal income without a corresponding decrease in the financial burden; it found itself with a growing proportion of the economically unproductive in the population, be they the very young, the very old, the sick or the unemployed. Moreover, the arrival of the post-war immigrants had contributed to a decline in the electoral base, and the gravity of the situation from the *Municipalité*'s point of view is illustrated by the fact that voting figures from the municipal elections between 1965 and 1977 dropped from 60 169 to 53 010 – a decline of 12 per cent.[74] For the *Municipalité*, developing tertiary activities was therefore a

---

as the panacea for the failure of the state: the Big Apple proclaimed narcissistically 'I♥NY', Mr Happy assured us that 'Glasg☺w's miles better', while the Spanish capital looked skywards, 'de Madrid al cielo'.

71 The issue of *image de marque* is discussed in Duriez and Cornuel, *Transformations économiques, évolution des rapports politiques et restructuration urbaine* and Cornuel and Duriez, *Le mirage urbain: histoire de logement à Roubaix*.

72 Many of these had originally been employed in administration or management in the textile industry, or in ancillary activities. With the onset of the textile crisis they began to look elsewhere for jobs.

73 Cornuel and Duriez, *Le mirage urbain: histoire de logement à Roubaix*, p. 164.

74 *Nord Eclair* (15 March 1965), pp. 1 and 5; *Nord Eclair* (15 March 1971), p. 1; *Nord Eclair* (14 March 1977), p. 1.

means of combating the employment crisis and revitalizing the city's economic and the demographic profile. Of course, it also had to consider its electorate, and the future of Roubaix's economy and employment structure was a perennial issue. The development of the tertiary sector therefore offered a means by which the town hall could demonstrate its commitment to improving the economic position of Roubaix's citizens.

In addition to lending its support to the tertiary drive, the *Municipalité* took direct measures to discourage the arrival of immigrants, particularly from 1973 onwards. For example, it forbade the opening of new cafes by North Africans and restricted the construction of *foyers* (residential halls) for migrant workers in renewal projects, despite advice to the contrary from specialist organizations. The *Municipalité* also rejected a proposal that Roubaix should become an official place of immigration, and in 1980 it opposed the purchase of a property by a Muslim organization that wished to construct a mosque.[75]

Clearly, while the *Municipalité*, the SPT and the town's commercial interests pursued a common agenda in their drive towards the development of tertiary services, there were diverse interests at play. In particular, there was a tension between the desire of the textile bosses to revitalize their industry through the development of tertiary activities, and the hope of the commercial sector that the growth of the tertiary sector would sound the death knell for Roubaix's industrial past. As for the *Municipalité*, there was certainly a recognition that what was good for the textile industry, in one manifestation or another, was also good for Roubaix. But, at the same time, the development of a healthy tertiary sector offered the town hall the chance to reclaim the initiative in urban affairs from the textile industry, which had directed the development of Roubaix for so long.

The ambition of these groups to see the tertiary sector rise from the ashes of Roubaix's industrial past were to remain largely unfulfilled. The linchpins of Roubaix's tertiary sector have been mail order sales, the public sector and insurance,[76] but beyond this there has been little development. Many of the service sector jobs which were created, particularly those in mail order, were unskilled and so failed to attract either the skilled French workers sought by the textile industry or the wealthier population courted by the *Chambre de Commerce et d'Industrie* and the *Municipalité*. In attempting to attract employment from outside, Roubaix and neighbouring Tourcoing put themselves

---

[75] Cornuel and Duriez, *Le mirage urbain: histoire de logement à Roubaix*, p. 176. Cornuel and Duriez have argued that the low level of qualifications in the textile industry were as a result of the employers' low-wage policy, and not vice versa. They claim that the industrialists employed the discourse of the immigrant workers' poor capacity to work in order to justify their own policy of low pay. Ibid., p. 64.

[76] Particularly the Verspieren Group. See Bruyelle, 'Roubaix face aux grandes mutations récentes', p. 312.

into direct competition with Lille, which generally proved to be a much more attractive town to new employers.[77] This was partly because Roubaix and Tourcoing's historical development had left these towns ill-equipped to provide services for the region, and as a result they exerted much less influence than their size alone would suggest. Moreover, in contrast to Lille, the conversion of industrial buildings to offices, shops or houses by the private sector in Roubaix was rare. Up until 1977, Roubaix's *Municipalité* tended to use land freed from industrial use for the construction of public sector housing, and it was only after 1977 that there emerged a policy which promoted available land for industrial use, encouraged private investment and advocated the re-use of empty factories. But even given this shift, tertiary activity preferred to locate outside Roubaix. Of the 214 000m^2 of office space created in the *métropole du Nord* from 1975 to 1982, only 27 000m^2 (12.5 per cent) was located in Roubaix, and 17 000m^2 of this was in a single development, the Mercure building, which was financed by the *Chambre de Commerce et d'Industrie* and lay on the boundary between Roubaix and Tourcoing. Moreover, much of this office development was associated with the administrative aspects of the textile industry. Tertiary activity was further hampered because development policies in the agglomeration tended to favour Lille and the new town of Villeneuve d'Ascq at the expense of Roubaix and Tourcoing. Indeed, the creation of Villeneuve d'Ascq in 1970 to act as a pole of attraction for tertiary activity in the region was a major factor in thwarting the dream of the *Chambre de Commerce et d'Industrie* and the SPT of a new Roubaix founded on tertiary activity. Perhaps one of the most painfully ironic episodes from this history was the decision to locate a research centre and laboratory for the textile industry in Villeneuve d'Ascq rather than in Roubaix.

The *courées*: these doors that led to despair

As noted, conditions in the *courées* were already a source of concern in the nineteenth century and, from around the turn of the century, calls from doctors, reformers and philanthropists for the demolition of this form of housing became more frequent. These protests, however, had no effect, partly because two world wars, the housing shortage and the impact of rent laws ensured that the *courées* survived, and partly because, as Cornuel and Duriez point out, they continued to play a valuable role in providing cheap housing for the workforce

[77] It is interesting to note that Roubaix and Tourcoing placed themselves in competition with Lille in a period when the emphasis seemed to be on the unification of the towns and the removal of barriers, particularly with the creation of the *Communauté Urbaine de Lille*.

of the textile industry.[78] Moreover, as we have seen in Chapter Two, the issue of housing only came onto the political agenda in France during the 1950s.

The spatial arrangement of the *courées* remained more or less unaltered until the introduction of legislation for urban renewal in 1958, at which time there were still 1034 *courées* in the town (as compared to the maximum of 1324 in 1912). In 1954, as much as 85.8 per cent of the housing in Roubaix had been built prior to 1914. This figure had fallen to 71 per cent by 1962, with the start of the *Municipalité*'s demolition programmes, but this was still exceptionally high given that even neighbouring Lille had a figure of 55 per cent for the same year.[79] Roubaix's old housing stock lacked basic sanitary facilities, a key factor in the designation of housing as *insalubre*: only 13.8 per cent of all houses in Roubaix had a bath or a shower in 1954, while only 29.6 per cent had an inside WC.[80] Indeed, the correlation between the *courées* and housing officially designated *insalubre* was striking. For example, in 1956, 9534 houses in Roubaix were classified as *insalubre*, representing approximately one-quarter of the town's total housing stock. Of these, some 9000 (94 per cent) were located in the *courées*. Housing density in the *courées* was around 8530 units per km^2 in 1962. This would not have been particularly high for apartment buildings, but for individual houses like the *courées* this represented an extremely dense built environment.[81]

If the physical layout of the *courées* had changed little over the years, the social composition had undergone continuous transformation since the *courées* now served as a reception area for successive waves of immigrants. This process was exacerbated by the restructuring of the textile industry in the post-war period, which provoked considerable movement in the town's population. As the immigrants in the textile industry were paid low wages, the *courées* represented the only form of housing realistically available to them, and the spatial concentration of the non-French which this produced further contributed to their 'visibility'. In 1971 a survey of the population of the *courées* of Lille, Roubaix and Tourcoing was carried out by the *Organisation pour la Suppression des Courées de la Métropole Nord*.[82] This survey found that 30 per cent of the *courées*' population were immigrants, with just over half of these – that is, 16 per cent of the total population – being of North African origin. Often

[78] D. Cornuel and B. Duriez, *Les courées de Roubaix: 1884–1974* (Villeneuve d'Ascq: Centre d'Analyse du Développement, 1975), p. 1.

[79] Bruyelle, 'Roubaix face aux grandes mutations récentes', p. 324.

[80] Ibid., p. 335.

[81] Ibid., p. 324.

[82] The following figures are cited in ABAC-Paris and APU-Roubaix, 'Roubaix: le quartier de l'Alma-Gare', pp. 171–3, and 'Roubaix: L'APU 2. Stratégie du capital et stratégie populaire', *Place*, no. 5 (autumn, 1976), p. 12. INSEE figures for 1968 had recorded a total of 16 821 people living in *courées* in Roubaix. The percentages which are cited are therefore roughly applicable to this total figure.

the inhabitants of the *courées* who were in work belonged to the most exploited elements of the workforce, those who were least able to defend their interests. They often made up the reserve labour force for the textile factories, being called upon to work at low wages in periods of economic boom, then laid off in periods of recession. Amongst the economically active, 24.3 per cent were classified by the survey as unskilled manual workers, 35 per cent were skilled workers, 16 per cent fell into the category of professional workers and 9 per cent were *personnel de service*.[83] Thus 60 per cent of the active population fell into the category of manual workers of one kind or another. Increasingly, the *courées* also came to house a population which was economically inactive; only 60 per cent of heads of household were in full- or part-time work, with the remainder being unemployed, retired (25 per cent, rising to 35 per cent in some *courées*), suffering from long-term illness or without known employment. The population of the *courées* was also characterized by a large proportion of both elderly and the young; more than 20 per cent were 65 years old or over (the national average in 1968 was 13 per cent), while 51 per cent of the population were less than 25 years old (the national average in 1971 was 41 per cent). In addition, 28 per cent of the population were found to live alone, the majority of these being the elderly or single male immigrant workers, and there was also a high proportion of large families, a feature which reflected the significant immigrant population. Not surprisingly, household income in the *courées* was low, and the young and the immigrant populations were especially likely to be without work or exploited in the black economy. Poverty and poor housing inevitably led to health problems, and Vincenti and Vilment cite a Dr Boyaval who, from his study of the distribution of infant mortality in Roubaix in 1965, felt able to speak of a 'pathology specific to the *courées*' when considering the levels of tuberculosis, infant mortality and so on.[84] The situation was such that the term *courée* became synonymous with poor housing conditions.

While studies of the *courées* have emphasized their negative aspects, one should not overlook the advantages offered by this form of housing. For example, immigrants often employed informal networks distinct from those of their French neighbours to find housing – networks based on family, friendship or cultural bonds. The *courées* allowed people of the same nationality or religion to live in proximity to one another and thus to benefit from mutual support systems and common cultural experience. Nor was this experience limited to the non-French; for the elderly, in particular, the *courées* represented a rich social resource and an environment invested with memories. On a more practical level, houses in the *courées* were also flexible in their internal

[83] *Personnel de service* is a category that refers to service and administrative staff. The remaining 15 per cent fell in to other employment categories.

[84] '... pathologie propre aux courées.' Cited in Vicentini and Vilment, 'L'Evolution du cadre de vie à Roubaix de 1945 à 1977', p. 41.

arrangements, being adaptable to both single people and large families. It is also interesting to note Benarab's findings in her study of the appropriation of space in the *courées* by different cultural communities, and especially the analogy she suggests between traditional *maghrébin* housing and the *courée* form:

> The entry passage to the *courée* plays the role of a filter reminiscent of the cul-de-sac or *driba* (hall) of the North African's traditional house, creating a degree of distance and therefore of intimacy with respect to the street (public space), which is an important feature for the North African ... . The courée therefore offers the North African an urban structure which, *a priori*, is not unfamiliar ... . The habitat of the *courée* is a horizontal habitat in the image of the North African home (2 storeys maximum).[85]

An early initiative to improve conditions in the *courées* was the formation of PACT – *Propagande et Action Contre les Taudis*.[86] PACT was founded in 1950 as a Catholic voluntary association and was originally made up of young people who contributed some of their spare time to the upkeep, repair and rehabilitation of old housing – particularly houses inhabited by the elderly. During the 1960s, the organization developed a more technical approach, took on a number of permanent employees, and increasingly became involved in the ownership and management of property, buying up houses or even whole *courées*. In this way it became the largest owner of old housing stock in Roubaix. These properties were then rented out at a 'normal' rent to those members of the population who could not qualify for, or were expelled from CIL or HLM housing. Thus it was PACT that dealt with the most marginalized population of the *courées* – immigrants, travellers, the sick, those with large families and so on – providing them with transition homes in the old housing stock so that they could undergo a process of 'socialization'.[87] From 1969 PACT began to receive financial and legal support from the government, and by 1976 it was managing 600 houses in Lille and 1900 in Roubaix,[88] after which the impact of the various clearance programmes in Roubaix caused a reduction in the organization's housing stock.

The role of PACT was to ensure the physical maintenance of the houses in the *courées*. The first important initiative to *remove* the *courées* was taken on 14 January 1957, when the *Municipalité*, with the promise of considerable financial backing from central government, decided to embark on the renewal

[85] N. Benarab, 'Appropriation d'une courée Roubaisienne par des communautés culturellement différentes et les rapports sociaux induits par ce type d'appropriation', unpublished thesis, University of Lille (1981), p. 12.

[86] This title is an example of the word *taudis* – slum – being associated with the *courées*.

[87] For immigrant workers, for example, a period in the old housing was a necessary precondition for access to a CIL apartment.

[88] G. Lamarche-Vadel and A. Cotlenko, 'Alma-Gare – le singulier et le politique', *Autrement*, no. 6 (1976), p. 63.

of the area around the rue de Longues Haies in the centre of Roubaix.[89] The second operation planned in Roubaix was at Trois-Ponts to the south-east of the centre. This was started in 1962 and consisted of 1650 housing units. The third area earmarked for renewal was Alma-Gare to the north-west. The operation was originally scheduled to start in 1966, but was consistently delayed until it was finally initiated under legislation for *résorption de l'habitat insalubre* in 1973.[90] The Trois-Ponts operation was seen as the potential *opération tiroir* for Alma-Gare, but this aspect never materialized, partly because of the long delays involved in the Alma-Gare project.[91]

The growing desire of the *Municipalité de Roubaix* to take the initiative in the town's affairs, combined with the national concern over the condition of France's housing stock, the plight of the homeless and the need to valorize France's urban structure (messages transmitted not only through political channels, but also through the media), tended to encourage the interpretation of the *courées* as the slum inheritance of the nineteenth century. This meaning had always been present, but had almost always been overlooked. Without doubt, the discomfort of *courée* life was palpable and, in this new context, could hardly have failed to inspire the town's elected representatives to push for improvements. Certain councillors had lived or continued to live in the *courées*, many had friends or family – not to mention electorate – who lived in them, and the proximity of these areas to the town centre reminded council members daily of the conditions the inhabitants had to endure. In particular, Victor Provo, Roubaix's long serving mayor, was recognized for his personal commitment to improving housing conditions. As Provo pointed out in an open letter published in 1970: 'I lived in a *courée* until adulthood, my mother lives there still. I know the human comfort one can find there. I also know the servitudes.'[92] These 'servitudes' were given an official definition – *insalubrité* – a definition supported by 'objective' surveys which quantified the degree to which the *courées* failed to meet contemporary housing standards. This, in turn, justified a particular treatment – demolition – and created an expectation of modern public

[89] This decision was taken before the legislation of 1958 had officially made the legal tools for *rénovation* available. The *Société d'Aménagement de Roubaix* (SAR), a *société d'économie mixte*, was created for this purpose.

[90] The poor quality of construction of the *courées* made most of them unsuitable for rehabilitation and so the law of 4 August 1962 was not applied to them. Nor were they considered to offer sufficient historical, aesthetic or architectural interest to warrant designation as *secteurs sauvegardés* – conservation areas.

[91] An *opération tiroir*, literally a 'drawer operation', was intended to rehouse the population of an area undergoing renewal in nearby new housing which had been constructed in a previous phase. Thus it was planned that the population displaced from Alma-Gare would be decanted to Trois-Ponts.

[92] 'J'ai vécu jusqu'à l'âge adulte dans une courée, ma mère y vit encore. Je connais les réconforts d'ordre humain qu'on peut y rencontrer, j'en connais aussi les servitudes.' Cited in Descamps, 'La résorption des courées de la Métropole Nord', p. 52.

housing constructed according to rational land use principles. The removal of the *courées* thus came to be understood by the *Municipalité* as a moral crusade, and Provo, writing to the *préfet* of the Lille region in June 1968, explicitly linked the demolition of the *courées* with the dignity of the town's population:

> The municipal administration has never failed to draw to the attention of the public powers the immense needs of Roubaix and the lamentable state of a housing stock which was of poor quality from the start, and which is now doomed to large scale demolition if we are to maintain a minimum of dignity for our population.[93]

Removing the *courées* was, as the mayor of Roubaix succinctly put it, 'in short, a social, human and fraternal undertaking'.[94] In employing a discourse on human dignity and assuring the citizens of their right to a better housing future, the *Municipalité* tapped into themes concerning the moral dimension of poor housing that were the heritage of nineteenth-century philanthropy and charitable work. In this way, the *courées* were presented as symbols of shame – a collective shame that in the second half of the twentieth century a sector of the population should have to live in 'a degraded, unhealthy and dangerous housing stock'.[95] The August 1974 edition of the municipal magazine included a series of photographic images of doors and passageways leading to the *courées* under the title, 'ces portes qui conduisaient au désespoir' – 'these doors that led to despair' (Figure 3.3).[96] Each picture is taken from the street, thus creating a distance between the viewer and the dark world of the *courées*, a world which, according to the municipal discourse, is destined to be swept away.

In this period, when the CIL had a strong influence on Roubaix's housing output, the textile industry was still the guarantor of the town's well-being and the presence of a Socialist mayor in the town hall was sustained by a minority of centrist councillors, the *Municipalité* offered an uncritical and inconclusive interpretation of the origin of the *courées*. Indeed, Provo depicted the renewal of Roubaix as a kind of renaissance, reviving old qualities in a new context: 'We will be in a position to offer to all our visitors the spectacle of a workers' town which has found the way to open up to the future without forgetting that which, in the past, has made its reputation and its wealth.'[97]

---

[93] Letter from Victor Provo, President of *Conseil Général du Nord* and Mayor of Roubaix, to Monsieur Dumont, *Préfet de la Région de Lille*, 27 June 1968, p. 2. ADN, 1284/466.

[94] '... en bref, une œuvre sociale, humaine et fraternelle.', Victor Provo cited in 'Trois autres quartiers changent de visage', Roubaix, *Periodique d'information municipale* (August, 1974), p. 3.

[95] '... un patrimoine immobilier vétuste, insalubre et dangereux'. Ibid.

[96] Ibid., p. 16.

[97] 'Nous seront en mesure d'offrir à tous nos visiteurs le spectacle d'une Ville ouvrière, qui a su s'ouvrir sur l'avenir sans oublier ceux qui, dans le passé, ont fait sa renommée et sa richesse.' Victor Provo, cited in ibid., p. 3.

ces portes qui conduisaient au désespoir...

3.3 'These doors that led to despair'
Reproduced from 'Trois autres quartiers changent de visage', Roubaix, *Périodique d'information municipale* (August 1974), pp. 16–7.

The consensus over the need to remove the *courées* was underpinned by a range of other considerations. As discussed above, from the perspective of the *Municipalité*, the SPT and the *Chambre de Commerce et d'Industrie*, the tertiary sector appeared to offer the panacea for the town's post-war ills, but the development of this sector required nothing short of a radical restructuring of the Roubaix's urban space. The town displayed a lack of cultural activities, shopping facilities and services in comparison to other urban centres of a similar size. Its communications were generally poor, and there was a marked lack of green space, other than the impressive Parc Barbieux to the south, in the area which housed the wealthiest section of the population. In short, the spatial arrangements that had ensured the efficiency of the nineteenth-century textile industry were wholly unsuited to the development of the tertiary sector. Restructuring meant the creation of new spaces, new housing and new communications which would link Roubaix to the rest of the *métropole*. An essential element in this was the new expressway or *voie structurante* that was to provide an efficient link between Roubaix and Tourcoing, via the Mercure building, and beyond to the planned *autoroute du Nord*. The expressway was conceived as a dorsal spine, running along the Avenue des Nations Unies in the centre of Roubaix and traversing Alma-Gare and the neighbouring area of Alma-Centre. As a result of this project, the *Municipalité* claimed that the town would become seamlessly integrated with the rest of the country: 'from ROUBAIX, it will be possible to reach PARIS and the SOUTH without red lights.'[98] But the purpose of the roadway was not simply to facilitate traffic flow, it was also to serve as the axis for tertiary activity in the town: 'its functional impact is also reinforced by the wish to make the *Voie Nouvelle* not only a privileged axis of communication (vehicles and pedestrians) but also Roubaix's tertiary axis between the town centre and the "Mercure" operation.'[99]

Another essential element of this restructuring was the removal of the *courées*. In the context of favouring the development of tertiary activities, large-scale demolition would remove the physical evidence of a declining industrial town in the thrall of the textile industry, where the population lived in poverty in the labyrinthine *courées*. This housing, together with the nineteenth-century textile factories it surrounded, was the physical symbol of an outmoded economic system – a symbol that served to confirm to outsiders the stereotype which the *Municipalité* hoped to escape and which was hardly attractive to either new investment or to new residents. Moreover, the demolition of the *courées* and the construction of public housing would radically change the population profile of these old areas, substituting a poor, marginalized population by a wealthier, more stable one. Further, on the political level, this new population would bolster the town's declining electoral base. The project also offered Roubaix's socialist–centrist administration the opportunity to reinforce its own image in the eyes of the electorate as the benefactors and protectors of the 'working class'. Finally, the three proposed *rénovation* projects answered a desire on the part of the *Municipalité* and its architects and planners to apply the fashionable, functionalist principles of modernist planning to the 'outdated' urban fabric of the town and so rationalize the divisions between housing, infrastructure, services, industry and transport.

Despite the benefits that *rénovation urbaine* promised, such operations were not without their contradictions. Thus, for example, in initiating renewal operations and instigating a sorting of the population of the *courées* that this

---

98 '... de ROUBAIX, il sera possible gagner PARIS et le MIDI sans feux rouges.' Ibid., p. 31.

99 Communauté Urbaine de Lille, Ville de Roubaix, 'Aménagement de l'Ilot "Vieil Abreuvoir", Note de Présentation', p. 3, no date. ADN, 1284W/467.

involved, the *Municipalité* risked eroding its own support base. The *Syndicat Patronal du Textile* also experienced a degree of ambiguity. While happy to encourage a sorting of the population in favour of the most stable elements of the workforce, they were less enthusiastic about the functional separation of activities – industry, shopping, commerce and so on – which such operations involved, because this inevitably required the relocation of the textile factories (although factor- owners sometimes had significant real estate interests in the old areas of the town, and renewal held the promise of increasing land values). Also, while the provision of new housing with its selective rules for entry favoured skilled workers of European origin with 'average' sized families, it had the disadvantage for local industrialists that the higher rents in these developments would lead to pressure for higher wages.

The contradictions of renewal were also visited upon the inhabitants of the *courées* themselves. If the renewal process represented the rationalization of urban space according to modernist principles, it equally represented a rationalization of the population of these areas, tending to sift and subdivide the population according to their socioeconomic status and then concentrate these various subdivisions in distinct housing groups, ranging from CIL housing for the most 'stable' elements of the workforce with sufficient income to pay the relatively high rents, through HLM developments, apartments constructed by the *programme social de relogement* (a more economic version of HLM), to *courée* houses restored by PACT. As for the most marginal elements of the population, they were left to find their own housing solution, invariably in other areas of *logements insalubres*. This meant that it was not unusual, in the course of a renewal operation, for agencies involved in rehousing to come across families they had already encountered in earlier phases or in other areas. Even for those who qualified for a modern CIL or HLM apartment there were certain disadvantages, not least that new housing meant higher rents. The economic impact of moving house was even greater when service charges for the new housing, plus the expenses involved in the purchase of new furniture, carpets and so on, were taken into account.[100] In short, for skilled workers and their families the demolition of their home in the *courées* was compensated for by the promise of a larger and more comfortable (but, ultimately, more costly) apartment in a CIL or HLM project, while for many large families, immigrants, unskilled workers, unemployed and so on, housing in the *courées* represented the only form of dwelling they could hope to obtain. Of course, these groups lacked the political voice to oppose the *Municipalité*'s modernization programme.

[100] In part, new tenants felt that their old furniture was inappropriate and, in part, these new apartments were much larger than the *courée* homes, and so required more furnishings, carpets and so on.

At this point, it is worth briefly examining the impact of the first *rénovation* operation carried out in Roubaix, for it was to prove to be significant in shaping the perception of large scale renewal operations in the years to come. Initiated in 1958, the redevelopment of the area of Longues Haies was one of the earliest *rénovation* operations carried out in France and represented the first time that a municipal council, with the backing of the ministry of finance, became the instigator, planner and supervisor of such a project. The area of Longues Haies – an entire network of streets and some 70 *courées* containing 2160 houses and one factory – was completely erased and replaced by 1550 houses, 650 of which were municipal HLM, 450 were CIL, and another 450 were *logements primés*.[101] The style of architecture was a product of industrial construction techniques, and the concrete towers, ranging from nine to 18 storeys, embodied the desire to modify the town's *image de marque* and heralded a new phase in Roubaix's development.[102] These towers, along with the several squares which were constructed to provide greenery, could not have failed to offer a stark contrast to the huddled mass of brick-built *courées* in the adjoining areas. In addition to the housing, and in keeping with the growing emphasis on the tertiary sector, a large commercial centre was planned. This was given the optimistic and, at this time, even futuristic name of Roubaix 2000. The project also included a school, a sports hall, an old people's home and a four-level carpark. In short, the operation offered a good example of the modernist paradigm of the functional separation of urban activities into discrete spatial areas, a rational street plan and technological solutions for architectural production.

Clearly renewal had to start *somewhere*, but why in Longues Haies in particular? As Duriez and Cornuel point out, it was neither the oldest area of housing in Roubaix, nor was it the only run-down part of the town.[103] It did, however, occupy a large area very close to the city centre and, if a city is to seek to transform its image, there is clearly much to be gained from allocating priority to those areas that are most visible, though not necessarily most urgent. Longues Haies also occupied an important place in the collective memory of Roubaix's citizens, particularly for the role its inhabitants had played in the strike of 1931, during which the area had been the scene of serious confrontations. Longues Haies thus represented a symbol of a turbulent period in Roubaix's history which both the *Municipalité* and the textile industry were

[101] Vicentini and Vilment, 'L'Evolution du cadre de vie à Roubaix de 1945 à 1977', p. 50. *Logements primés* were a form of government-subsidized housing introduced under the legislation of 20 July 1950.

[102] Duriez and Cornuel, *Transformations économiques, évolution des rapports politiques et restructuration urbaine*, p. 59.

[103] Cornuel and Duriez, *Le mirage urbain: histoire de logement à Roubaix*, p. 179.

keen to erase, so much so that even the name of the area did not escape transformation: Longues Haies was replaced by the less emotive Edouard Anseele, taken from the name of a street in the area.

The Longues Haies/Edouard Anseele operation dragged on for almost 15 years and, moreover, there was a string of complications and delays associated with the Roubaix 2000 project, with the result that the contribution of the *Municipalité* had risen from an original figure of 8 350 544 francs to 23 647 000 francs by October 1974.[104] These delays not only meant that the town centre was visually scarred over a number of years by the presence of a large building site, but also that the project's commercial success was jeopardized. The financial burden on the *Municipalité* was made worse by the fact that it had undertaken the *rénovation* of Trois-Ponts over the same period. As for the 5000 or so former residents of the Longues Haies area, most found themselves excluded from the new housing. A little under 50 per cent of the original population were streamed into either HLM housing or other areas of *courées*. Many of those who were provided with HLM were decanted to peripheral developments which had been initiated during the 1950s. Those who were to be rehoused in the *courées* became the responsibility of PACT, and represented approximately 25 per cent of the households involved. Many of those who fell to PACT were elderly people, since there were insufficient places in special homes, while HLM, which was intended to cater for average-sized families, rarely provided one-room apartments.[105] Prior to the operation, 25 per cent of the population in Longues Haies was elderly, but afterwards virtually none remained. The other residents (a little over half of the households affected by the project) did not wait for assistance from the rehousing agencies, but simply left the *quartier* when the chance to take another *courée* house presented itself.[106] As for the 400 or so single, non-French males living in rented furnished accommodation, they were not included in rehousing measures and had to find their own housing solutions.[107]

Because of its cost, inefficiency and the timescale involved (all well illustrated by the example of Longues Haies), *rénovation urbaine* had only a limited impact on conditions in Roubaix's *courées*. During the 1960s, growing public concern over living conditions in French cities began to make the issue of the *courées* and the battle against *insalubrité* an important political issue, and various actors began to mobilize around the issue. One of the most dynamic of these actors was the CIL for Roubaix–Tourcoing. In 1968 the CIL produced a study on housing conditions in Roubaix which it presented to central

---

104 Descamps, 'La résorption des courées de la Métropole Nord', p. 65.

105 Cornuel and Duriez, *Le mirage urbain: histoire de logement à Roubaix*, p. 183.

106 Ibid., p. 182.

107 Ibid., p. 181.

government. In this study, the CIL sought to demonstrate that the *courée* was a direct descendant of the *bidonville* and, on the basis of this, it succeeded in persuading the government to extend legislation for the treatment of *bidonvilles* to include the *courées*.[108] This move suggests a recognition on the part of central government that the *courées* no longer had a role to play as an element in the nation's housing stock. We might also consider that the association of these two forms of human shelter reflected a change in the general perception of what was 'normal' or 'acceptable' in housing terms. If we understand a *bidonville* to represent temporary, makeshift housing which provides shelter to a marginalized population, one can argue that, by extending the legislation, the *courées* were being presented in the same way. As it turned out, the introduction of the August 1969 legislation was more significant than its impact. Before it could be usefully applied, the *loi Vivien* was introduced in 1970, marking the start of the second phase of the systematic treatment of *insalubrité*.[109]

The success of the CIL's initiative with respect to the *bidonville* legislation was partly due to the national attention that came to be focused on living conditions in Roubaix around this time. In September 1968 Dechartre, then minister for housing, made a trip to inspect Roubaix's *courées* and, while this did not directly produce any concrete measures, it served to raise awareness of the issues. A more significant development took place in 1969, when Roubaix celebrated the 500th anniversary of the *charte des drapiers* – the cloth manufacturers' charter. In these celebrations the *Municipalité* saw a useful opportunity to raise the town's profile, and André Diligent, who was, at that time, Roubaix's deputy mayor with the portfolio for social and economic issues, decided to organize a press day and bring journalists to the town by means of a special train. Part of the programme for the day included a visit to the *courées*, and it was this in particular that caught the journalists' imagination. As a result, living conditions in the *courées* became a major issue in the national press. For example, François Miralles, writing in *l'Express*, emotively compared living conditions in a town in the north of France with the Third World 'Other': 'We have visited some *courées*. This brought to mind some of the worst images of misery from Africa or South America.'.[110] The attention given to Roubaix's housing reflected similar concerns on a national level; living conditions in France were becoming an important issue, and in June 1969 the prime minister, Jacques Chaban-Delmas, launched the *croisade des bidonvilles*.[111]

---

[108] The decision was taken in August 1969.

[109] Specifically, RHI – *résorption de l'habitat insalubre*.

[110] 'Nous avons visité des courées. Cela nous a rappelé les pires images de misère d'Afrique ou d'Amérique de Sud.' Cited in Descamps, 'La résorption des courées de la Métropole Nord', p. 71.

[111] Literally, the 'bidonville crusade'.

In this context, and encouraged by the nationwide attention Roubaix had received, momentum gathered and by November 1969 the *Municipalité* had identified 8500 *courée* houses for demolition in the short term.[112] Subsequently, 22 associations and organizations variously interested in the redevelopment of the *courées* came together in a group called the *Association pour la Résorption des Courées* (ARC), with the aim of organizing a conference on the issue – the *colloque des courées*. These organizations included the *office public d'HLM*, the CIL, PACT, the SPT, three unions – the *Confédération Française Démocratique du Travail* (CFDT), the *Confédération Française des Travailleurs Chrétiens* (CFTC) and the CGT, the *Société d'Aménagement de la Région de Roubaix-Tourcoing* and the *Association Populaire Familiale* (APF).[113]

The *colloque des courées*, which was presented as an apolitical collection of organizations unanimously joined in their fight against *insalubrité* in the *courées*, took place on 29 and 30 November 1969. In the course of these two days a range of topics was addressed, including the historical evolution of the *courées*, social, health and sanitation issues, and possible approaches to tackle these problems. The conference proved to be successful both in generating publicity for the issue of the *courées*, which the press presented as the heritage of nineteenth-century industrialization, and in providing a springboard for future action. Through the publicity it generated and the united front it presented, the conference also offered a means whereby the participating organizations could exert pressure on public bodies.

On the second day of the conference, Robert-André Vivien, the secretary of state for housing, presided over a meeting at the *préfecture* in Lille at which it was decided to create the *Organisme Régional pour la Suppression des Courées de la Métropole Nord* (ORSUCOMN). This initiative had come largely from the CIL, which had lobbied Vivien, providing him with reports and articles in favour of setting up such an organization. The role of ORSUCOMN, which was in fact a private association, was to act as the operational organization for the application of the *loi Vivien* on its introduction the following year. Its aim was to coordinate and plan the preliminary studies for housing projects under the new law and so help overcome the complexities which had arisen in *rénovation* operations. In so doing, it would provide a test structure for the national application of the procedure for *résorption de l'habitat insalubre*. In its administration ORSUCOMN brought together representatives from a collection of private and public sector partners, but not

---

[112] Gantier, 'L'Evolution de la Politique Urbaine à Roubaix depuis 1970: Recherches sur un quartier', unpublished thesis, University of Lille (1986), p. 13.

[113] The *Association Populaire Familiale* was to have a key role in the events in Alma-Gare.

surprisingly, the CIL had a particularly strong influence on the methods it employed. The *Communauté Urbaine de Lille* assigned ORSUCOMN the tasks of acquisition, demolition and rehousing in its *résorption* operations and, from its creation in 1969 until 1982, when it was dismantled and its role assumed directly by the *Communauté Urbaine de Lille*, ORSUCOMN was responsible for the demolition of 5000 houses in Roubaix.[114]

With the optimism generated by the new legislation and the resolve inspired by attention from press and politicians alike, four major areas of *résorption* operations were outlined in Roubaix. One was around the rue de l'Epeule and involved 456 houses, another was the Ingouville project in Edouard Anseele, which involved 123 houses and was effectively an extension of the original Longues Haies project, a third was at l'Hommelet, where 388 houses were planned, and the fourth was in Alma-Gare, where delays and financial problems had meant that the planned *rénovation urbaine* had never taken place. With this new project, 123 new houses were scheduled for a small area called Barbe d'Or, and another 734 for Alma-Gare phase one.[115]

If the initiative to restructure Roubaix's urban space and sweep away its legacy of nineteenth-century workers' housing was broadly accepted and approved of, it was not without its critics. For example, while not denying the importance of ridding the town of the *courées*, the Communist Party rejected what it saw as the collaboration of the *Municipalité* with the class enemy, the textile industry. Another critic of the method, if not the general intent, was the *Association Populaire Familiale*. The APF was a voluntary organization which concerned itself with issues related to the domestic sphere. Its origins lay in the Catholic worker tradition (a tradition which was particularly strong in the north of France), having developed as a branch of the *Jeunnesse Ouvrière Chrétienne* during the Second World War.[116] The APF began to operate in Roubaix in 1952 and, over the subsequent years, its explicitly Christian identity gradually faded. Nevertheless, the fact that APF activists chose to work on behalf of a population such as that of the *courées*, which was not defined by distinct class interests, reflected the universalism of the organization's Christian origins.[117]

The early activities of the APF in Roubaix's *courées* were principally directed at pressing for the repair and maintenance of the housing stock, whether it was owned by private landlords or by PACT. The APF also lobbied the town hall in order to ensure the continued provision of services – electricity

---

[114] Bruyelle, 'Roubaix face aux grandes mutations récentes', p. 331.

[115] Cornuel and Duriez, *Le mirage urbain: histoire de logement à Roubaix*, p. 187.

[116] Jeunesse Ouvrière Chrétienne had, in turn, been founded in Belgium in 1925 in response to the concern of the Catholic Church over both the spiritual and material conditions of the growing industrial workforce. The Lille–Roubaix–Tourcoing branch was founded in 1927 and expanded rapidly thereafter.

[117] ABAC-Paris and APU-Roubaix, 'Roubaix: le quartier de l'Alma-Gare', p. 204.

and water – to *courées* which had been scheduled for demolition but which were still inhabited. During the events of spring 1968, the APF in Roubaix organized support for striking workers, and in 1969, fired by this experience, it declared war on housing conditions: 'THIS IS A CRY OF ANGUISH – A GREAT INJUSTICE THAT DEMANDS URGENT SOLUTIONS. IF MAY 68 HAS COME AND GONE ... WE WILL WRITE MAY 69'.[118] The APF activists saw themselves as explicitly political (though not party-political), in that they linked the poor condition of workers' housing to the level of wages paid by the textile industry, and located the struggle for decent housing within the broader struggle of the working class. Ironically, this view brought the APU, with its Catholic roots, very close to the position of Roubaix's Communist Party. The Roubaix branches of the APF defined their aim as ensuring as series of rights: the right to decent housing for those on low pay; the right to information on the planning programme and the delays it involved; the right to a minimum level of facilities and comfort for all; the right of retired workers, immigrants and large families to be housed like everyone else; the right of households to choose housing according their needs; and the right to participate in the housing and planning process.[119] During their 1969 housing campaign members of the APF organized meetings, issued press statements, published a *dossier noir du logement* – a 'black book' listing detailed housing problems – and, in the autumn of that year, sent a delegation to the secretary of state for housing. In November they organized a day of demonstrations in Roubaix's *courées*, during which they claimed to have mobilized some 800 people. In the same month, they withdrew their participation from the ARC's *colloque des courées*: at a preparatory meeting on 28 November, the eve of the conference, members of the APF demanded the right to speak on behalf of the inhabitants of the *courées*, whom they claimed were unrepresented. This request was refused by the conference organizers and the APF activists, who also objected to the apolitical way in which the conference presented Roubaix's housing problems, walked out, giving the lie to the unanimity claimed by the other participants in the *colloque*.

In the context of urban renewal, when the announcement was made that a neighbourhood was to be redeveloped, APF activists and sympathizers would organize a defence committee. These were generally ephemeral structures, lasting only as long as the population remained in the area. In February 1971, for example, there were nine such committees in the *commune de Roubaix*, each one organized by the APF.[120] These committees demanded information from

[118] Association Populaire Familiale, *SOS Logement*, Special number, Roubaix, (May 1969), p. 6. AIR.

[119] Ibid., p. 19.

[120] Duriez and Cornuel, *Transformations économiques, évolution des rapports politiques et restructuration urbaine*, p. 213.

the agencies charged with development, and made various claims, particularly with reference to the right to rehousing and, as clearance operations got under way, to the level of compensation paid both to home-owners and tenants. The APF also carried out a long campaign for the application of the fair rent law of 1948 – a campaign which was particularly intense in 1973.[121] These actions helped the APF to gain the confidence and support of many residents of the *courées*.[122]

One of the leading members of the APF in Roubaix was Marie-Agnès Leman, who had moved to Alma-Gare with her husband, Roger, in 1962. The Lemans recall that there was already the basis of a collective identity in the *courées* when they first arrived in Alma-Gare. They explain how the APF had bought a number of washing machines, which were mounted on trolleys. Households could then hire these washing machines for a small fee in order to do their weekly washing. The Lemans claim that the organization and personal contact this system required was an important element in creating social links and an informal information network amongst the population.[123] Not surprisingly, women played a particularly important role in the APF. In part this was because of the domestic basis of this organization: the APF drew much of its strength from those who remained in the *courées* during the day, and, with the structural changes in the textile industry discussed above, this increasingly came to mean the female population. Precise figures for the membership of the APF are difficult to come by, but a handwritten 'liste des adhérents pour l'année 1973' lists 118 names, of which 115 are from Roubaix and three from neighbouring Wattrelos.[124]

---

[121] Often the tenants of the *courées* were exploited by landlords and paid excessively high rents given the condition of their accommodation. The law of 1948 was intended to set rent levels according to the floorspace of an apartment and the living conditions therein, and tenants of a property designated *insalubre* were not required to pay any rent at all. The APF proved to be very successful in having the 1948 law enforced: 300 rents were reduced in the old areas of Roubaix by more or less 50 per cent, and in 1973 the APF led 13 successful court actions which allowed tenants to claim back several thousands of francs in rent which had been set too high. R. Leman and M-A. Leman, 'A l'Alma-Gare à Roubaix: une organisation collective des habitants pour un meilleur urbanisme', *Sauvegarde de l'enfance*, no. 2 (March–April 1980), p. 295.

[122] This point is also made by Duriez and Cornuel, who suggest that the APF enjoyed the support of certain religious groups and political parties such as the PSU. Duriez and Cornuel, *Transformations économiques, évolution des rapports politiques et restructuration urbaine*, p. 103.

[123] The story of the washing machines was recounted to the author by Roger Leman. Verbrackel also mentions the system, stating that the APF had as many as 120 washing machines. E. Verbrackel, 'L'Atelier populaire d'urbanisme de l'Alma-Gare à Roubaix', unpublished thesis, University of Lille (1980), p. 29.

[124] 'Gare Alma: Responsables – Sympathisants', handwritten 'liste des adhérents pour l'année 1973'. AIR.

The importance of the close links between the women of the *courées* is one of the themes that emerge from the personal notes of Marie-Agnès Leman. In the following notes from 1967 in which she describes the situation in Fort Frasez – one of the largest *courées* in Alma-Gare – she also touches on several of the other characteristics of the population of this area, including unemployment, large families, ill-health and a certain sense of helplessness:

> I've the impression of finding myself in the middle of a hospital.
> Thérèse: 50 years old has had an attack, she can hardly walk.
> Janine: hospitalised: the birth is approaching, obliged to stay lying down (it's the 8th).
> Elaine: has had her 6th: back after 48 hours in hospital.
> Odette's husband has had peritonitis: she tells me: afterwards he'll go into a nursing home, he can't stay at home any longer. Tuberculous.
> Nobody talks about anything: social security, urban planning.
> ... Many men are on sickness benefit (5)
> ... Janine's husband (Algerian) still unemployed ... .[125]
> Nobody speaks about Fort Frasez. ... They're all exhausted and live from day to day.
> – they do the washing when they have the time and when the weather's good.
> – the kids do what they want
> – the men want peace when they return home in the evening after a tough day in the factory
> – the women spend their time at their neighbours' where they often help each other out.[126]

In defining itself, the APF stated that it '... is to the *quartier* what the union is to the workplace'.[127] Indeed, in 1975 the organization became the *Confédération Syndicale du Cadre de Vie* (CSCV), a title which made its aspirations explicit. They considered that workers were not only exploited as producers in the workplace, but also as consumers in the home environment and urged, 'Workers organized in the workplace, we also want to organize the setting for our [daily] life [*cadre de vie*]'.[128] This phrase, featured in a *bulletin d'adhésion* for the CSCV (see Figure 3.4), was accompanied by a sketch of two men in work overalls, with their outstretched arms linking a depiction of a factory to one of a *courée* street, the domestic sphere. Below, a pair of cupped female hands, symbolizing the CSCV, frames a series of four images representing the organization's areas of activity: *école*, *santé*, *logement* and *consommation*.[129]

---

[125] Handwritten notes of Marie-Agnes Leman, 25 September 1967, AIR.

[126] Handwritten notes of Marie-Agnes Leman, 7 October 1967, AIR.

[127] Association Populaire Familiale, *SOS Logement*, Special number, Roubaix, (May 1969), p. 19. AIR.

[128] From CSCV, 'Bulletin d'adhésion', AIR.

[129] School, health, housing and consumer issues.

3.4 CSCV *bulletin d'adhésion*

Despite these claims, relations between the APF/CSCV on the one hand and the workers' unions on the other were generally weak. The APF/CSCV was regarded by the trade unions as an organization for the wives of workers – that is, as an organization involved in the sphere of social reproduction – while the unions saw themselves as concerned with the sphere of production. In addition, the APF/CSCV was involved with elements of the population that did not belong to the 'working class', such as children and the elderly, and even with elements who were considered to have a 'destabilizing' effect, notably immigrant workers. This difficulty was recognized by the activists themselves:

> We find ourselves in the presence of authentic popular levels of society, but they do not have a workers' integrated social base. On the one hand, many residents of the *courées* remain outside the field of production: that is, the elderly, the young, and a large proportion of women. On the other hand, those who are workers belong to the most exploited categories and the least well-defended elements of the working class: the reserve army of the proletariat ... .[130]

[130] 'On se trouve en présence de couches sociales authentiquement populaires, mais non d'une base sociale ouvrière intégrée. D'une part, nombre des habitants des courées restent en dehors du champ de la production : ce sont les vieux, les jeunes, une bonne partie des femmes. D'autre part, les travailleurs effectifs appartiennent aux catégories les plus exploitées et les plus mal défendues de la classe ouvrière: armée de réserve du

As a consequence the organizations which represented the working class almost never supported the activities of the APF/CSCV:

> ... because it concerns populations marginalized by the local development of capitalist production, in part outsiders to their historical base (and in the North, this means something), and therefore not fully integrated in the struggles going on in the sphere of production. Past and present events in the *courées* have found no resonance inside the workers' organizations. Or at best a very weak resonance, and not at the scale of the problem.[131]

Finally, it must be reiterated that the APF/CSCV was not against the demolition of the *courées per se* and, indeed, its members campaigned for their demolition. They were, however, opposed to what they considered to be the iniquities associated with the process of demolition and rehousing. In 1971, for example, the APF occupied the headquarters of ORSUCOMN for a day demanding that all residents of areas designated for renewal should be rehoused before demolition work got under way and that appropriate compensation be made available to residents of certain *courées*. Nor did the APF call for 'housing for all' imply *any* form of housing. They were opposed to the divisions in the population introduced by different categories of housing, to the activity of PACT in rehousing elements of the population in old houses, and also to the low cost new housing provided by the *programme social de relogement*, since they considered that all these solutions assigned the poorest housing to the poorest members of society.

Alma-Gare: 'Ce que doit disparaître!'

Alma-Gare was built between 1830 and 1880 and, until its redevelopment in the 1970s and 1980s, demonstrated the typical urban morphology of this period: textile factories embedded in a dense network of workers' houses which consisted of *courées*, *cours* and two large *forts* – Fort Frasez and Fort Watel. Alma-Gare had served as a reception area for the various waves of immigrants arriving in Roubaix in the different phases of the textile industry's development and, like the other areas of workers' housing in Roubaix, conditions in Alma-Gare's *courées* had began to deteriorate soon after their construction.

---

prolétariat ...', 'Roubaix: L'APU 2. stratégie du capital et stratégie populaire', *Place*, no. 6 (Winter 1977), pp. 12–13.

131 '... parce qu'il s'agit là de populations marginalisées par le développement de la production capitaliste locale, étrangères en partie à leur base historique (et dans le Nord ça signifie quelque chose), donc pas pleinement intégrées dans les luttes en cours dans le champ de la production, il n'y a pas eu d'échos au sein des organisations ouvrières sur ce qui s'est passé et se passe dans les courées. Ou du moins bien faibles et pas à l'échelle du problème.' Ibid., p. 13.

A survey of a limited area of seven blocks in Alma-Gare was carried out by ORSUCOMN in 1973.[132] This survey, a good example of the objective quantification of living conditions, found that 85 per cent of housing in the sample, a total of 748 houses, had been built prior to 1914. Moreover, 9.9 per cent of houses (72 units) were classified as being in a good state, 19.5 per cent (146) were in a mediocre state, while 70.6 per cent (530) were defined as *insalubre*. Thus, buildings classified by ORSUCOMN as either *médiocres* or *insalubres* represented 90.1 per cent of the total housing stock in the survey area.[133]

Not surprisingly, the population of Alma-Gare demonstrated the general characteristics of the population of the *courées* discussed above – that is, heterogeneity, instability and, in economic terms, marginality. In 1958, the population of Alma-Gare stood at approximately 6000 but, over the years, demolitions, rehousing and general uncertainty as to the future all took their toll on the population, which had fallen to 1500 by 1977.[134] These same processes had tended to lead to a concentration of the non-French population: in 1968, 24 per cent of the population of Alma-Gare was estimated to be non-French, while by 1974 this group represented 44 per cent.[135] Although it is difficult to produce precise statistics for the socioeconomic characteristics of Alma-Gare's population, some indication can be gained from the results of ORSUCOMN's 1973 survey. In the survey area there were, in all, 1812 inhabitants, of whom 122 were single foreign men living in furnished rooms (*garnis*);[136] 56 per cent of the total population was classified by the survey as 'French'; 26 per cent were of Algerian or Moroccan origin; and the remaining 18 per cent was made up of other immigrant groups, principally Spanish, Portuguese and Italian. Of the 574 households (*foyers*) in the area 304 (53 per cent) were made up of single people. The majority of single males in the area were Algerian or Moroccan, while most single females were elderly women of French origin. There was also a significant number of large families in the area, and 54 households (9.4 per cent) had more than five children. There were also 165 households (28.8 per cent) made up of people over 65 years old. Financial resources were low – in

[132] These blocks represented sector 1 of the renewal operation in Alma-Gare. Given that renewal had been an issue for some time, the uncertainty hanging over the area may already have provoked a movement of population, with the result that ORSUCOMN's findings paint a particularly pessimistic picture.

[133] ORSUCOMN, étude réalisée par le CERNA, 'Etude Socio-Démographique Alma-Gare', 20 August 1973, IV, p. 4. ADN, 1284W/466, folder, 'Opération de Rénovation Urbaine – Relogement des Habitants'.

[134] O. Desreumaux, 'Roubaix: deux opérations à suivre: Alma-Gare et Alma-Centre', *La Gazette*, 1 (1980), pp. 3–4.

[135] Cornuel and Duriez, *Le mirage urbain: histoire de logement à Roubaix*, p. 202.

[136] There were 50 refusals or absences recorded in the survey, and a large number of surveys were not completed, particularly by single men living in *garnis*.

1973 around 40 per cent of households received less than 500 francs per person per month.[137] With respect to the economic characteristics of the population, ORSUCOMN's study of this limited area in Alma-Gare revealed that 12.6 per cent of heads of family were *sans activité* – without work – and 32.6 per cent were retired.[138]

The same study also found that over 40.7 per cent of the French population had lived in their present home for over 20 years, while another 17.4 per cent had lived there for between 11 and 20 years. By contrast, 90 per cent of Spanish and Portuguese, and 69.4 per cent of Algerians and Moroccans had lived in their present home for five years or less. Indeed, 30.0 per cent of Spanish and Portuguese and 19.4 per cent of Algerians and Moroccans had lived in their present accommodation for less than one year (this was the case for only 8.2 per cent of the French population).[139] In considering these figures, it is important to take into account that the impact of long years of uncertainty over the future of Alma-Gare will have provoked a higher degree of movement in the population than would otherwise have been the case. An indication of this movement is given by the fact that, in 1973, ORSUCOMN estimated that 40.7 per cent of households had arrived in the *quartier* since 1968.[140] Moreover, as the population decreased it is also likely that the concentration of 'problem' households increased – that is, households that had slipped through the net of the rehousing organizations because of ineligibility due to their income level, nationality, size or 'antisocial behaviour'. This process of 'concentration' is illustrated by ORSUCOMN's findings that one-quarter of all French families in Alma-Gare were living below the poverty line by 1977 and, significantly, that the majority of these had arrived in the last two years.[141]

In political terms, the population of Alma-Gare demonstrated a voting pattern that was broadly similar to that of Roubaix as a whole, in as much as it gave consistent support to Provo's socialist–centrist alliance. All the same, throughout the 1960s it also tended to give more support to the Communist Party than did the town as a whole.[142] From 1965, however, while the Socialist

---

137 As a point of comparison, an apartment in the new Edouard Anseele development might cost as much as 800 francs per month, including charges, while rents in the *courées* varied between 50 and 250 francs per month. Gantier states that in 93 per cent of cases in 1970, rent in the *courées* was less than 125 francs per month. Gantier, 'L'Evolution de la Politique Urbaine à Roubaix depuis 1970', p. 12.

138 ORSUCOMN, étude réalisée par le CERNA, 'Etude Socio-Démographique Alma-Gare', 20 August 1973, III, p. 3. ADN, 1284W/466, folder 'Opération de Rénovation Urbaine – Relogement des Habitants'.

139 Ibid., VII, p. 7.

140 Ibid., II, p. 2.

141 ORSUCOMN, 'Quelques donnés du problème', 1976. AIR.

142 For example, in the municipal elections of 14 March 1965, in Roubaix as a whole Provo's Socialist list was victorious, taking 51.6 per cent of the votes, while in Alma-Gare the list took 45 per cent of the votes. The *Union pour la Nouvelle République*

share of the vote remained stable in Alma-Gare, there was a general shift in the voting base away from the more left-wing parties, although support for the Communist Party still remained relatively stronger than in Roubaix as a whole. The same period also saw a sharp drop in those registered to vote in Alma-Gare: from 2258 in 1965 to 1803 in 1971 (over the same period, the voting population in Roubaix as a whole also fell – from 60 169 to 54 874).[143] Finally, in the municipal elections of 13 March 1977, marked by a new polarization of political interests in the absence of the socialist–centrist list, Pierre Prouvost's *Union des Forces de Gauche* (which included the Communists) took 56.7 per cent of the vote in Alma-Gare, while Andre Diligent's centre–right list took 40.2 per cent. In Roubaix as a whole, the *Union des Forces de Gauche* took 52 per cent of the votes, compared to 46 per cent for Diligent's list.[144]

As noted above, towards the end of the 1950s the *Municipalité de Roubaix* produced a list which identified their priorities for *rénovation urbaine* within the town. The Longues Haies project was to be carried out first, followed by Trois-Ponts and then Alma-Gare. In May 1962 the council took the first concrete step towards *rénovation* in Alma-Gare, requesting a detailed study of the Notre Dame–Alma-Gare sector of Roubaix. For the next four years no further progress was made. The dossier was then reviewed in December 1966 and, at a meeting of 12 December, the *Municipalité* announced its intention to initiate a *rénovation urbaine* project in this same area. At this meeting, militants from the APF unfurled a banner in the public gallery of the council room: 'Urbanization OK, but when? For whom? While we wait, the houses are crumbling.'[145] The following day the local press heralded triumphantly, 'The *courées* of Alma-Gare are to disappear at last',[146] but this optimism proved to be misplaced. Jaques Maziol, Minister of Equipment and Housing, decided that all funds should be reserved for operations already under way, since these were proving to be more costly than expected. In Roubaix, the *Municipalité* was already committed to completing two projects, with the result that they were left with no hope of embarking upon the programme for Alma-Gare. In addition, central government had directed its support, both political and financial, towards the construction of Villeneuve d'Ascq, the new town project on the outskirts of Lille.

(UNR) in conjunction with the *apolitiques* took 20.9 per cent in Roubaix, but only 15 per cent in Alma-Gare. The Communists took 18.3 per cent of votes in Roubaix, but returned as much as 29.4 per cent in Alma-Gare. *Nord Eclair* (15 March 1965), pp. 1 and 5.

[143] *Nord Eclair* (15 March 1965), pp. 1 and 5; *Nord Eclair* (15 March 1971), p. 1.

[144] *Nord Eclair* (14 March 1977), p. 1.

[145] This banner features in a photograph in, Association Populaire Familiale, *SOS Logement*, Special number, Roubaix, (May 1969), p. 6. AIR.

[146] Cited in Verbrackel, 'L'Atelier populaire d'urbanisme de l'Alma-Gare à Roubaix', p. 28.

The urgency, and indeed the frustration, on the part of the *Municipalité* is apparent in a letter from Provo to the *préfet* in which the mayor complained in strong terms about the delays in obtaining funding for the Alma-Gare project: 'Delayed for various reasons, subordinated to the introduction of new procedures, paralysed by long-term plans which overlook immediate necessities, the decision has never been taken .... This is, in substance, a cry of alarm from the municipal council, for this operation, in reasonable terms, must no longer be put off.' Provo then concluded this official letter on a personal note: 'I express the great hope that the public powers are able to understand – as I, personally, no longer do – this permanent suspension of a ruling on a classic type of delimited operation [*opération limitée de type classique*].'[147]

Alma-Gare, like Longues Haies, was only one area of *courées* amongst many in Roubaix. The priority assigned to its restructuring by the *Municipalité* was partly to do with the poor condition of the area's housing stock and partly to do with what the *Municipalité* and the *Communauté Urbaine de Lille* described as, 'the necessity to revitalize Roubaix's town centre'.[148] On one level, Alma-Gare was unambiguously understood to be a 'slum' – an area that failed to meet modern levels of hygiene. Indeed, in describing Alma-Gare and the treatment it required, Provo employed a modernist, hygienist discourse which seemed to come directly from the nineteenth century: 'It concerns a veritable transformation of a degraded housing stock, unhealthy and dangerous. It is also the striving for and the conquest of open space to bring light and air, and to breathe better.'[149] On another level, the dense mass of *courées* and the 'inefficient' road network in Alma-Gare was considered to represent a physical barrier to the planned expressway, regarded by the *Municipalité* as so essential for the future of the town. In Provo's words: 'as a result of its geographical situation, it [Alma-Gare] constitutes an excessive bottleneck which hinders communication by road between ROUBAIX and TOURCOING.'[150]

---

[147] Letter from Victor Provo, President of *Conseil Général du Nord* and mayor of Roubaix, to Monsieur Dumont, *Préfet de la Région de Lille*, 27 June 1968, p. 2. ADN, 1284/466.

[148] Communauté Urbaine de Lille, Ville de Roubaix, Société d'Aménagement et d'Equipement du Nord, 'Aménagement du Quartier "Alma-Centre"', 1977, pp. 1–2. ADN, 1284W/467.

[149] 'Il s'agit d'une véritable transformation d'un patrimoine immobilier vétuste, insalubre et dangereux. C'est aussi la recherche et la conquête de l'espace libre pour éclairer, aérer, respirer mieux.' Victor Provo cited in 'Trois autres quartiers changent de visage', p. 3.

[150] Document Ville de Roubaix, 'Opération 'Alma-Gare-Notre-Dame'. Note de Renseignements', p. 1, included in 'Rénovation Quartier Alma-Gare', Société d'Aménagements de la Région de Roubaix, Tourcoing/Ville de Roubaix. ADN, 1284W/466, folder 'Opération de Rénovation Urbaine – Relogement des Habitants'. This document is undated, but the project 'Alma-Gare-Notre -Dame' dates from circa 1971. This theme also in document, 'Extrait du Registre des Délibérations du Conseil de

The cries of protest from the *Conseil Municipal* at the repeated delays in the Alma-Gare programme grew even more strident as it became clear that the right-wing national government could be blamed for delays in the redevelopment project, and in 1970 Provo himself took the head of the movement to unblock the funds necessary for *résorption de l'habitat insalubre*. The uncertainty over the future of Alma-Gare therefore also proved to be a thorn in the side for the local representatives of central government. As Pierre Dupuch, *préfet* of the *Région du Nord* and, in this capacity, representative of central government, pointed out in 1972, 'The representatives of the municipality, and its delegates in the council of the *Communauté Urbaine de Lille*, never miss the opportunity to denounce the responsibility of the state for the delay involved in the operation'.[151] Dupuch justified the need to redevelop Alma-Gare on precisely the same grounds as the *Municipalité*. In a letter to the minister of equipment and housing in 1972 he explained that:

> The execution of this operation must respond to the following three essential objectives:
> – The removal of the most insanitary housing in a *quartier* close to the town centre ...
> – A restructuring that facilitates the creation of an urban expressway between ROUBAIX and TOURCOING and beyond in the direction of the new town of LILLE-East ...
> – The development of a tertiary employment sector. The current situation of the region requires the development of a centre for tertiary activity ... .[152]

Over and above these justifications, the local representatives of central government had a more pressing interest in Alma-Gare: Pierre Herman – Gaullist and incumbent *deputé du Nord* – was facing a challenge from Leonce Clérambeaux – Socialist, Deputy Mayor of Roubaix and Vice-President of the *Communauté Urbaine de Lille* – in the 1973 legislative elections. Clérambeaux was basing part of his campaign on the future of the operation at Alma-Gare and was emphasizing the initiatives taken by the *Municipalité de Roubaix* since 1964, while blaming the lack of results on central government. On 18 October 1972, Herman, clearly under pressure, wrote to the *préfet* of the *Région du Nord* urging that the funds for the redevelopment of Alma-Gare be made available

---

Communauté, Séance du 19 février, 1971, No 93, rapport de M. le Président au Conseil de Communauté', emphasizing the importance of improving the road link. ADN, 1284W/466, folder 'Opération de Rénovation Urbaine – Relogement des Habitants'.

[151] Letter from Pierre Dupuch, *Préfet de la Région du Nord* to the *Services de la Délégation à l'Aménagement du Territoire et à l'Action Régionale*, 20 December 1972, Lille, p. 1. ADN, 1284W/462.

[152] Letter from Pierre Dupuch, *Préfet de la Région du Nord* to *Ministre du Logement*, Paris, 2 June 1972, pp. 2–3. ADN, 1284W/466, folder 'Opération de Rénovation Urbaine – Relogement des Habitants'.

in order to avoid anti-government sentiment and, implicitly, to protect his own political situation:

> I should be most grateful if you would stress the importance of this project to M. Olivier Guichard, Minister of Planning, Infrastructure, Housing and Tourism, as well as to the Prime Minister. You are aware that this operation is located in my constituency and that the population has become particularly sensitive to this issue. The operation must be unblocked urgently in order to avoid any anti-government reactions [*toute manifestation hostile au Gouvernement*] ... .[153]

Dupuch, the *préfet*, in turn wrote to Maurice Ulrich, Director of the Cabinet of the Minister of Planning, Infrastructure, Housing and Tourism, drawing Ulrich's attention to the political aspect of this issue. Dupuch observed that the absence of state intervention 'is, certainly, reproached by M. Herman, who has, moreover, had to speak to the Minister concerning this problem'.[154] He added that Herman estimated that a subvention of some 3 to 4 million francs, 'assigned to urban renewal would be most timely in order to support his campaign for this particularly dense and populous *quartier* of his constituency'.[155] Subsequently, Dupuch wrote directly to the Minister of Planning, Infrastructure, Housing and Tourism. In his letter he explained to the Minister that Alma-Gare, 'located scarcely 500 metres from Roubaix's Grand Place, and on the boundary with Tourcoing, features amongst the most defective areas [*les secteurs les plus défectueux*] of the *Métropole*'s agglomeration'.[156] In elaborating the nature of Alma-Gare's defects, it became clear that the problem lay as much with the nature of the population as with the housing itself: 'It consists of workers' housing laid out in numerous *courées* which have been insanitary for a long time. The population, for the most part, is made up of foreigners, and North Africans in particular.'[157] Thus, from the *préfet*'s point of view, Alma-Gare was regarded as a sensitive area for the government, inhabited by a politically undesirable population. For central government, however, Alma-Gare was also a price tag; in 1972, the project had run up an estimated deficit of over eight million francs.[158] In the event, central government finally unblocked the funds

[153] Letter from Pierre Herman, *Député du Nord*, to Pierre Dupuch, *Préfet de la Région du Nord*, 18 October 1972. ADN, 1284W/462.

[154] Letter from Pierre Dupuch, *Préfet de la Région du Nord*, to Maurice Ulrich, *Directeur du Cabinet de M. le Ministre de l'Aménagement du Territoire, de l'Equipement, du Logement et du Tourisme*, Lille, 20 November 1972, p. 1. ADN, 1284W/462.

[155] Ibid., p. 2.

[156] Letter from Pierre Dupuch, *Préfet de la Région du Nord*, to the *Ministre de l'Aménagement du Territoire, de l'Equipement, du Logement et du Tourisme*, Lille, 14 December 1972, p. 1. ADN, 1284W/462.

[157] Ibid.

[158] Ibid.

for *résorption de l'habitat insalubre* in Alma-Gare in 1973, but all the same, the fears of Herman and Dupuch proved to be well founded, and Herman lost his seat in the legislative elections in March of the same year.

With the end of the socialist–centrist alliance in Roubaix and the growing strength and unity of the political left in the town, the history of the *courées* began to be reassessed. While Victor Provo had contented himself with describing the need to 'efface the heavy heritage of the past',[159] the new Socialist alliance of 1977 used less ambiguous terms. From the 'present' of Alma-Gare they presented a past which was the product of capitalist exploitation – a 'wrong' which the central government was intransigently failing to put right. In the run-up to the 1977 municipal elections, *Nord Eclair* ran an interview feature with Pierre Prouvost, the leader of the Socialist alliance. Asked when he considered he would be able to inform the population of Alma-Gare as to what was going on in their neighbourhood, Prouvost encapsulated the Socialist Party's version of Alma-Gare's history:

> Effectively it has now been 10 years that the government has allowed this affair to drag on by assigning what is clearly insufficient funding to carry out the project in the best conditions. This despite the numerous interventions on the part of our elected representatives.
>
> It is for this reason that for the last 2 years, M. Clérambeaux and M. Prouvost have decided to take this operation into their own hands, in close cooperation with the *communauté urbaine* in order to ... construct together a new *quartier* in place of the slums [*taudis*] constructed by the capitalists of the 19th century.[160]

There are two interesting historical points to note in Prouvost's interpretation of the 'slums' of Alma-Gare. First, he asserts that the 'capitalists' constructed these slums rather than constructed houses which subsequently deteriorated into slums. The provision of substandard housing implies an element of exploitation from the outset – an interpretation which had, until then, been absent from Roubaix's mainstream politics. Second, the term 'capitalists', as employed by Prouvost, is undefined and tends to imply that the constructors of the *courées* were the factory bosses, the most famous of Roubaix's capitalists, rather than, as this chapter has discussed and the exhaustive research of Cornuel and Duriez has shown, a group of small investors and *rentiers*. In applying these vague terms, the leader of the *Union de Forces de Gauche* and future Mayor of Roubaix sought to place the moral responsibility for the living conditions in Alma-Gare upon the class enemy, and also aimed to evade any question of the *Municipalité*'s own involvement in the perpetuation of the housing conditions

[159] '... effacer le lourd héritage du passé'. Victor Provo cited in 'Trois autres quartiers changent de visage', p. 3.

[160] 'Roubaix: Nos lecteurs posent des questions aux candidats', *Nord Eclair* (11 March 1977), p. 9.

in Alma-Gare. This historical narrative led inexorably from the construction of poor-quality workers' housing by capitalist industrialists, incorporated the exploitation of the working class, catalogued the physical disintegration of the urban fabric, to arrive in a present in which the working population of the town was forced to live in slum conditions in the *courées*. This interpretation was then used to justify a golden future; the horizon of expectation was marked by a vision of modern housing and sanitation for all provided by the *Municipalité* via the rehousing organizations. In this sense, only the *Municipalité* had the ability, vision and democratic right to take charge of the creation of a new *quartier*.

While local interests on both sides of the political spectrum agreed that the funding for the renewal of Alma-Gare had to be unblocked, this conviction was not necessarily shared by all the population of the area. As already discussed, renewal operations generally brought contradictions to the surface, and in this Alma-Gare was no exception. Although living conditions in Alma-Gare's *courées* were undoubtedly poor, this form of housing offered the advantages that rents were low, housing could be adapted to the needs of both large families and single persons, and the location was convenient for access to the town centre, the station, the main bus routes to Tourcoing and often also to the workplace. The ORSUCOMN study in August 1973 for the first phase of Alma-Gare indicated that very few households in the survey area had the option of moving into the new housing which the *Municipalité* was planning to provide: as many as 94.2 per cent of households did not have the means to enter *habitations à loyer modéré*, and 74.6 per cent of households had revenues below even the level necessary for access to the cheaper 'safety net' housing provided by the *programme social de relogement*. ORSUCOMN's findings for the population's geographic preferences for rehousing, from the same survey, reinforce this contradiction: 39.4 per cent of households expressed a wish to stay in the area. In addition, 30.3 per cent wished to stay in Roubaix, while 24.9 per cent envisaged rehousing in another town.[161] These responses undoubtedly reflect the experience of a population living in an area which was facing imminent demolition, with all the insecurity and difficulty which this situation generated. The nature of the responses would also be conditioned by the unclear perception of the future for Alma-Gare and the limited amount of information available on this subject. It is therefore probable that, under different circumstances, a greater proportion of the population would have chosen to remain in Alma-Gare.

For those who owned, rather than rented, their house in Alma-Gare, *rénovation* or *résorption* represented a serious financial loss – the amount

---

[161] ORSUCOMN, étude réalisée par le CERNA, 'Etude Socio-Démographique Alma-Gare', 20 August 1973, VII, p. 7. ADN, 1284W 466, folder 'Opération de Rénovation Urbaine – Relogement des Habitants'.

provided in compensation through compulsory purchase was never enough to cover the cost of buying another property.[162] Many owner-occupiers were elderly, and for them the *courées* represented a social investment as much as a financial one. Other owner-occupiers were immigrants who had taken advantage of the low property prices in the *courées* once the textile industry had begun to decline and the *rentiers* had begun to sell off their properties. Measures included in the *loi Vivien* of July 1970 required that non-French people wishing to bring their families to France had to first demonstrate that they owned a house. This measure provided a greater incentive amongst the immigrant populations to buy property, and even encouraged the collective purchase of houses in the *courées*. Moreover, while the discourse of the *Municipalité* emphasized the terrible conditions in Alma-Gare, many householders had made a substantial investment in their homes and did not consider them to be *insalubre* (this was as true for the non-French as the French, despite the received wisdom that the presence of a large immigrant population contributed directly to the deterioration of the housing stock). For example, a certain Monsieur Brecan, a resident of Alma-Gare, wrote to the planning division of the *préfecture* in Lille on 1 July 1974. His testimony not only gives a particularly personal insight into the predicament of Alma-Gare's home owners, but also highlights the conflicting meanings constructed around housing in the *courées*:

> Sirs,
> My property is located at no. 85, rue Archimède, amongst the houses designated insanitary in the *quartier* of Alma-Gare, which features in the renewal plans for the town of Roubaix.
> I dispute that my house is insanitary.
> Since it was purchased, it has undergone considerable improvements, particularly with respect to its layout and its sanitary facilities (it was formerly a boarding house).
> I would only bring to your attention, amongst other things: WCs on 2 floors, running water, electricity, gas, plumbing and sewerage, the installation of an office etc. ... .
> I bought this house and renovated it in the hope of generating some revenue, and with my old age in mind.[163]

In similar vein, *Le Monde* cites the case of Germaine (who, it should be added, was an active member of the APF): ' "My house isn't a slum [*taudis*]!" exclaimed 65 year-old Germaine, who was born there and who, last year,

---

[162] Some 15 000 francs in 1976, for example. The figure represents the value of the land occupied by the property (the property itself, having been designated *insalubre*, had no market value), less the cost of demolition.

[163] Letter from M. Marin Brencan to the *Préfecture de Lille, services 'Urbanisme'*, 1 July 1974. ADN, 1284W/463, folder 'Déclaration Insalubrité'.

repainted and repapered.'[164] These examples clearly express the contradictions underpinning a seemingly objective, scientific measure of 'habitability'. Compensation from the authorities took neither the human nor the economic investment in these properties into account. Indeed, the contradiction goes deeper than this, for while the *Municipalité* considered that issues of human dignity and fraternal duty underpinned the drive to improve the town's housing stock, and employed a discourse which echoed these beliefs, the methods selected to achieve this future state prioritized objective assessments of the physical condition of the built environment while virtually ignoring any 'human' dimensions. From this sprang the sort of incredulity expressed by the two residents cited above.

These tensions, however, were covered over by the term *courée* which, by the second half of the 1960s, had assumed such negative connotations that few would have challenged any policy aimed at ridding Roubaix of this particular form of housing. In describing Alma-Gare as 'consisting principally of workers' housing laid out in numerous *courées* which have been insanitary for a long time',[165] this area of Roubaix became indisputably, 'that which must disappear!'.[166] The *Municipalité de Roubaix* presented the demolition of the *courées*, a key element in this fight against *insalubrité*, as bringing benefits to all citizens, either directly by erasing an outdated housing stock, or indirectly by promoting the development of the tertiary sector. In this chapter, however, I have argued that these benefits did not extend to all the population, a substantial element of whom stood to lose their only realistic housing solution as a result of the *Municipalité*'s renewal policy. Nevertheless, the *Municipalité*'s position was difficult to criticize, particularly given the political impotence of those most likely to suffer from the development. Alma-Gare thus became the just target of the bulldozer, which was itself a potent symbol in the history of renewal projects. Indeed, as noted in the previous chapter, the bulldozer came to represent the essence of these projects – a metaphor for progress and for the cathartic removal of the old and the creation of a *tabula rasa* for the construction of the new (see the frontispiece, from the back cover of the *Périodique d'information municipale*, 'Trois autres quartiers changent de visage', of August 1974).

In the construction of Alma-Gare, the physical structure of the area was privileged over its social networks: the justification for the municipal project was founded on the condition of the housing stock, and in this way avoided

[164] 'Quand Roubaix change de peau', *Le Monde* (5 May 1976), p. 24.

[165] Communauté Urbaine de Lille, Société d'aménagement de la Communauté Urbaine de Lille, 'Ville de Roubaix. Rénovation du Quartier "Alma Gare", Rapport Sommaire', Lille, January 1972, p. 2. ADN, 1284W/461, folder, 'Opération de Rénovation Urbaine – Relogement des Habitants'.

[166] '... ce qui doit disparaître!' 'Trois autres quartiers changent de visage', p. 13.

any problems which might be raised by the introduction of the issue of the inhabitants' social and cultural investment in their neighbourhood. When the challenge to the *Municipalité*'s project eventually came, it was formed precisely in these social terms.

CHAPTER FOUR

Alma-Gare: 'Maintenant je reste ici!'

This chapter opens at a point when there was a general, if uneasy, consensus between the *Municipalité de Roubaix* and the APF over the future of Alma-Gare. Although there were tensions between their specific positions, there was an understanding that this area of *courées* should undergo renewal, in one legislative form or another, as soon as possible. However, this consensus would prove to be short-lived, and soon the local activists began to promote another vision of Alma-Gare, one founded upon social priorities rather than housing conditions. They claimed the right not only to remain in their area – 'on reste' – but also to be provided with housing that was something more than mass-produced modernist architecture. During the 1970s, in a process of confrontation, bargaining and negotiation, the identity of Alma-Gare was transformed from one area of *courées* amongst many – and therefore an unequivocal target for renewal – to a dynamic *quartier* and an object of sociological and architectural interest. For the activists Alma-Gare became the positive expression of popular creativity, a symbol of what could be achieved when a population was freed from the yoke of technocratic planning. For the *Municipalité*, on the other hand, Alma-Gare became a thorn in the flesh and a challenge to its authority in urban affairs – at least until its innovations could be appropriated and presented as their own.

Alma-Gare: the breakdown of consensus

In 1967 there were already indications that elements of the population of Alma-Gare were growing impatient with the uncertainty hanging over the future of their area: the same APF banner that had appeared at the council meeting in 1966 – 'Urbanization OK, but when? For whom? While we wait, the houses are crumbling' – was hung across the street at Fort Frasez in Alma-Gare, and the activists organized a press day when journalists were invited to hear the APF and the inhabitants explain the problems of the area. As already noted, the APF did not oppose the plans of the *Municipalité* to demolish the *courées*, but rather drew attention to what it saw as the discrimination and iniquities inherent in this process. In particular, the APF activists were concerned with the level of rents in new public housing, which, they argued, was beyond the reach of many of the inhabitants of the *courées*. In addition they drew attention to the decline of both the physical and social structures in Alma-Gare – the population was becoming increasingly mobile and there was a growing number of empty houses in the area. The decline in the population also had a knock-on effect upon shops and other services, which began to shut down.

The APF took advantage of the celebrations in 1969 marking the 500th anniversary of Roubaix's *charte des drapiers* to draw attention to its misgivings concerning the direction which the town's development was taking. The *Municipalité* wished to present this event as a celebration of the origins of Roubaix's prosperity, but the APF chose to highlight the contradictions inherent in this position. Its members emphasized another history, arguing that the *charte* marked the beginning of the exploitation of the town's workers, not only in the sphere of production, but also, through the construction of the infamous *courées*, in that of reproduction. In a small way the APF appropriated the theme of the celebration and produced its own newsletter for the event. This included a parody of the *charte* in which a medieval herald, trumpet to lips, announced, '5th centenary of the charter. Centenary of the *courées*'. Alongside the herald was a shield that bore, instead of a traditional coat of arms, a rough sketch of a *courée* with a factory chimney rising in the background. The accompanying text read:

> IN ROUBAIX A QUARTER OF THE POULATION LIVES IN *COUREES* .....
> WE RECONSTRUCT .... CERTAINLY .... BUT HOW AND FOR WHOM?????
> 25.000 people still live in conditions of hygiene that are unacceptable in the 20th century and yet, they are human beings.
> ROUBAISIENS! DO YOU ACCEPT THIS SITUATION??
> DO YOU FEEL CONCERNED??
> Join our organization in order to challenge this housing policy.[1]

The protests associated with this alternative centenary message received some national coverage, with the result that the APF's campaign marred the town's celebrations and provoked the hostility of the *Municipalité* (in this way, a pattern of mutual animosity was established that would mark their relations in the coming years). In this early phase of the APF's activities, when its members were less sensitive to the quality of the environment and more enthusiastic about the *Municipalité*'s programme for Alma-Gare, the activists made use of graffiti to publicize their position, and walls were daubed with messages such as 'Centenary of the *courées*', 'There are still 10 000 slums [*taudis*] in Roubaix', '*Courées* = infant mortality', 'Decent housing for our children', '"Human beings" live here', 'The APF defends the poorly-housed', 'SOS housing' and

[1] Association Populaire Familiale, *SOS Logement*, Special number, Roubaix, May 1969, p. 1. AIR. Capitalized in original.

'Social housing – when?'.[2] In protest at the high cost of public housing one piece of graffiti depicted a group of tenants chasing away a figure representing the *office de l'HLM.* Although personifying a twentieth-century public organization, this top-hatted figure, with 'HLM' written across his body, was also an evocation of the classic nineteenth-century landlord associated with Daumier's sketches. Underneath this composition was an inscription that read 'Rent + charges = 500 francs. We don't want this'.[3]

As noted, 1969 was a year that saw particularly intense activity around the issue of the *courées*, including many press articles on the subject, demonstrations coordinated by the APF, the organization of the *colloque des courées* and the establishment of the *Organisme Régional pour la Suppression des Courées de la Métropole Nord* (ORSUCOMN). Despite this flurry of activity no substantial progress was made with respect to Alma-Gare. On 10 July of the following year the law for *résorption de l'habitat insalubre* was introduced, and in the same year central government gave an assurance that the financial means would be made available to enable the operation in Alma-Gare to be carried out. However, during the 1971 municipal election campaign, while the socialist–centrist list was claiming a victory in securing the funds for the operation, the Gaullist central government sent a well-timed telegram informing the Socialist majority that the operation would not go ahead after all.

Due to these delays it was only in 1973 that Alma-Gare was finally scheduled for renewal. In February of that year, the *Communauté Urbaine de Lille* created a *zone d'aménagement différé* in Alma-Gare, thus enabling the purchase of land to begin. Within this *zone*, two sectors of *résorption de l'habitat insalubre* were defined – the first to commence in 1974 and the second to start a year later. Another part of Alma-Gare was to be subject to *rénovation urbaine* starting from 1976, in order to permit the construction of the expressway through the area. It was also in 1973 that ORSUCOMN initiated a small housing operation in Alma-Gare called la Guinguette-Barbe d'Or, involving a limited programme of demolition, the rehousing of 112 families and the construction of 123 new housing units.

With the planning structure in place, central government finally confirmed its financial participation in the operation in the spring of 1974. On 26 March of that year the Ministry of Planning, Equipment, Housing and Tourism published *arrêté* No 74–26, announcing that:

> ... a subvention amounting to ... 10 882 000 (francs) is assigned to the *Organisation pour la Suppression des Courées de la Métropole Nord* (ORSUCOMN) with a view to an operation to clear blocks of insanitary

---

[2] Ibid., p. 6.

[3] 'Loyer + charges = 500F. On n'en veut pas'. Photograph from Carton & l'Atelier Populaire d'Urbanisme d'Alma-Gare – CSCV, 'Introduction', p. 16.

> housing in (North) Roubaix, operation Alma-Gare, 1st sector, *résorption d'habitat insalubre* involving 734 houses and 47 economic activities.[4]

The announcement that the operation was to go ahead was a critical moment for the activists of Alma-Gare: 'it's at this moment that everything caught fire: "they're going to demolish our *quartier*".'[5] During the years of uncertainty leading up to this announcement the consensus between the APF and the *Municipalité* over the need to redevelop Alma-Gare – a consensus based, in any case, on very different interests – had begun to crumble. The delays had enabled the APF to reassess its position, particularly in the light of the slow and costly transformation of Longues Haies to Edouard Anseele. When, in July 1973 the press published a letter from the *préfet* announcing that *résorption de l'habitat insalubre* would go ahead in Alma-Gare, the APF responded with an explicit parallel between Longues Haies and Alma-Gare:

> We do not want to be victims of this renewal operation, and we do not want, in a word, to share the experience of the inhabitants of the *courées* of Longues Haies, who, for the vast majority, have had to leave the *quartier*, since they do not have the means to pay the rents asked of them ... .[6]

Thus, although the APF activists of the continued to campaign for the demolition of the *courées*, the demands that accompanied this call became more refined and specific: the population should be entitled to rehousing in the neighbourhood – 'rester sur place' – (which in turn implied 'fair' levels of rent in the new housing), they should be allowed to participate actively in the planning of the new area, and there should be no modernist towers or blocks which, the APF claimed, destroyed community life because of the anonymity inherent in the organization of their space.

It was symptomatic of this new, prescriptive position that the Alma-Gare branch of the APF began to consider how to give concrete form to their own ideas for the area. In February 1973 it held a public meeting at which it was decided to set up a structure that would not only enable the local population to meet and discuss with officials and technicians involved in the planning process, but also to develop their own ideas for the future of Alma-Gare. Thus it

---

[4] '... une subvention d'un montant de ... 10.882.000 (francs) est accordée à l'Organisation pour la suppression des Courées de la Métropole Nord (ORSUCOMN) en vue d'une opération de suppression de cités insalubres à Roubaix (Nord) Opération Alma-Gare, 1ère tranche, résorption d'habitat insalubre comprenant 734 immeubles et 47 activités économiques.' 'Trois autres quartiers changent de visage', Roubaix, Périodiquex d'information municipale (August 1974), p. 12.

[5] Marie-Agnès Leman, CSCV official for Alma-Gare, text of presentation given at conference organized in Lille by the *Centre de Formation à l'Environnement*, 26, 27 and 28 October 1977, p. 2.

[6] APF statement, July 1973. Cited in E. Verbrackel, 'L'Atelier populaire d'urbanisme de l'Alma-Gare à Roubaix', unpublished thesis, University of Lille, p. 31.

was that the *Atelier Populaire d'Urbanisme* (APU) – the 'People's Planning Workshop' – came into being, and its organizers felt able to claim that it had been formed at the express desire of the population.[7] The APU took as its slogan 'It's possible. We act. We reflect. We build'.[8] The organization was open to all, and the only requirement for membership was part spatial and part social: 'to live in the *quartier* and want to fight to stay there.'[9] With the benefit of five years' hindsight, the APU described its early role as that of a defence committee for the *quartier*: 'At the start, the APU was almost a defence committee and functioned as such. The process of degeneration of the *quartier* had to be stopped, and a response had to be found to the most urgent, most vital problems of the people [*la collectivité*].'[10]

The majority of the APU's organizers came from the APF;[11] indeed, two of its founding members and most active participants were Marie-Agnès and Roger Leman. In time, the organization began to attracted participants from outside the area, especially students, social workers and teachers,[12] with the result that the social profile of its militant base did not necessarily correspond to that of the residents of the *courées* whom they sought to represent. But despite the influx of 'outsiders' attracted by the APU's efforts and ideals, Marie-Agnès and Roger Leman always maintained a central role in conceiving and directing its activities – they frequently appeared in newspaper photographs, were regularly cited in the press, and were the principal signatories of official documents. Given its origins, it is not surprising that the APU took up the themes of the APF, demanding that the population should have the right to decent housing, to remain 'sur place', and to participate in planning the future of Alma-Gare. It is worth noting, however, that while the APF (later the *Confédération Syndicale du Cadre de Vie* (CSCV)) and the APU had much in common, the two organizations were marked by a fundamental difference. While the APF/CSCV was founded in order to address socioeconomic issues connected with the domestic realm, the APU was specifically a place-based organization, conceived to direct the urban development of a particular *quartier* in Roubaix. As such, it could claim, paradoxically, to represent groups whose

[7] APU-CSCV, 'La démarche au quotidien', P. Prouvost, *Roubaix Alma-Gare. Lutte Urbaine et Architecture* (Bruxelles: Editions de l'Atelier d'Art Urbain, 1982), p. 26.

[8] 'C'est possible. On agit. On réfléchit. On construit.'

[9] APU-CSCV, 'La démarche au quotidien', p. 26.

[10] 'Après 5 ans d'existence l'APU: 2 méthodes de fonctionnement. Les documents de l'Alma Gare', no. 17, nd (c.1978), p. 1. AIR.

[11] The APU, with its open membership, was thus a means by which the APF could extend its action to include non-members.

[12] For an example of a study carried out by a sociologist, Gerard Grass, involved in the APU, see G. Grass amd P. Lemonier, 'Pour un schéma directeur de l'organisation de la vie sociale', *Autrement*, no. 6 (September 1976), pp. 230–49.

interests were not necessarily complementary but who, like owner-occupiers and tenants, shared the common experience of living in Alma-Gare.

In its early days, the APU had no permanent location and meetings were normally held at the house of one of the activists; however, the *Société d'Aménagement et d'Equipement du Nord* (SAEN)[13] soon offered the APU a permanent location in a disused shop. In this way, the APU became both an organization and a meeting place. It held regular Wednesday meetings which were open to all and at which decisions were taken by direct democracy. Local councillors were also invited, but they rarely attended (indeed, at this stage, the APU was given little serious consideration by the councillors and officers of the *Municipalité*). The outcomes of these meetings were widely publicized, not only in pamphlets, but also by word of mouth, especially by women and the elderly.[14]

In April 1974 the press published the 'official' and 'definitive' plans for the first sector of *résorption* in Alma-Gare – plans that made no concession to the APU's claims. The project included towers of up to ten storeys, three underground carparks, one primary school, two nursery schools, an old people's home and a system of walkways that were to lead to a central *place* occupied by a commercial centre and a social centre (Figure 4.1). In short, the project consisted precisely of the form of architecture and organization of space to which the activists associated with the APU had announced their absolute opposition.

It was also in 1974 that the evacuation of the population of Alma-Gare began and demolition of the *courées* got under way. Certain areas were cleared quickly, with the aim of establishing an *opération tiroir* to rehouse those who were to be allowed to stay in the area.[15] The first *opération tiroir* carried out was at the Magasins Généraux, a site occupied by warehousing belonging to the

---

[13] SAEN had its origins in the *Société d'Aménagement de Roubaix* (SAR), a *société d'économie mixte* which was created in 1957 by the *Municipalité de Roubaix* to carry out the renewal of Longues Haies. Soon after SAR became the *Société d'Aménagement de la Région de Roubaix* (SARR) as the commune of Wattrelos added its participation. In 1962 it became the *Société d'Aménagement de la Région de Roubaix-Tourcoing* (SART). Following the creation of the CUDL it was integrated with SACOMUL, the *Société d'Aménagement de la Communauté Urbaine de Lille*. Finally, in 1972, SACOMUL joined with the *Société d'Equipement du Nord*, which had responsibility for the whole department, to become SAEN, the *Société d'Aménagement et d'Equipement du Nord*.

[14] In other words, those who were most often at home during the day. See G. Lamarche-Vadel and A. Cotlenko, 'Alma-Gare – le singulier et la politique', *Autrement*, no. 6 (September 1976), p. 66.

[15] The *Municipalité* pointed out that for certain families who required 'solutions spécifiques' because of their size, or because of 'des problèmes particuliers qu'elles peuvent poser' (the particular problems they could pose) there was a plan to purchase old housing. See 'Trois autres quartiers changent de visage', p. 25.

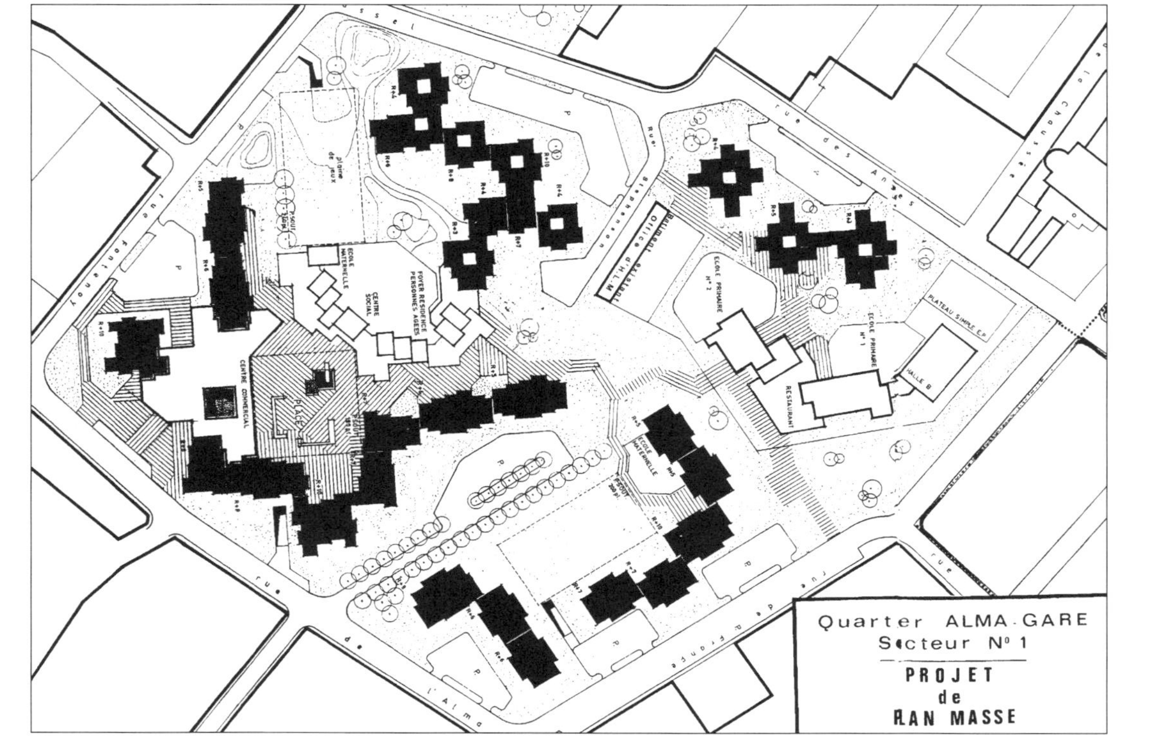

4.1 Quartier Alma-Gare, Secteur No. 1, Projet de Plan Masse, 1974
Reproduced from 'Trois autres quartiers changent de visage', Roubaix, *Périodique d'information municipale* (August 1974), pp. 26–7.

Chambre de Commerce et d'Industrie. The APU demanded that it should be consulted as to the nature of the development and, in response, SAEN and the *office de l'HLM* presented the plans for Magasins Généraux to the population of Alma-Gare on the evening of 8 January 1975. The meeting was held at the self-declared *Atelier* and was attended by some 50 residents of Alma-Gare.[16] The audience was told that the demolition of the warehouses was to start immediately, while the construction of housing was scheduled to begin in April, and the first tenants were due to move in by 1976. The project was to consist of 175 apartments, 28 of which would be reserved for the elderly and would be linked to communal dining facilities and the social centre. Although SAEN and the *office de l'HLM* claimed that the plan was sympathetic to the APU's demands, the activists were unconvinced, arguing that the '*concertation*' (consultation) was a fiction given that the project had already been officially finalized and approved. SAEN and the *office de l'HLM* conceded that they had been forced to push through the project in order to make sure that they could use financial credits from 1974 which were not automatically transferable to the new budget. According to the local paper, these events strengthened the activists' resolve to ensure that, in subsequent phases of the operation, they would obtain 'real' participation in the planning process.[17]

From 1974 to 1977 clearance activities in Alma-Gare continued, but other than the Magasins Généraux project, which was completed in 1976, there was little accompanying construction. This process clearly had implications for the area's population figures. In 1973, for example, the first sector of Alma-Gare identified for redevelopment had a population of 1812, but by 1977 this figure had fallen by almost two-thirds to only 642.[18] Faced with large derelict areas in Alma-Gare, the haemorrhaging of the population and little progress towards reconstruction, the opposition of the activists in the APF/CFCV and the APU intensified. The APU became more confrontational in its nature, organizing public protests, occupying building sites and halting the progress of bulldozers. In a *tract* from October 1975 it stated: 'the aim of this *atelier*: to confront the technocrats and political and administrative powers with a popular force [*une force populaire*], in order to oblige the "renewers" ["*rénovateurs*"] (such as SAEN and the *Municipalité*) to take into account our needs, our desires and our wishes.'[19]

---

[16] 'Le projet du premier îlot Alma-Gare présenté à la population', *Nord Eclair* (9 January 1975), no page nos. ANE, dossier 'Roubaix 1', folder 'Alma-Gare'.

[17] Ibid.

[18] J. Geus, 'Le nouvel Alma sera élaboré en concertation avec la population mais le schéma d'aménagement tiendra compte de la stratégie économique de la ville', *Nord Eclair* (3 June 1977), p. 8.

[19] APF-APU pamphlet. Cited in B. Duriez and D. Cornuel, *Transformations Economiques, évolution des rapports politiques et restructuration urbaine: Roubaix 1960–1975* (Villeneuve d'Ascq: Centre d'Analyse du Développement, 1975), p. 220.

In campaigning for the right of the population to influence the planning process the APU's greatest weakness was its lack of technical expertise. How were they to shape this process when they knew so little about the 'nuts and bolts' of town planning? The impact of the APU's protests would most probably have remained limited had it not been offered, in 1976, the opportunity to sign a contract with *Plan Construction*, a section of the Ministry of Equipment (and therefore of central government), that promised them funding to pay for their own technical assistance. This contract was the first of its kind in France and, in theory at least, not only gave a neighbourhood organization access to information, but also provided it with the technical means to put this information to its own use. The group that was to collaborate with the APU was called ABAC,[20] a Paris-based team consisting of three architects, a sociologist and a lawyer. Members of ABAC had been following events at Alma-Gare for as long as eight years and had already encountered the APU while carrying out research into the impact of *résorption de l'habitat insalubre*. The originality of the situation at Alma-Gare had prompted ABAC to submit a research proposal to central government, and the dossier had meandered through the ministry of equipment until it reached the *Plan Construction* unit (see Chapter 2), which was working on participation in the planning process. Clearly the APU's efforts found a certain ideological resonance amongst the personnel of *Plan Construction* and the project was given the green light. The opportunity to collaborate with the APU enabled ABAC to put into practice its theories concerning public participation and the production of the built environment. This initiative marked the second time that Roubaix had been identified as a test-ground for new planning practices by central government – the first instance being the formation of ORSUCOMN in 1969 to pilot the new legislation for *résorption de l'habitat insalubre*. Of course, *résorption* had been founded on a construction of Alma-Gare as a *quartier insalubre*, whereas the involvement of *Plan Construction* suggested a recognition that Alma-Gare contained a population capable of making a positive contribution to the planning process. Central government had little to lose in sponsoring an experiment that fitted so neatly into the emerging planning philosophy of small operations that incorporated renovation as well as renewal and offered greater scope for the involvement of the local population. Even the *Municipalité de Roubaix* gave the project its cautious support.[21]

With the signing of the contract with *Plan Construction* in November 1976, the APU not only obtained funding for technical support from ABAC, but also a huge boost to the morale of its supporters. This marked yet another evolution in the APU's outlook, as its members began to believe in the possibility of

---

[20] This was not an acronym.

[21] Some of the reasons for this will be discussed below.

taking charge of the development of their neighbourhood: 'With the arrival of ABAC, this defence committee was transformed into a true APU. Inhabitants + architect = our new *quartier*.'[22]

ABAC set itself up in Alma-Gare in an empty house that was provided by SAEN. The group was fortunate enough to arrive during a hiatus in the project – as noted, the land had been purchased and clearance had begun, but there was still considerable uncertainty surrounding the future of the plan itself. The ABAC team was not permanently based in the *quartier*; rather, certain members visited Alma-Gare on specific days. Their method consisted of forming working groups with the inhabitants, with the stated aim of 'helping the people give shape to their ideas'.[23] The first three working groups established were the group for the living environment (*cadre de vie*), the elderly people's group and the urban rehabilitation group, all of which met once every week.[24] The elderly people's group discussed the advantages and disadvantages of the various options for the elderly and came to champion the preservation of traditional social relations: 'What is clear is that the elderly know each other, and meet each other in the streets. They wish to preserve the neighbourly relations that they experience.'[25] The aim of the group for the living environment was to identify the requirements of the population and to incorporate these in the options for the new neighbourhood. Its participants reached two important conclusions: first, that they wanted to avoid the standard programme of collective facilities and infrastructure favoured by the *Municipalité*; and, second, that the provision of housing and services could not be separated from local economic requirements and the development of an employment base. Finally, as a result of the work carried out by the urban rehabilitation group there emerged a view that it was not necessary to demolish the entire area of Alma-Gare and that a proportion of the existing street-front housing might be of a sufficient standard to be retained. The novelty of this position owed much to the fresh perspective brought by ABAC. Indeed, as early as January 1976, even before the official signing of the contract, ABAC had floated the possibility of a limited amount of renovation: 'Our reflections lead us to think of the future *quartier* as much in terms of rehabilitation as in terms of renewal and new constructions.'[26] The urban rehabilitation group subsequently worked

---

[22] 'Après 5 ans d'existence l'APU: 2 méthodes de fonctionnement. Les documents de l'Alma Gare', no. 17, nd (c.1978), p. 1. AIR.

[23] ABAC architect quoted in, 'A l'Alma-Gare à Roubaix, expérience unique en France', *Nord Eclair* (14 January 1977), no page nos. ANE, dossier 'Roubaix 1', folder 'Alma-Gare'.

[24] On Mondays, Tuesdays and Thursdays respectively.

[25] 'A l'Alma-Gare à Roubaix, expérience unique en France', *Nord Eclair* (14 January 1977), no page nos. ANE, dossier 'Roubaix 1', folder 'Alma-Gare'.

[26] ABAC, 'Petite note pour la préparation de la rencontre avec la Mairie du 17/1/76', nd, folder 'Réflexions ABAC'. AIR.

to redefine the criteria of *insalubrité* that had been employed up to that point by ORSUCOMN and, between November 1976 and April 1977, it concentrated on drawing up a *fiche de santé* – a bill of health – for each house in Alma-Gare in order to either confirm or contest ORSUCOMN's findings.

By the time of the municipal elections of 1977, Alma-Gare had become an important issue, and all the parties promised that, should they come to power, they would embrace the concept of public participation in the planning process. Inspired by the events at Alma-Gare, André Diligent, leading the centrist assault on the town hall, advocated a form of planning that, 'must ... allow citizens to determine the conditions in which they wish to live',[27] and where the role of the elected representative was to reconcile the requirements of the technicians and the population in such a way that, 'housing and planning will be the business of everyone!'.[28] Diligent indicated that, in his vision, 'the planning of the town will respect the life of the *quartiers*',[29] and that, as far as possible, both the original population and local facilities, such as small shops, would be allowed to remain in areas scheduled for renewal.[30] Shortly after Diligent's statement came that of a seemingly enlightened Pierre Prouvost on behalf of the *Union de Forces de Gauche*:

> To rehabilitate is, above all, to preserve the experience of the population in a *quartier* by conserving the existing housing. It is, at the same time, to maintain the relations that are struck up between the members of this population and, additionally, to conserve or rediscover its collective forms of expression.[31]

He then went on to appropriate and paraphrase the aims of the APU:

> It would not be a good rehabilitation policy for the old environment if we did not impose two requirements:
> – a willingness to keep the inhabitants in their *quartiers*, while making notable improvements to living conditions for the occupants of old housing.
> – the fact that, whatever the regulations adopted for the operations, it [rehabilitation] will be preceded by consultation with and participation by the inhabitants.[32]

Furthermore, Prouvost sidestepped any suggestion that the socialist–centrist administration at the town hall was responsible for the delays in the Alma-Gare

---

[27] Diligent cited in, 'Urbanisme Logement', *A Propos* (February 1977), no. 2, p. 6.
[28] Diligent cited in ibid.
[29] Diligent cited in ibid.
[30] Of course, Diligent, as the political 'challenger' was much less restricted by political and practical factors than his rival in the *Mairie*.
[31] Prouvost cited in, 'Vers une politique de l'Urbanisme', *Le Métro*, (March 1977), Roubaix edn, p. 5.
[32] Prouvost cited in ibid.

project by neatly attributing the blame to central government which, he insisted, made 'promises quickly forgotten'.[33]

The elections of March 1977 saw Prouvost, who also held the position of vice-president of the *Communauté Urbaine de Lille*, elected as mayor. He immediately set up a working group for Alma-Gare with the intention of bringing together all the institutional actors. He wrote to Marie-Agnès Leman of the CSCV and APU on 14 April 1977, inviting the activists to join the working group rather than pursue a parallel initiative;

> The CSCV and the APU had suggested being represented at this group in the role of 'observers'. In reality, it appears impossible that there should be two parallel initiatives defining planning positions for the *quartier* of Alma-Gare.
> I therefore invite you to participate in a real way and, in this fashion, to take part in the efforts of the working group over which I preside.[34]

Although some members of the CSCV and APU had misgivings about participating in a working group organized by the *Municipalité*,[35] it was clear that, at this point, the practicalities of planning a new *quartier* demanded some degree of cooperation with the municipal authorities, and the APU decided to participate. The working group, the sole decision-making body for Alma-Gare, had initially envisaged drawing up a new planning document for the area, but the APU, keen to promote social issues and popular participation rather than technical solutions, presented their own vision for the area in the form of a *carte-affiche* – a large-scale annotated map – drawn up in conjunction with ABAC. This *carte-affiche*, which, on the basis of the APU's *fiches de santé*, included a proposal to rehabilitate up to 40 per cent of the buildings in Alma-Gare, provoked a hostile reaction from the *Municipalité*. The mayor rejected the proposals, not only on the grounds that they did not conform to the outline of the project as it had been laid down by the municipal working group, but also because it was felt that the APU had surpassed its brief in taking this initiative. In a public letter dated 22 April 1977, the Mayor wrote:

> Here, the *Atelier Populaire de l'Urbanisme* is a privileged place of information, a place for the reception of information, a place of activity and training. But the APU has wanted to enlarge its role: it has wanted, with the help of a team of technicians delegated by *Plan Construction*, to become the place of conception of the future *quartier*. However, the partners in the planning process are multiple. They are not limited to these single actors at the APU who are inclined to produce this outline.[36]

---

[33] Prouvost cited in ibid.

[34] Letter from Prouvost reproduced in Atelier Populaire d'Urbanisme, 'Rapport d'Activités 78, APU,' nd, p. 32. AIR.

[35] *Nord Eclair* (15 April 1977), p. Rx8.

[36] 'Ici, l'Atelier Populaire d'Urbanisme est un lieu privilégié d'information, un lieu de réception de l'information, un lieu d'animation et de formation. Mais l'APU a voulu

While there was clearly a question of 'legitimacy' involved in the dispute, where the stake was control over the 'conception of the future *quartier*', the discussions that followed concentrated on the issue of whether a certain proportion of housing in Alma-Gare was of a sufficient standard to warrant renovation, as the APU and ABAC argued, or whether it should be completely demolished – the solution advocated by Prouvost. Finally, at a press conference on 17 June, the mayor publicly confirmed his intention to demolish the area, asserting unambiguously that, 'the *quartier* is too run-down [*dégradé*], it must be razed'.[37] The shocked APU reacted by boycotting the working group. They sent an open letter to the Mayor explaining their disappointment and suggesting that the administration had betrayed its working-class identity:

> We placed much hope in the setting up of the new Municipality; all hopes were permissible; the left had all the elements to demonstrate what it was capable of ... . We had thought that Roubaix's new public image would be that of a town which knew how to imagine a new urban policy with and for the workers.[38]

If, according to the APU, the left-wing *Municipalité* had abandoned its Socialist principles, then, according to Prouvost, the APU, self-proclaimed champions of public participation, had abandoned the principle of consultation: 'If the APU does not feel able to assume its responsibilities, then the elected representatives will make their decisions. But have no doubt that they will be the first to regret this deficiency on the level of consultation.'[39] The *Municipalité*, Prouvost stated, refused to be dictated to by the APU and he reformulated his position on participation: 'in the last resort, decisions lie with the elected representatives.'[40]

This stalemate lasted for a month until, in July 1977, a compromise was negotiated whereby the working group agreed that the condition of the housing stock in Alma-Gare should be a reassessed and, on the basis of the findings of this new survey, a decision would be taken on whether or not to proceed with the rehabilitation of a proportion of the housing. The study, assigned to SAEN, gave a favourable assessment of some of the housing stock that had previously

élargir son rôle: il a voulu, avec l'aide d'une équipe de techniciens délégués par le Plan Construction, devenir le lieu de conception du futur quartier. Or les partenaires de l'urbanisme sont multiples. Ils ne se limitent pas aux seuls acteurs qui tendaient à produire ce schéma à l'APU.' ABAC-Paris & APU-Roubaix, 'Roubaix: le quartier de l'Alma-Gare', J-L. Flamand et al., *La Question du logement et le mouvement ouvrier français* (Paris: Editions de la Villette, 1981), p. 194.

[37] APU-CSCV, 'La démarche au quotidien', p. 26.

[38] Cited in M. Delberghe, 'L'avenir du quartier Alma-Gare, 1 – Un dialogue qui repose sur l'incompréhension et le rapport de force', *La Voix du Nord* (25 June 1977), no page nos. ANE, dossier 'Roubaix 1', folder 'Alma-Gare'.

[39] Atelier Populaire d'Urbanisme, 'Rapport d'Activités 78, APU,' nd, p. 37. AIR.

[40] Prouvost cited in Geus, 'Le nouvel Alma sera élaboré en concertation avec la population', p. 8.

been earmarked for demolition. On the basis of this study, and after no little contention, the working group finally accepted the concept of partial rehabilitation. The technicians from SAEN, working closely with the APU and ABAC, then presented a revised *schéma directeur* to the working group. This, with some modifications, was finally adopted on 11 October 1977 as the basis for the future development of Alma-Gare. At this point, the APU felt able to announce 'an important success for the *quartier*'.[41]

The new area was to house a population of 5000 – approximately twice the population of Alma-Gare in 1977. Some 1000 new housing units were to be constructed, and a working group was set up to consider the appropriate level of rent and apartment charges. The plan also allowed for the rehabilitation of 400 existing houses in rue de la Chaussé, rue de France, rue Vallon and rue Christophe Colomb. It was decided that this work would be started relatively quickly in order to have 50 houses ready by October 1978. In addition, a study would be carried out for Fort Frasez and the rue de Toulouse with the aim of ascertaining whether houses in these streets might also be retained. It was also decided that immediate improvements should be made to the area in order to ameliorate the conditions for the population who still lived there.[42] Finally, the *schéma* met the APU's demand that planning should not just be about housing, since it also addressed issues such as employment, public space and the quality of social life.

At the end of 1977 the working group decided to establish a permanent operational team in Alma-Gare – the *Equipe Opérationnelle Permanente pour Alma-Gare* (EOPAG). EOPAG, which came under the direct control of the *Municipalité*, comprised four full-time workers (an architect, a sociologist, a designer and a secretary) and five part-time workers (another architect, a landscape architect, an accountant, a structural engineer and a systems engineer). Its task was to carry out and supervise the operation at Alma-Gare, to oversee all the operational studies and to ensure the coordination of the various organizations involved in the project. The intention was that there should be one easily identifiable body to whom the population of Alma-Gare could refer for any aspect of the operation, with the philosophy of enabling participation rather than simply providing information.

The first operation carried out in Alma-Gare after the acceptance of the *schéma directeur* was that of Fontenoy-Frasez. This was the most symbolic and, subsequently, most visited of all the elements that were to form the new Alma-Gare. Fontenoy-Frasez was principally a residential area, covering some 3.8ha. Around 95 per cent of the buildings in area were to be demolished and replaced by a mix of housing, shops, workshops, public spaces and community buildings including a nursery and a school. Once the broad aims of the

---

41 '11 Octobre 1977: Un succès important pour le quartier', nd AIR.

42 Ibid.

Fontenoy-Frasez project had been outlined, the architects were selected. This selection involved considering a number of projects and making a number of study visits. A delegation from the *Municipalité* and a group from the APU made separate trips to visit a housing project at Wolluwe St Pierre in a suburb of Brussels, a development that appeared to correspond to the wishes and vision of the population of Alma-Gare. Meetings with AUSI A et P, the firm responsible for the development, showed these architects to be sensitive to the requirements of the Alma-Gare operation and they were subsequently awarded the contract for Fontenoy-Frasez. From April to June 1978, the architects engaged in 20 days of work alongside the *équipe opérationnelle* and some 12 evening sessions with the APU, at which they discussed and elaborated their plans for the area and obtained feedback from the population. This close cooperation between the population and their architects continued throughout the operation. The end result was a project that was much closer in form to Roubaix's traditional brick terraced housing than to the concrete blocks associated with modern public housing. Instead of the long corridors and dark stairwells associated with the latter, there was a complex structure of walkways and stairs that was intended to facilitate social interaction. The project included 350 housing units, with house sizes directly corresponding to the requirements of the local population – units were provided for both large families (numbering five, six or seven members) and for small households (one or two people). Additionally, there were some 80 houses reserved for the elderly, and these were distributed throughout the area rather than grouped in a *foyer*. A central public space was conceived, as well as numerous semi-public spaces, all based on Roubaix's traditional vocabulary of public and semi-public spaces – squares, streets, street corners, courtyards and so on – in order to guarantee their 'legibility' for the inhabitants. Rents were kept affordable, in part thanks to government participation in funding some of the collective infrastructure such as the large glass canopy over one of the public spaces, and in part due to a special agreement reached with the *office public de l'HLM*. The project was completed at the end of 1980 and, in 1981, the Fontenoy-Frasez operation at Alma-Gare won *le prix Européen d'Architecture*, awarded by the Council of Europe.

By 1978, the APU, which had started off as a defence committee for a semi-derelict area of Roubaix, had become the champion of human relations in a new urban environment. It opposed the modernist conception of clearly defined functions with a holistic, inclusive vision of the city: 'Fifteen years to make imperative [*pour imposer*], to cry, loud and strong that housing and planning are not ends in themselves, but means to enhance and develop social life, communication amongst people [*hommes*] and creation by and for people [*hommes*].'[43]

---

[43] Atelier Populaire d'Urbanisme, 'Rapport d'Activités 78, APU', nd, p. 25. AIR.

Driven by the aim of 'linking the social to the economic, the economic to the social',[44] economic projects were promoted alongside the architectural innovations in Alma-Gare, and the APU initiated an *atelier cuisine coopérative*, a building cooperative and a clothes shop. The *atelier cuisine*, established in Avenue Frasez, provided meals for the inhabitants, for the pupils at the new school and for children at the play centre. But it was more than a simple convenience; for the APU, 'the restaurant is also collective life',[45] and the *atelier cuisine* thus offered yet another means of reinforcing social bonds within the *quartier* – 'to eat together, work together, express ourselves together'.[46] The building cooperative employed up to nine roofers, masons, painters and joiners from Alma-Gare with the aim of allowing the inhabitants to shape their own built environment whilst also providing training opportunities for young people. The clothes shop collected unwanted clothing, which was repaired and resold. It employed three women, but many others from the area participated so that the shop also came to have a role as a meeting place.

The innovative nature of the work carried out in Alma-Gare demanded a similarly innovative programme of management for the new area – management that addressed issues of caretaking and the collective administration of housing, public spaces and public equipment, such as the school and, later, a sports hall. The solution was the establishment of the *régie technique du quartier*, a constitutionally autonomous structure which was described by the activists as 'an embryonic system for the trans-administrative management of spaces'.[47] The *régie*, which consisted of a group of three or four residents with a budget that allowed them to call upon external expertise, was intended to address questions concerning the *quartier*'s social life. It also had the role of relaying information and requests to the administrations and services that had a responsibility in the area and, in this way, the *régie* could guarantee a continuing dialogue between the population and the administration once the physical restructuring of the area had been achieved.

---

[44] '... lier le social à l'économique, l'économique au social.' AGIR, 'Pour un Pool de gestion dans une économie généralisée de quartier: projet de création et de développement d'activités et d'action formation', *Autrement*, no. 6 (September 1976), p. 252.

[45] 'Groupe de travail, "vie de quartier" du lundi 10 janvier 77', nd. AIR, folder 'Avenir du quartier'.

[46] '... manger ensemble, travailler ensemble, s'exprimer ensemble.' APU activist cited in B. Mattëi, 'Urbanisme populaire et économie de quartier', *Autrement*, no. 8 (March 1981), p. 20.

[47] 'Régie Technique: Alma Gare, 1982', p. 12. AIR.

Constructing the *quartier*: 'Notre force est d'être ensemble'

In the events outlined above, the modernist, functionalist approach to 'outdated' and 'inefficient' areas of the city was challenged by a construction that promoted Alma-Gare as a social entity – a vibrant place of human interaction and a font of collective strength and resilience. The term frequently used by the APU to encompass this idea was '*quartier*'. '*Quartier*', best translated in English as 'neighbourhood', combines both social and spatial dimensions. As many of the citations above confirm, the APU activists were neither the first nor the only group to speak of the '*quartier*', but they assigned a particular resonance to this term and, in the course of the 1970s, used it as a form of shorthand for the set of highly charged values they sought to assign to Alma-Gare. Drawing on material from elements of the Alma-Gare's past, they used the concept of *quartier* to give not only dynamism, but also coherence, to an area that, in fact, consisted of a myriad interest groups founded on age, ethnicity, gender, house tenure and so on.[48] Alma-Gare could thus be accorded an identity that was not class-based, but that nevertheless presented a united front amongst the residents of the *courées*. In this way, the *quartier* became something to be nurtured, and the APU became increasingly sensitive to the potential impact of their various initiatives on their neighbourhood: 'for example, such-and-such an activity, will it weaken or reinforce the *quartier*?'[49]

This construction of Alma-Gare directly opposed the 'common-sense' definition shared by the other actors. It confronted the technical with the social and the human, and the individual with the collective: 'Contemporary society imposes upon the individual a lifestyle founded upon individualism, social action must smash this logic and work to promote a harmonious collective life.'[50] This construction also challenged the *Municipalité* to look beyond the idea of *courées* as slums, with the moral dimension that this perspective implied, and it also challenged ORSUCOMN to look beyond individual households and the objective measurement of *insalubrité*. On the other hand, it encouraged the population to share in a wider concept of the idea of 'home'. It provided them with a collective identity that helped to overcome the fractures and conflicts of interest that otherwise characterized them and led them to believe that, as the APU claimed, 'it's possible'. Unmasking one 'reality', the APU replaced it with another, that of the militant *quartier* inhabited by a

---

[48] As a label for this diverse group of interests, *communauté*, primarily a social term, was never used by the APU. The diversity of the population, which included Spanish, Polish, Portuguese and North African groups, may have prevented the term from finding a resonance. Or perhaps the evident diversity of the population of Alma-Gare would have made it too easy for the opponents of the APU to discredit this identification.

[49] Atelier Populaire d'Urbanisme, 'Rapport d'Activités 78, APU', nd, p. 16. AIR.

[50] Ibid. AIR.

committed and innovative population united by a common purpose. This alternative construction relied on a proportion of the original population remaining in the area, both as an indication of a commitment to Alma-Gare and, more pragmatically, since the activists required a support base. Indeed, on an ideological level, the APU's proposal that the original population should remain in Alma-Gare challenged the very logic of capitalist real estate values: a capitalist city, to operate efficiently, should contain land uses that correspond to land-use values, and land of high value in or close to a city centre should be used for activities that provide a high economic return. In proclaiming 'on reste', the APU was directly challenging this logic by demanding that an area that lay a short walk from the very centre of the town should continue to house some of the least productive elements (in economic terms) of the population.[51]

This concept of Alma-Gare as a sociospatial entity was also projected into the future, for while it is not difficult to justify the demolition of a 'slum', the demolition of a 'neighbourhood' and the social life this term implies, appears little better than an act of bureaucratic vandalism driven by political expediency. From this perspective, if Alma-Gare was to be redeveloped, the project had to be innovative, creative and sensitive to the requirements of the population who would live there.

A key element in the construction of Alma-Gare as counter-place to the official interpretation of *logements insalubres* was the attempt of the APF/CSCV and the APU to develop a sense of a collective identity amongst the population of their *quartier*. This in turn would form the basis of the justification for remaining in Alma-Gare and having the 'right' to decide collectively on a coherent housing future. Generally, official activities had the effect of individualizing and isolating households: buildings were individually surveyed and classified according to their condition, compensation (where available) was given to individual householders; the social services assessed the needs and the eligibility of each household for new housing, and households that had lived side-by-side found themselves in different forms of housing in different areas of the town (or beyond) according to this assessment. At no stage in this process was there space for the interpretation of a collective identity based on something as seemingly vague as the fact of living in the same *quartier*.

A collective purpose requires efficient communication, and the activists placed much importance on ensuring that the population remained informed of

[51] For a full discussion of conflictual land-use values, see D. Harvey, *Social Justice and the City* (London: Edward Arnold, 1973). For an historical appraisal of the development of housing markets in France, and the separation of use-value and economic value, see C. Topalov, *Le Logement en France: histoire d'une marchandise impossible* (Paris: Presses de la Fondation nationale des sciences politiques, 1987).

developments and aware of forthcoming meetings. For example, they insisted on the importance of having noticeboards located around the *quartier*, and one of their concerns for the new flats built at Magasins Généraux was to obtain, 'noticeboards, so that everyone knows what's going on'.[52] Communication also helped legitimate the activists' position since, given that the APU had no direct mandate, it was important that their activities and discussions were seen to be open to all. Thus, meetings were well publicized in advance, all were made welcome, and the results found their way into a bi-monthly newsletter called *L'Atelier*, the first issue of which appeared on 1 May 1977. The newsletter was not only intended to communicate what was happening, but also what had already happened, and as such constituted a form of historical chronicle for Alma-Gare.

All communications intended for the population of Alma-Gare, be they *tracts*, posters or, latterly, articles in the newsletter, employed a grammar and vocabulary that addressed the reader directly. In these communications, however, the reader was never addressed as '*vous*' ('you') but always as '*nous*' ('we' or 'us' and so, by extension, '*notre quartier*' – 'our neighbourhood'). Statements were also frequently supplemented by terms such as '*tout le monde*' and '*ensemble*' ('everyone' and 'together') which further emphasized this collective project. For example, APU posters displayed in August 1976 with the aim of encouraging participation in the planning process declared, 'together, with the everyone's ideas, we're constructing our new *quartier*'.[53] Promoting the study trip to the Brussels suburb of Wolluwe St Pierre, the APU stressed the collective nature of the project: 'Currently, in Gare Alma, we're working together on our new *quartier*.'[54] And, in the late 1970s, when the attention of the planners turned to Alma-Centre, the activists were ready to extend their collective discourse to this neighbouring *quartier*, emphasizing social investment and ties in the area:

> To all the inhabitants of Alma-Centre.
> LET'S GET ORGANIZED TOGETHER
> THIS IS OUR STRENGTH
> Living in this sector of Alma-Centre, we know that the 'REDOUTE' operation is forcing us, in the long or short term, to leave the *quartier*.
> For the most part, we have lived in this *quartier* for many years.
> We know our neighbours, we have our friends ...
> As inhabitants of the *quartier*, either owners or tenants, WE HAVE RIGHTS[55]

---

[52] Atelier Populaire d'Urbanisme, 'Rapport d'Activités 78, APU', nd, p. 7. AIR.

[53] Cited in Descamps, 'La Résorption des courées de la Metropole du Nord', unpublished thesis, University of Lille (1976), p. 257.

[54] CSCV and APU, '15 Mai Voyage à Bruxelles', nd, AIR.

[55] APU, 'A Tous les habitants d'Alma-Centre', pamphlet, nd, *Les documents de l'Alma Gare*, no. 10. AIR. Capitalized and underlined in original.

By employing the first person plural – 'we' – no distinctions were made, either between the activists and the population in general,[56] or between the different economic and cultural groups within the population. The only exception to this rule seems to have been single male immigrants, mostly North African, who lived in *garnis* or rented rooms. Here is an example of a *tract* distributed by the APU with the aim of encouraging greater participation from this group. The use of 'you' – 'vous' – is striking, given their otherwise consistent use of 'we':

> YOU, WHO LIVE in FURNISHED ROOMS, DON'T REMAIN ALONE
> You know that from this point on the *quartier* is going to be transformed.
> YOU KNOW, TOO, that THE INHABITANTS OF ALMA-GARE HAVE ORGANIZED THEMSELVES IN ORDER TO REMAIN IN their [*leur*] *quartier*.
> You who live in furnished rooms, you too have wishes and ideas concerning the future of the *quartier*.[57]

In this text, the second person plural – 'you' – is set in opposition to 'the inhabitants of Alma-Gare', who have organized themselves to stay in *their* neighbourhood. On this evidence, it seems that the activists perceived a distinction between these immigrants and the rest of the population of Alma-Gare. Nevertheless, they made a conscious effort to involve this group in their actions, as indicated from this extract from CSCV/APU notes from *c.*1977: 'it is important that the unmarried [male] IMMIGRANTS are able to take part with us in all the *quartier*'s struggles ... . In conclusion, we take the phrase cited by an immigrant comrade "OUR STRENGTH IS BEING TOGETHER [*notre force est d'être ensemble*]".'[58] Despite the APU's resolve, it is certain that for some of the more recently arrived immigrants, the actions and the means of

---

[56] The APU appears to have had a policy that individual activists or authors of texts should remain unnamed in communications, statements and press articles, enhancing the idea of a collective undertaking. For this reason it is difficult to identify the source of texts. All the same, the recurrence of certain stylistic devices suggests that the statements attributed to the population are, in fact, the discourses and arguments of a small, dynamic and ubiquitous core group who are particularly adept at stage management. For example, in a letter dated 31 March 1977 to Madame Larthomas of ORSUCOMN, four elderly female residents of Alma-Gare complain about housing provision for the elderly: 'D'autre part, nous participons depuis des années à l'atelier populaire d'urbanisme et nous nous étonnons que de telles propositions continuent à nous être faites alors que nous sommes contre les ségrégations dans le logement.' Letter from Madames Sonneville, Vankoosbeke, Jannick, Delparte to Madame Lartomas, ORSUCOMN, Roubaix, 31 March 1977. AIR. The tone of this letter in general, and the phrase 'nous nous étonnons que ...' in particular, is typical of husband and wife Roger and Marie Agnès Leman, leading organizers of the APU and CSCV/APF in Alma-Gare.

[57] CSCV/APU, 'Vous, qui vivez en garnis ne restez pas isolés', pamphlet, nd, (reference is made to this meeting in other documents dating from 1977). AIR. Capitalized in original.

[58] CSCV/APU, 'Pourquoi un Groupe de Travail sur les immigrés vivant en garnis', nd, *c*. January–February 1977. AIR. Capitalized and underlined in original.

expression chosen by the organization remained marginal to their concerns. In particular, single North African males had little to gain from calls to take charge of the planning process or from actions to stop bulldozers. Often their aim was to incur the lowest possible living costs in order to be able to send as much of their earnings home as possible, in the hope that one day they too might return. In addition, the non-French imigrant populations had their own organizations, such as the *Amicale des Algériens*, while the common practice of working night-shifts also tended to restrict their participation. The sources give no hint of racial opposition, although it is possible that some of the French residents of the *courées* resented the presence of the North Africans, regarding them as being, in some sense, responsible for the decline of the textile industry. In 1981, in reflective mood, the APU admitted the difficulty of integrating certain groups into their activities and explicitly perpetuated the *nous–vous* dichotomy:

> what becomes apparent in Alma-Gare is that, as generous as the objectives and those who advance them are, not everybody plays an equal part in the project, and there lies the limit. There are inhabitants and there are inhabitants; and the immigrants, principally the single men, non-stabilized families, are less inhabitants than the others.[59]

Another characteristic of the communications from the APF/CSCV and the APU was an informality that lent itself to comprehension by all. This informality helped convey a sense of familiarity in the face of formal bureaucracy and offered an alternative to the abstract and distant discourse employed by the town hall and, even more so, by the clearance and rehousing agencies such as ORSUCOMN. For example, striving to encourage the participation of Alma-Gare's population, the APU activists declared: 'LET'S DO SOME ELBOWING [*serrons-nous les coudes*]. THAT'S THE WAY TO GET OUT OF THIS [situation] AND WIN'.[60] Often these informal expressions were a form of shorthand for technical terms. For example, one of the APU's preferred expressions to describe public housing was 'cages à lapins' (rabbit hutches),[61] less often 'cages à poules' (chicken hutches)[62] or, more elaborately, 'we don't

[59] '... ce qui se révèle à Alma-Gare, c'est que, aussi généreux que soient les objectifs et ceux qui les portent, tout le monde n'est pas également partie prenante dans le projet, et c'est là la limite. Il y a des habitants et des habitants; et les immigrés, célibataires au premier chef, familles non stabilisées le sont moins que les autres.' ABAC-Paris and APU-Roubaix, 'Roubaix: le quartier de l'Alma-Gare', p. 221.

[60] Atelier Populaire d'Urbanisme, 'Rapport d'Activités 78, APU', nd, p. 7. AIR.

[61] For example, announcing the study trip to Brussels: 'we are going in particular to see the social housing which, it seems, doesn't resemble rabbit hutches.' CSCV and APU, '15 Mai Voyage à Bruxelles', nd AIR.

[62] For example, reflecting on the architecture originally proposed for Alma-Gare: 'The model imposed by the *office d'HLM* appeared to us to be of the "chicken hutch" type.' Marie-Agnès Leman, CSCV official for Alma-Gare, text of presentation given at

want to be put in tins, normalized and sterilized [*mis en conserve, normalisé, aseptisé*]; we're not rabbits, down with the hutches'.[63] These were clearly emotive representations of the dehumanizing homogeneity associated with the modernist architectural future of towers and slab-blocks being offered by the *Municipalité*. The theme of coercion by the political authorities reflected in the use of the term '*cages*' (hutches) is echoed in the activists' equally emotive description of 'the politics of deportation to the suburbs'.[64]

It is also clear from many of the examples offered above that statements from the APF/CSCV and the APU echoed the union discourse from the workplace. All the calls for unity in the struggle to remain in the *quartier* are reminiscent of union calls in strike periods. The activists thus employed a language with which they and a large part of the population were already familiar, and they explicitly located themselves 'in the struggles of the labour movement, so that the workers can live in decent conditions in order to better organize themselves and wage their struggle'.[65] The main differences between the APU's position and that of the 'orthodox' unions was the shift from the sphere of production to that of reproduction and the substitution of the 'bosses' by the 'politicians' as the principal 'enemy'. While the discourse of the activists was undeniably similar to that of the unions, as too was their tactic of fly posting and distributing *tracts*, the point has already been made that the CSCV and the APU could not call upon a 'traditional' working-class support base.

The activists also contrasted the openness and informality of their own organization with the bureaucratic secrecy of the politicians, the administrators and the planning organizations. For example, when the APU obtained funding for technical support from ABAC they announced in their newsletter:

> An end to the secrets, the projects drawn up behind closed doors, the unilateral decisions that direct the destiny of city dwellers. Each citizen has, from now on, the possibility to put forward their opinion, to participate in the creation of a *quartier*.'[66]

In this form of localized othering, the population of Alma-Gare was defined with respect to decision-makers who came from outside the *quartier*. This

conference organized in Lille by the *Centre de Formation à l'Environnement*, 26, 27 and 28 October 1977, p. 2. AIR.

[63] 'Petite Note sur la Rue de la BARBE D'OR', nd, p. 1. AIR.

[64] CSCV, Union Locale de Roubaix et Environs, Commission Logement, 'Communique', Roubaix, 11 February 1980, p. 1. AIR.

[65] 'La Définition de nouveaux objectifs pour la rénovation du quartier du l'Alma remet en cause le projet de l'ABAC et de l'Atelier Populaire d'Urbanisme', *La Voix du Nord* (14 May 1977), p. z126.

[66] 'Finis les secrets, les projets établis en atelier clos, les décisions unilatérales qui orientent le destin des citadins. Chaque citoyen a désormais la possibilité d'apporter son avis, de participer à la création d'un quartier.' *L'Atelier* newsletter, February 1977, cited in ABAC-Paris and APU-Roubaix, 'Roubaix: le quartier de l'Alma-Gare', pp. 203–4.

tactic of identifying the 'enemy outside' was useful for the APU since it avoided the issue of who constituted 'us', the common interest group inside the *quartier*, by shifting the issue to 'them', those who did *not* belong to this group. Of course, this identification was only selectively applied; activists, sociologists, journalists and, naturally, the ABAC technical team from Paris were not labelled as unwelcome outsiders (although Gérard Grass, a Parisian sociologist who arrived in Alma-Gare around 1976, is cited as saying, 'at the beginning, they treated us like dogs'[67]). Rather, the tactic of exclusion was reserved for experts associated with the rehousing organizations and the planning department at the town hall, or for the politicians in the *Conseil Municipale*. For the *Comité Interprofessionnel du Logement* (CIL) the APU discourse extended into sarcasm. Speaking of the CIL's 'almost legendary public image', the activists described 'an impartial organization, committed to the common good, to satisfying the needs of wage earners and, moreover, ready, in its infinite goodwill, to collaborate with everyone while, with the modesty that characterizes it, being very careful not to overstep its role'.[68] As for the ORSUCOMN, which the APF/CSCV and APU considered to be the puppet of CIL, the activists, writing in 1977, recalled that it had been founded when Robert-André Vivien, Secretary of State for Housing (another unwelcome outsider) had decided to 'show the end of his nose'[69] in Roubaix.

> In the middle of the night, and in front of 50 deputies, he invented a law for the removal of the *courées*. He set ORSUCOMN in orbit, not through a desire to deliver the people from the servitudes of the *courées*, but to perpetuate a style of life that isolates, uproots and individualizes and, like it or not, ORSUCOMN set to it [*s'engage sur le chemin*].[70]

This citation has an additional interest for the way in which modernist architecture is presented by the APU as a continuation of, rather than a break with, the 'servitudes' associated with the *courées*.

The activists also contrasted the innovative work they were carrying out in the *quartier* of Alma-Gare with the *Municipalité*'s wasteful expenditure elsewhere in the town. For example, in April 1977 the APU and CSCV submitted a request for a financial subvention to set up the structures necessary for the EOPAG management group. By November of the same year, they had still received no response from the town hall:

> And meanwhile, we can read in the press that the fountain in the pedestrian precinct has cost 50 million old francs. We read on the notices posted on

[67] Cited in Champenois, 'La belle aventure des citoyens bâtisseurs de Roubaix', *Le Monde* (24 and 25 January 1982), p. 14.

[68] CSCV, Union Locale de Roubaix et Environs, Commission Logement, 'Communique', Roubaix, 11 February 1980, p. 1. AIR.

[69] CSCV and APU, 'A Gare-Alma ou en est-on?', 12 January 1977, p. 1. AIR.

[70] Ibid.

> the very walls of this *quartier* that they're going to spend 200 million old francs to restore the facade of the town hall ... . Are they going to continue for much longer mocking the inhabitants of a *quartier* that has been undergoing renovation for 15 years and which has been stricken by the negligence of the different parties involved? Are they going to continue for much longer mocking the work that the inhabitants of Gare-Alma have been carrying out for years, work that has greatly contributed to the evolution of ideas concerning planning in Roubaix and which thus serves the general interest of the town and its workers?[71]

They thus contrasted the worthy nature of their own project, one founded on hard work and solid social imperatives, with the frivolous expenditure by the *Municipalité* on aesthetic (and implicitly bourgeois) projects for a fountain and a face-lift for the town hall. In the same vein, the activists also located Alma-Gare, *quartier populaire*, in opposition to the tertiary future promoted by the *Municipalité* for the wealthy *classes aisées*, and particularly with respect to the neighbouring area of Alma-Centre: in a letter of 22 September 1977 from the CSCV and APU to the mayor, they complained that the *Municipalité* 'plays off Alma Centre, Roubaix's new façade, drawn up in secret meetings [*dans le secret des cabinets*], against Alma Gare, popular *quartier*'.[72] They felt that the dossier for Alma-Centre had been pushed through, 'and all this, conforming to your objectives: to realize the tertiary axis of "Mercure-Redoute-Vieil Abreuvoir" and attract the well-off classes to Roubaix'.[73] In contrast, they considered that nothing had been achieved for Alma-Gare because the political will was lacking: 'things are therefore clear: the attention given to Alma-Centre has been lacking in Alma-Gare, or more exactly, the care from which the wealthy classes have benefited does not extend to the inhabitants of Gare Alma.'[74]

The APU, as all the examples above illustrate, also made frequent use of the name 'Alma-Gare' and the word '*quartier*', thereby charging these terms with a significance that they had not previously enjoyed. And it went further than this, juxtaposing Alma-Gare with other areas of Roubaix in order to illustrate what their *quartier* should not become. In particular, it should not share the fate of Longues Haies, 'a *quartier* similar to Gare Alma',[75] whose transformation had seen the old urban morphology destroyed completely, new modernist blocks constructed and all the small, local shops swept away. The APU observed that this physical transformation was accompanied by the social

---

[71] Cited in, 'Rupture entre l'APU D'Alma-Gare et la Municipalité', *Nord Éclair* (16 November 1977), no page nos. ANE, dossier 'Roubaix 1', folder 'Alma-Gare'.

[72] Atelier Populaire d'Urbanisme, 'Rapport d'Activités 78, APU', nd, p. 33. AIR.

[73] Ibid.

[74] Ibid., p. 34.

[75] CSCV/APU, 'Gare Alma: Une expérience d'intervention de la population dans la création de son habitat', 4 April 1977, p. 1. AIR.

transformation of the area's population: 'In the new *quartier* ... there are none of the old inhabitants. The animation and the rich social life characteristic of the old *quartier* have disappeared.'[76] Not even the name of the area was allowed to survive, and so Longues Haies was transformed from what the APU described as, 'an old and strong workers' bastion, in the very heart of the town'[77] to become Edouard Anseele: 'the former inhabitants of Longues Haies no longer recognize themselves in this new *quartier*, and the population, which is made up of people who have come from all over, live one beside the other and not one with the other.'[78]

But the modernist threat not only lay beyond the boundaries of Alma-Gare, it had also invaded the *quartier*, and the developments at Magasins Généraux and Barbe d'Or[79] symbolized exactly what the APU activists did not wish for their neighbourhood. In the passage cited here, they are explicit about the role of Barbe d'Or as the 'anti-Alma-Gare' and use it as a justification for their actions:

> For Alma-Gare, Barbe d'Or, an operation that was dropped from the sky [*opération parachutée*] and that nobody really asked for, is becoming the anti-Alma-Gare, the example of what should not be done. A degraded image that valorizes, in contrast, that which is being done elsewhere. A disquieting testimony to what could have been done to the whole *quartier*, and reassuring testimony to that which we believe we have escaped, a negative example that legitimates a positive action.[80]

Indeed, the developments at Barbe d'Or and Magasins Généraux were even more meaningful given that the activists had tried to influence the planning and construction of these projects, but had been almost completely unsuccessful. These developments, 'an ensemble characteristic of technocratic logic',[81] therefore stood as concrete, physical reminders of what awaited the whole *quartier* if the APU failed in its efforts.

If the APU activists employed language that both implied and encouraged the existence of a coherent identity for the *quartier* of Alma-Gare, they also wanted to be sure that this discourse was supported by evidence of collective activity. For example, they were concerned that meetings were well attended, as

---

[76] Ibid.

[77] '... une ancienne et forte bastille ouvrière, en plein cour de la ville.' 'Roubaix: L'APU. Naissance d'un mouvement populaire de résistance aux expulsions', *Place*, no. 5 (autumn 1976), p. 15.

[78] CSCV/APU, 'Groupe de Travail "Réhabilitation"', 2 February 1977, p. 1. AIR. Underlined in original.

[79] The name Barbe d'Or supposedly came from a tavern-owner who sported a particularly fine golden beard. It became the name of a street, and from there was extended to an area in Alma-Gare.

[80] Christian Carlier, (APU), 'Note sur Barbe d'Or', 23 April 1984. AIR.

[81] Atelier Populaire d'Urbanisme, 'Rapport d'Activités 78, APU', nd, p. 2. AIR.

is made clear in the 'Little Guide for our Street Meetings', produced by the CSCV/APU and dated 28 February 1977:

> These little street meetings have been organized in such a way that the large majority of the *quartier* is able to participate in them.
> Perhaps we should go and look for people, because perhaps there might be those who have never come to the *atelier*.
> On the other hand, while an agenda might be planned, it seems important to let the people express their problems and to take into consideration the questions asked and write them in the notebook ... .
> Equally, try to note the name and address of the participants for future meetings.[82]

The involvement of a substantial proportion of the population of Alma-Gare was important to the activists for several reasons. First, numbers equated to legitimacy for an organization that could claim no official mandate and was often criticized for its lack of representativeness by the members of Roubaix's *Municipalité*. Second, widespread participation offered confirmation to the activists themselves of the justness of their claim that all residents of the *quartier* were entitled to participate in the planning process. Third, the more people who witnessed a protest action, the more weight this action carried and, in turn, the more tangible the idea of Alma-Gare as a dynamic *quartier* became.

Despite this emphasis on participation, informal communication and simple messages, the APU eventually began to employ a more technical, abstract and theoretical discourse. This occurred particularly after the arrival of ABAC and was perhaps an inevitable development given the increased involvement of planning experts in the events at Alma-Gare. The activists were aware that a more technical approach would put the Alma-Gare operation beyond the understanding of those who were not specialists in the field (that is, the population of Alma-Gare, from whom the APU drew its support). Indeed, with the requirement to produce the *carte-affiche* and then the collaborative work necessary to convert this to the *schéma directeur*, the APU moved a little closer to the discourse of the authorities whom they sought to oppose. Even the concept of what it meant to live in the *quartier* was given a prescriptive and, indeed, exclusive dimension. While the APU had initially considered the fact of living in Alma-Gare and the will to remain there enough to qualify as participation – 'to live in the *quartier* and want to fight to stay there' – with the arrival of ABAC there emerged a more elaborate definition of participation founded upon *la vie sociale* – social life:

> To live in the *quartier*, is not simply to have a house in the *quartier*. To live in the *quartier* is to participate in its collective life of meetings and neighbourhood links [*voisinages*], to participate in and create social life.

[82] CSCV/APU, 'Petit Guide pour nos réunions de Rue', 28 February 1977. AIR, folder 'Groupe de travail "Réhabilitation"'.

> Social life is that which takes place in the courtyards, in the streets, in the shops, at meetings, in the Place Fontenoy etc ... . It concerns public spaces, infrastructure and services more than its does housing.[83]

Moreover, with the arrival of ABAC there emerged a thread in the theoretical arguments proposed by the APU that led directly to Marxist theories of space and, most obviously, to the ideas of Henri Lefebvre. In keeping with the theoretical foundation of Lefebvre's *La Production de l'espace*,[84] they argued that urban space was restructured (or produced) as a direct consequence of changes in the economic system of production.[85] For example, they considered that Barbe d'Or had been 'privatisé'[86] and had thus lost its communal riches. Spaces (*espaces*) had been replaced by emptiness (*le vide*) – that is, by residual areas in which sociability had gradually been stifled. Modernist techniques of functional zoning had produced an impoverished environment in the new development: 'They clear a space to make a desert of it.'[87] As for the street, this had been reduced to its most abstract expression, 'a no-man's-land'.[88] ABAC and the APU also echoed the Lefebvrian theme of natural space when they argued that, when planning became mere zoning, 'green space [*l'espace vert*] becomes merely the colour that masks dead space [*l'espace mort*]'.[89] Finally, in the APU-CSCV's contribution to the retrospective assessment of the Alma-Gare operation from 1982, *Roubaix Alma-Gare. Lutte Urbaine et Architecture*, they state explicitly that the project '... contains a reappropriation of the norms and state-controlled categories of *the production of space*'.[90] This serves to remind us that, in part, these concepts were woven into the APU's history of their own actions *post facto* as a means of giving their struggle additional intellectual legitimacy.

---

83 APU/CSCV, ABAC, 'Maintenant nous avons pratiquement gagné la bataille de la réhabilitation et de la restructuration', 28 March 1977, p. 2. AIR, folder, 'Groupe de travail, avenir du quartier'.

84 H. Lefebvre, *La Production de l'espace* (Paris: Anthropos, 1986).

85 See, for example, ABAC-Paris and APU-Roubaix, 'Roubaix: le quartier de l'Alma-Gare'.

86 'Petite Note sur la Rue de la BARBE D'OR', nd, p. 1. AIR.

87 Ibid.

88 Ibid.

89 Ibid. Lefebvre considered that 'natural' space had been destroyed by 'abstract' space. He argued that, in the second half of the twentieth century, advanced capitalist societies had been marked by the consolidation of the state, with the result that the production of abstract space had become increasingly tied to state attempts to plan and organize societies rationally, aided by knowledge and technological resources. H. Lefebvre, *The Production of Space* (Oxford: Blackwell, 1991), p. 23. Green areas represent a non-productive consumption of space and, since they do not serve capitalist interests, they are constantly under threat.

90 '... contient une réappropriation des normes et des catégories étatiques de la production de l'espace.' APU-CSCV, 'La démarche au quotidien', p. 19. My emphasis.

Unfortunately, the sources do not lend themselves to an assessment of the efficacy of the APU's attempts to mobilize the population. One may surmise that it was hard not to respond, at least to some degree, to a discourse that addressed 'us', or to promises to challenge the mechanisms that were so evidently at work in the area. In addition, the myth of the *courée* population as dynamic, unified and resourceful must inevitably have had a certain appeal, particularly for a marginalized population that was rarely, if ever, assigned a positive role. The Lemans, writing in a journal in 1980, claimed that although not all the inhabitants of Alma-Gare were members of the CSCV, many had wanted to participate in the struggle against the renewal project.[91] Moreover, if turn-outs for meetings and protest activities are any indication, calls by the APU to reject the rabbit hutches produced by modernist industrial construction techniques and to demand rehousing 'sur place' seem to have struck chords with the population. For example, on 4 April 1976 some 100 people protested outside Roubaix's town hall in order to make clear their intention to remain in the *quartier*, with the cry 'Alma doesn't plan to drop its guard'[92] (which was also a personification of the *quartier*). Given the importance assumed by the events in Alma-Gare and the attention they attracted, the perception of the *quartier* must have changed even amongst those who did not participate in the campaign. It may be significant that in none of the APU's well-publicized and well-reported actions was there ever an indication of active opposition on the part of the population. Furthermore, the *Municipalité* would have been unlikely to go along with the innovations proposed by the APU had the majority of the population in Alma-Gare not been in favour. The only evidence of popular discontent was in a claim by some councillors that they were regularly approached for information on the future of the Alma-Gare project by individuals who did not wish to use the channels of information provided by the APU.[93] Again, it is difficult to know the extent to which this really was a current practice or simply an attempt by the councillors to discredit the APU.

Despite the APU's efforts and the apparent lack of opposition to their initiatives from the population, the figures cited in Chapter Three indicate that a large number of people continued to leave the area of Alma-Gare throughout the period of the most intensive action by the APF/CSCV and the APU. This suggests that not all adhered to the activists' ideals or, at least, that even if these ideals were appealing, they were a luxury that could not be afforded in the most marginal of housing and employment markets.

---

[91] R. Leman and M-A. Leman, 'A l'Alma-Gare à Roubaix: une organisation collective des habitants pour un meilleur urbanisme', *Sauvegarde de l'enfance*, no. 2 (March–April 1980), p. 295.

[92] 'L'Alma ne compte pas baisser les bras'. APU-CSCV, 'La démarche au quotidien', p. 26.

[93] Verbrackel, 'L'Atelier populaire d'urbanisme de l'Alma-Gare à Roubaix', pp. 178–9.

'On reste': APU actions and strategies

The APU sought to construct a new identity for Alma-Gare and its inhabitants not only through the discourses it employed, but also through its activities. For example, many of the APU's actions were directed at maintaining or improving conditions in the *courées*, a tactic intended to encourage the population to remain in Alma-Gare. These same actions also challenged the official view of Alma-Gare as a collection of uninhabitable *logements insalubres* by valorizing the social dimensions of the *quartier*. The APF/CSCV and APU were well aware that *rénovation urbaine*, *résorption de l'habitat insalubre* or, indeed, even the threat of these procedures would lead to the emptying of the *quartier*, and they estimated that in normal renewal projects only 50 per cent or less of those living in the *courées* were rehoused in new housing, while the remainder were forced to leave the area in search of an alternative housing solution, often in another area of old housing.[94] With the departure of the population, the APF/CSCV and APU would lose both their support base and their relevance. Thus rose the clarion cry, 'on reste'.

When faced with a particular issue, the APU conceived of its actions on two levels. There were one-off initiatives – *actions ponctuelles* – intended to address the immediate source of a problem, and there were long-term strategies that were intended to develop permanent solutions. In its own 'code of practice' the APU prioritized negotiation towards a long-term solution and regarded confrontation as the final resort in resolving an issue: 'Resolve problems raised as far as possible by an amiable approach to the organization responsible. If this fails, we engage in a test of strength by the appropriate means. All decisions are taken together within the structure of the APU every Wednesday.'[95] The activists liked to assign a degree of spontaneity to their one-off actions, making them appear to be the outcome of the collective will of the population, but there was clearly, and necessarily, an element of orchestration. For example, describing a meeting in a *cour* in May 1969 attended by some 70 people, the APF claimed 'spontaneously, a banner was unrolled and a procession was organized ...'.[96] That a banner was at hand slightly undermines the claimed spontaneity of the event.

---

[94] P. Prouvost, 'Roubaix : L'APU 2. stratégie du capital et stratégie populaire', *Place*, no. 6 (Winter 1976), p. 16.

[95] 'Résoudre dans la mesure du possible les problèmes évoqués par des démarches amiables envers l'organisme responsable. Si échec, nous engageons l'épreuve de force par des moyens appropriés. Toutes les décisions sont prises ensemble dans le cadre de l'APU tous les mercredis.' Leman and Leman, 'A l'Alma-Gare à Roubaix', p. 295.

[96] Association Populaire Familiale, *SOS Logement*, Special number, Roubaix, May 1969, p. 11. AIR.

The twofold approach – long-term strategies and *actions ponctuelles* – was apparent in the APU's tactics for establishing its authority in matters concerning the future shape of Alma-Gare. While the long-term aim of the APU was to win a role in deciding on the form of their new *quartier* through negotiation, canvassing and lobbying, their *actions ponctuelles* included several attempts to block the progress of the bulldozers. Indeed, while the *Municipalité* used the bulldozer as a harbinger of good – the symbol of an inevitable progress – the APU used the same machine to represent the complete destruction of a community – along with the *courées* it would sweep away, indiscriminately, the life of the *quartier*. When, for example, at the working group of 28 April 1977, the mayor announced the '*reconstruction*' of Alma-Gare, the APU and CSCV responded with urgency:

> IT'S CLEAR; IF WE DON'T FIGHT, THE BULLDOZER THAT IS NOW IN RUE ARCHIMEDE, WILL CONTINUE ITS COURSE, IT WILL DESTROY ALL OUR HOUSES AND ALONG WITH THEM IT WILL DESTROY THE LIFE OF THE *QUARTIER*.
> THIS IS THEREFORE A SOLEMN CALL THAT THE CSCV AND APU ARE MAKING TO YOU[97]

As well as stopping bulldozers, the APU made several attempts to impede the progress of work on the building sites, and on at least two occasions the activists and members of the population occupied the building site of Barbe d'Or in protest at the perceived lack of public consultation.

Another good example of this twofold approach was provoked by the issue of water supplies to the *courées*. Water arrived in each of the *courées* from the public supply by way of a single water main located in one of the houses in the *courée*. The water meter, also located in this house, was a communal one, and therefore the periodic water bill had to be divided amongst the households of the *courées*. Problems arose as renewal, or the threat of renewal, provoked a degree of movement amongst the population. Residents would leave a *courée* without receiving a final water bill, which would then be left for the new arrivals to pay (if indeed there were new arrivals). If this share of the bill was left unpaid, the cost fell to the remaining residents of the *courée*. Worse still was the scenario whereby the resident responsible for the meter and the division of the bill left and nobody else assumed this task. Either way, when the municipal water service found that a *courée* was falling into arrears with water payments it would cut off the water supply. In one particularly extreme case, the local

[97] CSCV/APU, letter re. meeting of the working group, 8 June 1977. AIR. Capitalized in original. Later, in 1979, the APU, in more reflective mood, was able to claim that it had delivered a large part of the *quartier* from this destructive force: 'it should be noted that it is thanks to the action of the APU that 40% of the buildings have been saved from the bulldozer.' Atelier Populaire d'Urbanisme, 'Rapport d'Activités 1979, APU', nd, p. 9. AIR.

newspapers of 11 February 1973 reported that 30 families had been without water for ten days.[98] The APU regularly negotiated with the water service on behalf of inhabitants of the *courées* who were deprived of water. Its aim in these negotiations was to develop a long-term solution to the problem rather than allowing the water service to find 'un pigeon'[99] amongst the population who was prepared to sign a paper accepting responsibility for water payments and eventual debts:

> THE PUBLIC SERVICE MUST PROVIDE 'A SERVICE' AND NOT REPRESS THE WORKERS
> IT ISN'T US WHO INVENTED THE COMMUNAL METERS[100]

The outcome of these negotiations was an agreement that every household located in a *courée* with a communal water-meter would pay a monthly sum of ten francs against any final bill (smaller households would pay a smaller proportion of the total amount). This facilitated the management of domestic spending for the residents of the *courées* by spreading the impact of the bill, and at the same time limited the risks involved for the water service.

Although the APU's code placed most importance on long-term solutions, in the case of the water supply the one-off, short-term action is particularly interesting. On 21 May 1975 the CSCV and APU, claiming that as many as 200 people in Alma-Gare were at that time without water, organized a demonstration. Armed with buckets, some 100 protesters marched from Rue de la Guinguette in Alma-Gare to the town's central square, beneath the windows of the town hall. While singing, '*De l'eau, rien que de l'eau*' – 'Water, nothing but water' – they drew water from the nineteenth-century fountain that adorns the square.[101] The symbolism was clear, the statement was eloquent: the needy of the town, for whom the *Municipalité* was supposedly responsible, took the water necessary to sustain life from the decorative fountain in front of the town hall. The fountain is a symbol of plenty, indeed, of excess, and also represents the municipal pride of the town. The protesters were thus forcing a juxtaposition between the need in their *quartier* and the excess in the 'other' Roubaix – a contradiction that was intended to shame the town's administration. Moreover, as the activists themselves pointed out, for a mere symbolic gesture it would have been enough for one person to fill a single

---

[98] This information was communicated to the papers by the APF. These articles were photocopied in the AIR archive – for example, 'Trente familles sans eau depuis dix jours', *La Voix du Nord* (11 February 1973).

[99] APU, '21 May 1975 MANIFESTATION!', pamphlet, nd. AIR.

[100] Ibid. Capitalized and underlined in original. This reference to the inhabitants of the *courées* as 'workers' is yet another example of the APU's attempt to develop a parallel with the unions of the workplace.

[101] 'Privés d'eau, ils se servent dans le bassin de la Grand-Place', *La Voix du Nord*, nd, no page nos, photocopy. AIR.

bucket from the municipal fountain. The fact that this operation was repeated by dozens of people from Alma-Gare shifted the operation from an individual initiative (or, at least, the initiative of a limited number of APU activists) to an initiative that was, apparently, an expression of the *quartier*'s collective will. The water protest also drew attention to the fact that, even though Alma-Gare had been identified for demolition, it still housed a substantial population whose needs did not diminish just because their *quartier* had been earmarked for destruction.

Another initiative aimed at maintaining the quality of day-to-day life in the *courées* was a system called *rond rouge*, whereby a red paper disc displayed in the window of a house owned by SAEN (and therefore due for demolition) was used to indicate a maintenance problem, such as a water leak, that required the immediate intervention of the authorities. This technique was necessary given that few residents in the *courées* had their own telephone. Eventually, the *Municipalité* agreed to meet the APU's demands for the employment of two permanent maintenance workers to carry out these minor repair and maintenance jobs in the *quartier*. The *rond rouge* initiative lasted from 1976 to 1978 and drew attention to the contradictions experienced by people whose houses, while fulfilling the role of homes, tended to be disregarded because they had been officially identified as *insalubres*.

The improvement of living conditions also lay behind the APU's initiative to undertake the unauthorized walling-up of vacant houses. These operations came about because houses defined as *insalubres* could not be re-let once they fell vacant. As a result, properties were often left empty for long periods while awaiting demolition and so became targets for pillaging and squatting, as well as locations for illegal rubbish dumping. ORSUCOMN, within whose competence this issue fell, did not, however, have the legal right to wall up houses without the permission of the owner – permission that was sometimes not forthcoming, especially if the house had been obtained by compulsory purchase or if the owner was absent. Moreover, ORSUCOMN's reluctance to wall up properties may have had something to do with their own agenda of encouraging the population to leave the area. Certainly, this was the opinion expressed by the APF: 'The APF asks itself if, voluntarily, they don't allow the situation to deteriorate [*pourrir*] so that the inhabitants of the *quartier* flee to other buildings, in other *quartiers*. This strategy would evidently permit construction for other people, the inhabitants of the *quartier* of Alma-Gare having disappeared.'[102] It was therefore to avoid the deterioration of conditions in the area that the APU demanded that empty properties be walled up, and even organized several 'shock' walling-up operations, the first of which took place in

[102] APF statement, 17 May 1974. Cited in Verbrackel, 'L'Atelier populaire d'urbanisme de l'Alma-Gare à Roubaix', p. 37.

November 1974 in three houses in Fort Wattel and rue de l'Alma. These sporadic walling-up initiatives were largely tolerated by the authorities, who were forced to recognize the contradiction between the individual rights of property-owners and the communal rights of the inhabitants of the *quartier*.

In another initiative with a similar scope, the APU, along with a group of children and youths from the *quartier*, transformed, on two separate occasions, an area of wasteland into a recreation area. The first of these operations took place on 1 May 1975, when the children of Alma-Gare cleared a piece of wasteland in order to create a play area. The second occasion was on 25 April 1977, when the children of Fort Frasez laid out a sports field on an area of wasteland behind the *fort*. In so doing, they were putting to a positive use an area of land that served no immediate purpose, but which had been earmarked by the town hall officials for construction at some future point, and for some future, unidentified population. The APU was challenging this conception of the future by appropriating the land in order to put it to use for the present community. Again, this action was conceived on two levels. The first was the immediate, short-term operation of removing rubbish that would otherwise attract rats and of providing somewhere safe where the children of the *quartier* could play (they would otherwise play on the derelict and dangerous gap sites). The second, more long-term goal was to encourage the authorities to recognize the importance of a *coordinated* clearance and rehousing programme and to demonstrate that cleared land, with a little work, could serve a positive purpose and make life more bearable for those who remained in the *quartier*. The action of encouraging young people to clear the wasteland also added to the sense of a collective undertaking in Alma-Gare, not only amongst those who participated in the action, but also amongst those who witnessed it. The significance was still greater since the participants represented the youth of Alma-Gare – that is, the future residents of the *quartier* if the APU succeeded in winning its fight.[103]

The contrasts between the APU's and *Municipalité*'s views of Alma-Gare were further highlighted by two symbolic rehousing operations carried out by the APU. The first of these took place on 1 May 1974, and was subsequently described by the activists in their own history of their struggle as, 'a key moment in the history of the quartier'.[104] A 74 year-old woman, who had been living in the *quartier* for 20 years, had been forced to remain in her *courée* home in Fort Watel, in dire conditions, and without electricity, for eight days, while houses on the street front, in much better condition than the woman's house

[103] As noted, a source of inspiration for this sort of action was very probably the theoretical work of Henri Lefebvre. In keeping with Lefebvrian theory, the creation of green, non-productive space (for example, recreational space) is a direct challenge to the capitalist organization of space.

[104] '... un moment fort de l'histoire du quartier.' APU-CSCV, 'La démarche au quotidien', p. 26.

were legally designated as uninhabitable because they had been classified by ORSUCOMN as *insalubre*. The woman had been offered an apartment on the outskirts of Roubaix, an offer which she had refused with the support of 'all the *quartier*'.[105] Instead, the APU undertook to rehouse the woman illegally in a street-front property. The symbolic aspect of the action was emphasized to the full, and a mock-official presentation of the keys was made to the old woman, who was known to one and all as '*Memère*' – grandmother – the personification of the memory and life of the *quartier*, of its past, its present and, therefore, its future. The conferral of the keys and the opening of the 'new' house in Avenue Frasez (the symbolic core of the *quartier*) was done with a degree of ceremony and was witnessed by many of the residents of Alma-Gare. The whole scenario was conceived in such a way as to carry the fullest impact at the level of the *quartier*: all the issues it addressed – the degradation of the environment, the precarious housing future, the apparent lack of logic in the label of '*insalubre*' – were common to the whole population of Alma-Gare. The action was repeated on 1 May of the following year, when an entire family who had recently been evicted from their home was 'rehoused'.

The reasons behind the APU's call for rehousing were outlined in a document entitled 'Why rehousing?'.[106] The first reason given by the APU was, 'a simple question of good sense': many of the street-front houses, although in relatively good condition, were lying empty, while the off-street housing in the *courées* was not only in much worse condition, but was also too small for the families who lived in them. The second reason was that rehousing people in street-front buildings would have the effect of stopping 'the haemorrhaging of the *quartier*, especially for the most poorly housed, and, in leaving people the possibility of staying in the *quartier*, this change allows a certain life to continue to exist in these sectors'.[107] Third, the APU considered that there was a value in preserving the built environment and the morphology of space in Alma-Gare for, 'their character and their architectural qualities'.[108] The APU appropriated the role of the rehousing authorities, but only temporarily, and, moreover, the solution it presented was in itself only temporary. Its aim was to persuade the rehousing authorities to take on this responsibility by confronting the technical definition of *insalubrité* with the social one – the definition as lived by the residents of the *quartier*. It took considerable pressure, as well as the symbolic rehousing of the grandmother, before ORSUCOMN recognized

---

[105] '... tout le quartier'. Ibid., p. 26.

[106] 'Pourquoi le relogement?', undated, but the technical nature of some of the discussion dates it to the period following the arrival of ABAC.

[107] APU, 'Pourquoi le Relogement?', nd. AIR, folder, 'Réflexions ABAC'. Reproduced in, 'Le relogement et les ouvriers d'entretien sont deux problèmes à résoudre dans l'immédiat', *La Voix du Nord* (28 January 1977).

[108] Ibid.

the logic of the APU's stance, relaxed its position and agreed to embark on a limited rehousing project, even if this was technically illegal.[109]

It was with a similar aim that, on 2 July 1977, the APU undertook the restructuring of a pair of street-front properties. This initiative was launched during the period of stalemate between the *Municipalité* and the APU over the issue of *réhabilitation*. On that particular day, members of the town council made a visit to Alma-Gare, but the APU chose to boycott this event. Instead, while the councillors were walking through the area, members of the APU were engaged in their renovation operation: they converted two houses, located on the corner of Rue de l'Alma and avenue de Fort-Frasez in the heart of the *quartier*, into a single dwelling. This action served not only to demonstrate the APU's determination and commitment, but also to confront directly the claim of the *Municipalité* that it was impossible to renovate the area's housing stock. It also established a striking dichotomy between the 'talk' of the town council and the 'action' of the APU.

Given the importance of maximizing the number of witnesses to protest actions, it is not surprising that the APU made full use of the possibilities presented by the media. For example, apart from the symbolic value of taking buckets of water from the fountain in Roubaix's main square, the action also made for good, digestible news. No actions were ever carried out without the local press being informed.[110] Indeed, at certain critical points in the story of Alma-Gare, media interest even became national; the *quartier* was invaded by journalists from across France, and *Le Monde* ran a number of features on the events taking place in this neighbourhood of a small northern textile town.[111] Not only did the presence of the media create the sensation of an 'event' amongst the participants, it also reinforced the idea of the *quartier* to 'insiders' and 'outsiders' alike, through the very act of reporting. The fact of having events reported in the press located them unambiguously in the public sphere and gave them a certain 'reality' and 'permanence'. And this in turn served

---

[109] ORSUCOMN was, in a sense, caught in a legal trap of its own making. A property, once designated *insalubre* could not be reinhabited and, as a result, the CSCV/APU's rehousing activities were technically illegal, as were the actions of ORSUCOMN when it finally collaborated with the activists.

[110] The APU was quick to take the press to task if they considered that the reporting of an event or statement was inaccurate. For example, following the occupation of the building site at Barbe d'Or on 28 March 1975, the APU sent an article to the local press explaining the motivations behind their action. The left-wing *Voix du Nord* printed the article in full. 'In contrast', the APU complained, ' "Nord Eclair" has once again interpreted this article and has masked the truth.' APF/APU, 'Suite de la manifestation du 28.2.75 sur le secteur de la "Barbe d'Or" ', nd. AIR. *Nord Eclair* tended to favour the CIL.

[111] See, for example, 'Quand Roubaix change de peau', *Le Monde* (5 May 1976), p. 24, and Champenois, 'La belle aventure des citoyens bâtisseurs de Roubaix', p. 14.

to reinforce these moments in the collective memory of the inhabitants of Alma-Gare. In addition, of course, press coverage also served to exert pressure on an intransigent *Municipalité*.

It seems, moreover, that despite the APU's claim to prioritize negotiation over action, the activists sometimes consciously orchestrated opportunities for protest, since these served to attract publicity and press attention. There also appears to have been a certain ritualized element in these events, whereby the APU would make urgent demands which it had no real expectation of having met. The events surrounding an occupation of the building site at Barbe d'Or cast some light on the way relations worked between the APU and the construction organizations.[112] The *Toit Familial*, a *société d'économie mixte*, had been assigned the task of constructing the new housing at Barbe d'Or, and the APU claimed the right to participate in determining the form of this new housing. When, in November 1976, the APU felt that it was being marginalized in this process, they sent a telegram to *Toit Familial*: 'Stop construction barbe d'or we await negotiations.'[113] This gesture was clearly intended to have more dramatic impact than efficacy, particularly since the APU had already taken the decision to occupy the building site at 3.30pm on the very same day. Half an hour before the occupation, activists distributed leaflets explaining their case to the site workers and calling for their cooperation and solidarity:

> Why construct housing that you'll never live in, because YOU know,
> **THAT THE COLLECTIVE BLOCKS**
> **are for rabbits!!!**
> **ALL TOGETHER IN THE STRUGGLE**[114]

The protesters made it clear that other occupations might follow, but the main thrust of the leaflet was to establish a degree of solidarity between the demonstrators and the construction workers, while tapping into the theme of the division of labour and the separation between those who produce a product and those who use it. The protesters moved on to the site, held a small rally, made the stirring call, 'All together in the struggle, be ready whatever the cost to see that our *quartier*, our town, is built with the participation of those who use it',[115] and then left. Their action was planned to gain publicity for their views and reinforce a collective sense of purpose and, as ever, the initiative was presented

[112] This occupation took place on 10 November 1976. An earlier one had occurred on 28 March 1975.

[113] CSCV/APU, speech prepared for occupation of Barbe d'Or, Roubaix, 10 November 1976, p. 2. AIR.

[114] 'Aux travailleurs du bâtiment du chantier "Barbe d'Or"', pamphlet, nd. AIR. Capitalized, underlined and bold effect in original.

[115] CSCV/APU, speech prepared for occupation of Barbe d'Or, Roubaix, 10 November 1976, p. 2. AIR.

by the activists as the *population* taking over the site. In response to the action, and in contrast to the urgency implied by the APU's telegram, the president of *Toit Familial* wrote to the APU six days later, with no little irony:

> We were very surprised to receive your telegram of the 10th inst. and we required the report of the press in order to understand that it referred to the 'Barbe d'Or' operation.... This dossier has obtained its building permit, was submitted to the Department's *Direction de l'Equipement* several months ago, has obtained its funding and has had its programme given the go ahead [*l'ordre de service lancé*]. Consequently, we are terribly sorry that we are unable – as you would wish – to stop the construction.[116]

The patronizing tone of the letter offers an insight into the nature of the relationship between the APU and one of the 'official' participants of the planning process.

The sense of occasion created by media coverage was often reinforced by the creation of festive moments – *fêtes* or parties – open to the whole *quartier*. Sometimes these events were held on 1 May, in this way linking them to a radical, workers' tradition. On 1 May 1975, for example, a parade of clowns moved through the *quartier* and the APU coordinated the appropriation of the wasteground for a playspace. In November 1975 the APU organized a day during which 'outsiders' were invited to visit the *quartier*. There were presentations on the history of Alma-Gare and the visitors were invited into homes for a meal and to chat with the residents about the events in the *quartier*. Afterwards, a play was staged on the subject of renewal in Alma-Gare and there was music and dancing. Once again, this action served both to reinforce the collective identity of the *quartier* and to encourage the visitors to see beyond the definition of *courée* slum and understand Alma-Gare as 'home' to a section of Roubaix's population. Even in moments of crisis, the *fête* was used as a means of imparting a sense of unity: on 2 July 1977, when the councillors were visiting Alma-Gare and the mayor had made a statement reconfirming that the area was to be demolished, the APU organized a *fête des habitants* in rue du Fort Frasez to celebrate the renovation of the two street-front houses. Later that same year, when the *schéma directeur* was accepted, the victory was marked by another *fête*, held on 24 October: 'WE HAVE THUS WON A VICTORY For us the inhabitants and workers of Alma, it is important to mark this victory: EVERYONE to the party ... .'[117] Yet another celebration was held on 1 May 1980: in the morning there were presentations at the headquarters of the APU, and in the afternoon there was the inauguration of the building site at Fontenoy-Frasez by some of the elderly residents of the *quartier*.

---

[116] Letter from president, *Toit Familial* to Rodger Leman, APF, 16 November 1976. AIR.

[117] '11 Octobre 1977: Un succès important pour le quartier', nd. AIR. Capitalized and underlined in original.

Finally, it is worth remarking that many of the tactics discussed in this section involved an element of game-playing. The appropriation of the role of the *Municipalité* or the rehousing organizations by the activists was marked by a certain playfulness. This form of activity by marginal groups has, of course, a long historical pedigree – the robber king in the Court of Miracles, medieval and renaissance festivals that mocked the religious hierarchy, early modern processions where town councils and guilds were the target, and the 'world turned upside down' of carnival. The conventional argument is that these were all actions tolerated by authority as means of reducing social tensions, but in the case of Alma-Gare, the actions were not sanctioned by the *Municipalité* and instead aimed to create a social solidarity through which its authority might be challenged.

'Cela fera du bien pour les autres qui viendront après'

The APU's attempts to promote Alma-Gare as a social entity marked by cohesion and cooperation was underpinned by the promotion of a collective memory that legitimated these efforts.

APU activists took every opportunity to recount their own history. For example, they produced a play entitled 'La vie et l'action des habitants' ('The Life and the Action of the Inhabitants'), which was performed in the school canteen in the rue des Anges in December 1975 and offered a simplified parable of *rénovation* and urban change. Moreover, the first issue of the newsletter *l'Atelier* in 1977 outlined the history and listed the achievements of the APU, numerous newspaper articles retraced its activities and, in planning their meetings in the 'Little Guide for our Street Meetings', the activists decided that the first meeting should open with an outline of their own history: 'recount a short history of the *atelier*' and list the 'the results arrived at'.[118] In the context of this collective memory, the meaning of the *courées* themselves was reassessed and they began to assume, at least partially, a positive aspect. Without denying the terrible living conditions households had experienced (and continued to experience), the APU promoted the myth of a cohesive community that had flourished in the spatial arrangement of this housing. It offered a Marxist explanation for the presence of the *courées*: in order to ensure the reproduction of the workforce there had been a division of labour between the *bourgeoisie* and the *petite-bourgeoisie*, whereby the former invested in industrial activity and the latter invested in a specific form of 'capitalisme rentier'.[119] They

[118] CSCV/APU, 'Petit Guide pour nos réunions de Rue', 28.2.77, folder, 'Groupe de Travail, "Réhabilitation" '. AIR.

[119] APU, 'Roubaix: L'APU. Naissance d'un mouvement populaire de résistance aux expulsions', p. 14.

pointed out that, from as early as 1900, the conditions of this housing had been criticized, but not, they argued, because of the levels of hygiene, 'but rather because such concentrations of workers create conditions detrimental to local industry, by favouring the development of a class consciousness and a system of close mutual support amongst all the inhabitants of the *cours*'.[120] It was this 'close mutual support' that, the APU claimed, had become the heritage of their own struggle: 'One could say that the thing that gives strength to the movement in the *courées* in Roubaix – its durability, its imaginative power in its objectives and in the forms of its actions, its partial successes – is its strong and vibrant popular roots.'[121] This perspective opened up the possibility of reappraising the *courées*, and consequently this architectural form, once universally and unambiguously vilified, came to assume certain positive aspects, both economic and social:

> A low rent, proximity to work and to the town centre, a simple and active form of solidarity, at ground level, and a history too – a history of individuals, some of whom, after more than sixty years, still live in the house in which they were born. And more than this, a collective history, a class history. And so, they say that they wish to keep their houses, and want to be helped in restoring them, to salvage the best, to demolish the most run-down in order to build in their place new housing and collective infrastructure for the *quartier*.[122]

The individual and collective histories of the *courées* were, according to the APU, ignored or suppressed by the most powerful actors in the town. In an act of mutual support, the CIL and the *Municipalité* had emptied the *courées* of much of the workforce, installing them in either CIL or HLM housing and leaving only the most economically marginalized in the old housing. The place of the workers was taken by immigrant populations, who were used by the

[120] '... mais plutôt parce que de telles concentrations ouvrières créaient des conditions préjudiciables à l'industrie locale, en favorisant le développement d'un sentiment de classe et d'un entr'aide étroite entre tous les habitants des cours.' Ibid., p. 14.

[121] 'On pourrait dire que ce qui fait la force du mouvement des courées à Roubaix – sa durée, son pouvoir "imaginant" dans les objectifs et dans les formes de luttes, ses succès partiels – ce sont ses fortes et vivaces racines populaires.' Prouvost, 'Roubaix : L'APU 2. stratégie du capital et stratégie populaire', p. 13. Here again emerges the tension in the APU position, for while it constantly sought to valorize Alma-Gare as a *quartier populaire*, rather than a working-class area in the strictest sense of the term, it never managed to renounce entirely its aspirations to participate in a class struggle.

[122] '... un faible loyer, la proximité du travail et du centre-ville, une solidarité simple et active, à ras de terre, une histoire aussi – histoire individuelle, pour certains ils sont nés dans la maison qu'ils occupent actuellement après plus de soixante ans, et plus encore histoire collective, histoire de classe. Alors ils disent vouloir garder leur maison, vouloir qu'on les aide à les restaurer, récupérer les meilleures, démolir les plus abîmées pour y reconstruire des logements neufs et des équipements collectifs pour le quartier, à la place.' 'Roubaix: L'APU. Naissance d'un mouvement populaire', p. 16.

industrialists to keep wages down. In time, the *courées* became a target of *rénovation* in order to satisfy real estate interests and to liberate the town's social services from the weight of the *courée* population.[123] This history brought the APU to a present in which, they considered, the Socialist administration of Roubaix had betrayed the popular classes. From this perspective there were two possible futures: one in which the *Municipalité* realigned itself with its natural support base, and another where the administration 'sold out' completely to the tertiary dream:

> The municipality must now express its views on this point: does it want to build a popular *quartier* with and for the workers? Or, on the other hand, does it want to build a residential *quartier*, determined by the Mercure operation and the projects for new roadways, where it will content itself by reserving certain enclaves (Magasins Généraux, Barbe d'Or, the rehabilitated block of rue de France, rue Vallon) for the former inhabitants? ... Is it realistic to base the future of Roubaix on a possible development of the tertiary sector?
> Isn't this where the real trap lies?[124]

One of the elements that linked the past of the *quartier* to the present, and from there to the future to which the APU aspired, was the continued presence of the elderly in Alma-Gare. For the APU, the elderly offered evidence of continuity in a situation where many of the residents of Alma-Gare were new arrivals in the *quartier*, having fled clearance operations in other parts of the town. It was essential that the elderly should be seen to wish to remain in the area, for, without them, any claim to historical continuity – to the *quartier* as an entity that existed across time and not just in space – would begin to sound hollow. This theme was clearly present, for example, in the APU's initiative to rehouse *Memère*. In this act, the activists were symbolically rehousing the *quartier*, its memories and its experiences. Moreover, the elderly came to represent the iniquities of the renewal process – exposed and vulnerable to a process that stripped away all that was familiar to them. It was not by chance, therefore, that it was stories involving the elderly that captured the imagination of Alma-Gare's population. It was recounted, for example, that a bulldozer had crashed into the kitchen of a 76 year-old disabled woman. Then, during the following night, pillagers stole the lead from the water main in the house next door, and when the woman awoke she found she had no water. Another unfortunate elderly woman was watching television when the image disappeared. She went to her window to see if there was a neighbour who might help her and, to her surprise, saw a figure making off with her television aerial. Whether accurate or not, these stories served to encapsulate the problems

[123] Ibid., p. 15.
[124] CSCV and APU, 'Communique de Presse', 12 May 1977, pp. 2–3. AIR.

associated with living in an area destined for demolition, where the weakest members of society – the elderly, disabled and isolated – were left to live in fear and insecurity.

The usual practice in operations of *rénovation urbaine* or *résorption de l'habitat insalubre* was to move the elderly population of an area into a *foyer* or home, with the result that they became segregated from the rest of the development. The activists in Alma-Gare organized a trip for some of the elderly residents of the *courées* to visit a *foyer*. It was reported afterwards that they had expressed a clear dislike of what they had seen and had stated their desire to continue to live in the *quartier*, surrounded by people of different ages. According to *Le Monde*, this position provoked surprise amongst the municipal councillors:

> What astonishes them most are the determined old ladies who declare, after having visited one of these *foyers* where there is a colour television, that they certainly would not like to end their days there. 'If I have to swap for a palace and I can't get used to it', says Germaine, 'what point is there? Here, when I stick my nose out the door, the first person to appear will say hello to me ... . We need young people around us.'[125]

It should be noted that Germaine, cited above, was not a representative of the elderly drawn at random from the population of Alma-Gare, but a regular participant in the APU. She therefore echoes APU theory concerning the positive aspects of the tight social networks developed in the *courées*. This only goes to emphasis the importance the APU placed on giving the elderly of Alma-Gare a strong and dynamic voice. In another example (Figure 4.2), an old woman is featured in a cartoon strip from the APU newsletter, along with an everyman character called Jules de l'Alma, explaining why it is important to fight for the right to stay in the *quartier* and to have a say in its planning.

The sprightly and spirited old woman personifies the dynamism of the *quartier*, while, paradoxically, representing an element of the population that would have, traditionally, been considered least dynamic. Her age and years in the *quartier* present a form of memory for the struggle.

Given the importance of the elderly for Alma-Gare, both symbolically and, as discussed in Chapter Three, numerically, the APU and ABAC decided to set up a working group that directly addressed the requirements of this group for the new *quartier*. At the meeting of the *groupe des personnes âgées* of 5 January 1977, there were six people present.[126] They concluded that they would

---

[125] 'Quand Roubaix change de peau', *Le Monde* (5 May 1976), p. 24.

[126] Apart from illustrating the importance given to issues concerning the elderly, this meeting provides a good example of the hidden tactics of the principal activists of the APU; the six people present are all active members of the APU, and although it is not recorded, the style of the minutes, exemplified in the quotations above, is very close to the style of the ubiquitous Marie-Agnès Leman.

4.2 A strong voice for the elderly[127]
Reproduced from 'Roubaix: L'APU. Naissance d'un mouvement populaire de résistance aux expulsions', *Place*, no. 5, special issue on 'l'Atelier' (Autumn 1976), p. 15.

127 Jules: 'You seem to be in good form!', Elderly woman: 'That's because we're fighting', Jules: 'They want to give you a hard time too?', Elderly woman: 'They'd like to dump us who knows where in homes ... full of old folks! But we all want to live, not die in there. I hate playing cards and I haven't worked 50 years to be treated like a kid. Now I'm staying put! Youngster!'

be happy with new housing if it preserved the advantages of the old, while assuming a degree of comfort that was currently lacking, by which they meant hot water, a WC and a shower: 'to live in new [housing] might be fine if we can find in it several things that make us prefer Fort Frasez to the Magasins Généraux.'[128] They did not want apartments that were 'rabbit hutches', where they would enjoy little interaction with their neighbours, nor did they wish to be segregated from the rest of the *quartier*. They valued the possibility of stopping on the stairs and chatting with friends, sitting in a garden or watching passers-by from their window (a characteristic of traditional street-front housing). On the other hand, they did not dismiss the idea of less traditional buildings of more than two floors, so long as there were mechanisms to promote human contact: 'there could be streets "in the air", why not?'[129]

If the elderly personified the values of the past, the future was evoked by the participation of children in the APU's activities, providing this construction of Alma-Gare with a sense of continuity. The initiative to take charge of the planning of Alma-Gare was therefore not only for the present generation of residents, but also for the next:

> And the old woman, young militant who had never taken to the streets when she was working, admitted, astonished at herself, 'I would never have thought that one could do things like that', and she added, 'This will do good for those who come after [*cela fera du bien pour les autres qui viendront après*].'[130]

This helps explain the initiatives to make playing fields and play spaces with the participation of the local children. In addition, young artists were encouraged to produce murals around the *quartier* (which was also a form of visual signposting, reinforcing the distinctiveness and innovative quality of Alma-Gare), and a vacant house was made available as a base for a youth organization. This organization, called the *Jeunes Bénévoles de l'Alma Gare* (JBAG) was founded in November 1978, with the aim of undertaking various tasks in the *quartier*, including a project for a free bicycle service, although it was never very active. Finally, a great deal of thought was given to the development of the local school. After much debate within the forum of the APU it was finally decided that this should be an 'open school' of 15 classes for 300 pupils at nursery and primary school level. As an 'open school' it was intended as a school open to *all* residents of the *quartier*. This not only meant that the school facilities were to be available for training courses and night classes during the evening, but also that there was no delimited playground and children were free to move around the *quartier* when they were not in class.

---

[128] 'Commission Personnes Agées', 5 January 1977, p. 12. AIR.
[129] Ibid.
[130] 'Quand Roubaix change de peau', *Le Monde* (5 May 1976), p. 24.

Equally, adults could walk through the school during lessons, by means of walkways suspended above the classrooms. In this way, it was envisaged that the school should merge seamlessly with the *quartier* – in the words of the APU, 'the *quartier* is also the school, we want to participate in the school, and the school should play a part in the life of the *quartier*'.[131]

A key event: the production of the *carte-affiche*

The various themes discussed in this chapter come together in the production of the *carte-affiche*, drawn up in 1977 by the APU in conjunction with ABAC. This was the concrete representation of the future of the *quartier* that so many of the APU's activities had been directed towards establishing. The production of the *carte-affiche* was one of the most difficult moments for the protest movement in Alma-Gare, for it marked the first time that the APU had to venture into the realm of the planning experts, and also the first time that it had to impose a physical form on the ideas that, until then, had had the freedom and flexibility to fill the nebulous utopia developed by the activists.

ABAC described their involvement with the population of the *quartier* of Alma-Gare in the following terms:

> We, technicians, have a project, you, the inhabitants, have ideas: we confront these and elaborate them together ... . This is the first time that technicians carry out planning that allows the will of the inhabitants to be perceived. We have witnessed the emergence of a type of inhabitants capable of visualizing a way of living together, not only in their homes, but also in a group [*un ensemble*]. This plan does not reflect the concerns of planners alone. It takes into account the wishes expressed by the population.[132]

In this text, ABAC even go as far as to suggest that the act of participation encouraged the development of a *type* of resident who was capable of conceiving the Alma-Gare project in collective terms. As discussed, various working groups collaborated with ABAC to draw up a preliminary *carte-affiche*, which was then explained, refined and modified in dozens of street meetings held between 28 February and 5 March. The *carte* was then presented at a general assembly and, finally, was displayed and commented upon at the Wednesday market and posted at various locations around the *quartier*. In this

---

[131] '... le quartier c'est aussi l'école, nous voulons participer à l'école, et l'école doit être partie prenante dans la vie du quartier.' Cited in Lemonier, 'La concertation produit le nouveau quartier', in A. Mollet (ed.), *Quand les Habitants Prennent la Parole* (Paris: Plan Construction, 1981), p. 225.

[132] 'Avec les techniciens de l'ABAC et l'Atelier Populaire de l'urbanisme les habitants de l'Alma-Gare ont élaboré leur projet d'aménagement du quartier', *La Voix du Nord* (19 March 1977), p. z118.

way, the *carte*'s legitimacy was considered to have been established through the widespread participation of the population of Alma-Gare.

In its final form the *carte-affiche*, dated 8 March 1977, was the fruit of four months of activity and, as with all the APU's initiatives, it was presented as the outcome of a collective effort and a common will:

> WE, INHABITANTS OF THE *QUARTIER*, ORGANIZED WITH THE CSCV AND THE APU, WE WANT THE NEW *QUARTIER* TO BE CONSTRUCTED ACCORDING TO THE IDEAS THAT WE HAVE DEFINED IN THIS PLAN ALONG WITH THE TECHNICIANS.[133]

The introduction to the *carte-affiche* evoked the threat of the bulldozer and the debilitating impact of more than ten years of uncertainty over the future of Alma-Gare:

> IN ALMA-GARE IT'S MORE THAN TEN YEARS THAT THEY SPEAK TO US OF A *RENOVATION-BULLDOZER* THAT RAZES THE WHOLE *QUARTIER* AND CHASES AWAY THE INHABITANTS.[134]

The APU and ABAC proposed an alternative future in their *carte-affiche*, one that was founded upon three principle points:

> WE WANT
> 1. to stay in the *quartier*
> 2. to keep our streets and a part of the present buildings which will be 'renovated' ... . We will only keep the buildings on the street, not the *courées* (except for one or two) ... .
> 3. in the spaces liberated by the demolitions, we want housing, services (post office, playgroups, a clinic, etc ...), social infrastructure (schools, secondary school, sports hall etc ...), shops and employment activities (workshops ... , artisans ...).[135]

Point 1, 'to stay in the *quartier*', was, as we have seen, an enduring theme of the APU. Point 3 reflected the APU's belief that a *quartier* was made up not only of housing, but also of social facilities, infrastructure, commerce and employment. Point 2, with its reference to renovation, was the most contentious, since it challenged the basic assumptions of the *Municipalité de Roubaix* and ORSUCOMN. The official project for Alma-Gare rested on the 'common-sense' assumption that the *courées* were slums, and therefore could and should be demolished. The fact that the residents of these 'slums' themselves demanded that a certain proportion of the buildings be retained directly challenged the logic of *résorption*.

ABAC and the APU proposed that the social interest of retaining a proportion of the old housing stock rested on four arguments. First, that these

133 Carte-Affiche, 8 March 1977. AIR. Capitalized in original.
134 Ibid. Capitalized in original.
135 Ibid. Capitalized and underlined in original.

buildings were a form of 'cultural heritage' that represented an important moment in the history of the provision of housing in France and possessed spatial qualities that it would be regrettable to lose:

> This patrimony is also a cultural heritage [*patrimoine culturel*], representing an important moment for social housing in France ... . In addition it possesses a certain number of spatial qualities which it would be a pity to lose: a rich relationship between public spaces and private spaces (the structure of the courtyard, street-front houses and their relation to the street, etc ...).[136]

The second argument returned to the deterministic theme that the built environment was the support of social life, and to destroy the buildings of Alma-Gare meant destroying the collective life of the *quartier*: 'It is in this patrimony that the social practices that form the basis of the present *quartier* have developed.'[137] Third, Alma-Gare was characterized by an intensive *vie de quartier* and highly developed social interaction, and the APU and ABAC felt that it would be difficult to recreate this social life in new housing. Finally, they considered that Alma-Gare's social life was at the heart of the spirit of creativity – *esprit de créativité* – that allowed the population to develop an original and innovative view of the future.[138] Following the logic of these arguments, ABAC and the APU were suggesting that the possibility of creating an innovative future derived directly from the accumulated experience of living in a distinct form of urban morphology, with the social relations and 'close mutual support' that it encouraged. Where the buildings could not be preserved, the new developments should seek to reproduce this particular organization of space so that the social practices associated with the *courées* could be perpetuated. Their aim in retaining a proportion of the buildings in Alma-Gare was to preserve *la vie collective* and, tapping into themes of spatial determinism, *réhabilitation* was regarded as a means of influencing the spatial arrangement of the *quartier* in order to reinforce social cohesion and avoid the production of the desert-like space found in public housing projects:

> 'Rehabilitation' is a privileged moment for redefining the roles that spaces and buildings are called upon to play in the *quartier* (or the town?). It is at this point that it is possible to decide to change the way a space or a building is used, to change its purpose. In particular, it is the moment to reflect how to develop and reinforce the social life of the *quartier*, the

136 ABAC, 'La Restructuration du quartier de l'Alma-Gare', nd, p. 2. AIR, folder 'Groupe de Travail, "Réhabilitation"'.

137 Ibid.

138 'A "Gare-Alma" (expérience qui intéresse des aménageurs du monde entier) la restructuration du quartier va remplacer une "Rénovation-bulldozer" désormais condamnée', *La Voix du Nord* (19 February 1977), p. z103. These points are also made in a two-page policy document, CSCV/APU, 'La "Réhabilitation" dans le quartier de Gare-Alma', 10 February 1977. AIR.

> neighbourliness, solidarity and collective creation that give it its great richness. This social life is made possible by, and can develop thanks to certain spatial solutions that are in opposition to the organization of spaces that one finds in the ZUPs and the HLM developments: a veritable desert.[139]

The production of the *carte* represented the capacity of the inhabitants of Alma-Gare to master the space of their *quartier*, and presented the *Municipalité*, ORSUCOMN and the other organizations involved with a striking representation of Alma-Gare as a coherent entity rather than a collection of individual housing units or blocks. It is the reactions of the *Municipalité* and ORSUCOMN that we turn to consider in the last part of this chapter.

Responses to the APU challenge

From the outset, the events in Alma-Gare are marked by the inability of the *Municipalité* and the APU to find a common point from which to initiate a constructive dialogue. The result was often bewilderment, frustration and resentment, not only for the *Municipalité* – 'Dialogue isn't easy ... because they are used to mass demonstrations and marches. It isn't always pleasant for the officials'[140] – but also for the activists: 'It isn't great. It's always up to us to maintain the effort. I think that we must be starting to get tired – they could make a bit of an effort, that would allow us to go further and perhaps it would ease the efforts of the APU.'[141]

The *Municipalité* deeply resented the APU's readiness to resort to confrontational tactics rather than relying on discussion and negotiation. For example, on 15 November 1977 there was a serious stand-off between the APU and representatives of the *Municipalité* who had learned of the activists' intention to stage a symbolic walk-out from a meeting they were all due to attend with the residents of Alma-Gare. At 6.00 pm, half an hour before the meeting was to start, the four councillors involved called the offices of *Nord Eclair*, one of the local newspapers, and explained that they had learned from dependable sources that the APU had decided to embark on a consultation boycott – 'une grève de concertation' – and that its representatives planned to read a declaration and then leave the meeting room. The councillors stated:

---

139 CSCV/APU, 'La "Réhabilitation" dans le quartier de Gare-Alma', 10 February 1977, p. 2. AIR.

140 Victor Provo, Mayor of Roubaix, cited in, 'Quand Roubaix change de peau', *Le Monde* (5 May 1976), p. 24.

141 APU, 'No3, Urbanisme, logement, promoteurs et quartier', 28 August/2 September, no year, but 1977 or after, p. 1. AIR.

> At the municipal council, we are very much in agreement over the policy to take regarding consultation. Participation is not dictated by one side or the other. We have been elected to direct a policy along with the population. But there is no question of pressure groups forcing us to draw up a policy for which we have not been elected.[142]

The frustration felt by Roubaix's councillors at actions of this kind by the APU is well illustrated by the following extract from an interview with Bernard Carton (H), Deputy Mayor for Planning, carried out for a Master's thesis by a member of the APU in Alma-Gare:

> H: We've put services [*permanences*] at their disposal, we've done a load of things, well, it must be said that on experience, they never come forward without blowing the difficulties and conflicts out of proportion and, generally, in a dialogue with the Municipality that's not always frank ... it's a deliberate choice by the APU, they do it that way, ah well, now I'm beginning to get used to it, they use conflictual situations and never discussion or negotiation.
> F: Why do you think that is?
> H: Well, I don't know why ... Me, listen, in a word, I'm genuinely open.
> F: Yes, but you've been seeing this phenomenon for some time now, do you have a way to interpret it?
> H: I don't know, but instead of coming to me and saying there's a problem first of all, they organize a demonstration and then they come to me to say there's a problem and they make a point when there's a meeting of raising a problem regarding which they've planned a demonstration two days later, it's extraordinary that ... they do what they want, it's a method that always gives one the impression that we're in conflict ... [143]

Carton suggests that the APU did not always follow its own code of practice and often chose to embark on protest actions without first attempting to resolve an issue by discussion. Moreover, he clearly resented the conflictual nature of the APU's tactics, which, he considered, were specifically conceived to provoke the *Municipalité*.

From their particular perspectives, the *Municipalité* and the APU saw Alma-Gare as two different places, founded on two different historical narratives. It was therefore inevitable that they should also see two different futures for the area. Confronted by the attempts of the APU and APF/CSCV to construct a new identity for Alma-Gare, the *Municipalité* could hardly afford to admit that this key area for the strategic development of Roubaix had, in fact, assumed a life of its own, animated from within by the collective will of the community. There was no place in the municipal construction of Alma-Gare to allow for the population righting its own wrongs, or for the conception of the *courées*

---

[142] 'Rupture entre l'APU d'Alma-Gare et la Municipalité', *Nord Eclair* (16 November, 1977), no page nos. ANE, dossier 'Roubaix 1', folder 'Alma-Gare'.

[143] Verbrackel, 'L'Atelier populaire d'urbanisme de l'Alma-Gare à Roubaix', p. 166.

as something other than a homogeneous mass of misery. The *Municipalité* rejected the idea that either the social or physical arrangement of the *courées* might have positive aspects and thus saw no justification for preserving elements of the urban fabric. Equally, since the *Municipalité* had adopted a stance against the town's immigrant population, the APU claim to remain – 'rester sur place' – was clearly unacceptable to the town hall.

Later, however, as the concept of public involvement began to gain ground in planning theory, municipal publications began to talk of 'consultation' with the population. In the municipal magazine of August 1974, in which the official plans for Alma-Gare were outlined, the *Municipalité* promised that:

> The population will be associated with the progress of this renewal. It will not only be called to witness the demolitions, but it will be given the means to express its needs and desires. The problems of the *quartier* will be discussed with its representatives.[144]

However, the APU did not consider that this approach went far enough and, moreover, regarded it as a means to contain protest within the existing political and planning structures.

Generally, the *Municipalité de Roubaix* was compelled to respond to APU initiatives and rarely succeeded in taking any of its own; indeed, their appraisal of the events at Alma-Gare was, for the most part, founded on a desire to maintain the status quo. From this, for example, sprang the *Municipalité*'s tactic of challenging the legitimacy of the claims of the APU and APF/CSCV to represent the population of Alma-Gare. The activists, they were always quick to point out, had been elected by nobody, while the *Municipalité* had a democratic mandate and was acting in the best interests of the population:

> We do not accept the APU as a counter-municipal council in this *quartier*, nor do we accept that it acts towards the elected representatives on the basis of a trial of strength [*il agisse en termes de rapport de forces avec les élus*].
>
> Because nobody has elected ... the members of the APU. They speak in the name of others, but without being representatives of the population as a whole.[145]

The theme of the activists' non-democratic tactics emerged again in the mayor's resentment at the APU's suggestion that a member of the *Atelier* should accompany social workers on their visits to families due to be rehoused. Indeed, Prouvost went as far as to suggest that the APU was capable of

---

[144] 'La population sera associée au déroulement de cette rénovation. Elle ne sera pas seulement appelée à constater les démolitions, mais on lui donnera les moyens d'exprimer ses besoins et ses désirs. Les problèmes du quartier seront discutés avec ses représentants.' 'Trois autres quartiers changent de visage', p. 13.

[145] 'Rupture entre l'APU d'Alma-Gare et la Municipalité', *Nord Eclair* (16 November 1977), no page nos. ANE, dossier 'Roubaix 1', folder 'Alma-Gare'.

manipulating the population in order to 'yoke' them to their own ideology. Just as the APU saw itself as nurturing the *collective* potential of the population of Alma-Gare, so the *Municipalité de Roubaix* saw themselves as protecting the rights of this group as *individuals*:

> If we, as elected representatives, are convinced of the importance of the population being able to organize itself to ensure that it is represented, we are, at the same time, guarantors of individual liberties. The inhabitants have the right to choose the path they wish in order to achieve their demands or their wishes.
>
> If the privileged consultation in which we have engaged with the APU, and which we intend to pursue, ends up in yoking the entire population [*enfermer l'ensemble des habitants dans un carcan*], we cannot be in agreement.[146]

Of course, one might also suggest that behind the *Municipalité*'s statements about the APU's lack of legitimacy lay a concern to protect its own privileged position of authority in the urban sphere and prevent the decentralization of local power. It was only latterly that the *Municipalité* began to pay something more than politically expedient lip service to the idea of participation and, ultimately, even claimed the initiative as their own.

As the protests in Alma-Gare gained momentum, so the *Municipalité* sought to downplay the significance of the APU's actions. In 1976, *Le Monde* cited the first deputy mayor of Roubaix: ' "They're good types who take an avid interest in their living conditions", says M. Clèrambeaux with a hint of paternalism. "It's an interesting initiative, and even a little touching" '[147] Prouvost himself spoke of 'The operation at Alma-Gare ... we want it to be exemplary. It already is on the level of consultation with the population',[148] without making any reference to the APU whatsoever. Instead, he chose to depict his Socialist councillors as the dynamic element in the developments in Alma-Gare: 'For several months, the Socialist councillors of Roubaix have been holding periodic meetings with the inhabitants of Alma-Gare, in the course of which a productive exchange of ideas has been established concerning the way in which this new *quartier* should be conceived.'[149] In a newspaper interview just before the 1977 elections, Prouvost once again spoke in glowing terms of the innovations at Alma-Gare, but once more failed to mention the involvement of the APU, choosing instead to comment on the collective work of his councillors, the planners and the residents of the area: 'Moreover, this operation

---

[146] Reported in, Atelier Populaire d'Urbanisme, 'Rapport d'Activités 78, APU', nd, pp. 36–7. AIR.

[147] Cited in 'Quand Roubaix change de peau', *Le Monde* (5 May 1976), p. 24.

[148] Prouvost, cited in, 'Vers une politique de l'Urbanisme', *Le Métro* (March 1977), Roubaix edn, p. 5.

[149] 'Alma-Gare: Un plan d'aménagement', *Le Métro*, (January 1977), Roubaix edn, p. 7.

is now cited as an example, not only in France, but also in Europe, for the way in which the elected representatives, the technicians and the inhabitants are collectively compiling the documents for planning and infrastructure.'[150]

Given its unwillingness to accept the legitimacy of the APU and its tendency to marginalize the role of the activists in Alma-Gare, why then did the *Municipalité* agree to support the *Atelier*'s request for its own technical assistance? First, although the agreement of the town hall was officially required to enable ABAC to take up official residence in Alma-Gare, the *Municipalité* would have found it difficult to justify the refusal of such an innovative and high-profile project. Second, it is possible that, in agreeing to allow ABAC to work with the APU, the *Municipalité* hoped that this gesture would have been enough to satisfy the demands of these 'good types'. Indeed, since ABAC were *urbanistes* like its own planners, the *Municipalité* may well have hoped that they would have shown the activists the logic of 'common sense' and that they would explain to them exactly why the official plans for Alma-Gare should go ahead. In other words, the *Municipalité* presumed that ABAC would have accepted the institutional view of Alma-Gare as *logements insalubres* and, in turn, would have transmitted this view to the *Atelier*. However, as we have seen, the arrival of ABAC only served to contribute to the sense of autonomy of the *quartier* and, furthermore, the planners from Paris infuriated the *Municipalité* by encouraging the population to question the validity of what was going on around them and to elaborate their own vision of the future *quartier*.

This alternative vision took the tangible form of the *carte-affiche*. When confronted with this interpretation of Alma-Gare, Prouvost rejected the proposals out of hand, not only on the grounds that they did not correspond to the general outline laid down by the working group for Alma-Gare, but also because the APU was seen, yet again, to have overstepped the bounds of its competence. Bernard Carton, Deputy Mayor for Planning, expressed his reservations in terms of the plan's impact on the traffic flow in Roubaix and the possible isolation of the *quartier*,[151] but the conflict became crystallized over the issue of *réhabilitation*. The *Municipalité* claimed to be perplexed by the growing emphasis on the idea of preserving and renovating a proportion of the area's housing stock, and Clérambeaux, President of SAEN, *député du Nord* and First Deputy Mayor, attempted to present this development as an impediment to progress and to depict the activists as reactionary: 'You have asked to be rehoused in the same area ... but as things proceed, you are

[150] Prouvost, cited in, 'Roubaix: Nos lecteurs posent des questions aux candidats', *Nord Eclair* (11 March 1977), p. 9.

[151] 'Une carte pour la rénovation de l'Alma-gare: Les habitants sont devenus urbanistes', *Nord Eclair* (17 March 1977).

becoming the curator of the state of things as they stand [*conservateur de l'état des choses existant*].'[152] The APU, for its part, refused to be categorized as 'passéistes' or 'conservateurs',[153] and explained in a press statement in May 1977 that 'our project is not to make a museum of Gare Alma'.[154] For the *Municipalité de Roubaix*, however, a version of Alma-Gare that contained old housing, even in renovated form, was suggestive of a period from which it was trying to distance itself. It also directly opposed the municipal vision of Roubaix as a new tertiary centre inhabited by a population that would serve this sector's employment requirements. In the eyes of the *Municipalité*, renovation would reproduce the very image of Roubaix which it was seeking to escape.

As for ORSUCOMN, the very *raison d'être* of this organization was challenged by the APU's reappraisal of the *courées*. ORSUCOMN viewed the area in technical terms, and employed statistics to confirm its analysis. Moreover, all these statistics indicated the negative aspects of Alma-Gare – high unemployment, low levels of schooling, high concentration of immigrants and other 'problems'. The issue of *insalubrité* was a particular sticking point, since this was a criterion applied by ORSUCOMN itself, with the implication that it was a rational, objective, scientific measurement. The APU, however, insisted that Alma-Gare was more than the sum of its statistics and spoke of the area as a collective, social entity. With the assistance of ABAC, the APU challenged ORSUCOMN's objectivity, as did each member of the population who protested that they considered their house was a home rather than a slum.[155]

In the midst of the crisis provoked by Prouvost's rejection of the *carte-affiche* and his announcement that Alma-Gare would be demolished, Carton stated that he did not wish to burn the bridges – '*couper les ponts*' – with the APU, but warned that this view was not shared by all his colleagues. This, it appears, held true as much for the Communists as for the Socialists. Emile Duhamel, a deputy mayor and leader of the Communist group in the town hall, made his party's position clear at a meeting of the Municipal Council in 1977: 'We want to extend dialogue, consultation and openness towards everyone and towards the different organizations that represent them: no speakers privileged *a priori* and no recognition of a single organization as having a calling to speak or express

152 Clérambeaux, cited in *La Voix du Nord* (8 November 1976).

153 'La Définition de nouveaux objectifs pour la rénovation du quartier du l'Alma remet en cause le projet de l'ABAC et de l'Atelier Populaire d'Urbanisme', *La Voix du Nord* (14 May 1977), p. z126.

154 CSCV and APU, 'Communiqué de Presse', 12 May 1977, p. 2. AIR.

155 ORSUCOMN's position with respect to the ABAC was especially hostile. In large part, this was because the two organizations were very similar – that is, they were both technical organizations, involving urban planners, sociologists and legal experts, and they both laid claim to expertise in the same field, albeit from two very different perspectives.

itself on behalf of a whole *quartier* or undertaking.'[156] Furthermore, when the APU invited each of the political elements in the municipal council to discuss separately the *carte-affiche*, Duhamel left little doubt as to his position: 'We will not accept an undertaking that aims at compromising municipal solidarity.'[157] Ironically, in this same period Communist councillors in neighbouring Lille had decided to support the action of the CSCV in a *quartier* of an area called Fives threatened by *rénovation*. The irony was all the greater given that this *quartier* was also called Alma. Perhaps, therefore, beneath Duhamel's concern about the unity of Roubaix lay a deeper concern about the location of power in Roubaix's urban politics and the threat that the APU posed to the *status quo*. In fact, Duhamel was explicit about his concerns over the divisive nature of the activists' actions in Alma-Gare: 'we have gone too far in allowing ABAC and the APU to think that they were going to be able to build an independent city [*cité*] outside the town [*ville*] as a whole.'[158]

The climb-down that followed on the part of the *Municipalité* over the *carte-affiche* in general, and the issue of *réhabilitation* in particular, must in part be attributed to the fact that the Alma-Gare counter-project had become a social reality to the extent that it was impossible to ignore it and fall back on the former construction of Alma-Gare. Although the activists liked to emphasize their long-term aims, I would argue that it was largely through their *actions ponctuelles* that they were able to establish this counter-project and counter-place. In other words, faced with large turn-outs of protesters, clever protest 'gimmicks' (such as drawing water from the municipal fountain) and the presence of the local press, the *Municipalité* was often forced to give ground on the particular issue at stake. At this point, the *Municipalité* not only jeopardized its own authority, albeit in a small way, but, more importantly, gave recognition to the version of Alma-Gare championed by the APU. Whenever the *Municipalité* agreed to meet the demands of the protesters, it was giving credence to the idea of Alma-Gare as a dynamic, innovative community and, with every small victory won, this version of Alma-Gare assumed a greater resonance, not only for the protesters themselves, but also for those who observed the events from outside the *quartier*. Indeed, this process was recognized to some extent by the activists themselves in their own assessment of the events in Alma-Gare: 'By means of concrete actions we show that our claims are legitimate, realizable and marked by a collective instinct ... . Through popular mobilization, we force the public powers to take charge of

[156] Duhamel, cited in M. Delberghe, 'L'avenir du quartier Alma-Gare, III – Pour les élus, c'est l'apprentissage de la concertation', *La Voix du Nord*, (29 June 1977) no page nos. ANE, dossier 'Roubaix 1', folder 'Alma-Gare'.

[157] Duhamel, cited in ibid.

[158] Duhamel, cited in ibid.

what initially emerged from an initiative of the inhabitants.'[159] So it was that, in effect, the APU planted the seed of a new vision of Alma-Gare, and the *Municipalité*, unwittingly, nurtured this seed by giving it a degree of recognition.

Alma-Gare gradually ceased to be a passive entity to be laid bare by the bulldozer and became an dynamic element in the urban politics of Roubaix – a *quartier* capable of making decisions about its own identity, and therefore about its own past, present and future. Additionally, the APU's actions drew attention to the political dimensions hidden within the supposedly non-political activity of slum clearance. When the APU was able to demonstrate the existence of contradictions within the institutional construction of Alma-Gare, confronting it with ideas of solidarity, creativity, initiative and so on, it had the opportunity to insert its own vision. The earliest stages of this process were the slowest, but once the idea of Alma-Gare as a vibrant *quartier* became conceivable, it began to gather momentum until it brought its own 'mutual corroboration',[160] to borrow Douglas's phrase. Alma-Gare received visits from the press, from television stations, from professionals in the field of architecture and planning, from academics and from students, including, in March 1977, engineers from the prestigious *Ecole Nationale des Ponts et Chaussées*.

As the new construction of Alma-Gare took form, the *Municipalité de Roubaix* began to make efforts to appropriate the initiatives of the APU and its supporters.[161] For example, at the end of 1977 the *Municipalité* created Roubaix's first *comités du quartier*. It announced that every *quartier* in the town should have a committee to represent its interests and communicate its views to the town hall. Moreover, the *Municipalité* began to claim credit for the activity at Alma-Gare. When the Alma-Gare story finally took the shape of a glossy publication, *Roubaix Alma-Gare. Lutte urbaine et architecture*, published in 1982, it was Bernard Carton, Deputy Mayor for Planning, who wrote the introduction. In this text he recounts the *Municipalité*'s history of Alma-Gare, blaming modernist planning initiatives on central government and

---

159 CSCV/APU, 'Après 5 ans d'existence l'APU: 2 méthodes de fonctionnement. Les documents de l'Alma Gare', no. 17, nd (*c.*1978), p. 2. AIR.

160 Douglas, *How Institutions Think* (Syracuse: Syracuse University Press, 1986), p. 92.

161 In contrast, ORSUCOMN never came to terms with the position of the APU with respect to Alma-Gare. The two visions of place were to remain incompatible and, significantly, when an organization was sought to oversee the construction of the new *quartier* and to manage its social and economic development, the task was assigned to the *Société d'Economie Mixte d'Aménagement et d'Equipement* rather than ORSUCOMN. The *Organisme Régional pour la Suppression des Courées de la Métropole Nord* found itself marginalized because it had been structured to respond to a version of place which, by the late 1970s, had become outdated and politically undesirable.

'technocrats' who had foisted these projects on unsuspecting city councils: 'What isn't justified in the name of technology!'[162] In his introduction, Carton resurrected the old issue of legitimacy, but this time it was not the legitimacy of the APU that was under scrutiny, but the legitimacy of the alliance of interests that had promoted modernist planning projects and had leapfrogged the local representatives of the population: '... the elected representatives are confronted by the *fait accompli* of technical rationality. When the local elected representatives lose their responsibility, it is the inhabitants themselves who are crushed by this machine that finds its legitimacy "elsewhere".'[163] The inaccessible and diffuse power of the state, he argued, had set in place a decision-making process that had marginalized local government. The solution to this crisis of legitimacy was found in the development of public participation, which forced the decision-makers to justify their actions: 'It is in giving a voice to the inhabitants that the elected representatives rediscover their legitimacy, because this voice obliges the arbitrariness of technocracy to express itself clearly on the notion of "public interest" that supposedly directs its action.'[164]

In embarking on the redevelopment of Pile, another *quartier* of Roubaix, in 1981, the *Municipalité* produced a text that examined the arguments for and against public participation in the planning process. It had clearly learned a lesson from the events at Alma-Gare – public participation was certainly an essential element in the planning process and was to be encouraged from the outset of a project, but it was a double-edged sword: 'we have seen that this participation can be neither optional [*facultative*] nor, still less, artificial [*factice*] – this results in the risk of conflictual situations and the necessity of managing them.'[165] The conclusion was that it was essential to put in place a structure that could guide the process of participation from the very beginning:

> ... it is therefore important to put, immediately, a multidisciplinary team of technicians at the disposal of the *quartier* with the brief to provide a permanent assistance to the population in order to facilitate the translation of its needs and to permit, lastly, the emergence of innovative relations between the different partners.[166]

[162] 'Que ne justifie-t-on pas au nom de la technique!' B. Carton and l'Atelier Populaire d'Urbanisme d'Alma-Gare – CSCV, 'Introduction', in *Roubaix Alma-Gare. Lutte Urbaine et Architecture*, p. 13.

[163] '... les élus sont placés devant le fait accompli de la rationalité technique. Quand les élus locaux perdent leur responsabilité, ce sont les habitants eux-mêmes qui sont écrasés par cette machine qui trouvent sa légitimité "ailleurs".' Ibid.

[164] 'C'est en donnant la parole aux habitants que les élus retrouvent leur légitimité parce que cette parole oblige l'arbitraire de la technocratie à s'expliquer clairement sur la notion "d'intérêt public" qui conduit soi-disant son action.' Ibid.

[165] 'Plan du Développement du Quartier du Pile à Roubaix: Mise en place d'une Equipe d'Animation Pluridisciplinaire'/ 'Opération du Pile', Ville de Roubaix, 3 February 1981, p. 4. ADN, 1284W/285, folder 'Aménagement du Quartier du Pile'.

[166] Ibid., p. 1.

Finally, based on the experience of Alma-Gare the *Municipalité* assessed that the need to institutionalize participation was particularly great in 'poor' neighbourhoods:

> The 'Alma-Gare' operation has revealed that the poorer a *quartier* is, the more it is necessary to ensure that the population is accompanied from the pre-operational stage throughout the operation in order to familiarize them with the project, maintain its dynamic and permit real participation.[167]

A postscript to Alma-Gare

Although the APU activists felt able to claim a remarkable victory, having successfully challenged the dominant power geometry in Roubaix and imposed a new vision of their *quartier*, this position could not be sustained. As noted, once the *quartier* had been planned and construction and renovation had begun, the APU increasingly came to emphasize the importance of stimulating socioeconomic development in Alma-Gare, but this, as one activist pointed out, was much more difficult than dealing with issues of bricks and mortar: 'Planning was hard, but the population was united around the same goal. The economy is less obvious. Less obvious than getting people interested in their housing.'[168] Thus, as physical planning became less important and the management of the area became more so, the APU began to lose its direction. The activists leant more heavily on institutional expertise and gradually they assumed the institutional perspective which they had so long fought to avoid. ABAC too became increasingly marginalized as architecture gave way to management and the initiative for the development of the *quartier* was assumed by the *Equipe Opérationelle Permanente pour Alma-Gare*. As a response to this, in 1978 ABAC changed its composition to one sociologist, one legal and financial adviser and only one architect. The establishment of the *régie technique*, with its stress on the facilitation of social coordination, was another response to this change in emphasis. Inevitably, in taking charge of the socioeconomic development of the *quartier*, the activists had to accept that they would assume the role of 'managers' in the eyes of the population. The alternative would have been to surrender this role to the *Municipalité* and remain experimental and provocative, but surrendering this role would have also signified surrendering the power they had struggled for so long to obtain.

---

167 Ibid.

168 'L'urbanisme c'était dur, mais il y avait unité de la population autour du même but. L'économie c'est moins évident. Moins évident que d'intéresser les gens à leur logement.' APU activist cited in Mattëi, 'Urbanisme populaire et économie de quartier', p. 20.

Despite the many initiatives, the task of setting up an oasis of economic productivity in a desert of economic decline proved to be beyond the scope of the APU. Its construction of Alma-Gare, a construction founded upon utopian principles, was not strong enough to sustain itself in the face of the difficulties of Roubaix as a whole, which could not escape its image as a run-down textile town, a sink-hole for unemployment and a breeding ground for racial tension.

The impossibility of sustaining the APU's version of Alma-Gare was also partly the result of the fragility of the *quartier*'s population structure: in this highly fluid, fragmented and extremely deprived group, it was difficult to sustain a collective memory. The passageways and staircases which had been intended to perpetuate the vibrant life of the community became dark and threatening obstacles to be negotiated by the population, vandalism increased, residents failed to appropriate semi-private spaces such as the walkways in front of their houses, drugs became an increasingly serious problem, the *régie* went bankrupt, the print shop was closed, the businesses envisaged in Fontenoy-Frasez never materialized and the small commercial initiatives in the *quartier* shut down one by one. In 1986 it was estimated that some 30 to 40 per cent of houses in Alma-Gare were lying vacant.[169] The 300 underground car-parking places provided with the new project proved to be not only unnecessary, but also too dangerous to use. There were also been problems arising from the close proximity of the elderly and the young of the *quartier*, and the school reverted to normal scholastic institution, with an enclosed playground to stop the children running through the area. Today, while the inhabitants of Alma-Gare may still be consulted over decisions concerning their neighbourhood, they have no decision-making powers. The APU changed its identity to the *Association Inter-quartiers de Roubaix* (AIR), which now represents ten *quartiers* in Roubaix, serving as a channel of communication between the population and official structures, including the town hall. The activists who remain at AIR continue to regard Alma-Gare as the militant *quartier*, and their greatest achievement.

The final comment in this chapter on the events at Alma-Gare comes from central government, in the form of a document from the *Ministère de l'Environnement et du Cadre de Vie*, published in 1979, which considered 'The social management of experimental works. The example of Alma-Gare' and examined possible means to extend the innovation in the built environment into the daily management of the *quartier*. This document, while recognizing the valuable innovations introduced in Alma-Gare, took a pessimistic view of the *quartier*'s future. Ironically, this pessimism stemmed from the very idea that

[169] C. Maillard, 'Alma-Gare, le mirage des années 70', *Urbanisme*, no. 256 (September 1992), p. 50.

the APU had so long sought to establish, namely that the *quartier* had a unique identity founded upon the unity and creativity of its inhabitants:

> How does one avoid the phenomenon of the 'protected area', that is, of allowing an urban sector in which there are produced at one and the same time, and in a cumulative way, innovations in the field of housing, social and even economic experimentation, without the rest of the town being touched, and without the normal procedures being modified? In other words, even if Alma-Gare was a success in and of itself, if this *quartier* were to become only a display case (cf. the troops of visitors, French and foreign ...) would it not, at the end of the day, be a failure?[170]

As we have seen, this document would prove to be prophetic, for the greatest problem facing Alma-Gare today is the fact that, despite diverse initiatives, its fate has remained tied to Roubaix's socioeconomic (poor) fortunes. Some, particularly in the town hall, would argue that Alma-Gare has become little more than a planning curiosity.[171]

---

[170] Ministère de l'Environnement et du Cadre de Vie, Direction de la Construction, 'La Gestion sociale des réalisations expérimentales. L'exemple d'Alma-Gare', 15 October 1979, p. 4. AIR.

[171] Here is yet another construction of past, present and future for Alma-Gare, but one which we shall pass over.

CHAPTER FIVE

The Gorbals: from *No Mean City* to Glasgow's miracle

This chapter introduces the second case study, which deals with the area of the Gorbals in Glasgow, Scotland. It opens with a brief discussion of Glasgow's urban development and, in particular, of the city's post-war housing policy. It then goes on to look specifically at this neighbourhood of the Gorbals. This investigation is divided into two parts, based on the myth of the 'old Gorbals' and construction of the 'new Gorbals'. These were terms commonly used by the press, politicians and even the residents of the Gorbals in the 1950s, 1960s and 1970s to distinguish between the Gorbals of nineteenth-century tenement housing and the modernist Gorbals which was constructed in the course of the comprehensive redevelopment of the area. The aim is not to describe 'how it really was' in the old and new Gorbals, but to analyse the various elements which combined to give meaning to the area at different times for different groups.

Glasgow: the social, political and economic contexts

One of the most frequently evoked aspects of Glasgow's identity is derived from its nineteenth- and twentieth-century industrial heritage. However, this tends to obscure other elements of the city's past: one of the earliest references to it concerned the founding of a church there in the sixth century AD. The settlement was located at a strategic fording point on the River Clyde, and represented the westernmost natural crossing point on this waterway. Glasgow developed on the north bank of the river, on the routeway which ran from Clydesdale in the east to Dumbarton in the west, and from there afforded access to the north-west of Scotland. The ford at Glasgow also allowed for the development of a north–south routeway, along which the town's first suburb developed, on the south bank of the river. This single-street village came to be called Gorbals, a name whose origins are uncertain, but which most likely derives from the Gaelic *gor baile*, meaning 'town land'.[1] By the twelfth century

[1] This derivation can be found in various texts, including Crown Street Regeneration Project, *Masterplan Report*, *c*. 1991. GI.

a cathedral had been established in Glasgow, and in 1178 the city received its burgh charter from King William. Glasgow thus acquired considerable powers, not least the right to hold a market and an annual fair. It was through the influence of the church that the university was established in 1451, by which time the city's population was estimated to be around 1500.[2]

Another key element in Glasgow's identity is derived from the river on whose banks it developed: 'the Clyde made Glasgow, and Glasgow made the Clyde.' Certainly, as early as the fifteenth century the city's commercial life, based largely on the export of salmon and herring to Ireland and mainland Europe, was beginning to flourish thanks to its riverside location. By the seventeenth century, Glasgow's export list had grown to include coal, wool and linen, while imports included brandy, wine, timber, iron and fruits. Economic development was accompanied by population growth, and towards the end of this century the city's population had grown to something between 12 000 and 14 000.[3] The 1707 Act of Union between Scotland and England offered important economic opportunities to Glasgow, opening the way to new trade links with England's colonies, particularly in the Americas. Enjoying an ideal location on the west coast, Glasgow merchants imported rum, mahogany, sugar, raw cotton and tobacco, and exported linen cloth and thread, glass, candles, gloves, handkerchiefs, shoes and hats.[4] Apart from the American colonies, the city also enjoyed regular trade with Italy, Spain, Portugal, France, Holland, Poland, Sweden, Russia, Norway and Ireland.[5] It was this breadth of trade which saved Glasgow from the most extreme economic implications of the outbreak of the American War of Independence in 1775. This effectively marked the end of Glasgow's tobacco trade, and the city's merchants shifted their operations to the West Indies.

The city's growing population required housing: given the restrictive nature of the burgh boundaries, it was necessary to build upwards, and in Glasgow, as in other Scottish towns, there developed a flatted ownership system in stone-built tenement buildings. The basic tenement form consisted of flats built to several storeys (as high as ten storeys in Edinburgh in the sixteenth century), accessed by a common stair and a passageway, known as the 'close', which opened on to the street. There were generally two or three flats off each landing in the stairwell.[6] With the growing wealth of the merchant class, ideas of

---

[2] Corporation of the City of Glasgow, *The First Quinquennial Review of the Development Plan, 1960: The Survey Report* (Glasgow: Corporation of the City of Glasgow, 1960), section 1.6.

[3] Ibid.

[4] F. Worsdall, *The Tenement: A Way of Life* (Edinburgh: Chambers, 1979), p. 3.

[5] Ibid., p. 4.

[6] The tenement form will be discussed more fully in the following section of this chapter.

comfort changed, and those who could afford it began to move out of the traditional tenements and built new, elegant housing beyond the city's boundaries. As we will see in this chapter and the next, this was the start of a rather chequered career for the tenement. But, vilified or celebrated, this housing form, in its various manifestations, would prove to be an enduring feature of Glasgow's urban landscape.

By the late eighteenth century, Glasgow and its hinterland was developing a significant cotton industry. This industry was concentrated in the Clyde Valley, and particularly in nearby Renfrewshire and Lanarkshire where there was a plentiful supply of water. The same locational factors that had assisted the development of the tobacco trade in Glasgow were equally advantageous for the importation of raw cotton and the distribution of the finished product. Moreover, the growing population of the area, swollen by agricultural workers leaving the land and by the thousands displaced by the clearances in Ireland and the Scottish highlands, provided a source of cheap labour.

The skill of the mechanics associated with the cotton mills contributed to Glasgow's development as a major centre of heavy industry in the nineteenth century. This, of course, was not the only factor: there were, at least initially, local deposits of coal and iron ore and, moreover, Glasgow's merchants showed a willingness to invest in these new activities. For shipbuilding, the city had the added advantage of being the lowest bridging point on the Clyde. It is estimated that in 1835 more than half the tonnage of the steamships launched in Britain was built on the River Clyde.[7] When the construction of the railways started in the mid-nineteenth century, the city took a leading role in the production of locomotives and rolling stock. The first railway works were established in 1836. By 1900 the North British Locomotive Company plants in the Springburn and St Rollox areas of Glasgow were employing some 8000 workers.[8] The range of heavy industrial products expanded during the nineteenth century to include sugar-refining plant, marine and electrical engineering products, and instrument making. In the early 1880s Singer founded the world's largest sewing machine factory downstream from the city at Clydebank.

Glasgow's economic development during the nineteenth century was accompanied by massive population growth (from 77 385 in 1801 to 784 496 in 1901[9]), which in turn created a huge demand for housing. As noted, many

---

[7] Corporation of the City of Glasgow, *The First Quinquennial Review of the Development Plan, 1960*, section 1.8.

[8] M. Keating, *The City that Refused to Die. Glasgow: The Politics of Urban Regeneration* (Aberdeen: Aberdeen University Press, 1988), p. 2.

[9] M. Horsey, *Tenements and Towers: Glasgow Working Class Housing 1890–1900* (Edinburgh: The Royal Commission on the Ancient and Historical Monuments of Scotland, 1990), p. 10.

immigrants arrived from the Scottish highlands and from Ireland – in 1851, the year of the Great Famine in Ireland, it was estimated that some 20 per cent of the city's population was Irish by birth.[10] Many of the migrants arriving in the city in the early part of the nineteenth century were unable to find work. The number of unemployed was further swollen during the trade recessions of 1816, 1819 and 1826. Inevitably, the large numbers of poor in the city were attracted to the oldest areas where rents were cheapest. Some found themselves in common lodging houses or labyrinthine old tenements to which, often, extra floors had been added. Those more fortunate were able to rent one- or two-room apartments in tenement blocks specifically constructed to meet the housing demand of the growing working-class population, while still others took rooms in the 'back lands' – poor-quality tenements constructed in the courtyards behind the street-front buildings where, not surprisingly, there was a shortage of both light and ventilation.

In 1848–49, Glasgow was struck by a cholera epidemic which killed 3772 people, and a second, in 1853–54, claimed another 3885 lives.[11] The principal cause of these outbreaks had been the defective water supply, which was drawn from the Clyde and a number of containment wells. The epidemics not only had the effect of spurring the city towards developing the Loch Katrine Water Scheme, which was opened in 1860, but also gave an incentive to slum improvement.[12] In 1859 a committee was set up to consider sanitary legislation. It recommended the introduction of building controls for new tenements in order to restrict their height in proportion to the width of the street on which they were built. Another significant outcome of the committee's work was the setting up of the City Improvement Trust in 1866 (whose powers were subsequently transferred to the City Corporation in 1895) with the aim of clearing areas of poor housing, building new streets and widening existing ones.

Glasgow's population growth, already rapid from around 1800, took off in the second half of the century. From 395 503 in 1861, the population rose to 565 839 in 1891 as the city, at the peak of its industrial productivity, acted as a pole of attraction to migrant populations.[13] This growing population created a massive demand for housing which was met by dwellings constructed for rent by private sector builders. In addition, as the middle classes moved away from the centre of the city, former middle-class areas of housing were converted to cater for the working classes, and large flats were subdivided or 'made-down' into one- or two-room apartments. Sometimes tenancies were by the month, or even shorter, and it was not unusual to find entire families in single rooms.

---

[10] Keating, *The City that Refused to Die*, p. 4.
[11] Worsdall, *The Tenement: A Way of Life*, p. 7.
[12] Ibid.
[13] Ibid., p. 91.

During the 1860s and 1870s, the City Improvement Trust demolished large parts of the old city, including the original core of the Gorbals village, in an attempt to improve the fabric of these overcrowded areas.

By the beginning of the twentieth century, Glasgow's natural resources were nearing exhaustion and its heavy industry was beginning to show some symptoms of decline, although the advent of the First World War and the short post-war boom which followed did not make the city's economic problems immediately visible. The inter-war decline of Glasgow's industries was then halted by the Second World War, but the conflict did nothing to alter the structural problems of a city dependent on a declining industrial base. Glasgow's private construction and rental sector fared little better in the new century. The first blow came in 1910 when Lloyd George's government, in the context of the 'People's Budget', passed a Finance Act which made it unprofitable to hold land or speculate in property. This made it uneconomical for private builders to continue to construct tenements for rent and for private landlords to maintain their properties in good condition. As a consequence, the construction of tenements virtually ceased and conditions in many existing areas began to decline, with the result that by the end of the First World War the city was experiencing an acute shortage of working-class housing. The House Letting and Rating (Scotland) Act of 1911 had the effect of pushing up rents, and this combination of high rents and poor conditions provoked a series of rent strikes by skilled and white-collar workers. In the war context, the government took the political decision to sacrifice the interest of the landlords in favour of the tenants and introduced the 1915 Rent Restriction Act. The Glasgow rent strikes have assumed a central position in the city's working-class mythology, although Miles Horsey has argued that:

> Glasgow's private market in house building for rent did not collapse of its own accord, as the result of some failure to provide accommodation for the unskilled poor. Rather, it was destroyed by pressure from middle-class and skilled working-class tenants pursuing their own grievances, which were concerned not with slum conditions, but with rent levels, sequestrations and inflexible letting arrangements.[14]

The government also shifted the responsibility for providing low-rent housing from private landlords to local authorities. The Housing and Town Planning (Scotland) Act of 1919 made it the responsibility of every local authority to provide houses for the working classes, while the Housing Act of 1920 authorized local authorities to borrow money to finance their housing schemes. Glasgow Corporation Housing Department began work on the city's first new housing scheme in 1920 at Riddrie, in the north-east of the city. This and other early schemes were based upon the garden suburb ideal of semi-detached

[14] Horsey, *Tenements and Towers*, p. 10.

houses set in their own gardens, but they soon proved to be too expensive and the Corporation reverted to a cheaper form of housing based on a flat-roofed, three-storey tenement form.

The Corporation's first slum clearance scheme was recommended in March 1922 by the Joint Committee on Slum Areas, with the aim of rehousing 700 families from an old area of the inner city, and the city boundaries were extended in 1926, 1931 and 1938 to meet the need for land for new housing and green space.[15] Between 1919 and the outbreak of the Second World War, a total of some 70 000 houses were erected in the city, of which 50 000 were built by the Corporation (half of which were in tenement blocks). Over the same period, some 18 000 houses were designated 'unfit', of which 15 000 were demolished.[16]

The issue of the provision of low-cost housing offered a platform from which the Labour Party was able to launch its bid to take political control of Glasgow's Corporation and, indeed, the theme of low-rent housing would continue to occupy an important place in the city's Labour Party ideology for many decades to come, even at the risk of provoking the hostility of right-wing national government from the 1950s through to the 1980s.[17] It was in the years immediately after the First World War that the Labour Party came to the fore in Glasgow's political scene, as it called, for example, for the continuation of wartime rent controls. Another element of Labour's success was the backing it enjoyed from the well-organized Irish political machine in the city. While in 1918 the Labour Party had only one MP elected in Glasgow out of 15 constituencies, it had ten MPs elected in the 1922 election, taking 43 per cent of the total vote.[18] It was not, however, until 1933 that Labour took control of Glasgow's Corporation, which, as Keating points out, was relatively late in the context of Britain's major cities, with only Birmingham and Liverpool taking longer to elect Labour administrations.[19] The main opposition to the Labour Party was provided by the Moderates, later called Progressives, who were a Unionist party. They long resisted the influence of the national Conservative Party, and it was only in 1965 that they changed their name to Conservatives, having been given the choice of contesting elections under the party name or facing a Conservative opponent at the next election. While Glasgow's socioeconomic development ensured that a large proportion of the city's

---

[15] Worsdall, *The Tenement: A Way of Life*, p. 129.

[16] Corporation of the City of Glasgow, *The First Quinquennial Review of the Development Plan, 1960*, section 13.3.

[17] For a discussion of the connections between tenants' movements and the emergence of the Labour Party in Glasgow see J. Melling, 'Clydeside Rent Struggles and the Making of Labour Politics in Scotland, 1900–39', in R. Rodger (ed.), *Scottish Housing in the Twentieth Century* (Leicester, Leicester University Press, 1989).

[18] Keating, *The City that Refused to Die*, p. 9.

[19] Ibid., p. 10.

population belonged to the 'working classes', this did not automatically mean unconditional support for the Labour Party from this group. The city's religious divisions, which echoed those between the Catholic and Protestant populations of Ireland, were also played out in Glasgow's politics. Although the majority of the working class generally gave its vote to the Labour Party, the backing received by Labour from the Irish political machine and the Unionist label of the Moderates ensured that the latter drew a significant working-class and middle-class Orange vote. Despite this, Labour formed administrations in the Corporation of Glasgow right up until the local government reorganization of 1975 (when the Corporation became Glasgow District Council) and beyond. On only three occasions did the Labour Party lose control of the city: from 1948 to 1951; again, 20 years later, from 1968 to 1971; and once more from 1977 to 1980. All three losses reflected the electorate's discontent with the national Labour Party as much as problems on the local level.

While Glasgow's Labour Party might have appeared monolithic, it was by no means free from internal divisions. In the post-war period in particular, the city's Labour group became divided between the left and right wing. Keating argues that this was a conflict which was, 'ostensibly based upon ideology but with ideology often used as a pretext for personal and factional rivalry'.[20] The implications of this divide often came to the surface in dealings with community groups, with left-wing party members more likely to support the more radical demands of these groups.

Apart from the Moderates/Progressives, Labour's other significant opponent in the city, particularly in the late 1960s and the 1970s, was the Scottish National Party (SNP). In 1968, largely thanks to public discontent with the Labour Party's record both in London and Glasgow, 12 SNP candidates were elected to the Corporation and gave their support to the Progressive's minority administration. A similar situation occurred in 1977, this time with 16 SNP councillors being elected (representing a gain of 15 seats). In this case, the Labour Party had been forced to concede the Hutchesontown seat in the Gorbals after the local councillor had been found to be involved in a housing scandal, an event which in turn led to an investigation into widespread house-letting irregularities.[21] The Communists, while having a high degree of influence in the local trade union movement in the shipyards and engineering works, and despite the still-current popular myths surrounding Red Clydeside

[20] Ibid., p. 59.

[21] 'Mrs Cantley Quits Polls in House Transfer Row', *The Glasgow Herald* (18 April 1977), p. 1. The article explains that Cantley had stepped down as Labour candidate for the Hutchesontown ward, having already resigned as housing vice-chair. She had been accused of 'serious misconduct in an affair in which her son and his mistress were transferred from their 3 apartment house in the Gorbals to a bigger one in the plusher, high amenity area of Mansewood.'

and the figure of John MacLean, never succeeded in obtaining a seat on the city council.[22] Sean Damer, no admirer of the city's entrenched machine politics, argues that, despite many public feuds between the Labour and Communist groups, the difference between the two was difficult to discern:

> The similarity was one of mentality ... both saw power as residing ultimately with the (male) workers organised in trade unions rather than in tenants' groups which have a tendency to be dominated by women. Their rhetoric was therefore well-nigh indistinguishable, with the exception that for the Communists the Soviet Union was the Good Society. In any event, the two groups could do business with each other and often did.[23]

The form of politics pursued by the Labour Party in Glasgow relied a great deal on popular loyalty to both the party and individual representatives rather than on active participation in the party structure, and Keating argues that the popular conception of Glasgow as a dynamic socialist city was not borne out by the level of support given to the Labour Party:

> Folk legends continued to maintain the picture of Glasgow as a very left-wing city. This was distinctly misleading. Labour's high level of electoral support went along with a low membership and an organisation which as times was quite moribund. Its increasing vote must be attributed to demographic change (the migration of the middle classes) together with the gradual decline of the religious factor, although the latter continued to affect politics up to the 1970s.[24]

Political machines developed in the older, working-class areas of the city such as the Gorbals, and Keating points out that particular issues – above all, the provision of housing – became perennial themes: 'The ideology of the Labour Party as Glasgow Corporation can best be summed up as "municipal labourism", a concern with a limited range of policy issues with an immediate impact on their constituents – notably housing matters – but little consideration of wider policy issues.'[25]

Tackling the city's housing crisis

In the wake of the Second World War, the city's Labour administration found itself facing a major housing crisis. While the city of Glasgow itself had

---

[22] John MacLean (1879–1923) was a schoolteacher and Marxist activist. He is credited with inspiring many of the activists involved in the industrial unrest on Clydeside during and after the First World War (Red Clydeside). He was appointed both an honorary president of the first Congress of Soviets and Soviet consul to Scotland.

[23] S. Damer, *Glasgow: Going for a Song* (London: Lawrence & Wishart, 1990), p. 197.

[24] Keating, *The City that Refused to Die*, p. 11.

[25] Ibid., p. 12.

suffered relatively little bomb damage,[26] the war years had seen the continued neglect of the its housing stock, which had started to decline from the early years of the twentieth century as a result of rent control measures. By the late 1940s the system of factoring and maintenance of privately rented housing had broken down almost completely, and by the end of the war it was generally considered that Glasgow's housing conditions were amongst the worst in Europe: according to Markus, housing densities in some areas were as high as 750 persons per hectare.[27] Moreover, 29.2 per cent of houses lacked an inside toilet and 43 per cent had no bath, while the equivalent figures for London were 5.5 per cent and 1.7 per cent respectively.[28]

The planners in the Corporation, in keeping with the post-war report produced by the Barlow Commission recommending the overspill of population from the large industrial centres of Britain, advocated, within a context of centrally-controlled urban and industrial reconstruction, the reduction of urban population densities, the physical limitation of city growth by the creation of green belts and the construction of new towns to house the decanted populations and factories. The planners' recommendations were formalized in the Clyde Valley Regional Plan, produced by a team of consultants working in conjunction with the Scottish Office and published in interim form in 1946, and then fully in 1949.[29] The aim of the Plan was to move a population of 500 000 people out of Glasgow's slum areas, while limiting the city's peripheral development by means of a green belt on its margins. The Labour-controlled Corporation was initially sceptical, preferring to solve the city's housing problems within its own boundaries, in part because this would maintain both the city's rates income and its working-class electoral base, and in part because of municipal pride and the desire that Glasgow should remain a significant city.[30] Indeed, in the late 1940s and early 1950s, the Corporation embarked upon the construction of major housing developments on the edge of the city which encroached upon the green belt. These schemes – Castlemilk to the south, Drumchapel to the west, and Easterhouse to the east – were to become notorious for the poor quality of their architecture and their lack of facilities. Castlemilk, a vast development covering 466 hectares and consisting of 8300

---

[26] The main target of bombing raids were the shipyards further downstream in Clydebank.

[27] T.A. Markus, 'Comprehensive Development and Housing, 1945–75', in P. Reed (ed.), *Glasgow: The Forming of a City* (Edinburgh: Edinburgh University Press, 1993), p. 152.

[28] Damer, *Glasgow: Going for a Song*, p. 187.

[29] One of the consultants was Sir Patrick Abercrombie, perhaps Britain's most influential post-war planner. Another was Robert Matthew, who would be one of the architects of the new Gorbals.

[30] It was a source of pride that Glasgow was known as 'the second city of the Empire', however strange it may seem to celebrate a second place.

houses, all in four-storey tenement blocks, would come to house many former residents of the Gorbals who were displaced by slum clearance programmes.

By the early 1950s Glasgow Corporation had a housing waiting list of 80–90 000 families.[31] The 1951 census recorded a population of some 1 090 000 people, living at an average density of 990 persons per hectare. It was estimated that 50.8 per cent of the city's houses consisted of only one or two rooms and that 24.6 per cent of the population lived at a density of more than two persons per room.[32] In short, the city was full. Faced with the enormity of the 'slum' problem, as well as pressure from the Scottish Office, Glasgow's councillors began to accept that an overspill policy, in conjunction with a high rate of house building within the boundaries of the city, was the only practical solution open to them.

The Corporation was not only concerned with issues of overspill and new housing, it also took steps in this period to eradicate the city's slum areas. The Comprehensive Development Area (CDA), introduced under the Town and Country Planning (Scotland) Act 1947, was selected as the chief planning instrument to achieve this goal. This designation allowed the Corporation to exercise compulsory purchase rights, demolish existing buildings, erase the road network and undertake complete rebuilding. In a 1957 report it was proposed to create 29 major housing developments in the city, of which 17 were CDAs. These 29 areas incorporated 100 000 houses – that is, virtually all Glasgow's nineteenth-century housing – the equivalent of one-third of the city's entire stock.[33] Densities were to be reduced from 1112 persons per hectare to 405 per hectare, which required the removal of 60 per cent of the population from these redevelopment areas.[34] The first CDA, approved in 1957, was for the Hutchesontown/part Gorbals area. It was phased over 20 years, was to cost £13 million, and would reduce the population of the area from 26 000 to 10 000. At the time it was the largest such development in the United Kingdom. A second CDA, for the area of Pollokshaws, was approved in 1958, and a third, for Anderston, in 1961. Later, the 1965 Highway Plan for Glasgow, one of the most ambitious in the United Kingdom, was drawn up to complement the CDA programme, and this too required substantial demolition.[35] There were those

---

[31] Markus, 'Comprehensive Development and Housing, 1945–75', p. 152.

[32] Damer, *Glasgow: Going for a Song*, pp. 186–87.

[33] Keating, *The City that Refused to Die*, p. 23.

[34] Glasgow Corporation subsequently increased the population density in the CDAs to 445 per hectare in 1958, but the Scottish Office refused to give permission for anything over 410. See Markus, 'Comprehensive Development and Housing, 1945–75', pp. 157–8.

[35] Glaswegian commentators were, and still are, quick to point out the incongruity of such an ambitious highway plan given the city's very low car ownership figures. An article entitled 'Ammunition for Campaign from Housing Report', *The Glasgow*

who suggested, even as early as the late 1950s, that a proportion of housing in the CDAs was of a sufficient standard to be renovated, but the concept of assisting private owners to improve their homes was anathema to Labour Party orthodoxy at the time.[36]

The CDAs were to include only a limited number of high-rise blocks, in keeping with their restricted rehousing density, but Glasgow Corporation did not demonstrate the same reserve when it came to gap sites which lay outside the CDAs. It was here that the Corporation overturned the overspill principles of the Clyde Valley Plan, by planting high-rise flats in any corner of the city where space allowed.[37] Backed by the new industrial construction techniques promoted by large contractors, Glasgow's Corporation embarked on the most concentrated multi-storey construction programme of any British city. Beyond the technical and financial reasons for choosing multi-storey flats (they benefited from a system of central government subsidies, at £30 per flat for 60 years, which substantially offset their real cost[38]), this form of architecture was undoubtedly a symbol of municipal prestige in this period and, in the case of Glasgow, also a symbol of defiance in the face of the regional priorities promoted by central government and the Scottish Office. By May 1969 there were close to 50 000 people living in the city's 163 multi-storey blocks,[39] and by the end of the 1970s the number of blocks had doubled to 321.[40] The Scottish Office, which disapproved of Glasgow Corporation's activities and was concerned by the combined implications of the policies of high-rise flats and peripheral estates, wrote in its 1963 *Housing Density Report* that Glasgow was:

> ... producing an image of itself it may regret and which we may regret in relation to what we are attempting to achieve for the Scottish economy as a whole ... it would appear no effort has been seriously made to consider whether the Glasgow housing policies are really suitable to meet the conditions of the later half of the 20th century; there would appear to have

Herald (1 July 1967), p. 1, puts the Scottish figure for car ownership at 34 per cent of the population, while Glasgow could only manage 18 per cent.

36 For a discussion of the possibility of renovating a proportion of the housing stock, see T. Brennan, *Reshaping a City* (Glasgow: The House of Grant, 1959).

37 Horsey attributes this phenomenon to one man, David Gibson, who was the housing convenor of Glasgow Corporation from 1961 to 1964. Gibson considered it a moral imperative to build as many houses in the shortest time possible in order to eradicate Glasgow's problem of substandard housing. He assigned a strong moral dimension to the question of slum housing, speaking of 'the unpardonable offence that bad housing creates against human dignity'. Horsey, *Tenements and Towers*, pp. 45–46.

38 P. Jephcott with H. Robinson, *Homes in High Flats: Some of the Human Problems Involved in Multi-storey Living*, Occasional Paper no. 13 (Edinburgh: University of Glasgow Social and Economic Studies, 1971), p. 17.

39 Ibid., p. 131.

40 Keating, *The City that Refused to Die*, p. 24.

> been no pause to consider whether or not the actual requirements of the population were really being met; there would appear to have been no consideration as to whether this kind of investment would stand the test of time.[41]

As we shall see, when Glasgow's chickens finally came home to roost in damp and deserted post-war housing projects, the Corporation, or Council as it was by then, had consigned the above advice to oblivion, and preferred to remember that it was central government that had encouraged them to adopt this particular housing strategy. Ironically, the city's Labour group had not always been supporters of the high-rise format. The Progressives had suggested the use of multi-storey blocks of nine stories in 1943, but Labour had fiercely opposed the project. Ostensibly this was on the grounds of cost, but Markus suggests that this refusal was based on Labour's perception of the tenement, 'which was at that time associated with the very worst squalor, and which, with a shared staircase, somehow came to be identified with high-rise blocks'.[42] The Labour ideal was the cottage or suburban semi-detached house. This attitude only began to change when the urgency of Glasgow's housing problem became evident. Indeed, in its post-war form, with its industrial construction techniques, multi-storey housing looked like an appropriately modern antidote to Glasgow's nineteenth-century slum inheritance. For example, Wimpey Construction claimed to have produced 1412 houses in Glasgow in 107 weeks.[43] These new houses, 'planned by computer', represented a substantial time saving for anxious city corporations with respect to traditional construction techniques: 'Taking a 15-storey block with six flats to a landing, providing 90 flats, the site man-hours by traditional means would amount to 2000 as against only 750 by the Wimpey system, a time saving of 60 per cent.'[44] Given the massive number of housing units constructed in these years, it is hardly surprising that Glasgow's post-war housing history has been tainted by allegations of scandal and corruption, both over construction contracts and housing allocations.

The high-rise flat drive in Glasgow represented the triumph of housing department imperatives over those of the planners in the Corporation, who had always argued in favour of overspill policies. The press had also made a significant contribution to the perception of the seriousness of Glasgow's housing situation, with headlines such as 'Glasgow Slums a National Responsibility', 'Enduring Slums of Glasgow', '£140m. Housing Problem in

---

[41] Cited in Markus, 'Comprehensive Development and Housing, 1945–75', p. 161.

[42] Ibid.

[43] 'Speed and Saving in Wimpey Building: Equipment Kept in Continuous Use', *The Glasgow Herald* (16 June 1964), p. 14.

[44] 'New Houses Planned by Computer', *The Glasgow Herald* (16 June 1964), p. 14.

Glasgow', and 'City's Intractable Housing Problem'.[45] Given these social and political pressures, the Corporation started to offer flats in multi-storey blocks to almost anyone on the housing list, including the elderly and families with young children. This was to prove one of the key reasons for the failure of the high-rise flat programme, as families and old people found themselves physically and socially isolated in high blocks where the lift system was all too frequently out of order. The physical fabric of the blocks deteriorated quickly, communal spaces, such as entrances, were poorly maintained, and the 'landscaped' areas of ground between the flats became wastelands.

At first, the reaction to free-standing multi-storey point blocks and slab blocks took the form of medium-height deck-access units, the first example of which was constructed in Glasgow in 1964. A deck-access unit was defined in Glasgow's *Housing Condition Survey* as a 'block of less than 8 storeys which has a central staircase or lift from which access is gained to individual dwellings along decks. These decks may be either over the living areas of dwellings in a lower floor, or project beyond the face of the block.'[46] The door of each apartment opened on to these decks, or extended balconies, and the concept was promoted by the emotive idea of 'streets in the air' and the human contact which this implied. The various deck-access schemes in Glasgow soon became the targets of vandalism and began to exhibit major structural problems, not least heat loss, condensation and water penetration. Faced with the failure of both point and deck-access blocks, the Corporation's enthusiasm for high-rise flats in any form began to wane. In November 1974 Councillor Dick Dynes, chair of the housing committee, officially announced the end of Glasgow's enchantment with the multi-storey flat and, with a clever bit of verbal footwork, attributed the blame for this housing failure to 'the planners':

> In Glasgow we will not be building any more after this. It is just not worth the candle. We have had a large number of complaints from both young and old people. The planners should have told us about the difficulties before they were built – but they did not. We had to find out for ourselves.[47]

Despite this announcement, the construction of high-rise flats in Glasgow dragged on into the second half of the 1970s, although the Council tried to ameliorate the situation by transferring the elderly and families with young children to the lower floors, or by moving them out of the flats completely. All

---

[45] *The Glasgow Herald* (13 January 1967), p. 1; *The Glasgow Herald* (29 March 1965), p. 8; *The Glasgow Herald* (6 April 1967), p. 1; *The Glasgow Herald* (16 September 1969), p. 12.

[46] City of Glasgow District Council, *Housing Condition Survey 1985, Vol 3: The District Council's Housing Stock* (Glasgow: Glasgow District Council, 1990), p. 23.

[47] 'High-Rise Housing Now Reaches Low Ebb', *The Glasgow Herald* (19 November 1974), p. 12.

the same, in 1979 it was estimated that of the city's 26 000 flats in multi-storey blocks, 10 000 housed families with small children.[48]

By the 1970s the Comprehensive Development Area, the other flagship of Labour's post-war reconstruction of the city, was also in trouble. Progress in these areas had been slow and large parts of the city had deteriorated as a result of planning blight (in 1971 there were estimated to be 17 000 empty dwellings awaiting demolition in Glasgow).[49] Of the 29 major housing treatment areas in the city, only 14 had received government approval by 1974 when the CDA programme was finally halted, and only four, at Hutchesontown/part Gorbals, Pollokshaws, Anderston and Cowcaddens, had been completed. The programme was coming to be seen as not only too costly, but also too disruptive to long-standing communities which found themselves broken up and shifted to various peripheral estates or beyond. It was also proving to be unpopular with the electorate.[50] Although CDAs were intended to be mixed-type developments, they inevitably came to be associated with multi-storey architecture – yet one more reason for their unpopularity. Finally, there was also a growing concern that the amount of public housing in Glasgow was reaching socially undesirable levels: in 1979 the proportion of public housing in the city was 64 per cent, compared with a Scottish average of 54 per cent and a UK average of only 32 per cent.[51]

By the mid-1970s, greater emphasis was being given to socioeconomic regeneration and the encouragement of new employment. This reflected national developments which were formalized in measures such as the Urban Programme of 1969. A parallel development saw a movement away from overspill policies towards the concept of inner-city regeneration: it was indicative of this changing perspective that the project for the development of a new town at Stonehouse was abandoned,[52] and instead the resources were channelled to the Glasgow Eastern Area Redevelopment (GEAR) scheme, which was set up in 1976. This was in keeping with the broad change in planning philosophy discussed in Chapter Two and characterized by a movement away from physical 'blueprint' planning and a greater emphasis on traditional urban forms and more piecemeal urban change. Concern began to mount over the phenomenon of multiple deprivation, which was found to

---

[48] '"Great Escape" Plan for High-Rise Families', *The Glasgow Herald* (21 March 1979), p. 3.

[49] Keating, *The City that Refused to Die*, p. 28.

[50] Ibid., p. 117.

[51] Horsey, *Tenements and Towers*, p. 69. Public housing refers both to council housing and Scottish Special Housing Association housing, which was directly funded by central government.

[52] Stonehouse was designated as a new town in 1973 but, with Glasgow's population falling, its future had never been certain.

extend well beyond the boundaries of the city's 'slum' areas.[53] In this context, the designation of a tenement flat as either fit or unfit for human habitation appeared rather one-dimensional, and the tenement form *per se* was freed from its direct association with slums. It was this new perspective which eventually led to a fresh appraisal of Glasgow's remaining nineteenth-century tenements. Many of the larger working-class tenement flats, especially those bordering middle-class areas of the city, underwent extensive rehabilitation and improvement. As Reed points out, the image of the tenement was transformed and, in the rush to rehabilitate those which remained, they became what he describes as 'the essential urban artefacts of the city'.[54]

It is not by chance that these changes coincided with a generational change in the city's administration following the Wheatley Commission's recommend-ations for local government reform in 1975. Glasgow Corporation became the City of Glasgow District Council, with responsibility for drawing up local plans, as well as for the construction and management of council housing, while Strathclyde Regional Council dealt with concerns such as transport and education and was responsible for drawing up a structure plan for the whole of Strathclyde Region in order to provide a framework for the integration of the various local plans.

The changes in the field of housing and planning, and particularly the idea that private housing stock should benefit from public funding for the purpose of rehabilitation, presented a serious challenge to the orthodoxy of Glasgow's Labour group and was opposed by many Labour councillors, particularly on the party's traditional left wing. Another factor contributing to the resistance of the 'old school' of councillors was that the movement towards rehabilitation threatened to deprive them of the valuable source of patronage that new-build represented.[55] Although the younger officials and councillors of Glasgow District Council were more receptive to the new ideas in urban planning, the weight of tradition and ideology remained for years to come, and would re-emerge, as Chapter Six shows, whenever the issue of municipal housing stock was raised.

---

[53] 'Shelter, the national campaign for the homeless, has produced a report entitled, "Reprieve for Slums". In a blueprint for improvement, the report calls for a massive injection of Government money and special treatment for areas of multiple deprivation.

Mr William Roe, Scottish director, Shelter, said that the idea of comprehensive redevelopment of city centres had turned sour as it had benefited only commercial interests.

"The people who live in these areas have come off worst of all" he said, "Our plan is to rebuild communities and give them the resources they need to regenerate their own lives."' 'Shelter's Plan for Slum Areas Launched', *The Glasgow Herald* (15 September 1972), p. 3.

[54] P. Reed, 'The Tenement City', in Reed, *Glasgow: The Forming of a City*, p. 104.

[55] Thanks to Michael Keating for this point.

Public sector 'slums'

In the mid-1970s there emerged yet another problem for the District Council, in the form of structural problems in their housing stock, and particularly the problem of dampness. There were still the familiar doom-laden headlines, '£500m Needed – or Glasgow will be the Worst Slum in Europe', but now the term 'slum' was being used in a new context, to refer to the city's inter-war and post-war municipal housing.[56] Authors have tended to underemphasize the importance of this phenomenon for the city's recent housing history, but the massive cost of treating thousands of council houses and flats was a factor that weakened Glasgow's bargaining position with respect to central government and, ultimately, contributed to the city's administration accepting Thatcherite urban policies, including the programme of council house sales.

Initially, stop-gap measures were introduced. In November 1975, for example, the Council launched a mobile exhibition unit which was intended to tell householders how to treat dampness in their homes and, in particular, to advise on heating and ventilation. Then, in 1978, nearly 200 000 leaflets were distributed in the city explaining that the use of paraffin heaters was one of the main causes of condensation in houses. With the city seemingly staggering from one financial crisis to another, the Council could not afford to accept responsibility for defective housing. It claimed that 95 per cent of the dampness cases it had been called to investigate were caused by condensation (that is, from cooking, bathing, washing clothes and using paraffin heaters), rather than from water penetration as a result of structural faults.[57] However, by 1980, largely as a result of militant and legal action by tenants in the Gorbals area (which will be examined more closely in the next chapter), Glasgow District Council had been forced to accept that dampness problems were inherent in the design of some of their housing stock.

It was estimated that £140 million was required to treat the 35 000 council houses affected by dampness (in addition to the cost to the Council of loss of rent, and, in some cases, the payment of compensation).[58] Forgetful of the Scottish Office warning in 1963 that Glasgow had demonstrated 'no consideration as to whether this kind of investment would stand the test of time', the Council began to argue that central government should meet the cost of this work, on the grounds that it had exerted pressure on local authorities to use non-traditional building methods during the 1950s and 1960s:

---

[56] *The Glasgow Herald* (30 June 1975), p. 7.

[57] Bailie John Kernaghan, chairman of the District Council's housing committee, cited in 'Nothing But Damp Expense to City', *The Glasgow Herald* (6 December 1978), p. 8.

[58] '£140m Needed to Beat Dampness', *The Glasgow Herald* (14 March 1980), p. 5.

> Most of these defects are in the system-built houses we were pressed by the government to build in the 1960s. They all carry National Building Agency certificates and quite clearly are a central government responsibility. We will be seeking representations with the Scottish Office for additional financial aid to cope with this problem.[59]

In 1981 central government's response to this claim was to suggest that an extra £4 million might be allocated to the city if Glasgow District Council achieved the figure of council house sales which the Conservative government believed was possible. The Council swallowed its socialist pride, stepped up its council houses sales programme and obtained additional funding as a result, only to find that, in the 1984–85 housing allocations, it had lost another £5.5 million for having allocated excessive subsidies to their tenants from their rates in defiance of central government policy and budgeting.[60]

By February 1984 Glasgow had a total of 3792 council tenants complaining of dampness problems, which left the Council little room to manoeuvre.[61] Once more, there were ominous predictions over the city's future, in part, no doubt, intended to encourage funding from central government. Glasgow's housing chairman used the city's past to conjure up a vision of the future, foreseeing the city's 'worst housing crisis since the turn of the century'.[62] The historical implications in this statement became explicit in March 1985 when the spectre of Glasgow's slum housing past was resurrected by Glasgow's director of housing who first warned of 'new slum clearance' if there was not a massive government investment in post-war public housing, and then expressed fears over a 'return to slum conditions'.[63] Confirmation of this seemed to come in December of the same year when the results of the District Council's *Housing Condition Survey* suggested that as many as 44 500 houses, representing approximately 15 per cent of the city's housing stock, were below the official 'tolerable standard' – a 'standard ... drawn up in the days of major private sector slum clearance'.[64] Overall, 38 per cent of Glasgow District Council housing stock was found to suffer from some kind of condensation or dampness,

---

[59] '800m Dampness Bill hangs Over New Councils', *The Glasgow Herald* (20 May 1980), p. 7.

[60] 'Glasgow Scorns its £127.2m share of finance for housing', *The Glasgow Herald* (31 March 1984), p. 3.

[61] 'Rents Freeze Hits Plans to Tackle Dampness', *The Glasgow Herald* (28 June 1984), p. 5.

[62] 'Crisis Fear as £21 Million Housing Appeal Fails', *The Glasgow Herald* (10 July 1984), p. 5.

[63] 'Housing Chief Warns of "New Slum Clearance" ', *The Glasgow Herald* (23 March 1985), p. 3; 'Housing Chief Fears Return to Slum Conditions', *The Glasgow Herald* (28 March 1985), p. 1.

[64] 'Anger over Survey on City's Slums', *The Glasgow Herald* (11 December 1985), p. 9.

although, in the tenants' view, this figure was as high as 53 per cent.[65] In September 1986 Glasgow's Labour group broke with its traditional dogma and borrowed an extra £75 million privately in order to treat the city's new slums.

It would be too simple to suggest that the wheel had come full circle, but certainly the concept of 'slum' had proved to be not only flexible, but also evocative and enduring. Of course, the major difference between the 'slum' in the 1980s and the 'slum' 100, or even 50, years before lay in the issue of housing tenure. The private landlord could no longer be depicted as the exploiter of the working class; rather, the problem lay squarely on the shoulders of Glasgow's socialist municipality, a victim, in part, of its own long-term, low-rent policy which had denied it the financial resources necessary to maintain its housing stock. And in facing up to its responsibilities, the Council had been forced to compromise on its own ideology, accepting the sale of council property and private sector borrowing, while retreating from the subsidy of council tenants' rents.

The myth of the 'old Gorbals'

> ... of Glasgow's 17 wards, it is the only one whose name is known 50 miles beyond the city limits, the reason being that it is the most notorious single slum district in the British Isles, and among the most notorious in the world.[66]

Like Alma-Gare (or Gare-Alma), there is a degree of uncertainty surrounding the name of Glasgow's first suburb. The point of contention is the use of the definitive article; while the area is sometimes referred to as 'Gorbals', it is more commonly referred to as 'the Gorbals'. Why it should be distinguished by a definite article is unclear.[67] Perhaps it is a derogatory usage, in the same way that the expression 'the Ukraine' is considered to belittle the status of Ukraine. On the other hand, it perhaps represents the assignation of a positive status, as the Gorbals History Research Group has argued: 'The Gorbals is unique among the districts of Glasgow. It is unique in that its history is just that bit different from all the other areas and also because Gorbals is almost always referred to as *the* Gorbals as if to stress that very uniqueness.'[68] It is certainly true that

[65] City of Glasgow District Council, *Housing Condition Survey 1985, Vol 3: The District Council's Housing Stock*, pp. 53–54.

[66] S. Watts, 'New Miracle in the Gorbals', *The Evening Times* (11 January 1960), p. 5, (copyright 1959, the *New Yorker Magazine*, Inc.).

[67] In Glasgow, the Gorbals shares this status with the Calton, an old weaving area to the east of the city centre, where housing conditions were also particularly poor.

[68] Gorbals History Research Group, *Third Time Lucky? The History and Hopes of the Gorbals* (Glasgow: ABC, nd, *c*. 1995), p. 7.

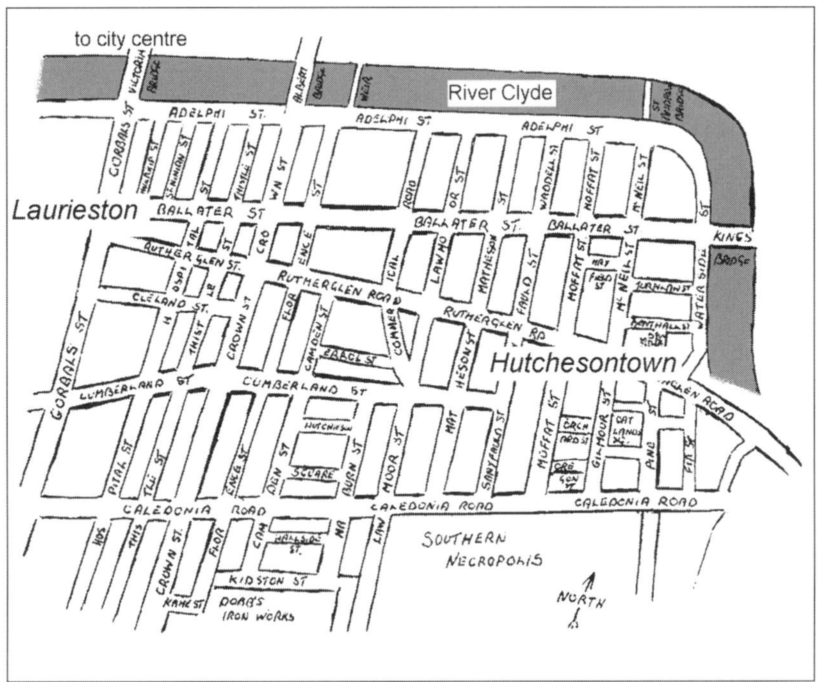

5.1 Sketch map of the Gorbals area prior to urban renewal
Reproduced from Gorbals History Research Group, *Third Time Lucky?: The History and Hopes of the Gorbals* (Glasgow: ABC, nd, *c*. 1995), p. 7.

the addition of the definite article suggests a rather folkloric status (Glasgow's answer to 'the Bronx'?), but more likely it is simply a linguistic usage which has developed over time, since geographical names which are plural, or appear to be plural, are often preceded by the definite article. For example, in Glasgow, people speak of the area called 'the Shields' (although always of 'Pollokshields', with no article), while in Edinburgh there are 'the Links', and, further afield, Paris has 'les Halles', Barcelona 'las Ramblas', and even Florence can provide the example of 'le Piagge', a modern neighbourhood with significant socioeconomic problems which is excluded from the essentialist view of *Firenze, la bella città*.

As noted, the Gorbals developed as a suburb of Glasgow. When the city received its charter in 1178, this effectively limited business within its boundary to burgesses and imposed taxes on goods brought in for sale in its market. This in turn provided an impetus for the growth of the Gorbals which, as a suburb, was not subject to the charter's regulations. As well as a location for unregulated commerce, in this period the Gorbals was also the site of the St Ninian's leper colony. In the fourteenth century a bridge was built at the ford on the Clyde, linking the city to its suburb at the point which came to be known as Bridgend. The growth of Gorbals was modest, and by the mid-eighteenth century it was still nothing more than a small village on the river's south bank, surrounded by farmland. However, it was around this time that weavers began to settle in the Gorbals, and by 1790 the population had grown to around 5000.[69] It was also at this time that the real estate value of the Gorbals area began to become apparent to the expanding city, and in 1790 the land was purchased by Glasgow's town council, with money borrowed from the Trades House and from Hutchesons' Hospital, which was located close to the Gorbals village.

The Trades House took the most westerly section of the Gorbals estate, naming it Tradeston and developing it, during the 1790s, as an area of speculative housing laid out on a grid plan. With the rapid development of Glasgow in the nineteenth century, Tradeston began to lose its housing function and increasingly became a location for industry and warehousing.[70] The eastern part of the Gorbals lands were developed from 1794 by Hutchesons' Hospital, also as a speculative residential development, and also on a regular grid plan. The new suburb of Hutchesontown was intended to house the city's growing wealthy classes, an ambition reflected in the area's construction standards: the buildings, in tenement form, were of a uniform height of four storeys, and the flats, of which there were two to a landing, often had three, four or even five rooms. The minimum width for streets was fixed at 70 feet (21.3 metres) (including 10-foot pavements on each side), while the width of lanes was fixed at 30 feet (9.1 metres).[71] Unsure of the success of their new venture, the patrons of Hutchesons' Hospital spread their risk by selling the westernmost section of the lands to a Glasgow merchant, James Laurie who was to undertake the most ambitious of the new housing developments, again, with Glasgow's growing wealthy classes as his target. Development of Laurieston began in 1800, starting at the river and moving southwards. The ambition of this project was reflected in the street names, which echoed the names of English aristocracy, including Norfolk, Portland, Oxford and Sussex. Like Hutchesontown, the form was an east–west grid plan of elegant, classical four-storey tenement blocks containing flats of five to seven rooms.

The Hutchesontown and Laurieston projects proved to be unsuccessful, principally because the city's fashionable classes chose to move westwards, first to the Blythswood New Town and then beyond. By the nineteenth century, the remaining parts of these Gorbals schemes were being developed for more modest tenements, and in 1807 the area had a population of some 26 000,

[69] Corporation of the City of Glasgow, *Laurieston/Gorbals Comprehensive Development Area, 1965. Survey Report* (Glasgow: Corporation of the City of Glasgow, 1960), p. 3.

[70] Worsdall, *The Tenement: A Way of Life*, p. 77.

[71] Ibid.

the majority of whom were working-class.[72] In 1839, the Govan Iron Works (locally known as Dixon's Blazes after William Dixon, the Northumberland miner who founded them) were established in the area. By 1850 Glasgow was connected by rail with other parts of the country, and Bridge Street station in the Gorbals served as the terminus for rail services to the south and down the Clyde estuary to Greenock. Thus, the Gorbals became increasingly hemmed in by industry and railways. By this time, the housing in the original village of Gorbals was deteriorating, and the poor sanitary conditions meant that the population fell victim to various epidemics, including cholera and typhoid. All these factors made the Gorbals less attractive to the skilled working classes, and the area began to attract a less stable, more marginal population, augmented by the arrival of poor migrants from the Scottish highlands and Irish immigrants seeking to escape famine conditions at home.[73] Given the conditions in the area, it was not surprisingly that the old core of the Gorbals became a target for the City Improvement Trust when it was set up in 1866. The Gorbals Main Street was thus demolished and rebuilt in the 1870s under the City Improvement Act. The new street was straighter and wider and lined with four-storey tenements with shops on the ground floor.

Construction in the Gorbals spanned some 80 years, but nonetheless the area exhibited a high degree of architectural unity, partly because of the slate and honey-coloured sandstone used in construction (although the sandstone was soon blackened by air pollution) and partly because of the uniformity of the four-storey tenement form. The working-class tenements were constructed on a grid iron plan, such that each block was formed by a continuous wall around a central space, known as the 'back court'. Before it became a legal requirement to provide WCs in the tenement blocks, the brick-built outhouses, which contained either plumbed WCs or lime pits, were located in these back courts. The back courts also provided the location for the communal wash-house, the 'middens' for the disposal of refuse, the drying greens and even housed small industries. They were entered either directly from the street through an alley or pend, or by means of the close. The close was a semi-private space, a dog-leg passageway which led from the street through the ground floor of each tenement (either with or without a main door at the entrance) and gave access to both the back court and the common stone stairs in the interior of the building. Depending on the design of the tenement there could be from eight to 13 separate houses opening on to each staircase. In the working-class tenements one of the most common designs was the 'two-one-two' pattern – that is, two

[72] Crown Street Regeneration Project, *Masterplan Report*, *c*.1991. GI.

[73] The Irish found work in mines, mills and railway works, and Protestant workers viewed them with hostility, fearing that they would have the effect of lowering wages. This resentment contributed to the religious rivalry and discrimination which has been a characteristic of Glasgow's twentieth-century history.

two-roomed houses and one one-roomed house (the 'single-end') on each floor (Figure 5.2).[74] Brennan describes the layout as resembling, 'a capital letter E, with the staircase rising at the end of the short middle arm. The staircases themselves are apt to be cold and dark and, since they are for common use ... they are often damp and uncared for.'[75]

The single end, which became notorious in Glasgow's housing folklore, and which sometimes housed an entire family, incorporated a bed recess, a grate with a coal fire and oven, and a sink with running water. As building legislation evolved it became necessary for landlords to provide internal WCs. These were normally located one above the other on each landing, thus forming a 'stack' which extended from the rear wall of the tenement. The pipes ran down the exterior of this wall, with the result that they were prone to freeze in the winter and foul water would wash down the staircase.

By the late nineteenth century many of the four- and five-room houses in the Hutchesontown and Laurieston parts of Gorbals were being 'made down' – subdivided – by landlords exploiting the massive demand for cheap housing in the city. The resultant overcrowding, combined with minimal maintenance, caused the deterioration of the tenement interiors, and the wide streets filled with children (since domestic space was short) contrasted with the increasingly constricted interiors of these tenement blocks. Conditions were exacerbated by the Finance Act of 1910, which made it unprofitable for landlords to carry out repair and maintenance of their properties.

In the twentieth century, the Gorbals continued its role as reception area for immigrant groups, including Irish, Italians, Jews fleeing persecution in Lithuania, Poland and Russia, and latterly Indians and Pakistanis. In 1931 the population of the Gorbals stood at over 85 000, and overcrowding was extreme. By 1951, in part due to a drift of population to the new council estates, the population had fallen to 68 000, but there was still serious overcrowding, made worse by the fact that the decline of the physical environment had continued unchecked. One should not assume, however, that the Gorbals was entirely populated by marginalized new arrivals. In a sample survey of the Hutchesontown/part Gorbals Comprehensive Development Area published in 1959, Tom Brennan, a sociologist from Glasgow University, found that of the 1014 interviewees, 45 per cent had been living in the area for over ten years, 25 per cent for over 20 years, and one in eight more than 30 years.[76]

[74] As Rodger points out, this arrangement of 'undifferentiated rooms meant food preparation and eating, sleeping, work, births and deaths, nursing and children's play all took place within the same area.' R. Rodger, *Housing in Urban Britain, 1780–1914. Class, Capitalism and Construction* (Basingstoke and London: Macmillan, 1989), p. 37.

[75] Brennan, *Reshaping a City*, p. 64.

[76] Ibid., p. 65.

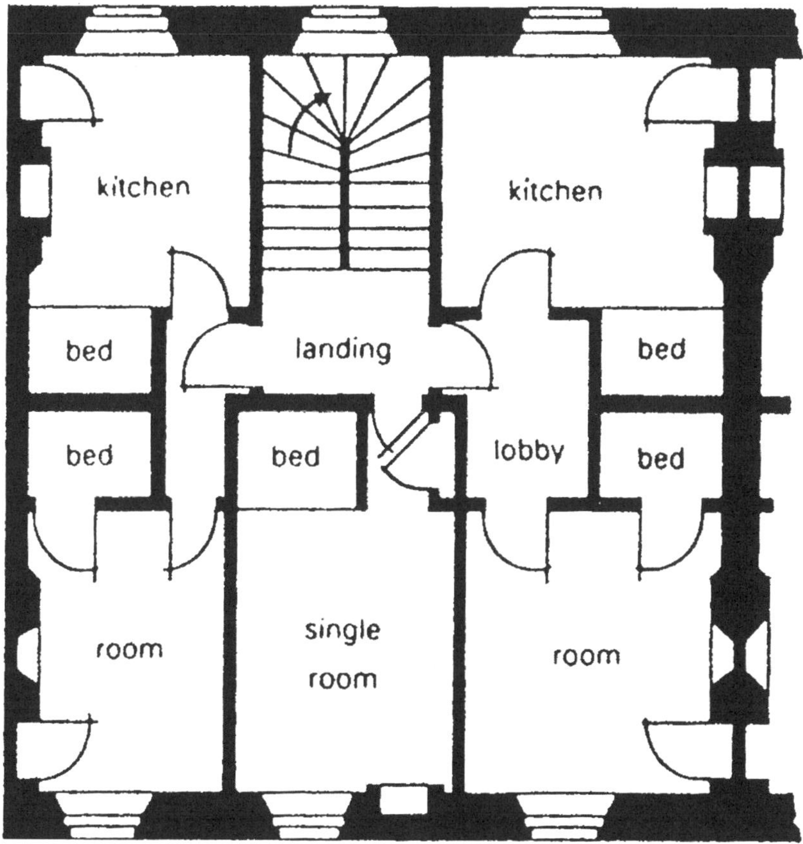

5.2 Plan of a typical nineteenth-century Scottish working-class tenement
Reproduced from R. Rodger (ed.), 'Construir la historia de la vivienda: dimensiones historiográficas del paisaje urbano británico', *Historia Urbana*, no. 2 (1993), p. 47.

The Hutchesontown/part Gorbals CDA, some 45 hectares covering the western part of the Gorbals, was designated in 1957. It was so named because, of its total area, some 60 per cent lay in the Hutchesontown city ward and 40 per cent in the Gorbals ward. According to the survey report, the CDA included 7605 dwellings, the majority of which were in four-storey tenements between 60 and 100 years old. Of these dwellings, 87 per cent had only one or two rooms, and there was a density of 597 rooms per hectare. While all houses had an internal water supply (normally a sink), only 3 per cent had baths and only 22 per cent of homes had their own WC, the majority making use of shared external toilets located on the stairs, with an average of three households to each.[77] For the purpose of the survey, the structural quality of each building was graded according to a six-point scale, from A to F, where A represented the best condition and F the worst. In the Hutchesontown–Gorbals area, 95 per cent of all houses were classified as D, E or F – that is, belonging to the three lowest structural categories.[78] As for sanitary conditions, these were, if anything, worse. The survey used four classes, derived from the Medical Officer of Health's categories:

- Class I: those dwellings which are fully acceptable from a sanitary aspect.
- Class II: unacceptable dwellings, but capable of improvement to class I.
- Class III: unacceptable dwellings and incapable of improvement to class I.
- Class IV: totally unacceptable dwellings.

As Table 5.1 shows, according to the classification of the time, 6905 of the 7605 dwellings in the area (90.8 per cent) were found to be incapable of improvement.

The total population of the development area was 26 860, which gave an average of 3.53 persons per house and 1.89 persons per room. The residential density was 1133.2 persons per hectare.[79] Of all the households in the survey, 46 per cent had children, 7 per cent consisted of six or more persons, and over 12 per cent were elderly persons.[80] The 1951 census stated that 24.4 per cent of the population of Glasgow was living more than two to a room, while in the Gorbals and Hutchesontown wards this figure was almost double, at 41.9 per cent and 44.2 per cent respectively.[81] In the Laurieston part of the Gorbals, conditions were no better. In 1960, when the population stood at some 18 000, 69 per cent of houses fell into the two lowest sanitary classes (classes III and IV), and in 1963, 99 per cent of houses were estimated to belong to the three lowest structural categories (D, E and F). In short, houses in the Gorbals were old and, both in terms of structure and sanitation, in poor condition. They were

[77] Corporation of the City of Glasgow, *Hutchesontown/Part Gorbals Comprehensive Development Area, 1956: Survey Report* (Glasgow: Corporation of the City of Glasgow, 1960), p. 4.

[78] Ibid.

[79] Ibid., p. 5.

[80] Ibid.

[81] While the Hutcheson ward, broadly speaking, covered the east part of the area known as the Gorbals, the Gorbals ward covered the centre and west of the area, including Laurieston. According to the 1951 census report for the City of Glasgow, while 37.47 per cent of households in the city as a whole only had access to a shared WC, these figures were as high as 81.85 per cent (the highest of all city wards) and 57.10 per cent in the Hutchesontown and Gorbals wards respectively. As for a 'fixed bath', 44.09 per cent of city households had this facility, while in Hutchesontown and Gorbals the figures were 7.01 per cent and 5.91 per cent (the lowest in the city).

Table 5.1 Summary of the structural and sanitary condition of houses in Hutchesontown–Gorbals

Sanitary Condition	Structural Condition						
	A	B	C	D	E	F	Totals
Class I	–	180	6	10	4	9	209
Class II	–	–	9	364	93	25	491
Class III	–	–	160	3157	2697	173	6187
Class IV	–	–	–	56	444	218	718
Totals, all classes	–	180	175	3587	3238	425	7605

Source: Corporation of the City of Glasgow, *Hutchesontown/Part Gorbals Comprehensive Development Area, 1956: Survey Report* (Glasgow: Corporation of the City of Glasgow, 1956), p. 4.

individually small and overcrowded, and their development was extremely dense. As in Alma-Gare, the households occupying these tenement apartments were often large families, although there was also a high proportion of elderly people. However, let us add a degree of balance at this point by referring to the findings of Brennan's survey of the clearance area: in over 300 households in the two blocks which were supposed to be in the worst physical condition Brennan observed that a large proportion of the houses showed evidence of improvements carried out by their tenants, and only a very few were found to be dirty or badly kept.[82]

It should be noted that the 'objective' measures of density, structural quality and sanitary conditions found in the *Survey Report* of 1956 and cited above, echo hygienist preoccupations and, as such, differ little from nineteenth-century discourses on the slum. The theme is also present in some of the more descriptive versions of the conditions in the area. These descriptions normally take one of two forms; either the population was depicted as helpless victims, living in 'a sump of human degradation', whom it was our moral or Christian duty to save, or as frightening denizens of a twilight world.[83] Not surprisingly, for the Christian Action Report on the Gorbals, published in 1965, the population fell into the first of these categories:

> Waste in the Gorbals is everywhere from the decaying houses and the rubbish to the malnutrition of its inhabitants. Crime and drunkenness

[82] Brennan, *Reshaping a City*, p. 182.

[83] The Gorbals was described as 'a sump of human degradation' in *The Gorbals 1965. A Christian Action Report on an Investigation into the Housing and Social Conditions of the Gorbals and Adjacent Slum Areas of Glasgow* (London: Christian Action, nd, *c.*1966), no page nos.

> follow hand in hand. Fear and insecurity is at the root of the problem amongst people whose needs are very real. On Saturday nights in particular, after much drinking, fights and rowdyism lead to serious breaches of the law.[84]

In this analysis, anti-social behaviour, fuelled by alcohol consumption, derived directly from the deteriorating living conditions. The report described the environment as degraded, infested and dangerous:

> Hardly anywhere is there a complete set of window panes and curtains are an exception. At the backs of houses, and up the stairways, the windows are all broken, leaving gaping holes in the wall, the frames holding sharp pieces of glass on which children can injure themselves. At night the windows are lit by naked light bulbs, sometimes behind a flimsy curtain or a piece of cardboard in place of a window pane. The back courts that had once been green lawns protected by iron railings are now infested wastelands; scarred with troughs holding pools of stagnant yellow water. Everywhere there is filth and rubbish; the ally of disease and vermin.[85]

This reference to vermin would not seem to be an exaggeration; in 1960 it was reported that 10 389 rats were killed in the Gorbals,[86] and in June 1964, the Gorbals and Hutchesontown Tenants' Association sent a petition signed by seven doctors in the area to the secretary of state for Scotland in a protest against the infestation of rats and the resultant risk to public health. A mother of four was reported as saying that rats were being exterminated, but their bodies were being left to float in pools of green scum in the back courts of the tenements: ' "Our children are running about the backs throwing dead rats at each other" the woman said.'[87]

In the same vein, in 1964 a local minister wrote to the medical officer of health for Glasgow to request the closure and demolition of a tenement property in the Gorbals, not only on the grounds that it was, 'a public health risk', but also because it was 'an affront to human dignity'.[88] In February of the same year W.G. Fyfe, another minister living in the Gorbals and member of an interchurch body working to protect tenants, wrote a series of articles for *The Glasgow Herald* under the title of 'Glasgow's Forgotten Slums'. In one of these articles he described a tenement block formed by South Portland Street, Nicholson Street and Abbotsford Place, which contained 139 multi-occupancy houses containing a total of 450 families – that is, just under 1500 people. In one case,

[84] Ibid.

[85] Ibid.

[86] Ibid.

[87] 'Rat Infested Houses: Petition to Mr Noble', *The Glasgow Herald* (12 June 1964), p. 18.

[88] 'Priest wants Gorbals Property Demolished', *The Glasgow Herald* (23 June 1964), p. 5.

three households, comprising 75 people, made use of a single WC.[89] In another article Fyfe cited the case of three houses inhabited by 59 people, where:

> The lavatories have not worked for a year and have to be flushed with a bucket. Tenants cook either on their own spirit stoves or on an open fire. The lighting was rigged up by tenants and in one place repaired by a plastic head square. In houses where the light had failed the tenants have to do without it and are expected to pay their rents as usual.[90]

As Fyfe suggests, the terrible living conditions did not seem to be any guarantee of paying a low rent: in 1964, the average rent being paid in Gorbals was 31 shillings a week, although it might have been as much as 60 shillings for a single room. A tenant who took his or her case to the rent tribunal would normally have seen this figure reduced to 19 or 20 shillings, or even less, but tenants did not always follow this course of action, sometimes because they were unaware of their legal rights, and sometimes because of intimidatory tactics on the part of landlords.[91] Indeed, the rent tribunal had given rise to a practice called 'Rachmanism' amongst unscrupulous property owners. Once the tribunal had set a fair rent for a property, a landlord was only entitled to raise this rent on the departure of the tenants. Following the lead of a London 'slum landlord' called Rachman, landlords employed harassment and even violence to persuade their tenants to move on, and so supplant them with tenants who would pay a higher rent. Apart from this particular form of exploitation, landlords frequently failed to issue rent-books, evicted tenants without due legal process and indulged in illegal money-lending. It even happened that the pension books of elderly tenants were transferred to the name of the landlord. Often those who fell victim to these practices were immigrants – either from abroad or from rural districts of Scotland – who found it difficult to find rented accommodation. Others had lost their house or had seen their family broken up during the war, while still others were considered by Corporation officials and 'respectable' landlords to be socially undesirable and a bad risk from the point of view of paying rent.

Fyfe considered the inhabitants of the Gorbals to be victims, both of inhuman conditions and of inhuman treatment at the hands of landlords, but, as noted, there was another very prevalent view which saw the 'slum-dwellers' as a race apart. Whatever the root cause of the conditions, this view equated the physical decline of the Gorbals with the moral vice of its inhabitants, whose principal activities appeared to be fighting and drinking. Stephen Watts, in an

---

[89] 'Glasgow's Forgotten Slums I. Exploitation in Gorbals', *The Glasgow Herald* (4 February, 1964), p. 6.

[90] 'Glasgow's Forgotten Slums II. The Inadequacy of Authority', *The Glasgow Herald* (5 February 1964), p. 8.

[91] 'Glasgow's Forgotten Slums I. Exploitation in Gorbals', *The Glasgow Herald* (4 February 1964), p. 6.

article he wrote for *The New Yorker Magazine* in 1960, admitted to being, 'born in another part of Glasgow', but nonetheless explained, 'Even years of absence, which tend to put a sentimental gloss on any place one knew when young, evoked no nostalgia for the Gorbals in me: I recall it simply as depressing and foul-smelling: a region of brawling toughs and frightening drunks; of poverty and crime.'[92]

In this context, it was in the 1930s that the Gorbals received one of the most damning blows to its reputation, with the publication of a novel by a Glaswegian baker called Alexander McArthur and a London journalist called H. Kingsley Long. The novel, entitled *No Mean City*,[93] was first published in 1935 and told the story of Johnnie Stark, a fictitious Gorbals' gang leader and 'razor king' – that is, a street fighter who carried in his waistcoat a pair of cut-throat razors with which he 'marked' the faces of his victims;

> 'Ah'm no mug!' he shouted, as his razor laid open the face of one of his opponents from cheekbone to chin. His movements were incredibly swift. He fought with two hands at once, slashing like lightening at faces hands and necks ... . Razor King had marked all three of his enemies before the fight had lasted two minutes ... . They shouted and cursed and the blood flowed in streams.[94]

This depiction of violence seems to have been widely and rather uncritically accepted. Damer cites the following leader from the *Evening Citizen* at the time of the book's publication and suggests that, 'it would be fair to say that this was typical of the reaction within the city':[95]

> The book is an appalling but undoubtedly faithful picture of life amongst the lowest of the low – the corner boys, the so-called 'gangsters', the dwellers of the filthiest slums. Naturally, the incidents which the authors describe, and the language which their characters use, are hideous. Nor is there any exaggeration. In fact, the authors have evidently felt compelled to exercise some restraint although, we think, they have gone to the utmost limits of what would be tolerable and permissible to print.[96]

---

[92] Watts, 'New Miracle in the Gorbals', p. 5. This was the first of four articles by Glasgow-born Watts reprinted in *The Evening Times* from *The New Yorker Magazine*. The other titles were 'Abject Poverty' (13 January 1964), p. 5; 'Bleak, Cold, Dirty!' (12 January 1964) p. 5; 'Fewer Pubs. The Drinking Men are None Too Pleased' (14 January 1964), p. 5.

[93] A. McArthur and H.K. Long, *No Mean City* (London: Corgi Books, 1957). The title derives in turn from a biblical reference, Acts 21:39, 'But Paul said, I am a man which am a Jew of Tarsus, a city in Cilicia, a citizen of no mean city.'

[94] Ibid., p. 100.

[95] S. Damer, 'No Mean Writer? The Curious Case of Alexander McArthur', in K. McCara and H. Whyte (eds), *A Glasgow Collection: Essays in Honour of Joe Fisher* (Glasgow: Glasgow City Libraries, 1990), p. 31.

[96] Ibid.

As for the Gorbals itself, *No Mean City* depicted the area as an overcrowded hive, both by day, '... Gorbals, with its children swarming in and out of the tenements into the spacious streets that mock the squalor and the misery of the tall hives which line them!',[97] and by night:

> Night brings no kindly silence to the tenement dwellers in the Empire's second city ... . The tenements themselves are never silent. There are sick children who wail and healthy ones who get restless; half-drunken men who snore and mutter; half-sober ones who quarrel with their wives. In the 'hoose' next door, or in some other 'hoose' on the landing above or below, there may be a party in progress which will last for forty-eight hours. And ever and anon front doors will open to allow some hurrying figure to reach the single landing closet which serves three households.[98]

McArthur and Long depicted a pathology particular to 'slum life' which, in the following quote, is equated with 'tenement life':

> Battles and sex are the only free diversions in slum life. Couple them with drink, which costs money, and you have the three principal outlets for that escape complex which is forever working in the tenement dweller's subconscious mind. Johnnie Stark would not have realized that the 'hoose' he lived in drove him to the streets or that poverty and sheer monotony drove him in their turn into the pubs and the dance halls or into affairs like the one he was having with Mary Hay. But then, the slums as a whole do not realize that they are living an abnormal life in abnormal conditions. They are fatalistic and the world outside the tenements is scarcely more real to them than the fantastic fairy-tale world of the pictures.[99]

The residents of the Gorbals were depicted as belonging to the lowest social stratum of city life, and even neighbouring Govanhill, where housing conditions were little different than those in the Gorbals, was presented as preferable: 'Most of the tenants were working-class people, but of a type much above the Gorbals average. They kept their homes cleaner and they did not use their sinks as latrines.'[100]

It should be noted that it was not only McArthur and Long who made the link between physical deterioration and the human condition in the Gorbals. The same theme, couched in very similar terms, appeared in Watts' article in the *New Yorker Magazine*: 'The Gorbals was always prolific of news, almost invariably of the violent sort ... there is nothing like enforced idleness and apparently hopeless poverty for stimulating the anarchic spirit in people naturally energetic, tough and sceptical of authority'.[101] As a novel, *No Mean City* did not shine for its literary quality, but it gained a notoriety which

[97] McArthur and Long, *No Mean City*, p. 88.
[98] Ibid., p. 22.
[99] Ibid., p. 44.
[100] Ibid., p. 223.
[101] Watts, 'New Miracle in the Gorbals', p. 5.

assured its commercial success.[102] In November 1935, the library committee of Glasgow Corporation decided that the city's libraries should not stock the work. The Labour administration felt that Glasgow's working-class culture had suffered enough negative coverage and claimed that the book, 'gave an unfair and inaccurate representation of working-class life in Glasgow'.[103] Certain booksellers in the city decided to boycott the work, while Smith's, the largest bookshop, decided against displaying and promoting it. As if all this was not enough to guarantee the novel's success, the *Sunday Mail* took the decision to serialize it from November 1935, and *No Mean City* entered Glasgow's mythology.

Alexander McArthur died in 1947, having drunk a bottle of disinfectant. Sean Damer adds: 'A final comment on this tragic affair is that the book has always been much more successful in England than in Scotland, where it is regarded with amused contempt.'[104] This is a rather offhand dismissal of a work whose impact on the identity of the Gorbals, 'old' and 'new' alike, has been both profound and ambiguous. As we shall see, *No Mean City* is sometimes employed to represent the 'truth' of the old Gorbals and sometimes to illustrate the fallacy of the myth. The book continues to sell well and is, not surprisingly, resented or ridiculed by the older inhabitants of the Gorbals, but sometimes also confirmed. In any case, there is no doubt that the Razor King has left his scars on the Gorbals. For example, in 1965, when Christian Action produced its report on the Gorbals, its opening chapter was entitled 'A Mean City', and in April 1975, when a Department of Environment report named Glasgow and Clydeside as the most deprived area in Britain in terms of housing, overcrowding and unemployment, *The Glasgow Herald* ran the headline, 'Is It Still No Mean City?'[105] In 1995 Ron McKay, a journalist, published a novel with the unimaginative, but nonetheless resonant title of *Mean City. The Shocking Novel of Glasgow Gangland Life*.[106] This book picked up the story of the Razor King dynasty from where McArthur and Long had left off, bringing it to a present of organized crime and drug-dealing. It differed from its predecessor by the fact that the quality of writing was even poorer, but it still

[102] There are no precise figures for the sales of the book, but Sean Damer offers the following analysis: the first hardback edition ran to eight impressions between October 1935 and August 1939, suggesting a total of 16 000 copies. In 1956, the paperback rights were acquired by Neville Spearman, who printed three impressions. From 1957, Corgi has printed 27 impressions, selling some 539 000 copies in all (1990 figures). The book continues to be popular , and some 3000 copies are sold annually. Damer, 'No Mean Writer?', pp. 33–34.

[103] *The Glasgow Herald* (19 November 1935), p. 9, cited in ibid., p. 32.

[104] Damer, *Glasgow: Going for a Song*, p. 193.

[105] *The Glasgow Herald* (15 April 1975), p. 1.

[106] R. McKay, *Mean City. The Shocking Novel of Glasgow Gangland Life* (London: Hodder & Stoughton, 1995).

evoked the same themes when dealing with the Gorbals, particularly the 'nature' of the 'slum-dweller'. Describing the 1930s Gorbals, McKay wrote: 'It had not changed much. For over 200 years it had been a leper colony and it was still occupied by the wretched, the dispossessed and vanquished, the disenfranchised.'[107] A little further on, he says:

> This outland created for uncounted lepers had grown from a smattering of houses along five streets immediately south of the river, to a smoky, raucous, dense barracks ... . The law, such as it was, was harsh and unforgiving. Thieves were branded on the face ... and scourged through the streets and banished. Women escaped the fiery brands but were still thrown out of the Gorbaile, now called the Gorbals by the Lowland tongue. But few knew the history of the place and even fewer cared. It was a place without a past or, for most, a future. Escape was in the head, or in the glass, more like.[108]

In no more than eight sentences McKay invoked leprosy, pollution, raucousness, marginalization, thievery, ignorance, hopelessness and alcohol abuse to describe the Gorbals. No mean list.

Apart from *No Mean City* and its more recent sequel, the Gorbals has also inspired a play by Robert Leishman called *The Gorbals Story*, and a ballet entitled *Miracle in the Gorbals*, which was first staged in 1944 by Saddlers Wells Ballet and recounts the story of a Christ-figure ultimately stabbed to death by the crowd. Damer claims that 'both productions said more about middle-class guilt than the reality of life in the Gorbals'.[109]

Whether the residents of the Gorbals were depicted as victims or fatalistic slum-dwellers, the Gorbals itself was inextricably associated in the city's collective consciousness with danger and violence. In fact, it is difficult to assess the extent of violence in the interwar Gorbals of *No Mean City*. Certainly economic conditions, and particularly widespread unemployment, in the 1920s and 1930s encouraged gang membership, and divides would have been sharpened by Protestant–Catholic rivalries. Percy Sillitoe, who was Glasgow's chief constable from 1931 to 1943, is remembered for his crackdown on gang activities and the severity of punishments for gang leaders. But many who recall this period emphasize that the extent of gang violence in the Gorbals was exaggerated. In an informal interview with a Gorbals resident who had been born in the area in 1920, I was told that *No Mean City* was an inaccurate depiction of the Gorbals: although he had lived there all his life, the interviewee had never once seen a fight in the Gorbals and suggested that maternal control had been so strict that no youths would have dared become involved in gangs. This is also the recollection of the participants in the Gorbals History Research

[107] Ibid., p. 19.
[108] Ibid., p. 20.
[109] Damer, *Glasgow: Going for a Song*, p. 192.

Group: 'there was very little bullying because the discipline in the homes was strict … . Street fights were rapidly transferred to the back courts where the local community made sure they were fought fairly.'[110] One might equally argue that the institutionalization of these brawls by the community is in fact an indication that violence was commonplace and accepted. The fact that violence was present, but contained, is also implied by the ambiguity of the recollections in 1994 of a man born in the Gorbals in 1923:

> You had gangs in those days fighting with bicycle chains and razors … . There were open-air gyms where they kept themselves fit for battles. They had their territory, but if you weren't a gang member there was no possibility of being assaulted. That book, No Mean City, exaggerated it out of proportion. It gave you the impression this was the Somme, that it was endless war here. It wasn't the case that all citizens were involved.[111]

On the other hand, Ellen McAllister, in her reminiscences on her Gorbals childhood, recalls that:

> Razor gangs were prevalent and a lot of trouble was caused by these gangs in the dance halls … . The Beehive Gang stood at the corner of Cumberland Street and Hospital Street. There was an ironmongers there called the Beehive … . Their arch enemies seemed to be the San Toi from Calton and no Calton man was allowed to cross the Albert Bridge to Crown Street without being claimed. I believe this practice continued until the late 1950's.[112]

Stephen Watts, the author of the article in the *New Yorker Magazine*, admitted to never having seen any violence, despite his colourful prose. All the same, he could not bring himself to renounce the myth – indeed, he chose to compound it with a reference to 1920s Chicago:

> I never happened to see a razor, a bottle, or a sharpened bicycle chain actually being used as a weapon (nor did most of the million-odd citizens of Glasgow, just as many a Chicagoan of the period never heard a shot fired), but I often arrived on the scene to see the effect of their use.[113]

Certainly gang violence, to whatever extent it existed, was curbed by the outbreak of the Second World War, which had the effect of removing a large proportion of the young male population and thus of breaking up gangs, while the economic boom after the war, albeit short-lived, brought comparative prosperity and high employment to the Gorbals. Brennan observed that during his survey, published in 1959, the most common remark from those who expressed a wish to stay in their existing houses, rather than have them

---

[110] Gorbals History Research Group, *Third Time Lucky?*, p. 14.

[111] 'Rebirth of the Gorbals', *The Guardian* (20 December 1994), p. 13.

[112] E. McAllister, *Shadows on a Gorbals Wall* (Glasgow: Gorbals Fair Society, 1986), p. 28.

[113] Watts, 'New Miracle in the Gorbals', p. 5.

demolished, was that the Gorbals had quietened down and was not such a bad place to live:

> Things were better than they used to be, we were told, and in any case the Gorbals had never deserved more than half the stories told about it. There had, of course, been razor fights and there had been a few methylated spirits drinkers; and elsewhere there had been groups of idle men crowding in the close mouth around some gambling game and fouling the passage with their spitting – and worse. But, the same informants told us, now the rougher element had moved out, it was not such a bad place. Few would admit that they themselves were 'the toughs' and 'the rougher element' and that they had changed.[114]

Brennan argued that the 'pacification' of the Gorbals was also partly to do with the altered economic status of women in the city after the Second World War. Thanks to new employment opportunities, the Gorbals no longer bounded their horizons (for some at least) and they developed social aspirations, while households benefited economically from their earnings.[115] Yet the theme of violence in the Gorbals was never far away, even if the importance of the gang had declined. In the Christian Action report from 1965 on the old Gorbals, it was stated that 'Gang warfare was a feature before the war. Today it is more prominent amongst the children in the area.'[116] But all the same, the report makes the point that 'It was reported to us that, by comparison with a few years ago, there is a great deal more violence and knife carrying', and provides some examples:

> Mrs Josephine Collins, Chairman of the Hutchesontown–Gorbals Tenants Association, recently had a petrol bomb thrown through her letter box. Only a fortnight before our investigation team arrived in the Gorbals there was a case of an 18 year old girl who had been slashed. She had to have 30 stitches in her face. A week before there had been a shooting in a pub called *Molls Mire*.[117]

Accounts of deprivation and violence might, of course, be attributed to any number of socioeconomically deprived areas in any number of large cities but, in the case of Glasgow, the scapegoat for many years was the Gorbals. The same was true for alcohol consumption. In Glasgow the stereotype of the hearty Scot with a taste for whisky became twisted into that of the hard-drinking hard man, and, again, it was the Gorbals that became the spiritual home of this stereotype. It is no coincidence that in almost every quotation about violence in this section there is also a reference to alcohol or drunkenness. Certainly, middle-class concern for working-class alcohol abuse has a long pedigree in Great Britain.

---

[114] Brennan, *Reshaping a City*, p. 182.
[115] Ibid., p. 184.
[116] *The Gorbals 1965*, no page nos.
[117] Ibid.

In Glasgow the trustees of the City Improvement Trust, established in 1866, forbade the use of any of their property as public houses or whisky shops on moral grounds. This policy was inherited by the Corporation and, encouraged by a mix of Presbyterian and Catholic morality, survived until 1969. Not only did this mean that Corporation members were condemned to drink tea at public occasions hosted by the Corporation, but, more significantly, it also meant that many of the inter-war council estates were 'dry' – that is, devoid of public houses and therefore lacking a valuable focus for social interaction. At the time of the designation of the Hutchesontown/part Gorbals CDA in 1957 there were 48 public houses in the development area, which were to be replaced after redevelopment by only nine. Whilst the original figure was high, it was not exceptional: in 1956, at the time of the public inquiry into the Hutchesontown–Gorbals CDA, the secretary of the Glasgow and District Licensed Trade Defence Association was reported as saying that, if anything, the old Gorbals was under-licensed, with a ratio of one public house for every 565 persons. He claimed that while Glasgow as a whole had only one pub for every 819 persons (doubtless reflecting the extensive 'dry' estates constructed by the Corporation), Edinburgh had one for every 544, and Birmingham one for every 582.[118]

Whether or not the Gorbals was under-licensed, there is no doubt that the negative aspects of its identity have been an enduring theme. As journalist Kenneth Roy put it, writing in March 1967, 'The Gorbals is a legend for all the wrong reasons; violence, poverty, social and physical degradation, drunkenness, depravity. Such legends die hard and painfully and slowly.'[119] Yet there is another important aspect of the old Gorbals myth, one which both complements and contradicts the themes discussed above: that of the vibrant neighbourhood, of the tight-knit community, of people who were always willing to share what little they had to help a neighbour. The Gorbals History Research Group remembers that 'The people were a God-fearing caring community ... . People were interdependent and supportive of one another at times of births and marriages. A death in the family was felt by the entire community – everyone was affected',[120] while Frank Worsdall, in his introduction to *Gorbals Children* explained that 'from its very beginning the Gorbals seems to have attracted a particular kind of person, fundamentally hard-working and shrewd, and with an astute business sense'.[121] This was a

---

[118] 'More Public Houses Sought in the New Gorbals', *The Glasgow Herald* (21 September 1956), p. 9.

[119] K. Roy, 'The Gorbals Still Waits for its Miracle', *The Glasgow Herald* (27 March 1967), p. 5.

[120] Gorbals History Research Group, *Third Time Lucky?*, p. 14.

[121] Worsdall, 'Introduction', in J. McKenzie, *Gorbals Children: A Study in Photographs* (Glasgow: Richard Drew Publishing, 1990), p. 7.

description far distant from that of Christian Action's 'sump of human degradation' and, paradoxically, closer to that of the *No Mean City* school's environmentalist position whereby certain human types colonize specific environments. Certainly, the overcrowded conditions and the shared facilities in the tenements, including the middens, the drying greens and wash-houses, the common stairs and the closes, all facilitated interaction, especially amongst women, since many of these spaces belonged to the domestic realm. The mouths of closes were favourite points for chatting, but women in particular also engaged in an activity called 'hingin'' – that is, leaning out of their windows to chat with their neighbours (whilst also supervising children playing in the street below). The street offered the principal recreational space for children: 'The street was wide and made of asphalt paving, great to play on, especially ball games, skipping ropes, rounders, peever and chuckies',[122] while 'Boys played football, cycled or played at cowboys. Some built carts with old pram wheels and pushed each other's carts along the pavements.'[123]

The old Gorbals was not only a residential area, it also played host to many economic concerns. The 1956 survey report for the Hutchesontown/part Gorbals Comprehensive Development Area found that there were over 100 industrial concerns in the area, employing a total of around 12 000 people. Most of these activities were located in small factories in back courts, and 75 per cent had ten or fewer employees, while only five in the whole redevelopment area employed more than 50 people.[124] The largest activities in the area produced food and drink products and hosiery, while the smaller firms were involved in a bewildering array of activities, including upholstery and chairframe-making, manufacturing of sugar confectionery, cigarette storage, scrap metal storage, rag storage, spirit dealing, printing, olive oil bottling, brass finishing, fish-curing, chemical manufacturing, and there was even a sausage skin merchant's warehouse.[125] In the same development area there were 444 shops of one kind or another, located on the ground floor of the tenements.[126] Of the inter-war period, the Gorbals History Research Group recalls:

> ... in the old days there were countless shops. In Cumberland Street everything from a needle to an anchor could be bought. The butcher's shop was possibly the least hygienic as the meat hung on big hooks against the wall and in summer flies were all over the meat. On Saturday afternoons, half an hour before closing, crowds used to gather at the open window of

[122] McAllister, *Shadows on a Gorbals Wall*, p. 4.

[123] Gorbals History Research Group, *Third Time Lucky?*, p. 26.

[124] 'The New Gorbals Plan Approved: £13,000,000 Scheme Phased Over 20 Years', *The Glasgow Herald* (9 February 1957), p. 6.

[125] Corporation of the City of Glasgow, *Hutchesontown/Part Gorbals Comprehensive Development Area, 1956: Survey Report* (Glasgow: Corporation of the City of Glasgow, 1956), Appendix IV.

[126] Ibid., p. 6.

> the fishmonger's waiting for the fish to be sold at half price ... at most corners was the public house ... . Another very necessary shop was the pawnbroker's where good clothes could be pawned on Mondays to be redeemed on Fridays.[127]

The presence of a Jewish community meant that there was also a commercial life on a Sunday. Moreover, the CDA survey indicated that there were all the other services a community requires, including 19 doctors' and dentists' surgeries, three banks, a post office, three cinemas, one wash-house and baths, a library, police station, six halls and meeting rooms, and eight churches with six church halls.[128] All these figures would seem to support the image of Gorbals as a lively, busy neighbourhood, although the majority of commercial premises were located on the main traffic routes going in and out of the city centre, while other streets presented a more monotonous pattern of flats on the ground floor. Moreover, the CDA survey found that 50 shops were vacant, and 'many are small and do not appear to be prosperous'.[129]

In contrast to all the descriptions in this section, the sociologist Tom Brennan saw in the Gorbals not a colourful exception, but a rather grey rule, an area similar to other parts of the city. Without denying the poverty of the internal conditions, Brennan provides a 'de-mythologized' vision: 'The area as a whole, though not attractive, is very much like other parts of Glasgow, congested and rather grey and dull, without playgrounds or much open space available for public use, with an occasional scrap yard or untidy storage yard mixed up with houses.'[130] Given all the colourful stories – not only of razors, vermin, squalor and crime, but also of human comfort and company – which go to make up the myth of the old Gorbals, it seems incongruous to hear the area described as 'grey and dull' and 'very much like other parts of Glasgow',[131] but this only

---

[127] Gorbals History Research Group, *Third Time Lucky?*, p. 16.

[128] Corporation of the City of Glasgow, *Hutchesontown/Part Gorbals Comprehensive Development Area, 1956: Survey Report*, p. 6. Given Glasgow's policy of religiously segregated schools, the corporation had to assess the proportion of Catholic and Protestant schoolchildren in the area, which in turn indicates the general proportions in the population of Hutchesontown–Gorbals – approximately one-third Catholic and two-thirds Protestant.

[129] Ibid.

[130] Brennan, *Reshaping a City*, p. 64.

[131] The same sentiment, this time in a literary rather than academic form, is present in the observations of Cliff Hanley, a Glasgow writer and journalist, from 1990; 'The Gorbals ... is more of a legend than a geographical location; a legend, that is, to people who have never seen the place ... . The Gorbals ranks, in the myth world, with the Barbary Coast and Tiger Bay and Chicago's Loop, Harlem, Chinatown and old Dodge City, as one of the insalubrious places where "anything goes".

To see the place in reality is to endanger the legend, maybe to endanger all legends. Each of these places must have contained a steady population of shopkeepers, clock repairers, music students and milliners, who went about their business every day and retired to their respectable beds every night, without even realising that the outside

goes to reinforce the argument that the elements which make up the identity of this area of the city are varied and contradictory, and they have been variously celebrated and suppressed, exaggerated and dismissed, forgotten and rediscovered at different historical moments by various actors. We now turn to a closer examination of this process, starting with the miracle of the new Gorbals.

The miracle of the 'new Gorbals'

The Hutchesontown/part Gorbals CDA – the first step towards the eradication of the old Gorbals – was not only the first CDA to be designated in Glasgow but also the largest, in population terms, to be designated nationally. The reasons for the importance given to this development are fairly clear from the previous section: the institutionalized view of the Gorbals was that of the archetypal slum, and the area was recognized as such even in an international context. The reputation of the Gorbals was a source of civic shame: this would have been the case for any city government in this post-war period of optimism and social improvement, but especially one which such a strong reputation for its socialist principles. A Labour administration, such as that of Glasgow, could not be seen to be anything less than efficient in dealing with the city's working-class housing crisis.

The weight of meaning attached to the Gorbals makes it difficult to imagine how Glasgow's programme of slum clearance could justifiably have been started anywhere else in the city. This was explicitly acknowledged at the time: at the 1956 public inquiry for the proposed development scheme, counsel for Glasgow Corporation stated that 'The very name Gorbals has come to epitomize all that is worst in living conditions, not only in Glasgow, or, indeed, in Scotland, but in Britain'. Significantly, there was virtually no opposition to the project for the new Gorbals, with the exception of one or two voices. For example, in 1955 a Progressive councillor urged an amendment to the Corporation's resolution approving the new plans for the Gorbals. His objections rested mainly on the treatment of economic activities which would be displaced and on the lack of information regarding the cost of the scheme, which he described as 'some Utopian dreamer's plan'.[132] He feared that the Gorbals project would cost so much that the Corporation would be unable to pursue other operations, but this lone councillor could not even find a seconder for his amendment amongst the ranks of his own party. Tom Brennan also raised questions about the cost of the project, suggesting that it might be closer to £20 million than the estimated £13 million, but his prediction made no impact

world thought they were living in hell.' Cliff Hanley, Foreword to McKenzie, *Gorbals Children*.

[132] 'Utopian Plan', *The Glasgow Herald* (25 November 1955), p. 8.

on civic resolve. The Corporation did not, therefore, have to struggle to find a general consensus for the project, dramatic as it was in the planning context of the time. Indeed, the comprehensive nature of the project was regarded as entirely necessary, for there seemed little worth saving in the old Gorbals.

The official reasons for the comprehensive redevelopment of Hutchesontown–Gorbals were outlined in the written statement for the comprehensive development area, published in 1956. It is possible to identify two distinct but complementary themes in the Corporation's argument. First, there is a justification, already touched upon in the previous section, founded on nineteenth-century hygienist arguments against the slum – arguments based on criteria of sanitation, overcrowding, sunlight and ventilation: 'The Survey Report ... shows that, in general, these properties are old, in poor condition from both a structural and a sanitary point of view and lack modern facilities. Individually, the houses are very small, overcrowded and extremely densely developed, while the whole area lacks amenity.'[133] The second justification is founded on the modernist conception of the functional zoning of the city and the facilitation of traffic flow, involving the rationalization and separation of land uses: 'The Land Use Survey illustrates the indiscriminate mixture of residential, industrial and commercial uses within the area; the unsatisfactory road layout which encourages through-traffic, and which contains numerous dangerous crossings; the lack of adequate school sites, etc.'[134] Taken together, these themes led to an inevitable conclusion: 'It is the opinion of the Corporation that the area is one of bad layout and obsolete development, and that the only satisfactory way of dealing with it is to define it as an area of Comprehensive Development under the Town and Country Planning (Scotland) Act, 1947.'[135]

The very first stage of the redevelopment project – what would come to be known as Hutchesontown 'A' – was approved in late 1956 and covered only one hectare.[136] While it formed part of the overall development plan for the Gorbals, the area was distinct from the CDA, which only received official permission in 1957. This first stage consisted of 96 housing units in 'low-rise' blocks – two of four storeys and one of three storeys. Care was taken over the open space around the blocks, and there were few private gardens and no traditional back greens. The scheme was opened in May 1958 and received the Saltire Society Award for that year on the grounds that it was 'Probably the most striking of all local authority housing completed in Scotland in 1958, both as a symbol of the new Glasgow and by contrast with its appalling surroundings. Here is new life

[133] Corporation of the City of Glasgow, *Hutchesontown/Part Gorbals Comprehensive Development Area, 1956: Written Statement*, p. 3.

[134] Ibid.

[135] Ibid.

[136] The successive stages of the Hutchesontown–Gorbals redevelopment were indicated by letters of the alphabet, from 'A' to 'E'.

growing out of the slums of the worst crowded city in Western Europe.'[137] This juxtaposition of 'the slums' of the old Gorbals and the 'new life' in the new Gorbals, or in this case 'the new Glasgow', was to be a recurrent theme in the discourse of planners, politicians and the media in these years of optimism.

A more significant step towards the exorcism of the old and the birth of the new was the approval of the £13 million plans for comprehensive development, first by the Corporation of the City of Glasgow – a unanimous decision – and then, on 8 February 1957, by the secretary of state for Scotland.[138] The scheme was an ambitious one: the 7605 existing tenement houses in the area of 45 hectares were to be replaced by 3502 'modern' houses, about half of which would be in tower blocks of ten storeys or more, producing a density of 371 habitable rooms per hectare.[139] As *The Glasgow Herald* put it, comparing this blueprint for the future with the Gorbals as it existed then, the 'spacious layout is in striking contrast to the closely built mass of property'.[140] Only 180 of the existing houses were to be allowed to remain standing. The population of the area would be reduced from 26 860 to 10 179, and the aim was to rehouse in the area a cross-section of the existing population which would include single-person households, but exclude households of six or more members.[141] Larger industrial establishments were to be moved elsewhere, while some of the smaller concerns would be relocated on a 1.2 hectare site reserved for service industries. In all, 25.1 hectares (56 per cent) of the total 45 hectares were assigned to residential use, 7.7 hectares (17 per cent) to schools (one secondary school and two primary schools), 2.4 hectares (5.7 per cent) for community facilities including churches, 2.2 hectares (5 per cent) to public open space (the planners counted on making use of two large public parks existing nearby), and 4.9 hectares (11 per cent) for roads and carparks.[142] Just over 1.2 hectares were allocated for commercial purposes, with the intention of providing one main and three subsidiary shopping centres containing, in all, 57 shops, nine public houses, a cinema, a community centre and accommodation for offices, banks,

[137] Corporation of the City of Glasgow, *The First Quinquennial Review of the Development Plan, 1960: The Survey Report*, section 13.6.

[138] 'The New Gorbals Plan Approved: £13,000,000 Scheme Phased Over 20 Years', *The Glasgow Herald* (9 February 1957), p. 5. The Written Statement for the Development Plan estimated that the total redevelopment cost would be £12 915 000, of which £1 250 000 was the estimated cost of acquisition, £500 000 the estimated cost of demolition, and £11 165 000 the estimated cost of development.

[139] Corporation of the City of Glasgow, *Hutchesontown/Part Gorbals Comprehensive Development Area, 1956: Written Statement*, p. 4.

[140] 'New Gorbals Plan', *The Glasgow Herald* (9 February 1957), p. 6.

[141] Corporation of the City of Glasgow, *Hutchesontown/Part Gorbals Comprehensive Development Area, 1956: Written Statement*, p. 4.

[142] J.H. Rae, *Gorbals Local Plan. Draft Survey Report* (Glasgow: Glasgow District Council, 1984), p. 24.

surgeries and so on.[143] It was decided that only a clinic, a library, a police station and nine churches should be retained from the old Gorbals.

The only dissenting voices at the public inquiry for the Hutchesontown/part Gorbals plan were economic interests concerned at the implications of the transformation of the area. Objections to the project were lodged by: the Licensed Trade Defence Association, which was concerned that the number of public houses was to be reduced from 48 to nine; the Glasgow and District Branch of the National Federation of Newsagents, Booksellers and Stationers, which was also concerned with the reduction in commercial premises and a fear that, with fewer shops, street vendors would benefit from their trade; the National Union of Small Shopkeepers, which felt that the compensation system was unfair and that displaced shopkeepers should be given the first opportunity to take over new shops in the Corporation's suburban schemes; a knitwear firm which was required by the plan to move out of the area; and several individual businessmen. The Corporation gave no ground to these objections, telling the shopkeepers, for example, that 'the corporation would give them more than sympathy and would do anything they could to minimize any hardship they might suffer', but offering no concessions.[144] The knitwear firm claimed that it would be entitled to compensation of £356 245 if it had to move its factory, but even this did not blunt municipal resolve.[145] The presence of a large factory in the middle of their new residential area was anathema to the principles of modernist functional planning, and the symbolic meaning of the new Gorbals could not be compromised by what the Corporation called that 'old-fashioned factory sticking up there'.[146] Ironically, the firm did remain in the new Gorbals and, indeed, the building stands to this day.[147]

The development was scheduled to last 20 years. The first five-year programme covered one-third of the total area of the plan and involved the clearance of 2030 houses and the construction of 876. It was to be divided into two parts: Hutchesontown 'B' and Hutchesontown 'C'. In an unusual move, the

---

143 The zonings in the CDA were subsequently reviewed in the Quinquennial Review of 1965.

144 ' "More than Sympathy" for Displaced Traders', *The Glasgow Herald* (22 September 1956), p. 6.

145 'More Public Houses Sought in the New Gorbals', *The Glasgow Herald* (21 September 1956), p. 9.

146 ' "That Old-Fashioned Factory" in the Gorbals', *The Glasgow Herald* (10 October 1956), p. 8. Moreover, the Corporation could not afford to set a precedent which might have allowed firms in a similar position to remain in other redevelopment areas.

147 In December 1968, the Progressives, supported by the SNP, outvoted Labour by 58 votes to 39 to change the zoning in the area to allow the firm to stay. The Progressives were afraid of the job losses involved in relocation, as well as of the amount of compensation the Corporation would be required to pay. The site occupied by the factory had originally been zoned for a community centre.

Corporation employed two well-known private architects, both of whom were based in Edinburgh, to carry out the detailed design of these developments, the city architect and planning officer having intimated that, because of work commitments and staffing problems, his department would be unable to carry out this task. Whether or not this was the case, the chance to employ two high-profile architects enabled the Corporation to make a clear statement about their intentions for the redevelopment of the Gorbals. Robert Matthew and Partners carried out the Hutchesontown 'B' scheme, which was a mixed development of low-rise blocks and four high-rise towers reaching 17 storeys. These towers flanked the Clyde and thus offered an important riverside frontage to the city centre on the opposite bank.[148] There was also a number of shops and services in the 'B' scheme, but no industry.

The Hutchesontown 'C' development was to prove to be much more controversial. The project was assigned to Basil Spence and Partners, and was to contain not only residential elements, but also service industries, community facilities and the main shopping centre for the new Gorbals.[149] The Corporation's planners had already specified that the shopping centre (including clinics, a post office, a police station and so on) should take the form of a semi-covered, pedestrianized area located beneath and around blocks of multi-storey flats. Spence designed two 22-storey residential blocks raised on *piloti* to allow free passage underneath. The blocks included inset communal balconies or gardens, which Spence apparently represented to the housing committee as the perpetuation of the tenement back green tradition and thus as a means to foster social interaction amongst the residents. Miles Horsey recounts that 'a former senior Corporation architect, present at that meeting, recalls that "he [Spence] told them, 'on Tuesdays, when all the washing's out, it'll be like a great ship in full sail!' ".'[150] In June 1961 the Queen arrived to lay the foundation stone of what was to be called Queen Elizabeth Square. The two slab blocks reached a height of 55 metres and, with their bright-white concrete and their association with hanging gardens, came to symbolize the new Gorbals. More than this, they also came to be a flagship for tower block developments in other parts of the city.

---

[148] This development came to be called Waddell Court and Commercial Court.

[149] Apart from his contribution to the Gorbals, Spence was also responsible for the controversial rebuilding of Coventry Cathedral after the Second World War, having won the design competition in 1951. He also designed the terminal building at Glasgow airport, and won major contracts at the universities of Southampton, Sussex, Liverpool, Exeter and Durham. From 1961 to 1968 he was professor of architecture at the Royal Academy, and was president of the Royal Institute of British Architects from 1958 to 1960. Despite the criticisms levelled at his buildings in the Gorbals, and especially at his tower-blocks, his project was one of the few post-war public housing schemes in Glasgow that showed any concern for aspects of architectural composition.

[150] Horsey, *Tenements and Towers*, p. 39.

The new Gorbals was one of the earliest redevelopment programmes in Great Britain and consequently there was virtually 'no space of experience, to use Koselleck's term. On the other hand, the institutionalized view of the old Gorbals as a slum demanded a radically new future, and the new Gorbals seemed to provide just that – new architectural forms, new arrangements of space, new technology and new materials. It was commonly reported that residents of the old Gorbals who were rehoused in the new flats were overcome by the space and privacy they afforded, by the fact that each family member had a bedroom for him or herself, and, perhaps above all, by the novelty of having their own bathroom (in an interview with the author, a Gorbals' resident described getting a bathroom as 'like getting a million dollars'). Their good fortune was confirmed by public rhetoric, which was future-oriented and continually associated the Gorbals with 'newness'. In February 1957 Lord Strathclyde called the plan ' "this most impressive undertaking" which aimed to produce a completely new and finer environment for the people of Hutchesontown–Gorbals; it was a "new deal" – a long term investment in a new Glasgow in which human environment would be worthy of the greatness of the city'.[151] The novelty of the project was such that it was regarded as an experiment, and Watts, writing in the *New Yorker Magazine* proclaimed:

> Five years from now ... the name of the Gorbals will be on the lips of the world's leading architects, but no longer as that of Britain's most painful and publicised slum ... their eyes will be looking up and taking in a picture of one of the most progressive social and architectural experiments this country has seen.[152]

At the opening of the first of the Spence slab blocks in 1962, Noble, Secretary of State for Scotland, dismissed the Gorbals' past whilst heralding the 'miracle' of the new Gorbals:

> People who don't know Glasgow have a picture of the Gorbals. It is often a bad one and a wrong one ... . In putting Glasgow into focus in the world's eye it was a masterly stroke to begin at this point. Here, ladies and gentlemen, the world is going to see the real miracle of the Gorbals.[153]

The next stage of the new Gorbals, Hutchesontown 'D', was assigned to the Scottish Special Housing Association (SSHA) rather than to Glasgow Corporation. The SSHA was a government agency originally established in the 1937 with the aim of accelerating the pace of house-building in the public sector. Central government funded the construction of SSHA housing, thus

---

[151] 'The New Gorbals Plan Approved: £13,000,000 Scheme Phased Over 20 Years', *The Glasgow Herald* (9 February 1957), p. 6.

[152] Watts, 'New Miracle in the Gorbals', p. 5.

[153] Cited in *The Gorbals 1965*, no page nos.

alleviating financial pressure on local government.[154] SSHA housing was built to a higher specification than was normal for local authority housing, but rents were generally higher too. The scheme, which was to provide 326 houses at an estimated cost of £1.3 million, was approved in 1965. The houses were in maisonette form, built in four-storey blocks around pedestrian courtyards. Then in 1968, even as central government was beginning to lose its enthusiasm for high-rise flats, the Corporation approved three eight-storey SSHA blocks, containing 96 apartments in all. It was during this phase that the Hutchesontown Tenants' Association (HTA) was formed by tenants who felt that the new area needed additional facilities, including a post office, shops and a pedestrian crossing in Caledonia Road. Originally the HTA only represented SSHA tenants, but its constitution was changed in 1971 to allow Corporation tenants to join. The HTA would become one of the most influential tenants' associations in the area.

Meanwhile, the western part of the Gorbals area had also come under the planner's scrutiny; Laurieston–Gorbals had originally been identified as a housing area in the *Quinquennial Review* of 1960. It had then received outline approval from the secretary of state for Scotland in 1964, and finally gained full approval in 1966. The plan, covering 14 acres, envisaged replacing 5500 old tenement flats with 2702 units in seven 24-storey blocks, and various deck-access blocks of six to eight storeys. The deck-access proposal was a novelty and was met with enthusiasm by *The Gorbals View* which described it 'In layman's terms, [as] an experiment in housing, to be tried out here in Gorbals, which might revolutionize the city of the future'.[155] The population would be reduced from 18 000 to 10 000. Part of the plan involved a riverside zone on the banks of the Clyde which would feature civic buildings fronting the river. These eventually included Glasgow sheriff court, a College of Nautical Studies and a mosque. As in Hutchesontown–Gorbals, the proposals for the redevelopment of the area met with little opposition other than from the licensed trade, concerned at the reduction in the number of public houses.

In 1969, the last phase of the Hutchesontown/part Gorbals scheme was initiated at an estimated cost of £6.7 million for 1143 housing units, a health clinic, a nursery school, a new church, three public houses and five or six shops.[156] The secretary of state for Scotland gave his approval in July 1969, but added that the scheme was expensive and not as well designed as he would have

---

[154] For a detailed discussion of the role of the SSHA in the provision of housing in Scotland, (the organization was abolished in April 1989), see R. Rodger and H. Al-Qaddo, 'The Scottish Special Housing Association and the Implementation of Housing Policy, 1937–87', in Rodger, *Scottish Housing in the Twentieth Century*.

[155] 'Comment. The Gorbals Experiment', *The Gorbals View*, no. 4 (July 1967), p. 1. ML.

[156] 'Mr Ross does not like Flats Proposal', *The Glasgow Herald* (24 July 1969), p. 14.

wished for the redevelopment of Glasgow. In particular, he was concerned about the number of families with children who might have to live in the upper levels of the two 24-storey blocks which were proposed, as well as the limited amount of open space provision. Apart from the two high-rise blocks, the 'E' scheme also included 12 seven-storey deck-access blocks which escaped the secretary of state's criticism. Once again, the deck-access design was hailed as an exciting experiment at a time when public opinion was turning against high-rise flats. Glasgow Corporation's chief planner at the time, James Rae, described the principle of the deck-access system in terms that mixed innovation with the evocative image of the traditional urban scene that had been lost with the introduction of high-rise flats: 'These "streets in the air" will form definite places and thoroughfares and will contain familiar street objects such as telephone kiosks, post boxes, seating benches, planting etc., and also shops.'[157] The 'familiar street objects' never materialized, and instead the development was marked by long, featureless access balconies. The deck-access flats were constructed using a patented system of prefabricated panels assembled on-site. This system, called Tracoba, had been developed in France and patented in 1958. It was first used there in 1959, and then subsequently in Algeria and in England, where the British concessionaires were Gilbert Ash (Structures) Ltd. In 1972, the Queen made a return trip to the Gorbals to open this new development which finally completed the Hutchesontown/part Gorbals programme.

The physical restructuring of the Gorbals was accompanied by a complementary social restructuring. Almost two-thirds of the Gorbals' population in 1957, when the CDA was approved, had to leave the area to take a house in the city's peripheral estates. A survey of almost 9000 employed people in the redevelopment area carried out by the Corporation's planning department in the same year found that 56 per cent of workers in the Hutchesontown–Gorbals area would have preferred to be rehoused in the same area after redevelopment.[158] This figure would certainly have been higher had the retired population also been consulted. The right to remain in the Gorbals was partly decided by length of time on the Corporation's housing list, household size and so on but, over and above this, the Corporation actively pursued a selection procedure to ensure that only the most 'suitable' tenants were able to qualify for a flat in the new Gorbals, even if it was not keen to publicize this process. 'Suitability' was assessed by a housing visitor, 'usually', according to *The Gorbals View*, 'a middle-aged lady with no special training', who called upon applicants for a new house. This housing visitor would fill in a

---

[157] 'Decked-Housing: A Special Article', *The Gorbals View*, no. 5 (August 1967), p. 13. ML.

[158] 'Attraction of Living in the Gorbals of the future', *The Glasgow Herald* (11 September 1957), p. 9.

report on the household and, in what *The Gorbals View* termed the 'most interesting and disturbing part of the form', gave their opinion on the family and their home: 'She grades them very good/good/medium/fair/poor under three categories; "Type of people", "Cleanliness", and "Furniture".'[159] To get a house in Hutchesontown, three marks of 'good' were required. 'So', *The Gorbals View* explained, 'if for example a family has been holding off buying new furniture till they get a new house they may only rate "medium" for furniture and they won't rate for a Hutchesontown house – the houses most families in this area want.'[160]

Despite the miracle only being available to selected tenants, the programme had continued to avoid dissenting voices throughout the 1960s. Certainly for some, especially the elderly, the prospect of leaving their old houses was tinged with regret. In November 1967, for example, *The Gorbals View* featured Mrs Mary Galloway, an 80 year-old woman living in a rat-infested single end with barricaded windows, who explained that:

> This building is not condemned yet. When it is, and I am told to go – then of course I will leave. Of course, on condition that I am given a decent place to go. In the meantime, I'm paying ten bob a week for this place, and I'm happy enough. ALL I WANT IS FOR PEOPLE TO LEAVE ME IN PEACE. I have wonderful friends and neighbours in the Gorbals here, and that is really something money cannot buy.[161]

Mrs Galloway's comment about 'wonderful friends and neighbours' is interesting because it offers an early example of the evocation and prioritization of the identification of the old Gorbals as a place of close social ties over its established meaning as a slum. A more extreme case, this time from 1971, offers an example whereby the social interaction in the old Gorbals was evoked even when the physical evidence of this 'community' had been swept away. Mr and Mrs John Mullen and their four children were the last household remaining in a tenement located at Gorbals Cross, in the heart of the old Gorbals. All the houses around them had been razed, and the bulldozers had even pulled away most of the building around their apartment with the result that there was a nine-metre drop from the back landing and the parents had forbidden their children to play in the house in case they were injured. Vandals had repeatedly lit fires in the derelict property below the flat and the police had evacuated the family on several occasions. The newspapers showed the Mullen's home perched precariously on a pile of masonry with nothing around it, like a rock stack in the Arizona Desert. Given their absolute isolation, their reasons for wishing to

[159] 'Mrs McLeish has lived in Gorbals for 35 years', *The Gorbals View*, no. 57 (January 1972), p. 1. ML.

[160] Ibid.

[161] Quoted by Jack Caplan in 'Gorbals Gossip', *The Gorbals View*, no. 8 (November 1967), p. 3. ML.

remain seemed incongruous: 'Apart from convenience for buses we have lived in Gorbals for 25 years since we came over from Ireland and this is where all our friends are.'[162] In July 1971, when the Mullens finally agreed to move out, they had been without neighbours for a year and a half, yet Mrs Mullen still insisted on the social importance of the Gorbals: 'I'll be sorry to leave Gorbals, as our relatives and friends live in this area, but it's a nice house we are going to.'[163]

The Mullens may have had other reasons for defying the bulldozers. By the early 1970s there were isolated incidents of families defying eviction orders because they claimed that the Corporation had reneged on rehousing promises. Often these tenants insisted that the Corporation had undertaken to rehouse them in the Gorbals area and repeatedly rejected offers for new houses in the peripheral estates. The Corporation, on the other hand, believed that the tenants were 'holding out', a tactic by which they hoped to secure themselves better housing offers. Since the Corporation had contractual agreements with construction companies, delays in clearing an area could have serious financial implications. In one case it was reported that because of ten families 'holding out' in Laurieston–Gorbals for a period of seven weeks, the Corporation had been obliged to pay an additional £280 000 to Crudens Ltd in compensation for delays in starting the construction of the multi-storey flats, and housing officials openly suggested that some families had been awkward in order to pressure the Corporation into offering them better houses.[164]

There is little doubt that those who were assigned a place in the new housing were considered particularly fortunate. For example, the Christian Action report of 1965, describing the Gorbals landscape of derelict tenements, added: 'In the background loom the new tower blocks of the Hutchesontown Redevelopment Scheme; some finished, some still being constructed. For a lucky few these are home, but to most of the 18 000 people in the Gorbals they remain and will remain only a promise on the skyline.'[165] The contrast between old and new was stark, as the 'Comment' page of *The Gorbals View* emphasized:

> Huddled behind the gleaming new flats, dwarfed by them both physically and in terms of propaganda, crouches the old Gorbals ... the Gorbals of 'No Mean City', of numerous Television and Press stories. The old Gorbals – jumbled crazily, precariously, aggressively smack up against the new.'[166]

---

[162] 'Family Defy Bulldozers', *The Glasgow Herald* (20 March 1971), p. 6.

[163] 'Gorbals Family Agree to Move out', *The Glasgow Herald* (9 July 1971), p. 11.

[164] 'Ten Families Caused £280 000 Housing Delay', *The Glasgow Herald* (9 January 1975), p. 3.

[165] *The Gorbals 1965*, no page numbers.

[166] 'Comment', *The Gorbals View*, no. 10 (January 1968), p. 1. ML.

The proximity of the modern apartment blocks only served to highlight the conditions in the old tenements – conditions which, in any case, were worsened by the phenomenon of planning blight. Themes which we have already seen in Alma-Gare began to emerge as people grew concerned about the authorities' neglect of the older areas which were awaiting redevelopment. For example, in 1964 the newly formed Hutchesontown–Gorbals Tenants' Association organized a demonstration of 'more than 20 housewives some with young children' at the City Chambers in order to protest against the living conditions in the Hutchesontown–Gorbals area.[167] Josephine Collins, the chair of the Association, claimed that some parents had to sit up all night with dogs, hammers and axes to protect their babies from rats and threatened to send a message to the Queen to inform her of the living conditions in the area.[168] In March 1969 the Gorbals Action Group was founded with the aim of ameliorating conditions in the Laurieston part of Gorbals, where redevelopment had been consistently delayed. The group expressed anger at the fact that many streets in the 'redevelopment' area were 'being allowed to die a slow, lingering, and filthy death by the powers that be',[169] and pressed the Corporation to take more action in repairing old houses and clearing debris-strewn back courts. In June 1969 the prospective Conservative parliamentary candidate for Gorbals tried to turn the situation to his political advantage and accused the Corporation of leaving 'a filthy, stinking desert of rubble and water', before swapping geographical metaphor with the rallying cry, 'let's build a new Gorbals in the rubble jungle'.[170] Significantly, more immediate results were obtained when the Lord Provost himself received a complaint from an Edinburgh schoolmaster who claimed that conditions in Abbotsford Place, Gorbals, 'were as bad as those in Calcutta'.[171] The master, from an exclusive public school, had visited the Gorbals with 30 of his pupils in order to clear rubbish from back courts as part of a Christian Action project. This comparison with the 'Third World Other', rather like the description of Roubaix's *courées* as bringing to mind the worst images of misery from Africa or South America, stung the Corporation into action, and officials were quickly dispatched to assess the situation.[172] One might also speculate that there were other dynamics in this event, not least the eternal rivalry between Glasgow and Edinburgh.

---

[167] 'Gorbals Housewives Demonstrate – Living Conditions Scandalous', *The Glasgow Herald* (11 August 1964), p. 5.

[168] Ibid.

[169] 'Gorbals Action Group', *The Gorbals View*, no. 32 (November 1969), p. 3. ML.

[170] 'The Two Faces of the Gorbals', *The Glasgow Herald* (19 June 1969), p. 18.

[171] 'Gorbals Clean-up After Complaint to Lord Provost', *The Glasgow Herald* (24 October 1969), p. 9.

[172] François Miralles in *l'Express*, cited in J. Descamps, 'La résorption des courées de la Métropole Nord', unpublished thesis, University of Lille (1976), see Chapter Three.

As in Alma-Gare, concern was expressed that it was particularly the elderly who were being left isolated in old housing. *The Gorbals View* asked, 'Why do the Corporation always leave old, sick and lonely people to face the problems of the sudden deterioration and wrecking of the building they live in?', and cited the examples (which might equally have come from Alma-Gare) of the old lady who was 'left in a building where water and gas pipes were being cut, doors kicked open, and where the whole structure was rapidly deteriorating'[173] and of the old man living in a semi-derelict tenement who had been forced to beat off intruders with a sweeping brush.[174] The same article also drew attention to the contradictions which had so much troubled the APU in Roubaix, asking, 'Why do [the] Corporation evacuate good buildings that are not insanitary or dangerous?'[175] However, the rehousing tactics used by the APU were never employed in the Gorbals, although it was recognized that 'The planners must be immobilizing thousands of houses each year which could provide excellent homes for people who are at the moment shuffled around like animals'.[176]

Perhaps the tension between old and new in the Gorbals was best summed up in the opening article of the first edition of *The Gorbals View* in April 1967. The article explained:

> We care about the past of Gorbals – we know it wasn't just all slums and street gangs ... . And we care about the present in the Gorbals – mainly because we live in it. For thousands of us, the 'miracle' of the Gorbals has not yet happened: we still live in one of the worst slums in Europe, we watch our children grow up in overcrowded and insanitary houses, we grow weary of the endless promises while the years roll our lives away.[177]

This text, marked by contradiction, challenges the construction of the old Gorbals of 'slums and street gangs', and yet goes on to confirm that it is still 'one of the worst slums in Europe'. From the past and the present from which the inhabitants of Gorbals ('we') draw their 'space of experience', the text moves to the future through the image of a new generation of children growing up. The key to this future lies in the miracle/non-miracle of the new Gorbals, where the horizon of expectation of escape from 'overcrowded and insanitary houses' disappears as 'endless promises' remain unfulfilled. The perspective on the future is made more explicit further on in the article: 'And we care about the future of Gorbals, because it's OUR future, or it should be – and it's the future of our children.'[178] There was an attempt to influence this future

---

173 'Violence: A Symptom?', *The Gorbals View*, no. 16 (July 1968), p. 4. ML.
174 Ibid., p. 5.
175 Ibid.
176 Ibid.
177 'The Reason Why', *The Gorbals View*, no. 1 (April 1967), p. 1. ML.
178 Ibid.

by organizing a series of public meetings to allow residents to examine the proposals for the Laurieston–Gorbals area which had not yet undergone redevelopment: 'COME AND SAY WHAT YOU WANT THE "NEW" GORBALS TO LOOK LIKE!.'[179] The first of these meetings was held on 23 April 1967 and was attended by over 40 people: 'The opinion of the meeting was that there was a pressing need for public opinion to be raised and expressed on the sort of "new" Gorbals we were being offered.'[180] At best, however, these meetings became a means for the Corporation to channel information to the residents rather than a real forum which could influence the form of the Gorbals. Here, participation was held up as an ideal, but unlike Alma-Gare, it was never fought for.

Despite this scepticism, the general consensus amongst the faithful was that a miracle had indeed taken place. As early as 1960, Steven Watts reported in the *New Yorker Magazine* that there had been a belief prevalent in Glasgow that the new housing in the Hutchesontown/part Gorbals CDA would be 'reduced to slums in a few months', not because of the quality of the new construction, but, to return to a theme discussed earlier, because of the nature of the inhabitants of the Gorbals. One day Watts 'walked by for a look' at Hutchesontown 'A', and described the following scene:

> In the flagged courtyards between the modern blocks, women were hanging out washing; there were neat, well-stocked flower and vegetable gardens, and the playgrounds were swarming with children, while there were none playing in the street beyond.
>
> At the windows of the houses there were flower boxes, and on the inside sills I saw china ornaments and more flowers in vases. Every window was curtained and each had a fringed yellow shade.[181]

This rather utopian description is a deliberate contrast to the elements which went to make up the institutionalized view of the old Gorbals (of which *No Mean City* was first and foremost – Watts mentions this novel several times in his article): curtained windows and fringed shades rather than 'windows lit by naked bulbs' and curtains 'an exception'; paved courtyards and 'well-stocked flower and vegetable gardens' instead of back courts which were 'infested wastelands'; and playgrounds swarming with children rather than 'children swarming in and out of the tenements into the spacious streets'. Watts was not alone in noting this transformation; for example, in the first edition of *The Gorbals View*, Alice Cullen, local Labour MP and widely respected

---

[179] *The Gorbals View*, no. 1 (April 1967), p. 1. ML. Capitalized in original.

[180] 'First Public Meeting on New Gorbals', *The Gorbals View*, no. 2 (May 1967), p. 1. ML.

[181] Watts, 'Every Window is Curtained', *The Evening Times* (20 January 1960), p. 5. Copyright 1959, *New Yorker Magazine*.

housing campaigner ('Vote for Alice an' she'll gie ye a palace') wrote: 'We have watched the redevelopment of the Gorbals. We have seen an area, having a reputation for bad housing, overcrowded families, rife unemployment, and an exaggerated over-publicized crime record, experience a vast and continued change.'[182]

By January 1968 even the editorial staff of *The Gorbals View*, who in April 1967 had claimed, as we have seen, that 'For thousands of us, the "miracle" of the Gorbals has not yet happened', had come to accept the miraculous transformation from old to new. The leading article in this issue picked up on the spirit of the new year in order to reflect upon the changes taking place in the area, and proclaimed unambiguously:

> The miracle of Gorbals! After years of wordy and empty promises from politicians, and highly coloured sensationalism in press and on television, it all began to happen ... . And not only buildings were new created in Hutchesontown. A people were created – with a common voice to be heard, in Ward Committee and Tenants Association.[183]

The rejection of the old in this statement goes to the extreme of suggesting that the reconstruction of the Gorbals was not only physical, but also social, and that 'a people were created' who were best suited to living in this new environment, indirectly lending support to the Corporation's selection procedure. The implication contained in this argument that the dwellers of the old Gorbals were somehow tainted by their slum environment would, as the following chapter shows, be employed by Glasgow Corporation as their miracle began to go awry. The piece continues: 'And now – 1968 – we are at the beginning of the end. Now the bulldozers, mindless avengers of years of neglect, are grinding out at last the final solution for Gorbals.'[184] The imagery here is particularly strong, although the echoing of Holocaust discourse in the 'final solution' is almost certainly unintentional. The bulldozer is portrayed as a 'mindless' or neutral force which, in this case, is being put to positive use, as the avenger for the suffering experienced in the old Gorbals. The piece finishes with a sentimental celebration of the Gorbals people, who, in contradiction to the earlier claim that the new Gorbals had created a new people, are depicted as the element which provides continuity in this period of massive change: 'Still – old or new – there are always the people – struggling, up or down – failing, celebrating, giving birth and dying – living and loving in towering multi-storey or condemned multi'slums.'[185]

---

[182] 'From our Member of Parliament, Mrs Alice Cullen, JP, MP', *The Gorbals View*, no. 1 (April 1967), p. 2. ML.

[183] 'Comment. The Old – and the Nearly New', *The Gorbals View*, no. 10 (January 1968), p. 1. ML.

[184] Ibid.

[185] Ibid., pp. 1–2.

The strength of conviction in the Gorbals miracle and the interplay between the meanings of the old and new Gorbals is also apparent in the distress caused by Corporation plans to site a public house close to the new SSHA multi-storey blocks in the Hutchesontown 'D' development. In April 1967 some 500 local residents sent a petition to the Corporation's planning committee protesting about the location of the pub which, they said, was too close to the new housing development and, in particular, to a children's playground. Frank McElhone, a local councillor for the area, claimed that 'The majority of tenants are completely against the site of the public house'.[186] The protest was led by the Hutchesontown Tenants' Association, which claimed that the tenants of the new blocks were being condemned to the old environment of 'no mean city'.[187] It was supported in its campaign by local churches, Glasgow Trades Council, youth leaders, other tenants' associations and MP Alice Cullen. The Corporation stood firm over its decision to license the property, but it is informative to note some of the comments made at a meeting organized by the HTA on 12 June 1967. At this meeting, the public house proposal was described as taking the area 'back to the old Gorbals'.[188] Cullen, pointing out that she had been a political worker in the area for the last 40 years, tapped into the Gorbals' reputation for alcohol consumption: 'If we're going to have a new Gorbals let us make it new without a pub at every corner. I think the site of the public house is disgraceful and I'll fight it to the bitter end.'[189] This was echoed by a local minister – 'The days of a public house on every corner have gone forever' – while another speaker yet again made use of the evocative power of the Gorbal's most famous literary product to distinguish the old from the new: 'The women especially have lifted their families above the dreary image of Gorbals depicted in "No Mean City" and our councillors should be urged to raise at all levels the question of the siting of the pub.'[190] The events surrounding the public house proposal indicate the desire shared by a large proportion of the population to ensure that no vestiges of the old Gorbals should remain to taint their new environment.

Of course, given the massive scale of change, contradictions were never far from the surface in attempts to put the transformation of the Gorbals in perspective. A writer for *The Gorbals View* interviewed some of the residents of Spence's high-rise flats in May 1967, and while one woman described them as

---

[186] 'Attempts are to be Made Today ...', *The Glasgow Herald* (4 April 1967), p. 5.

[187] 'Hutchesontown Tenants Angry at Pub near New Flats', *The Glasgow Herald* (12 May 1967), p. 13.

[188] 'Tenants to ask the Secretary of State to Meet a Deputation ...', *The Glasgow Herald* (13 June 1967), p. 20.

[189] Ibid.

[190] Ibid.

'A miracle of modern architecture', another tenant compared them to 'A bloody great slab cake'. He went on to explain that the different blocks in the Spence flats had been given prison nicknames by their residents: 'Alcatraz for A Block, Barlinnie [Glasgow's own prison] for B Block, and C Block being called Sing Sing!.'[191] But the paper's contributor added, 'I didn't find many people who were prepared to swap their new houses for the old property they had just come from.'[192]

Nostalgic recollections jostled with memories of the living conditions. The same edition of *The Gorbals View* carried a letter from a resident of the new SSHA flats in the Hutchesontown 'D' development who claimed that he and his wife still found 'the old friendly spirit' in the multi-storey flats and concluded that 'Our two apartment is just a dream home, and cheaper to run on electricity than our old home on coal and gas'. But this letter contains a plea for a degree of selective memory, for while the correspondent was happy to promote the memory of the old Gorbals as friendly community, he wished to consign to oblivion the view of old Gorbals as the archetypal slum and asked 'Why does TV and the Press keep reminding us of the squalor from which we have emerged and wish to escape'?[193] The same contradictory feelings are epitomized by the advice of *The Gorbals View* from 1969: 'Gorbals needs patient adjustment as the friendly old slumminess goes down before antiseptic modernity. The old was largely lethal, the new rich in promise.'[194]

The recollections of the living conditions in old Gorbals were still sufficiently strong to ensure that no one suggested that the loss of 'friendly old slumminess' was not a necessary sacrifice to endure for a healthier future: 'The new Gorbals, where 8000 are rehoused, parks its cars at the close. The vehicles their fathers knew were the ambulance and the hearse.'[195]

This chapter has sought to demonstrate that the meaning of the Gorbals was complex and often contradictory. By the time of its redevelopment, the institutionalized vision of the area was of a degraded slum, characterized by violence and alcohol abuse. This view was tempered somewhat by the idea of 'the old friendly spirit' of the Gorbals, although virtually all references to

---

[191] 'What's It Like Up There?', *The Gorbals View*, no. 2 (May 1967), p. 3. ML. I cannot say to what extent these names were commonly used. Indeed, although the interview states that they applied to the different blocks of Spence's development, they may, in fact, have been used in connection with the different phases – A, B and C – of the Hutchesontown development as a whole.

[192] Ibid.

[193] 'Your View', *The Gorbals View*, no. 2 (May 1967), p. 3. ML.

[194] 'Towards the By-Election', *The Gorbals View*, no. 31 (October 1969), p. 14. ML.

[195] Ibid., p. 13.

this aspect emerged from the 'inside', from the tenants themselves or from their local paper, and they found little resonance in 'external' reports, whether serious studies or sensationalist journalism, which tended to dwell on the area's negative associations. In this respect, the myth of the Gorbals spirit had a redemptory dimension since it offered the inhabitants themselves a means to rise above the damning identification of 'slum-dwellers'.

As for the 'miracle', it would appear that there was a general consensus amongst the population and its associations, as well as amongst politicians and in the press, that the Gorbals was undergoing a real and necessary transformation and that this transformation was to be welcomed as liberating the people of the Gorbals from their slum existence. At this point, the population's common experience of the new housing was limited, while the expectation was immense, and even the loss of the old social networks was deemed to be a reasonable sacrifice in order to obtain a new housing future.

CHAPTER SIX

From hell and back again: (re)constructing the Gorbals

This chapter takes as its starting point the general consensus at the beginning of the 1970s around the meaning of the new Gorbals as a modernist 'miracle' that had replaced the old Gorbals of slums and violence. From different perspectives, and with different motivations, Glasgow Corporation, the new tenants' associations and the residents of the Gorbals – particularly those who were able to remain in the area – welcomed this dawn of the new Gorbals and the twilight of the old. For a short time this consensus was maintained, but soon cracks began to appear. As the physical structure of the new flats, and the Hutchesontown 'E' phase in particular, began to deteriorate, so the definition of the new Gorbals as a 'miracle' became increasingly unsustainable.

It was in the events surrounding the new flats that different identities of the Gorbals were constructed, confronted and negotiated. As discussed in Chapter One, when a meaning for an area is constructed, this meaning is never entirely new. Material for this construction is found 'lying around' amongst the debris of the old. In this example, the materials were found lying around in the myth of the old Gorbals.

The miracle: seeds of doubt

While the consensus over the miracle of the Gorbals was widely shared, this does not mean it was founded on parity or equality amongst the groups who adhered to it. Rather, it was marked by tensions and unequal power relations. The new Gorbals was a solution imposed by the Corporation of the City of Glasgow, which enjoyed a dominant position based on its control of expertise, information and communications. For the Corporation, the miracle was a reflection of the success of its post-war housing policy and a showcase for the rest of the city. In terms of economic logic, it represented a valorization of a valuable inner-city site without assigning it to commercial purposes. The population felt the loss of family, friends, local facilities and familiar places, but the consensus was founded on the idea that this was a price worth paying for new housing, the luxury of a bathroom and so on.

The feeling of a new start was grasped by the tenants' associations, which saw theirs as a management, or 'fine-tuning' role. At first these associations directed their efforts in three principal directions. First, they tried to ensure that the Corporation or the Scottish Special Housing Association (SSHA) dealt with the relatively minor maintenance issues which arose in the new flats, such as faulty lighting, defective paintwork and incidents of vandalism. The second aspect of their activities was directed at keeping down the levels of rent and rates in the new flats which, coupled with the 'hidden' expenses of moving into a modern home – new furniture, curtains and carpets, expensive heating systems and so on – provoked a degree of unease amongst the residents (for example, in 1968, a tenant moving from an old tenement to an SSHA flat in Hutchesontown Court saw her rent and rates bill rise from £6.15 a *quarter* in her old home, to £8.16 a *month* in Hutchesontown Court[1]). The Hutchesontown Tenants' Association was particularly active in this sphere: its tactics involved not only direct lobbying of the SSHA, but also demonstrations,[2] petitions[3] and a rates strike.[4] This strike, in protest at rates increases, saw tenants of both Corporation and SSHA homes continuing to pay rates at the old level, while withholding the balance.

The third aspect of the tenants' associations' activities concerned improvements to the general environment of the new Gorbals. One of the most serious aspects of this was the issue of road safety, particularly for children.[5] For example, in June 1969, 200 residents of the new flats who were concerned at the risk presented to children by heavy traffic on Old Rutherglen Road demonstrated on the stretch that crossed the Gorbals, shouting 'Close this road', and booing passing motorists. They eventually succeeded in persuading the Corporation to close the road to through traffic.[6] The HTA also put pressure on the Corporation and the SSHA to landscape the areas around the new flats, was involved in organizing a senior citizens' club and a youth club in the area, and successfully opposed the application for a licence for a betting shop. The Association even had something to say about what, in 1956, the Corporation had described as that 'old factory sticking up there'[7] (see Chapter Five): 'We

---

1 '9000th SSHA House in Glasgow', *The Gorbals View*, no. 11 (February 1968), p. 5. ML.

2 'HTA to March on Edinburgh Over Rents Increase', *The Gorbals View*, no. 43 (October 1970), p. 2. ML.

3 'In Hutchesontown the Tenants Association sent in on behalf of their members and residents a massive 1300-plus appeals against the new [rates] valuations.' 'Over-Rated', *The Gorbals View*, no. 54 (October 1971), p. 1. ML.

4 '1500 in Rates Protest', *The Glasgow Herald* (6 October 1971), p. 1. ML.

5 'We feel proper provision for their safety must be made.' 'No Bridge Till '76', *The Gorbals View*, no. 43 (October 1970), p. 3. ML.

6 'Motorists Booed in Protest March', *The Glasgow Herald* (19 June 1969), p. 18.

7 ' "That Old-Fashioned Factory" in the Gorbals', *The Glasgow Herald* (10 October 1956), p. 8.

certainly hope that all political parties will not allow this building (built 1810/1820) to be left in the New Gorbals.'[8]

All these activities suggest a commitment and belief in the miracle of the Gorbals and seem to confirm the hope of the editorial board of *The Gorbals View* that, with the creation of the new Gorbals, 'A people were created – with a common voice to be heard, in Ward Committee and Tenants Association.'[9] In 1971, the HTA, in an article entitled 'The Spoilers', even complained that 'Several tenants are making a practice of hanging out washing on their balconies – by doing this they spoil the external appearance of the SSHA property'. The Association then went on to request 'that all tenants use the drying facilities provided'.[10]

It was not long, however, before the tenants and their associations were forced to confront more serious problems in their new homes, and cracks began to appear in the consensus. Complaints included excessive noise, flooding, dampness, lack of privacy, a scarcity of drying spaces and play space and persistent lift failures. For example, in September 1973 the HTA page of *The View* reported that:

> Over 500 tenants living in the SSHA multi-storey blocks at Caledonia Road, Hutchesontown are furious at the continuous LIFT BREAKDOWNS within their tower blocks .... Old age pensioners having to wait for over an hour at ground level – pregnant women released from lifts by means of ladders. Old people unable to obtain the district nurse. Home helps unable to get to the needy tenants. Workers unable to get to work on time.[11]

The emerging doubts were not only founded on the technical limitations of the new flats. As early as 1967 a well-known Glaswegian folksong humorously lamented the passing of the social organization associated with the tenements and, in particular, drew attention to the impracticality of mothers throwing a 'jeely piece' – jam sandwich – out of the window to their children playing in the street below:

> Oh ye cannae fling pieces oot a twenty-storey flat,
> Seven hundred hungry weans'll testify to that.
> If it's butter, cheese or jeely, if the breid is plain or pan,
> The odds against it reaching earth are ninety-nine tae wan.[12]

---

[8] 'Hutchesontown Tenants Association', *The Gorbals View*, no. 22 (January 1969), p. 3. ML.

[9] 'Comment. The Old – and the Nearly New', *The Gorbals View*, no. 10 (January 1968), p. 1. ML.

[10] 'Hutchesontown Tenants Association Newsletter', *The Gorbals View*, no. 51 (June 1971), p. 2. ML.

[11] 'Hutchesontown Tenants Association', *The View* (September 1973), p. 8. ML.

[12] A. McNaughtan, 'The Jeely Piece Song', in H. Whyte (ed.), *Mungoes Tongues. Glasgow Poems 1630–1990* (Edinburgh and London: Mainstream publishing, 1993), pp. 192–93. First published in 1967.

But the physical separation of the home and the street had implications other than dietary ones – it effectively removed the possibility of parental supervision, with the result that smaller children were more often confined to home, while the older ones were free to roam unsupervised. It also removed the opportunities for social interaction on the stairs, landings, in close-mouths and back-courts, while the activity of window 'hingin'' was scarcely practical. The social isolation of households, particularly the elderly, was made worse by the unreliable lifts, while even the rationalization of shopping facilities had an impact, as did the removal of communal wash-houses – the steamies – as the use of washing machines became more widespread.

Many of the concerns emerging in the new Gorbals were echoed in Pearl Jephcott's 1971 study of high-rise flats in Glasgow in which she identified key problems associated with lifts, service and facilities on the estates, the anonymity of life, logistical difficulties for pensioners, the disabled and families with young children and, as becomes apparent in the history of the new Gorbals, relations with the local authority.[13] All in all, the result was that the new Gorbals began to appear a little less miraculous and a little more tarnished. Even so, the transformation of identifications is not a simple, linear process, and new and old meanings can exist simultaneously. As late as June 1974, the Hutchesontown Tenants' Association's page in *The View* returned to the role of the population in shaping Hutchesontown, proclaiming:

> A great deal of imaginative planning has been put into the design of Hutchesontown – now it is up to us tenants who enjoy living here to do our best to make the new Hutchesontown a place of which we can be proud. We must encourage our fellow neighbours to join the Hutchesontown Tenants Association.[14]

The Association closed its appeal to the population of the new Gorbals by paraphrasing the motto of the City of Glasgow: 'LET HUTCHESONTOWN FLOURISH'.[15]

It proved to be the deterioration of the physical fabric of the new buildings which crystallized the inhabitants' perception of the new Gorbals. Of all the problems present in these blocks and towers, it would be the issue of dampness which was most effective in uniting the residents and capturing the imagination of the population of the city in general. The remainder of this chapter will concentrate on this issue, for it was here that the Corporation's vision of the new Gorbals experienced its most extreme crisis and was most vehemently

[13] P. Jephcott, with H. Robinson, *Homes in High Flats: Some of the Human Problems Involved in Multi-storey Living*, Occasional Paper no. 13 (Edinburgh: University of Glasgow Social and Economic Studies, 1971).

[14] 'Hutchesontown Tenants Association', *The View* (June 1974), p. 2. ML.

[15] Ibid. Capitalized in original.

challenged. Dampness became a widespread problem in the new Gorbals, but the phenomenon was most serious in the deck-access flats in the Hutchesontown 'E' development. These flats, where tenants and protesters claimed that more than 70 per cent of the units were suffering from dampness by 1977, became the symbolic centre of a long-term campaign.

'Heavy breathing' and the breakdown of consensus

The 'E' phase of the Hutchesontown project consisted of 12 low-rise deck-access blocks of seven storeys and two high-rise blocks of 24 storeys. In all, there were 1143 flats of between one and four rooms, 759 of which were included in the low-rise development and 384 in the high-rise. The population of this, the last phase in the Hutchesontown/part Gorbals redevelopment, was something over 2500, rehoused from their 'slum' homes in the old Gorbals. Construction of the flats began in 1969 and lasted until 1973, with the first tenants moving in to the deck-access development in December 1971. The official opening ceremony, carried out by the Queen, was held in 1972.

At least two sources claim that there was a problem of dampness in the deck-access flats from the very beginning; one of these sources, a report on the Gorbals Anti-Dampness Campaign produced by the Scottish Council of Social Services, suggests that intimations of dampness were made to the contractors, Gilbert Ash Ltd, as soon as the first tenants moved in at the end of 1971. Over the next two years individual tenants made official complaints about dampness in their flats, but at this stage neither the contractors nor Glasgow Corporation made any attempt to assess the cause of these problems.[16] The second source that reports the early presence of problems associated with dampness in Hutchesontown 'E' is McPhee, whose evidence is more anecdotal:

> When the complex was completed and the decorators moved in they were faced with walls running with water and doors lying off straight lines and moss growing *inside* the buildings. A painter who worked on the job told me that as he put the wallpaper on it just fell off.[17]

McPhee adds that workmen had to work overnight in order to prepare the flat that the Queen was to inspect at the opening ceremony because all the wallpaper had fallen off the walls.[18] In any case, by 1974 tenants were making regular complaints concerning the presence of dampness in their new flats. In April

---

[16] R. Bryant, *The Dampness Monster: A Report of the Gorbals Anti-Dampness Campaign* (Edinburgh: Scotish Council of Social Services, 1979), p. 3.

[17] P. McPhee, 'Hutchie E – A Monument to Corruption, Stupidity and Bad Planning', in F. McLay, *Workers' City* (Glasgow: Clyde Press, 1988), pp. 47–48.

[18] Ibid., p. 48.

1975, *The View* ran its first major feature on the issue, entitled 'Dampness – Whose Problem?' in which it was reported that 'the incidence of dampness in recently-built Corporation flats in Laurieston and Hutchesontown is reaching alarming proportions'.[19]

It is important to note that, throughout the history of Hutchesontown 'E', there was considerable confusion over the meaning of the term 'dampness'. The Gorbals tenants used it indiscriminately as a generic term to refer to the presence of water in their flats, while Council officials insisted on making a technical distinction between 'dampness' and 'condensation'. This technical distinction is encapsulated in the Glasgow District Council *Housing Condition Survey* of 1985 which makes a further distinction between 'rising damp' and 'penetrating damp'.[20] According to the Castlemilk Law Centre's tenants' handbook, 'rising damp' refers to water that enters the structure of a building through its foundations due to inadequate or absent damp-coursing, with the result that 'Walls and floors soak up moisture from the ground',[21] while 'penetrating damp' is the term used when 'moisture comes through the walls or roof due to failure of the structure eg leaking roof, holed gutter' and may be caused by 'blocked or leaking rainwater gutters, missing slates, faults in cavity walls etc'.[22] 'Condensation' differs from these two forms of dampness because it refers to water which is naturally present in a building as a by-product of human activity:

> People sweat, bathe, wash clothes, boil kettles and cook. This causes moisture. When warm air meets a cold surface the air cools. As warm air can carry more moisture than cool air, so moisture has to condense out of the cooling air. As the air cools, the moisture moves from the air to the cold walls or ceilings. Thus they become damp.[23]

Even then, the definition of condensation remains ambiguous, for while water vapour is always present to some degree, excessive condensation may result from technical faults in a building's physical structure, such as 'poor building materials and a lack of insulation' which 'allow a lot of heat to escape from inside the house and interior walls become cold', from 'inappropriate ventilation' or from problems that arise when 'the heating system is either too costly to run or too inefficient to warm walls and prevent condensation'.[24] In short, condensation may have a 'technical' cause related to failings in the

[19] 'Dampness – Whose Problem?', *The View* (April 1975), p. 11. ML.

[20] City of Glasgow District Council, *Housing Condition Survey 1985, vol. 5: Condensation and Dampness* (Glasgow: Glasgow District Council, 1989).

[21] *Dampness: Council Tenants' Rights* (Glasgow: Castlemilk Law Centre, 1983), p. 2.

[22] Ibid.

[23] Ibid., p. 4.

[24] Ibid.

building, or a 'human' cause as a result of 'inappropriate' behaviour on the part of residents, such as the excessive use of calor gas or paraffin heaters or failing to ventilate rooms properly.

In the case of Hutchesontown 'E', the distinction between human and structural causes went far beyond mere technical precision to impact on the very meanings assigned to the Gorbals by different groups. Nor was it a question of whether or not 'dampness' in its generic sense was present. The key issues were the severity of the problem and whether this 'dampness' was caused by technical and design faults, or by the lifestyle of the tenants. As the saga of Hutchesontown 'E' illustrates, it is not always easy to determine which of these factors is to blame or, indeed, the degree to which both are to blame. Moreover, the situation was complicated by the fact that, while a house may be declared 'below tolerable standard' because of rising or penetrating damp, even a building plagued with condensation could not legally be classed as falling below this standard. This being the case, even when considering one of the worst affected flats, the chairman of the housing management committee could report that 'Officials consider that this tenant's house is habitable and meets the required building regulations fully'.[25]

Whatever the cause of these conditions, for the tenants of the affected flats the day-to-day experience of dampness was far from pleasant: early dampness reports listed 'black fungus on walls, peeling wallpaper, furniture and clothing ruined'.[26] In addition, beds were constantly damp, furniture and carpets, often specifically bought for the new homes, were damaged, there were infestations of beetles (prompting visits from the Council's pest control department), and a constant unpleasant odour in the houses. Moreover, although it is extremely difficult to prove a direct link between a specific health complaint and the presence of dampness in a house, *The View* had no doubt over the link: 'It is disgraceful that young children and old people should be suffering from constant colds, influenza and bronchial trouble in nearly-new buildings.'[27]

And beyond the threat to physical good health, there were also risks to the tenants' psychological health due to the stress induced by these living conditions. The impact of damp conditions was often most severe for those, such as 'housewives', the unemployed and the housebound, who spent a large part of their day indoors. The report by the Scottish Council of Social Services suggests that the smell of damp was a particular source of social embarrassment: 'In many cases, when visitors are admitted to one of these flats for the first time, the main topic of conversation is associated with an

[25] Cited in 'Dampness – Public Meeting Hayfield School', *The View* (March 1976), p. 6. ML.

[26] 'Dampness – Whose Problem?', *The View* (April 1975), p. 11. ML.

[27] Ibid.

explanation of why there is a smell and why the decor is stained and discoloured.'[28]

It was not only *The View* that carried reports of these conditions; *The Glasgow Herald*, for example, cited the case of Mrs Agnes Marshall, a resident of Hutchesontown 'E' who, implicitly turning the meanings of the old and new Gorbals upside down, was reported as saying 'I came from a clean house and I'm not going to allow my home to be anything else'. She had 'spent a fortune on redecorating and cleans constantly'. Indeed, her flat had been redecorated every six months or so since she and her family had moved in four years earlier. The last redecoration took place just before Christmas 1975, and by the end of March 1976 there were already damp mouldy patches on the corners of the bedroom and the beginning of mould on the back of bedroom furniture.[29] In some cases, losses to individual households over a four-year period were estimated to be as high as £1000 – a figure calculated on the basis of damaged furniture, carpets and clothes, the cost of redecorating, and time lost at work due to ill-health.[30] It was said that some tenants simply burned their ruined furniture on the local wasteland.

When a tenant reported dampness in their flat, the Corporation sent officials to carry out a visual inspection of the property. The response of these officials did not please *The View*: 'A visit by Housing Department officials usually produces the statement, "it's only condensation – that's your problem" and some "helpful" advice about keeping electric heaters on and the windows open.'[31] This was hardly a practical suggestion for low-income households, particularly during the Scottish winter. Moreover, the flats in Hutchesontown 'E' had an electric heating system which proved to be extremely expensive to run, and high heating bills only added to the tenants' anxiety. Mrs Mary Kelly, who had a four-apartment house in Hutchesontown 'E' was reported as having electric fires on most of the time in her all-electric house. She also left windows open for as long as possible in order to encourage ventilation, with the result that her electricity bill over a two-month period was equivalent to half the sum she paid in rent over the same period. Despite this, she had mould in the corners of the bedrooms, damp patches on carpets and fungus growing under her bed.[32] Due to the expense of the heating system in the flats, tenants sometimes kept paraffin gas heaters in their homes and, when officials found these, they were identified as the cause of condensation to the exclusion of any other possibilities. It was also reported that the Corporation had suggested to

[28] Bryant, *The Dampness Monster*, p. 9.

[29] J. Cunningham, 'When Tenants Take on the Council', *The Glasgow Herald* (1 April 1976), p. 7.

[30] Bryant, *The Dampness Monster*, p. 6.

[31] 'Dampness – Whose Problem?', *The View* (April 1975), p. 11. ML.

[32] Cunningham, 'When Tenants Take on the Council', p. 7.

tenants that their curtains were 'too long'[33] – presumably preventing efficient ventilation – and, famously, that, 'heavy breathing during the night would cause dampness'.[34]

The tenants experiencing dampness in their homes were not satisfied with the Corporation's explanations and advice. 'What can be done to combat this growing menace?' asked *The View*, 'It seems only a long and vigorous campaign by tenants associations and all those people affected by the dampness issues – and those who may be affected in the future – will succeed in moving the corporation to action.'[35] In April 1975, James Carlin, a tenant in the Hutchesontown 'E' deck-access flats decided to withhold rent. 'Mr Carlin', *The View* reported, 'has tried everything possible to get the Corporation to carry out remedial work to stop the dampness, but the Corporation would not accept liability. Mr Carlin could only do one more thing to bring his protest to the ears of the City Fathers – he has withheld his rent.' *The View* added that the Hutchesontown Tenants' Association, 'fully support Mr Carlin and call for immediate action'.[36] Soon, other tenants were joining the rent strike, prompting *The Glasgow Herald* to report that 'More than 200 Glasgow tenants have threatened to withhold their rent unless the district council takes steps to combat dampness in their low-rise blocks of flats, which cost around £10,000 each to build'.[37]

In May 1975 the two local tenants associations – the Hutchesontown Tenants' Association and the Laurieston Tenants' Association – held a public meeting in a local school in order to assess the extent and severity of the dampness problem and decide on a course of action. Of the two associations, the HTA was much the larger, having 937 members in 1972,[38] while in the same year the LTA, for whom participation was a constant problem, had around 100 members, and only some 16 of these attended monthly meetings.[39] This joint meeting was attended by 120 tenants and two local councillors, and it was resolved to send a delegation to Glasgow Corporation in order to make clear the tenants' concerns. At the same time, the Laurieston Tenants' Association organized a petition in the flats it represented and then, two months later, 'noticed with amusement the corporation's attempt to combat the problem by putting air vents on the windows of the damp rooms'.[40]

---

[33] Bryant, *The Dampness Monster*, p. 14.

[34] 'Dampness. Tenants to Sue', *The View* (December 1975), p. 1. ML.

[35] 'Dampness – Whose Problem?', *The View* (April 1975), p. 11. ML.

[36] 'Hutchesontown Tenants Association', *The View* (June 1975), p. 4. ML.

[37] 'Rent Strike Threat by Tenants', *The Glasgow Herald* (10 June 1975), p. 3.

[38] 'Hutchesontown Tenants Association', *The Gorbals View*, no. 59 (March 1972), p. 2. ML.

[39] 'Laurieston Tenants Association', *The Gorbals View*, no. 62 (June 1972), p. 3. ML.

[40] 'Laurieston Tenants Association', *The View* (July/August 1975), p. 7. ML.

The response in the City Chambers to this growing unrest took the form of a report issued in August 1975 by the department of architecture, which not only reiterated the position that lack of ventilation and heating was at the heart of the problem, but also stated that, in many of the cases investigated, the mechanical ventilation systems were not operating and ventilation points had been blocked by tenants.[41] *The View* described the findings as 'RUBBISH!', and pointed out that an independent review carried out for the paper had stated 'that though condensation of a very severe type was the cause of much of the dampness in these flats, it was a result of the design of the building and that in many cases even if heating and ventilation were perfect, the damp would still be there'.[42]

Ever more frustrated that the problem should be explained in terms of the tenants' lifestyle, the two tenants' associations called a second public meeting on 27 October 1975. At this meeting, attended by some 150 people, it was decided to take legal action against the District Council under the Public Health (Scotland) Act 1897.[43] In addition, the decision was taken to set up the Gorbals Anti-Dampness Campaign, and an organizing committee was appointed. For the first two years, this committee consisted of only six members – a chairperson, a treasurer, a secretary and three others – who communicated with tenants by means of regular meetings open to all. At the start, according to the report by the Scottish Council for Social Services, the tenants involved had little or no experience of campaigning:

> With one or two exceptions, none of the hard core of regular activists was previously involved in community or political activities in the Gorbals prior to the start of the campaign. The majority of them had never before been involved in organising public events, lobbying politicians, running committee meetings and taking any form of direct action (eg rent strikes, demonstrations).[44]

In the early stages the Campaign would rely heavily on the two tenants' associations, but gradually it developed its own organizational structure. Apart from the support of the these associations, the Campaign was able to use the local Laurieston information centre as an administrative base and a source for technical help and support.[45] From a political point of view, the Campaign claimed to be entirely independent: 'The committee of the Dampness Campaign would like to emphasize that the campaign is an independent organization

[41] 'Tenants are Told How to Fight Damp', *The Glasgow Herald* (5 August 1975), p. 5.

[42] 'Dampness', *The View* (September 1975), p. 4. ML. Underlined in original.

[43] The Campaign planned to claim compensation on the grounds that, under the Act, the conditions in the flats represented a nuisance, although technically the Act did not allow for compensatory claims, but only for abatement measures. See Bryant, *The Dampness Monster*, p. 64.

[44] Ibid., p. 48.

[45] Ibid., p. 33.

which has no affiliation with any political party. The campaign exists solely to fight for decent, dry, damp-free houses in the Gorbals.'[46] This impartiality was borne out in the Campaign's activities, and it frequently criticized the Labour Party's record on dampness and other housing issues, despite the support given by the population to the Labour Party in local and general elections.

Meanwhile Glasgow District Council, following up on its August report, and prompted by reports of dampness in other public housing developments in the city, decided to launch a mobile exhibition aimed at confronting this growing problem. The 'Combat Condensation' exhibition, costing some £10 000, was launched on 10 November 1975 by Bailie Gordon Kane, chairman of the Council's building committee. After two days in George Square, in front of the City Chambers, the exhibition embarked on a four-week tour of the city. The main message of the exhibition was that heating without ventilation led inevitably to dampness problems, and Kane, opening the exhibition, stated that around 95 per cent of complaints received by the Council concerning penetrating damp turned out, on investigation, to be condensation problems which householders could cure themselves.[47] Visitors to the exhibition could register their particular complaint with the Council and also receive advice on the best ways to reduce condensation in their homes.

When the exhibition arrived in the Gorbals, more than 50 tenants, most of whom were members of the newly formed Gorbals Anti-Dampness Campaign, mounted a demonstration, and some members maintained a picket throughout the exhibition's two-day stay 'in a protest against officials attempting to blame them for deteriorating living conditions'.[48] The demonstration attracted considerable attention from the media; it was covered widely by the local evening papers, and even by some of the daily national papers, while Glasgow's local radio station broadcast a number of interviews with people from the area. It also received five minutes' coverage on Scottish Television's *Scotland Today* evening news and affairs programme – the Campaign's first television coverage.

By 1976 the Anti-Dampness Campaigners claimed that, at a conservative estimate, 60 per cent of the 1200 flats in the 'E' scheme were affected by dampness.[49] In April of that year, the Council took James Carlin, the first tenant to have withheld rent, to the small debt court, but withdrew their action the day before the hearing. This situation was repeated with another tenant in June and

[46] 'Dampness', *The View* (December/January 1976–77), p. 8. ML.

[47] 'Dampness Exhibition to Help Tenants', *The Glasgow Herald* (11 November 1975), p. 3.

[48] 'Gorbals Tenants Picket Mobile Exhibition', *The Glasgow Herald* (9 December 1975), p. 3.

[49] Cunningham, 'When Tenants Take on the Council', p. 7.

The View announced, 'VICTORY!'[50] This second climbdown by the Council encouraged large numbers of tenants in the damp flats to participate in the rent strike. However, the Campaign's plans to sue the Council under the 1897 Public Health Act received a setback when, in February 1976, the chairman of the housing management committee called upon the Council's chief executive to carry out a detailed investigation into the dampness complaints. The report which was produced recognized that dampness was a problem in the flats and stated that there was a requirement for the Council to take action to remedy the situation, although it remained vague on the issue of responsibility. This recognition on the part of the Council effectively removed the Campaign's legal grounds for action under the Act. Following up on the report, the Council recommended that the National Building Agency (NBA) should be invited to study the issue, despite the Anti-Dampness Campaign's objections on the grounds that the NBA had been responsible for certifying the flats 'fit for habitation' in the first place.

On 6 December, having officially recognized the problem of dampness, Glasgow District Council's housing committee agreed that flats which were badly affected should not be re-let when they fell vacant and suggested that the Council should also consider freezing rents in these properties.[51] Despite this resolution, the Campaign claimed that damp houses continued to be re-let. Shortly afterwards, the Council also decided to rehouse a couple from their damp house (this couple had been featured on Scottish Television at the time of the 'Combat Condensation' picket). Soon this offer was extended to all tenants living in flats which were officially recognized as being damp. The rehousing issue became one of the Anti-Dampness Campaign's major themes in 1977, and as early as January 1977 it had compiled a list of 342 tenants who had expressed an interest in being rehoused. The Council made no response, frustration amongst the tenants grew, and on 24 February over 60 tenants demonstrated outside the headquarters of the Council's housing management department to complain about delays in rehousing, once more attracting press and television coverage.

In April the long-awaited NBA report was published. This found that 238 of the 759 flats surveyed suffered from dampness and reported that in 94 of the flats examined the dampness was identified as 'severe', while a large percentage of the total number were 'affected to an unacceptable degree'. The estimated cost of remedial measures provoked a scandalized tone from *The Glasgow Herald*: '£500,000 needed to dry out new flats.'[52] The report

---

50 'Victory!', *The View* (July–August 1976), p. 1. ML. Capitalized in original.

51 'Rent Freeze in Damp Flats Urged', *The Glasgow Herald* (7 December 1976), p. 8.

52 '£500,000 Needed to Dry Out New Flats', *The Glasgow Herald* (14 April 1977), p. 4.

unambiguously identified the cause of the dampness as condensation, while the reasons for its excessive presence were considered to be largely, but not exclusively, technical rather than social. It noted that the flats were made of dense concrete panels which were unable to absorb moisture or to respond quickly to changes in temperature (thus presenting cold surfaces).[53] Moreover, there was an area at the edge of the external walls which was solid concrete rather than the normal prefabricated sandwich of concrete and polystyrene. Without this insulation, the concrete served as a 'cold bridge' where moisture could accumulate. These problems were exacerbated by the fact that deck-access flats tend to have many exposed surfaces, making them more difficult to heat. Another point made by the report was that tenants could not afford to pay for the level of heating necessary to counteract condensation build-up (electricity costs were shown to have risen by 119 per cent in three years). Additionally, the report stated that ventilation systems were poor, a situation exacerbated since modern flats without open fires have little natural ventilation. The report considered that social factors contributing to the conditions included the use of paraffin heaters and the fact that, with a growing number of women going out to work, flats were more frequently left inadequately heated and ventilated. On the basis of this report, the Council decided to carry out a pilot project in conjunction with the NBA on eight flats.[54]

Heartened by these findings, but frustrated at the lack of progress towards rehousing, the Anti-Dampness Campaign organized what was to be its largest meeting. Held in the Citizens Theatre in the Gorbals on 1 May, two days before the District Council elections, the event was attended by some 1000 Gorbals tenants, as well as the local political representatives and prospective candidates in the imminent elections. The following month, Glasgow District Council agreed to relax the restriction on their rehousing procedure for the Hutchesontown tenants by broadening the choice of rehousing areas and speeding up the rehousing process. While the campaigners welcomed these concessions, they continued to complain about the Council's policy of re-letting houses in the Hutchesontown 'E' scheme that were not suffering from dampness. They considered that this policy undermined their assertion that there were basic design and construction problems in the low-rise blocks, and they consequently pursued a tactic of dissuading prospective tenants from accepting a flat in the development. The end of June also saw the District Council open an office in the Gorbals, staffed by the housing department's area supervisor, in order to

---

[53] Bryant, *The Dampness Monster*, p. 11.

[54] Six of the eight flats were to be repaired, while two were to be left as they were as a 'control'. Four of the six would be tested empty, while two would have tenants living in them. The two control flats would also be inhabited. An element of this test was clearly to ascertain the significance of the 'lifestyle' factor.

answer complaints about dampness, and the Anti-Dampness Campaign hailed this as another victory.

At this stage, the main efforts of the Campaign were being directed towards two objectives. One of these was the preparation for a rates appeal which was due to be heard in September 1977. The basis of the appeal was that the 1976 rates valuations had not taken into account the worsening conditions in the buildings caused by dampness, and the Campaign therefore requested a nil valuation on the flats. The Campaign was under no illusion as to the importance of the event, and James Wray, the regional councillor for the area, announced that 'this is the biggest and most important appeal to be held in Glasgow and the decision could have nation-wide implications for tenants in similar prefabricated blocks of houses'.[55] The other focus for the Campaign's efforts at this time was the attempt to press the District Council for a reduction in rent and for compensation amounting to £40 000 for damage to personal belongings caused by dampness. By September 1977, the tenants had withheld a total of £30 000 in rent and rates over a 14-month period, lodging their payments in a bank account rather than paying the District and Regional Councils.[56] After considerable negotiation, the Campaign received a written offer from the Council of a one-third reduction in rent backdated to the date when the Council had officially recognized the presence of dampness in the flats.[57] In addition, the Council made an offer of £100 compensation to every household where belongings had been damaged. This offer was met with 'mixed feelings', since, while it established a principle of compensation and a basis for negotiations, the amount was small.[58] After a survey of the tenants who would be entitled to compensation, it was decided to reject the Council's offer.

The rates appeal was scheduled over two days – 15 and 22 September. On the first day, the Campaign coordinated a march through the city centre, and the six-hour hearing in the Burgh Court Hall in Glasgow was attended by nearly 200 Hutchesontown tenants.[59] The appeal resulted in the region's valuation appeal committee awarding a reduction for the 600 flats which had been earmarked for remedial work in the NBA report out of the total of 759 flats in the deck-access development. The gross annual value of this reduction ranged from 5 to 7.5 per cent, a figure much lower than the Anti-Dampness Campaign had hoped for. It was reported that 'The reduction, which would work out at less

[55] 'McElhone Joins fight for Tenants', *The Glasgow Herald* (6 September 1977), p. 9.

[56] 'Rebel Tenants Win Cut in Rent', *The Glasgow Herald* (10 September 1977), p. 3.

[57] Bryant, *The Dampness Monster*, p. 40.

[58] 'Dampness', *The View* (October 1977), p. 10. ML.

[59] 'Mildewed Settee Goes to Court as Angry Tenants Seek Rates Cut', *The Glasgow Herald* (16 September 1977), p. 5.

than 75p per month, was hailed ... as a "moral victory" by the chairman of the anti-dampness campaign, William Roxburgh'.[60]

These 'moral victories' scored by the Gorbals Anti-Dampness Campaign marked a critical point in the organization's development. While it had succeeded, in principle, in achieving its goals, having persuaded the Council to admit responsibility for the condition of the housing and offer compensation, the members were disappointed by the levels of compensation and rent and rate reductions they could expect: 'They have offered us peanuts' said Roxburgh.[61] Many of the most active members of the Campaign were also exhausted after years of intensive activity: 'It has been a long hard slog for many people ...'.[62] Moreover, they were, in a sense, victims of their own success, for as the residents of Hutchesontown 'E' were rehoused, so too the organization saw its support base dwindling. Not surprisingly, this process had a particularly skewed effect since the tenants who were rehoused first were those living in the flats worst affected by dampness, and therefore also tended to be those most actively involved in the Campaign. By January 1978 some 120 residents had been rehoused and, according to the Report of the Scottish Council of Social Services, 'it was rumoured in the area that the whole campaign was in a state of collapse'.[63] The outcome was a major reorganization; the secretary and treasurer resigned from the committee 'because of work pressures'[64] and two separate committees were formed, one which dealt with tenants waiting to be rehoused and to press for the complete evacuation of the flats ('We believe that everyone in the scheme should be given an opportunity to move'[65]), the other dealing with tenants who had already been rehoused but who were awaiting compensation (by April 1978 claims for compensation had reached over £85 000[66]). Of the 12 new committee members, nine were women. After this transformation, of the original committee only William Roxburgh, the Campaign chairman, remained with a leadership position.

By this time the problem of dampness in Scotland's public housing stock was widely recognized, and in March 1978 the issue was debated in the House of Commons. At the end of the year the District Council launched a new 'Combat Condensation' campaign, provoking the ire of the Anti-Dampness Campaign

---

[60] '"Moral Victory" for Damp Tenants', *The Glasgow Herald* (1 October 1977), p. 3. *The Herald* added that, 'A tenant in a four apartment house, at present paying £41 a month in rent and rates, would be around £11.40 a month better off if both the rent and rates reduction were accepted.'

[61] '"Moral Victory" for Damp Tenants', *The Glasgow Herald* (1 October 1977), p. 3.

[62] 'Gorbals Dampness', *The View* (December/January 1977/8), p. 5. ML.

[63] Bryant, *The Dampness Monster*, p. 43.

[64] 'Gorbals Dampness', *The View* (February 1978), p. 3. ML.

[65] 'Anti-Dampness campaign', *The View* (May 1978), p. 12. ML.

[66] 'Gorbals Dampness', *The View* (April 1978), p. 5. ML.

and other tenants' associations by distributing the same leaflets that it had handed out in its 1975 initiative. By the end of 1978 the rent arrears due to the tenants' rent strike amounted to more than £50 000, and over 250 tenants from the scheme had been rehoused, although the Campaign maintained pressure to speed up the evacuation.[67] In October 1979 the District Council made a revised offer of compensation to the tenants of Hutchesontown 'E', whereby all past and present tenants of damp flats would receive a payment equivalent to one-third of the rent paid from the date of entry to the flats, and compensation would be agreed on the merits of individual cases, with tenants having the right to sue the Council if a satisfactory agreement could not be reached. Uncharacteristically, the Campaign, always keen to emphasize the collective nature of their efforts, announced that 'it is now up to each individual tenant to make his or her own mind up about how to pursue their interests'.[68] In June 1980 Glasgow District Council announced 'We're no longer blaming dampness on people',[69] and drew up plans to deal with dampness in the city's council houses and to provide help in the form of compensation and rehousing for tenants living in damp houses.

As the blocks in Hutchesontown 'E' were emptied, they came to be used as meeting places for groups of youths and homeless, creating a sense of insecurity amongst the residents who still remained, so much so that the Council even hired security guards for a six-month period to prevent vandalism and threats to tenants. The Campaign continued to monitor closely the rehousing operation, and put pressure on the Council to board up vacant flats immediately, maintain the lift services and so on, in order to make life more bearable for those who still remained in the 'E' blocks. In October 1980 the Council announced that it had also recognized the severity of the dampness problem in the neighbouring Laurieston flats and stated its intention to carry out another rehousing programme there. By September 1981, the Campaign estimated that the average settlement for Hutchesontown 'E', including compensation and the rent reduction, worked out at approximately £580 per tenant.[70] The gradual exodus from the 'E' blocks continued until, in August 1982, all residents of what had come to be known as the 'Dampies' had been rehoused. At this point, *The View* could joke, ' "E" for Empty'.[71]

---

[67] Bryant, *The Dampness Monster*, p. 69.

[68] 'Huge Public Meeting', *The View* (November 1979), p. 10. ML.

[69] Cited in 'Damp', *The View* (June 1980), p. 1. ML.

[70] 'Council Renege', *The View* (September 1981), p. 5. ML.

[71] 'Ten Years After Hutchesontown. "E" for Empty', *The Gorbals View* (August 1982), p. 1. ML.

(Re)constructing the Gorbals

The events outlined in the previous section are characterized by a shift in power relations around the meaning of the Gorbals and, in particular, by the ascendancy of the Anti-Dampness Campaign's view that the new development was a social and financial disaster and the decline of the Council's definition of the 'miraculous' new Gorbals. In simple terms, the meaning of the new Gorbals as a modernist dream inhabited by former slum-dwellers was eclipsed by the meaning of the new Gorbals as slum housing inhabited by a group marked by a collective will. The material for these conflicting versions of place were already present in the meanings of the old Gorbals. The actors – principally the Anti-Dampness Campaign, the residents of the damp flats and Glasgow District Council – reactivated them in a new context, and used their resonance to promote their particular visions of the Gorbals.

This section will concentrate on two defining and interlinked themes in the (re)construction of the meaning of the Gorbals during the 1970s and early 1980s. First, there is the theme of the population of the Gorbals and the conflict over whether they were individuals or part of a collective organization. More specifically, this concerns the Council's explanation of dampness as 'condensation' resulting from the living habits of individual tenants, and the Anti-Dampness Campaign's attempt to organize a collective response to this view. The second theme is that of the 'slum' as a historio-geographical identification which was transferred from the old Gorbals to the new Gorbals. The activists took the initiative in this, claiming that the residents of the Gorbals had been better off before the alleged 'miracle' – a view that challenged the very core of the meaning the Corporation/Council had constructed for the area.

From 'lifestyle' to an injustice collectively sustained

From the moment the first complaints of 'dampness' in Hutchesontown 'E' were investigated, Corporation officials were adamant that the conditions were the result of tenants failing to heat and ventilate their flats properly. This explanation was founded on the tenant's lifestyle and the assumption that their behaviour was somehow 'inappropriate' for the new flats. Officials would visit a flat where dampness was present and explain to the tenant that condensation would continue to form unless they improved ventilation and turned up their heating. Many tenants experiencing dampness accepted this explanation and followed the Corporation's advice, but the measures made little impact on the conditions in the flats which, indeed, often continued to deteriorate.

Since the officials were understood to be 'experts', and the Corporation was the owner and landlord of the flats, it was hardly surprising that it took some time before tenants began to question the authority of this interpretation. Moreover, the Corporation had certain vested interests in placing responsibility on individual households. First, taking single cases, it was easier to suggest that the problem was due to the inappropriate behaviour of tenants and so deflect attention from the possibility that there were systematic flaws in the structure of their buildings (with the massive financial implications this would have for the Corporation). This is not to suggest that the Corporation's explanation was entirely cynical – one might surmise, given the expense and the newness of the development, reinforced by the widespread adherence at this time to the modern 'miracle' of deliverance from the tenement slums, that this possibility was scarcely considered even by the Corporation officials themselves. Second – and this aspect became more important as the tenants' groups began to organize against the Corporation – the treatment of individual cases represented a means of isolating tenants and discouraging the formation of a collective response, which would have been (and ultimately was), much harder for the Corporation to control.

But the Corporation's 'lifestyle' explanation had a much deeper implication than a mere criticism of the tenants' heating and ventilation practices in the new flats. As a concept, 'lifestyle', or living habits, bridges the gap between what one *does* and what one *is*. In this sense, the fact that the Corporation accused the tenants of inappropriate behaviour implied that the tenants themselves were not adapted to these flats – the modern housing failed because the tenants did not know how to behave in modern housing. This construction drew its resonance from the negative meaning of the old Gorbals and, in particular, from the concept of the Gorbals slum-dwellers as a distinct type, a breed apart (see Chapter Five). In this way, the stigma that had always been an element in the identity of the population of the old Gorbals was reactivated in this new setting. From this point of view, the former slum-dwellers had to be assisted in achieving the transformation their new environment required, and so the Council initiated its mobile 'Combat Condensation' exhibition (even the title placed onus on the tenants), where individual tenants could register their dampness problems and receive advice on appropriate preventive measures.

One of the principal aims of the Anti-Dampness Campaign was to shift the stigma from the people to the buildings they inhabited. When the Council's 'Combat Condensation' exhibition arrived in Gorbals, the reaction of the Anti-Dampness Campaign was to mount a picket and, in so doing, literally confront the two conflicting interpretations of 'dampness'. *The View* reported that 'the tenants felt the exhibition gave only a one-sided account of the problem and it was blaming the dampness on the LIVING HABITS OF THE PEOPLE and ignored such factors as faulty design and lack of insulation.'[72] Amongst the banners carried by the protesters there was particular emphasis in the breathing theme – 'STOP! BREATHING', 'Heavy Breathing Causes

[72] 'Dampness', *The View* (January 1976), p. 12. ML. Capitalized in original.

Dampness', 'Stop Breathing to Stop Dampness', and, in more detail, 'This Exhibition is Blaming Dampness on the Tenants' Living Habits – RUBBISH'.[73] The tactic of picketing the Council's mobile dampness exhibition not only allowed the Campaign to challenge the technical reasons for the dampness, but also to confront the *individual* lifestyle explanation with a show of *collective* will. Moreover, challenging the lifestyle explanation helped to enlarge the Campaign's support base: the Corporation/Council's argument implied that, if an individual could create damp conditions, then others might equally be able to avoid such conditions, but the Campaign's emphasis on the buildings made every resident a potential victim of dampness (indeed, the Campaign considered this to be a real possibility). The Campaign could thus argue that giving support to some ultimately meant support for all, seeking in this way to overcome the resistance produced by self-interest.

On another level, the implications of the Corporation/Council's 'lifestyle' explanation clashed head-on with the optimistic appraisal from *The Gorbals View* that '... not only were new buildings created in Hutchesontown. A people were created – with a common voice to be heard ...'.[74] Paradoxically, the identity of these 'new' people was derived from the 'spirit' of the Old Gorbals. This spirit was not only to do with social ties and gregariousness, it was also characterized by a combination of determination and defiance in the face of officialdom. In 1968 *The Gorbals View* explained: 'Gorbals people are often "treated like dirt" – though a few give as good as they get!'[75] This was to prove to be an enduring auto-identification; the gritty people of the Gorbals defying bureaucrats, officials and politicians who (and in this there was also, implicitly, a class dimension), they considered, looked down on them. From this point of view, the Campaign's ultimate success would be ensured by the collective determination of the Gorbals people. *The View*, reporting on a meeting during the early stages of the Anti-Dampness Campaign, 'attended by over 100 people (despite clashing with the European Cup Final!)', concluded that such a turn-out, football or no football, 'showed that the people of Gorbals are sick and fed-up with the Corporation's continued inactivity over this problem and are prepared to get together and stick together to get something done'.[76] As we shall see, the theme of the Gorbals 'spirit' became ever more important in the course of the 1980s as it increasingly came to be associated with the concept of 'community'.

The construction of a 'collective identity' by the activists took a rather different form from the equivalent process in Alma-Gare. We have seen how,

---

[73] Bryant, *The Dampness Monster*, photograph, p. 19.

[74] 'Comment. The Old – and the Nearly New', *The Gorbals View*, no. 10 (January 1968), p. 1. ML.

[75] 'Officialdom', *The Gorbals View*, no. 15 (June 1968), p. 1. ML.

[76] 'Dampness', *The View* (June 1975), p. 6. ML.

in Roubaix, the activists spoke unconditionally of a collective 'we' which united the APU and the population. In the Gorbals, however, there was never such a seamless identification of activists and residents. The discourse most commonly used, even while urging unity, distinguished between 'us', normally the Anti-Dampness Campaign, and 'you' the residents, in a fight against 'them' – that is, Glasgow District Council and its officials. Unlike Alma-Gare, participation was a choice rather than a *de facto* designation. During their meetings, for example, the Campaign committee frequently called upon the tenants to give their support: 'Do nothing ... and you support the Council.'[77] The same message was regularly carried in the pages of *The View*: 'YOUR ACTION IS NEEDED FOR VICTORY',[78] 'THE CAMPAIGN NEEDS YOUR SUPPORT FOR SUCCESS'[79] and so on. Following the rates appeal, the Campaign launched another plea for unity, aimed at encouraging the involvement of those who had so far not participated: 'To all those tenants who have not supported the Campaign – can you not see that we are achieving results – with more support, YOUR support we could achieve even more.'[80] In the following month's issue it linked the fate of the population with the fate of the Campaign: 'It does not matter how hard the campaign fights it must have your support. The fight for a dry home is your personal fight. You are the person who will win – if we lose, you lose.'[81] A little less than a year later the Campaign made explicit what it had previously only implied: 'The Campaign has achieved much over the last four years but everyone has got to make a contribution. Some people are enjoying the benefits of the campaign – the rehousing, the successful rent strike, the prospect of compensation – without contributing anything to our work! Everyone must pull their weight.'[82] In a sense, this introduced a division in the category of 'you, the residents' between 'you who participate' and 'you who do not'. This is an important point, for the Anti-Dampness Campaign was seeking to engender unity amongst a population that was marked by differences in interests and perspectives, not least the difference between those who lived in damp flats and those who did not. For this reason, the Campaign was interested in emphasizing the potential of the dampness to spread, as well as the actual conditions in the currently stricken flats.

Of course, it was not only in its discourse that the Campaign members sought to encourage tenant unity and present a collective response to the Council. A key element for the Campaign was its 'dampness clinic', held on a weekly or

[77] 'Dampness', *The View* (March 1976), p. 12. ML.
[78] 'Dampness Campaign News', *The View* (October 1976), p. 7. ML.
[79] 'Dampness', *The View* (February 1977), p. 10. ML. Capitalized in original.
[80] 'Dampness', *The View* (October 1977), p. 10. ML.
[81] 'Dampness', *The View* (November 1977), p. 12. ML.
[82] 'Dampness', *The View* (September 1978), p. 12. ML.

fortnightly basis (the term 'clinic' implying that dampness was a disease[83]). The clinic, which doubled as a committee meeting, offered a regular opportunity for tenants from damp flats to come together and exchange information and in this way helped to show that dampness was a shared problem. In practical terms, the clinic kept tenants informed of their rights, dealt as best it could with dampness problems and even offered a letter-writing service for the tenants' official correspondence and complaints. In all its aspects, it served as a means to instil a collective sense amongst the residents and to overcome any impression of isolation that the District Council's individualistic approach might have engendered. The clinic was judged by the organizers to be a 'great success', not only because it enabled the Campaign to improve its organization but also because it increased the accountability of the Campaign committee: 'So come along, listen, talk, ask questions, make decisions and ensure your views are heard where it matters.'[84] It was estimated that attendance at the dampness clinic varied between 12 and over 100, depending on the particular circumstances at the time.[85]

Apart from writing on behalf of individual tenants, the Campaign also maintained an intensive level of letter-writing and petitioning in the name of all the tenants. Letters headed:

Laurieston and Hutchesontown Tenants Association
ANTI-DAMPNESS CAMPAIGN
for Healthy-Habitable-Homes[86]

were sent to everyone from Glasgow District Council to the prime minister and even the queen. The Campaign sometimes sent over 50 and even as many as 100 letters in one week. The majority of these complaints, however, inevitably found their way to the environmental health department of Glasgow District Council, which insisted that the situation was being dealt with, but which was, understandably, unenthusiastic about taking measures that might implicate the Council itself. In the words of Willie Roxburgh, the Campaign chairman: 'Tenants' correspondence had no more impact than letters to Santa Claus.'[87] But this correspondence did, however, serve as a constant reminder to the

---

[83] This is not the only example of such a usage. In the June 1978 edition of *The View* for example, it was noted that 'The Gorbals dampness disease has spread into the Laurieston area!'. 'Laurieston Anti-Dampness Action Group', *The View* (June 1978), p. 4. ML.

[84] 'Dampness', *The View* (February 1976), p. 12.

[85] Bryant, *The Dampness Monster*, p. 49.

[86] The letterhead also depicted a stylized house (a traditional detached 'home' rather than deck-access flat), which is crying: dampness/tears roll from its windows/eyes. Scottish Consumer Council, *The Tenants' Handbook: A Guide to the Repair, Maintenance and Modernisation of Council Houses in Scotland* (Glasgow: Assist Architects, 1983), p. 16.

[87] Cunningham, 'When Tenants Take on the Council', p. 7.

authorities of the Campaign's activities and represented a tangible symbol of collective discontent.

One of the Campaign's most enduring tactics was the rent strike. A rent strike is, almost by definition, a collective activity, for while an individual may strike, the financial and 'propaganda' impact is limited. If, however, a group strikes, the action becomes not only financially inconvenient for a hard-pressed municipal council, but also a symbol of collective will and defiance likely to attract widespread attention. As noted, the Hutchesontown Tenants' Association had already employed this type of action, coordinating a rates strike in 1971 which involved around 1500 tenants of both Corporation and SSHA homes.[88] The Anti-Dampness Campaign's rent strike continued over several years, and even by 1978, when the Council was making important concessions, the Campaign committee called for its extension:

> The rent strike is gathering momentum and more and more people are expressing their anger at the dampness through withholding rent. The Campaign urges all tenants who have not, as yet, taken rent strike action to consider this possibility. The rent strike has proved to be very successful and has certainly had an important influence on the development of the Campaign.[89]

It was crucial that tenants who participated in the rent strike did not feel isolated, especially since the Council's response to strikers was to send out notices threatening eviction. For this reason the Campaign held regular support meetings and, in April 1978, reminded the tenants that 'no one has yet been evicted for withholding their rent'.[90] The tactic of the rent strike has particular resonance in the West of Scotland: the myth of the 1915 Glasgow rent strikes discussed in the previous chapter is a myth of the poor and exploited joining together to stand up for their rights in the face of private sector exploitation. In the collective memory of the city the result was a glorious success for the tenants – a success that even caused the government of the day to change its housing policy. In the rent strike, therefore, the Campaign had an activity that not only united all those involved in a common endeavour in the present, but also provided them with a link to a 'heroic' and optimistic past.

The Campaign's legal actions, research, surveys, letter-writing, petitioning and publicizing required a constant round of fund-raising, and the 'dampness clinic' provided a regular appointment for local fund-raisers to submit financial contributions to the Campaign. The Campaign's fund-raising initiatives included door-to-door collections, jumble sales, raffles, dances, sales of work, collections at meetings, appeals for donations from outside organizations such as trade unions, and a weekly football lottery. It raised approximately £1800

88 '1500 in Rates Protest', *The Glasgow Herald* (6 October 1971), p. 1.

89 'Gorbals Dampness', *The View* (March 1978), p. 12. ML.

90 'Gorbals Dampness', *The View* (April 1978), p. 5. ML.

over a three-year period – an impressive amount, but never sufficient to cover all its legal and technical advice, much of which it received free of charge.[91]

Many of the more regular fund-raising activities also served to strengthen the Campaign's local communication network, and much Campaign news was passed by word of mouth. Gradually, however, the idea of a network was expanded to include tenants' organizations from outside the Gorbals concerned with similar issues. With the involvement of groups from areas such as Pollok, Milton, Dalmarnock, Maryhill and, further afield, Cumbernauld, Livingston and Edinburgh, the collective nature of the protest was still further reinforced. Sometimes the support took the form of statements of solidarity, but on other occasions it was more tangible. For example, during the legal discussions at the small debt court in April 1976, when the Council finally dropped its case against James Carlin, the first rent-striker, the Gorbals tenants demonstrating outside the court were joined by representatives of the Wester Hailes Dampness Campaign from Edinburgh. Wester Hailes tenants were also present to give support on the first day of the rates appeal, as were representatives of other community groups. On 5 June 1978 there was a joint meeting of community groups from across Glasgow held in the clubroom of a block of flats in the Gorbals in order to discuss 'rehousing from redevelopment areas, dampness, highway and traffic, [and] planning questions'.[92] Two years later, tenants' groups from all over Glasgow met in the trade union centre to plan a concerted action to tackle dampness in the city's public housing stock. The meeting was organized jointly by Shelter, the national campaign for the homeless, which had already provided support to the Anti-Dampness Campaign, and the Laurieston information centre. On 28 April 1979 the first national meeting of anti-dampness campaigns from around Britain was held in Birmingham, and three representatives from the Gorbals attended.

In a sense, the fight by the Anti-Dampness Campaign to have the Council accept responsibility for the dampness problem in Hutchesontown 'E' was also a fight to have itself recognized as representative of a group of tenants who were united as a community of interests. The Campaign considered that, in establishing an informal information network amongst the tenants and providing a common point of reference in the shape of the 'dampness clinic', they possessed a degree of *de facto* legitimacy. This view, however, was not shared by Glasgow District Council which, like the *Municipalité de Roubaix* in Alma-Gare, sought to undermine the credibility of the Campaign by suggesting that the organizing committee was not representative of the population of the damp flats. To counter this criticism the Campaign decided to hold a major public meeting in the local community centre on 28 November 1976. There is some uncertainty as to the size of the audience at the meeting – *The Glasgow*

[91] Bryant, *The Dampness Monster*, p. 50.

[92] 'Laurieston Anti-Dampness Action Group', *The View* (June 1978), p. 4. ML.

Herald reported 300, while *The View*, with a vested interest, claimed over 900.[93] In any case, the community centre had a capacity of 500, and it seems that some people had to be accommodated in an overspill hall, so perhaps the 600 estimated by the report for the Scottish Council of Social Services is closest to the actual attendance.[94] The meeting was also attended by all the local political representatives, including the MP for Gorbals, although none of the Council officials who had been invited made an appearance. At the meeting it was resolved: 'To continue the anti-dampness campaign for dry homes; to have the rent and rates frozen; to continue if necessary with the legal action; *to give a mandate to our committee to represent us at public meetings and deputations*.'[95] The meeting was covered by the press and radio, and was also reported on the national Independent Television news that same evening. Whatever the exact attendance was, the Campaign considered the event a great success and henceforth felt free from any requirement to justify its representativeness to the Council.

Generally speaking, media coverage was essential for the Campaign since coverage from the 'outside' confirmed its existence, not only to a wider audience, but also to the tenants themselves. For example, after the considerable media interest in the picketing of the 'Combat Condensation' exhibition, *The View* reported: 'The publicity received must have brought a lot of embarrassment to the Glasgow District Council officials and it also strengthened and united the efforts of the local residents in their fight to eradicate the dampness in Gorbals.'[96] At the end of the first day of picketing, Willie Roxburgh, who seems to have been naturally given to 'sound-bites', made the sort of statement the press likes to hear: 'I understand the council have spent about £10,000 to mount their mobile exhibition on dampness. The money would have been better spent trying to get rid of the damp.'[97] It is interesting to note that the household featured on Scottish Television's *Scotland Today* programme after the picket was also the first to be evacuated from Hutchesontown 'E' by the Council. Often, the Campaign's initiatives, including demonstrations and meetings, were conceived to attract media attention, and one of the biggest media coups was the BBC's decision to dedicate an edition of *Grapevine*, a programme on self-help, on 5 May 1979, to the Anti-Dampness Campaign and the issue of dampness in Hutchesontown 'E'.

---

93 'Row over Dampness in Homes', *The Glasgow Herald* (29 November 1976), p. 3; 'Dampness', *The View* (December/January 1976/7), p. 8. ML.

94 Bryant, *The Dampness Monster*, p. 24.

95 'Dampness', *The View* (December/January 1976–77), p. 8. ML. My emphasis.

96 'Dampness', *The View* (January 1976), p. 12. ML.

97 'Gorbals Tenants Picket Mobile Exhibition', *The Glasgow Herald* (9 December 1975), p. 3.

As the Campaign sought to challenge the Council's depiction of the tenants as individuals who were not fully adapted to life in the new flats by constructing a positive collective identity, so too it increasingly assigned a negative identity to the Council. Just as the Campaign and the population it claimed to represent characterized themselves by dynamism, determination and the 'spirit' of the Gorbals, so the Council was depicted as, variously, incompetent, insensitive and secretive.

The infamous 'heavy breathing' quote, for example, was used by the Campaign and *The View* to highlight the distance between the reality of daily life in the damp flats and the Council's interpretation of the situation. Moreover, by associating the Council's 'lifestyle' argument with an essential function of the human organism, the Campaign sought to discredit its rivals and create resentment amongst the tenants at the Council's suggestion that their normal behaviour in their domestic space – breathing, boiling kettles and so on – was the cause of the deterioration of the flats. The tone adopted in these cases tended to be wryly ironic; for example, under a photograph of an area of wall covered in mould, *The View* placed the rhetorical caption 'Result of heavy breathing???'.[98] Similar irony was apparent, for example, when the Laurieston Tenants' Association, commenting on the subject of 'unidentified insect life' in damp flats, noted that 'An official who called to investigate had been variously identified as a pest controller and a health visitor'.[99] While Glasgow District Council was the main target for this irony, other symbols of authority also received the same treatment, although much less frequently: reporting on the parliamentary debate in 1978 on dampness in Scottish local authority housing, *The View* opened with the announcement: 'The problem of dampness has at last reached the House of Commons! We are assured that those hallowed chambers are NOT damp – unlike the homes of many tenants in the Gorbals.'[100]

The Council's incompetence was reinforced by stories reported in *The View*. For example, its efforts at rehousing tenants from Hutchesontown 'E' were described as 'A complete botch-up!'[101] on the grounds that rehousing priority was decided on the basis of how long tenants had been living in the district, not how long they had been living in a damp flat or on how extreme the dampness problem was. Moreover, *The View* reported that, as the flats were emptied, they were sealed with steel vandalproof doors. The Council, however, neglected to turn off the water supply and, following a freeze, the flats began to flood. Flats which were still inhabited suffered water damage, while plumbers were unable to gain entry to the sealed flats because they had no keys for the steel doors.

[98] 'Dampness', *The View* (December 1975), p. 12. ML.

[99] 'Laurieston Tenants Association', *The View* (November 1975), p. 6. ML.

[100] 'MPs Demand Government Action on Damp Houses', *The View* (April 1978), p. 4. ML.

[101] 'Common Sense?', *The View* (November 1980), p. 1. ML.

It took almost 12 hours to have the water switched off. The following day the same problem occurred in another block, and again the plumbers could not gain entry. 'Some houses', *The View* reported, 'were so badly flood damaged that families and isolated old age pensioners had to be urgently decanted.'[102]

The wry humour which often accompanied these stories was not present, however, when the Campaign reported what it regarded as the Council's efforts to intimidate its own tenants. For example, the Council's attempt to take the original rent strikers to court was described as 'bullying, oppressive behaviour' by the Campaign,[103] while, in applying its rehousing policy to the residents of Hutchesontown 'E', the 'supposedly Labour council' was accused of 'harassment and intimidation' for the way it compelled tenants to make 'hasty decisions' about their rehousing options.[104]

One of the Campaign's most enduring criticisms of Glasgow District Council was founded on what it considered its uncooperative and secretive nature. For example, as the Campaign prepared to take legal action against the Council under the 1897 Public Health Act, *The View* reported that the Council 'have no intention of releasing the plans, drawings and schedules requested 8 weeks ago. Their policy is to be one of complete non-cooperation. No mention was made of the investigation by their 6 man team. No report is being issued – WHY THE SECRECY?'[105] Later, when the Council had initiated its own investigation into the dampness issue, pre-empting the Campaign's legal action, the Campaign reported: '... the Council's investigation continues in private .... The District Council seems determined to act as judge and jury in its own trial. We feel the people of the Gorbals deserve more openness than this.'[106] As for the findings of this investigation, the Campaign described these as 'the non-event of the year. A flimsy document of 7 pages, telling us nothing we had not known for 4 years.'[107] Two years later, having again failed to obtain from the Council the detailed plans for the flats and the specifications of the materials which were used, the Campaign was still asking, 'Will the full facts about the building of the flats ever be made available to the Gorbals tenants and the ratepayers of the city?'[108]

The Campaign also contrasted its own dynamism with the Council's lack of action: 'The campaign has continued to meet and work throughout the summer. It's a pity the authorities don't do the same! Communication with Glasgow District Council has got worse – unanswered letters, broken promises about

[102] 'End of the Line', *The View* (February 1982), p. 2. ML.
[103] 'Victory!', *The View* (July/August 1976), p. 1. ML.
[104] 'Gorbals Notes', *The View* (November 1981), p. 2. ML.
[105] 'Dampness', *The View* (February 1976), p. 12. ML. Capitalized in original.
[106] 'Dampness Campaign News', *The View* (June 1976), p. 10.
[107] 'Victory!', *The View* (July/August 1976), p. 1. ML.
[108] 'Gorbals Dampness', *The View* (June 1978), p. 9. ML.

meetings, requests for information on rehousing being refused etc.'[109] Echoing the comment in *The Gorbals View* from 20 years previously, that 'Gorbals people are often "treated like dirt",'[110] they added resentfully that 'The authorities are still treating the tenants of the Hutchesontown "E" scheme as "second class citizens" '.[111] The resentment of the Gorbals residents is summed up in a cartoon featured in *The View* from 1976 (Figure 6.1), which not only plays upon the 'unnatural' condition of living up in the clouds (in this case, in an SSHA flat), but also features Bailie Patrick Lally, then chair of the Council's housing management committee, as an omnipotent, but not necessarily benevolent, God.

It should be noted that the Campaign did not appear to change its critical position according to whether it was dealing with a Labour-led Council or the Conservative–SNP Council of 1977–80, and Council officials seem to have been vilified without distinction. Only with respect to their own political representatives did Campaign members make some distinctions: their MP at the time, Frank McElhone (Labour), was also a Scottish minister, and it was felt that he was not always fully committed to the Campaign: 'Mr McElhone, our M.P. again made his usual speech about having nothing to do with housing and the difficulties he has a Minister. This is accepted by tenants, but it is considered he could exert more pressure and be seen to give more active support.'[112] McElhone was, however, applauded for representing the tenants so well at the rates appeal. James Wray (Labour), their representative at Strathclyde Regional Council, was generally respected: 'Unfortunately, Cnr Wray is not directly involved in housing matters but it is known he works very hard in this area.'[113] Until 1977, the Gorbals was represented in the District Council by two councillors – Catherine Cantley and John Lavelle, both Labour. Lavelle gave evidence on the tenants' behalf at the rates appeal, but he was still not considered to be entirely satisfactory: 'Cnr. Lavelle gave his account of events but as usual he had little of consequence to tell the tenants. In fairness, however, Hutchesontown is not his area.'[114] In 1977 it emerged that Cantley had been involved in serious house-letting irregularities and she was forced to resign. She was replaced by George McAulay (SNP) who worked very efficiently with the Campaign, undoubtedly benefiting from belonging to a new and more sympathetic Conservative–SNP administration in the City Chambers which felt free from any stigma attached to the city's modernist public housing schemes.

---

[109] 'Dampness', *The View* (September 1978), p. 12. ML.
[110] 'Officialdom', *The Gorbals View*, no. 15 (June 1968), p. 1. ML.
[111] 'Dampness', *The View* (September 1978), p. 12. ML.
[112] 'Dampness', *The View* (June 1977), p. 9. ML.
[113] Ibid.
[114] Ibid.

6.1 Cartoon from *The View*
Reproduced from *The View* (July–August 1976), p. 6. ML.

The Anti-Dampness Campaign, *The View* and the local tenants' associations all maintained considerable pressure on their elected representatives and made it very clear that their loyalties should lie with their constituents, not their party hierarchy. In a way, even this emphasis on the role of elected representatives reinforced the collective nature of the Campaign's case.

The resurrection of the 'slums'

As the tenants' associations and the Anti-Dampness Campaign sought to assign the 'spirit' of the old Gorbals to the population of the new, so the negative dimension of the old slums was increasingly directed at the physical structure of the new flats.

In the early phases, one of the Campaign's key tactics was to give substance to the issue of damp homes and so make the problem tangible. One way of achieving this was to cover the issue thoroughly in *The View* by means of reports, photographs and residents' comments. This eventually became a regular feature in the paper under the title of 'Dampness', although the issue also frequently found its way on to the paper's front page. Given the limited circulation of *The View*, one can assume that these articles were largely intended to consolidate support for the Campaign amongst the residents of the Gorbals area, although the paper would also have been read by their political representatives. In part to furnish these reports and in part as a foundation for their legal actions, much of the activity of the Campaign members was directed at collecting information concerning the technical aspects of dampness, the architectural and structural characteristics of the Tracoba blocks and the medical implications of damp conditions.

The 'factual' reports on the damp conditions and the activities of the Anti-Dampness Campaign were augmented by accounts of the losses experienced by households, which served to give the dampness a human meaning. At the same time, these reports were complemented by humorous or ironic cartoon references to the damp conditions. The 'reality' of the damp conditions was also communicated by inviting officials, press and politicians to view some of the flats, thus impressing on them the severity of the situation.

One of the first important steps towards the resurrection of the old slum identity in this new context was marked by the letter sent on behalf of the Campaign to Glasgow District Council on 10 November 1975, informing the Council that there was a nuisance present in the flats in Hutchesontown 'E', of which they were both owners and managers. On these grounds, the letter stated, the District Council was in breach of its statutory obligations under the Public Health (Scotland) Act 1897, sections 16 and 17. Under Section 16(1) of the act, the tenants had to demonstrate that '... the premises or part thereof of such a construction are in such a state as to be a nuisance or injurious or dangerous to health'. Since the presence of a nuisance must be proved, the Campaign had to show that the dampness was a health hazard, or likely to cause one, and that this hazard was not caused by living habits, but by fundamental design flaws or construction faults.[115] The paradox of applying the Public Health Act to Council-owned housing had not escaped the Campaign organizers. Willie Roxburgh commented, 'If our flats had been owned and managed by a private landlord, the council would long ago have recognized the health hazard and issued an abatement notice.' Moreover, he explained, the fact that the landlord was the Council created legal complications: 'Unfortunately, as the environmental health officers who are responsible for deciding if a statutory nuisance exists are council employees, it is nearly impossible to expect them to go against the council in the court.'[116] In preparation for their legal action, Jim Friel, the Campaign secretary and a trainee solicitor, began gathering evidence and taking experts on conducted tours of the mouldy walls and fungal growth. In addition, a number of architects and health inspectors interested in the Campaign offered consultative services free of charge. By February 1976 the Campaign claimed to have evidence from 14 doctors that dampness had exacerbated bronchial conditions of tenants living in the flats, and threatened that, if the District Council did not take action within the next ten weeks they would be taken to court.

[115] While the Campaign's action was novel, it was not without precedent; in July of the same year, a similar action had been initiated by a group of tenants in Bowhouse, Alloa, who took Clackmannan District Council to court over the dampness and lack of repair to drains and pipes in their houses. The Council took swift action to remedy the complaints and the tenants were awarded costs.

[116] Cunningham, 'When Tenants Take on the Council', p. 7.

As it was, the Campaign's initiative was thwarted by the Council which produced a report recognizing that a dampness problem existed. All the same, the Campaign's move was highly significant because it confronted the Council's definition of the new Gorbals with a legal tool drawn up in the previous century to protect tenants living in poor-standard, privately rented housing – the 'slums'. That this legislation should be used against those whose task it was to enforce it epitomized the changing attitude towards both the housing in the new Gorbals and the role of the District Council. On 9 December 1975 Willie Roxburgh went a step further to suggest that not only were the residents of New Gorbals inhabiting slums, but that living conditions in the old Gorbals had been preferable: 'The fault is in the construction of the houses with materials such as concrete, which is difficult to insulate. Most of the tenants in the new houses were better off in their old tenement homes.'[117] In short, they had been better off for two reasons. The first was simply that conditions in the deck-access blocks were considered to have deteriorated to the point that they were worse than in the old tenements. Indeed, in the most extreme cases even the advantage of spaciousness was lost, as damp conditions in the new flats made some rooms uninhabitable, while in other rooms furniture had to be moved away from the walls and into the centre of the floor in order to avoid the spread of mould, with the result that tenants unwillingly re-created the cramped conditions of the old tenements. *The View*, reporting the conditions in James Carlin's flat, explained, 'their new home is plagued with dampness – so bad that he and his wife and family are forced to sleep in the one dry room in the house.'[118] The second reason for the rejection of the new housing in favour of a lost housing past was that the old tenements had provided the home for what was coming to be remembered as a 'community'. It was felt that this community, which had developed from the collective memory of the 'spirit' of the Gorbals and was informed by a discourse which had emerged from the social sciences and the planning profession, was all but lost in the new flats. We shall examine this aspect in more detail in the section on 'Remembering the community' later in this chapter.

I have argued that establishing a meaning for a place in the present shapes expectations for its future – thus, if the new Gorbals was a slum, then the appropriate treatment ought to be the treatment reserved for slums. The June 1976 edition of *The View* featured on its front page a photograph of the demolition of the Pruitt-Igoe public housing scheme in St Louis, USA in 1972.[119] The

[117] 'Gorbals Tenants Picket Mobile Exhibition', *The Glasgow Herald* (9 December 1975), p. 3.

[118] 'Hutchesontown Tenants Association', *The View* (June 1975), p. 4. ML.

[119] Priutt-Igoe was a massive public housing project in St Louis. Demolition started on 15 July, 1972, and the scheme became a symbol of the failure of large-scale public urban projects of this kind.

headline, 'FAULTY TOWERS?', parodied the title of a popular television sitcom of the time. Underneath the photograph, *The View* asked if this was 'the ultimate solution to high rise problems?' and 'How long before this happens in Scotland?'.[120] This is one of the first occasions when the possibility of demolition was aired. Being sure to include the deck-access flats in their assessment ('In Gorbals many of the complaints about dampness come from medium rise blocks ...'), the article concluded with a question that was increasingly finding resonance in the Gorbals: 'Are they likely to be the new slums of Glasgow?'[121] Again, in 1978, as the Campaign waited for the results of the NBA pilot project to be made public, *The View* asked: 'Will the scheme be improved? Or will it be allowed to degenerate into Glasgow's first "modern" slum?'[122]

Increasingly, the new flats came to be referred to in terms that echoed descriptions of the old Gorbals. For example, at the public meeting in November 1976 at which the committee of the Anti-Dampness Campaign claimed to have received its mandate, Jim Friel described the flats as 'uninhabitable, unhealthy hell holes'.[123] But such comments were not limited to Campaign members. In statements to the press after a visit to the damp flats in December 1976, the theme was employed by two government ministers and a local councillor. Hugh Brown, Under-Secretary of State at the Scottish Office, responsible for housing in Scotland, announced that he thought that the houses were 'really deplorable'. The same adjective was also employed by Frank McElhone, the local MP, whose comments directly challenged the modernity of the flats: 'I have seen them before and I think they are absolutely deplorable. They are not the type of accommodation people should have to be using in the 1970s. But there is no easy answer.'[124] District councillor, John Lavelle, was even more cutting, describing some of the flats as 'cave dwellings' with water pouring down walls and fungus sprouting overnight.[125] Jim Friel, commenting after the ministers' visit, used an interesting expression: 'I think it was a fairly successful meeting. We have finally alerted government ministers to the problem of living in these middens.'[126] 'Midden' was the term for the refuse collection area in the

---

[120] 'Faulty Towers?', *The View* (June 1976), p. 1. ML.

[121] Ibid.

[122] 'Uncertain Future?', *The View* (November 1978), p. 1. ML.

[123] 'Dampness', *The View* (December/January 1976/7), p. 8. ML.

[124] In September 1977, McElhone was even more explicit about the growing perception of the New Gorbals, echoing the words of the Campaign chairman: 'Tenants are actually worse off than they were in the Gorbals slums from which they were moved.' 'McElhone Joins Fight for Tenants', *The Glasgow Herald* (6 September 1977), p. 9.

[125] 'Ministers Back Tenants in Damp Row', *The Glasgow Herald* (21 December 1976), p. 4.

[126] Ibid.

back-courts of the old tenements, and it is not unusual to hear it used in normal speech to describe dirty conditions, but here Friel's choice of vocabulary invokes a particular inversion: the flats of the new Gorbals have themselves become 'middens' – the filthiest part of the filthy old tenements.

The rehousing activity by Glasgow District Council marked another important step in the resurrection of the Gorbals' slum past. The emptying of Hutchesontown 'E' mirrored precisely the action it had carried out in the same area only ten years before, and the motivation was the same; a moral duty to provide acceptable living standards for a population inhabiting substandard housing. Of course, the key difference this time around was that these substandard properties did not belong to private landlords, but to the District Council itself. Just as the new housing increasingly came to be perceived as slums, so too the Council gradually ceased to be a miracle-worker and became an uncaring 'slum landlord'. In 1978 *The View* observed:

> From reports over the years tenants in Gorbals and Govanhill know well that even new properties are often sub-standard and badly maintained. Slums used to describe the old crumbling tenements but we know now that many newer Council houses are becoming slums because the landlord does not maintain them and, combined with bad design, this is creating the new slums of the 80's.[127]

From Labour's point of view, the Council could no longer depict itself as a socialist administration answering the housing concerns of its working-class citizens who would otherwise be exploited at the hands of private interests, and there can be little doubt that this provoked considerable unease amongst Labour Party councillors. It is hardly surprising that in this context they sought to shift the responsibility for Hutchesontown 'E' on to planners, architects and central government. Commenting in April 1977 (shortly before Labour lost control of the Council) on the findings and recommendations of the NBA survey of the Tracoba flats, Bailie Patrick Lally (Labour), chairman of the housing management committee stated:

> The cost of implementing these recommendations is very high. We can only continue to be appalled that we are having to face bills of this magnitude for what we thought would be good family housing.
> How it is possible to design houses that have these basic weaknesses and have them accepted by the powers that be at every level is really unbelievable.[128]

The Campaign was not prepared, however, to let the Council avoid its share of the responsibility. When, for example, a tenant of Hutchesontown 'E', who was clearing up prior to being rehoused, discovered, 'a "REJECT" mark in bold

---

[127] 'Rents Up Standards Down', *The View* (May 1978), p. 1. ML.

[128] '£500,000 Needed to Dry Out New Flats', *The Glasgow Herald* (14 April 1977), p. 4.

red letters printed on the inside of his kitchen cupboard'[129] and an investigation revealed another two such cupboards in the same block, the Campaign concluded that: 'These discoveries raise politically serious questions about the building standards which were used in the construction of the flats and the degree of supervision which was exercised during the construction period.'[130] Moreover, the very word 'REJECT' seems to offer an ironic confirmation of the position taken by the Campaign all along: not only were the flats substandard, but also their inhabitants were treated as if they too were somehow flawed.

Two key events

Two events in the course of the Anti-Dampness Campaign's efforts are worth particular consideration because they illustrate the ways in which the themes discussed above were put into practice. The first of these events is the meeting held in the Citizens' Theatre on 1 May 1977, and the second is the rates appeal in September of the same year.

The Citizens' Theatre meeting

The choice of 1 May for this meeting was not by chance – not only is this the traditional socialist May Day celebration (making it the preferred date for major events in Alma-Gare too), it was also two days before the District Council elections were due to be held, and the Campaign could be sure of attracting the attention of politicians and the media alike. The Citizens' Theatre, located in the Gorbals, has a large capacity, and even a turn-out of 500, impressive by local standards, would have left the theatre conspicuously empty. Thus, in order to arouse interest and encourage as large an attendance as possible, the Campaign organizers had around 100 posters and 2000 leaflets printed to publicize the event. An announcement in *The View* (Figure 6.2) proclaimed, 'Everybody Welcome!!!' and not only promised the 'Biggest Meeting in 10 Years!!!', but also the opportunity to 'Meet Mr Fungus!'.[131]

On the day itself, messages and music broadcast from a car fitted with a Tannoy system encouraged people to come to the meeting. Prior to the event, four bagpipers led a procession through the streets to the theatre, helping to create a sense of occasion. The pipers were accompanied by a figure in a sinister 'Mr Fungus' outfit, and a five-man 'Dampness Monster'. On arriving at the theatre, Mr Fungus was confronted by a superhero, 'Mr Anti-Dampness'. In the words of one of the local organizers, 'This fight ended, of course , with Mr

[129] 'Gorbals Dampness', *The View* (June 1978), p. 9. ML.
[130] Ibid.
[131] 'Anti Dampness Campaign', *The View* (May 1977), p. 12. ML.

6.2 Announcement in *The View* for the Citizens' Theatre meeting, featuring Mr Fungus
Reproduced from *The View* (May 1977), p. 12. ML.

Anti-Dampness triumphing over Mr Fungus and the Dampness Monster, to the cheers of everyone in the procession.'[132]

The meeting itself was attended by between 900 and 1000 people, leaving 'standing room only'.[133] All the Gorbals political representatives were there, as well as all the prospective candidates in the forthcoming elections. The event served as a forum for the tenants to air their demands, which included full compensation for damage to property and disturbance, a rent reduction for those living in damp property, no re-letting of damp houses, a special parliamentary inquiry into dampness in the Gorbals, and immediate rehousing in the area of their choice for all tenants living in damp flats.[134] The meeting was not, however, without problems: there was disagreement over the Campaign's 'space of experience' – from the point of view of the Campaign activists, the local Labour Party had not given them adequate support, while the Labour representatives accused the Campaign of employing unnecessarily aggressive tactics. Inevitably, with candidates of all parties present there was a diversity of views, and it was suggested, from different political perspectives, that the Campaign was a front for a rival group variously defined as Marxist, anarchist or Scottish Nationalist.[135]

The rather tense atmosphere of the meeting was moderated by a skit produced by two drama students which featured an encounter between Mrs Ivy

[132] Bryant, *The Dampness Monster*, p. 31.
[133] 'Dampness', *The View* (June 1977), p. 9. ML.
[134] Bryant, *The Dampness Monster*, p. 28.
[135] Ibid., p. 32.

Mould, a council house tenant, and the housing manager of Glasgow District Council. This served to unite the audience through the re-enactment of a common experience: 'how many tenants have found themselves in the past in Clive House [the housing department's headquarters] experiencing the same situation but not acting?'[136] The audience was also encouraged to join in a rendering of 'The Dampness Song', composed and performed by a tenant of Hutchesontown 'E' ('It is hoped the politicians learn the song and perhaps even sing it at Westminster and the City Chambers'[137]). To the tune of 'Clementine', the song opened with the lines:

> Oh the dampness
> In these houses, is the worst
> You've ever seen
> The furniture and the walls
> Have turned a shade of green[138]

Much of the 'entertainment' around the meeting was carnivalesque, a characteristic which, as we have seen, was also very present in the APU's activities in Alma-Gare. The personification of the tenants' problems in the form of Mr Fungus and the Dampness Monster, and their solution in the shape of Mr Anti-Dampness, appealed because they offered a simple representation of a shared problem. *The View* explained that 'The monster was no joke; dampness is a monster'.[139] (Dampness had already been depicted as a monster in *The View*: 'Loch Ness has Nessie! – We have our monster – Dampness!'[140]) Mrs Ivy Mould represented all Gorbals tenants, and expressed their frustration with the housing department of the District Council. Mrs Mould's confrontation with the housing manager reiterated the enduring theme of the Gorbals people being ' "treated like dirt" – though a few give as good as they get!'.[141] Even the song, simple too, served to create unity amongst the audience and emphasize their collective experience – and not only the collective experience then and there in the theatre, but also with respect to the common nature of the problem present in individual homes.

The rates appeal

Much preparation went into the rates appeal, and the case, consisting of two volumes, was submitted to the Assessor's Department in March 1977. It should be noted that rates were paid to Strathclyde Regional Council and not Glasgow

---

136 'Dampness', *The View* (June 1977), p. 9. ML.
137 Ibid.
138 Bryant, *The Dampness Monster*, p. 31. Written by P. Torrance.
139 'Dampness', *The View* (June 1977), p. 9. ML.
140 'Loch Ness has Nessie!', *The View* (November 1976), p. 3. ML.
141 'Officialdom', *The Gorbals View*, no. 15 (June 1968), p. 1. ML.

District Council, so in this instance the Campaign's case was against the region, although a ruling in their favour would also have significantly strengthened their position against the district.

Provocatively, the Campaign had even cited Charles Murdoch, Chief Executive of Glasgow District Council, Bailie Derek Wood, Chairman of the District Housing Committee, and Malcolm Smith, Director of Housing, as witnesses. The Council witnesses refused to appear, claiming that they did not wish to intervene in a Regional Council matter, with Wood adding, 'If I don't give evidence then I will no doubt be crucified for it. However, I don't think it would be proper for me to give evidence.'[142] Willie Roxburgh remarked that the decision did not surprise him: 'We had an idea they wouldn't come. We issued the citations to ensure they couldn't claim at a later stage that they had never been invited.'[143] In any case, their refusal only served to reinforce the negative identification of the Council in the eyes of the tenants. The Campaign, however, was less ambivalent about support from the residents of Hutchesontown 'E' and announced that 'It is now vitally important that we receive FULL SUPPORT FROM ALL THE TENANTS'.[144]

Like the Citizens' Theatre event, the first day of the rates appeal was marked by a festive, carnival atmosphere. Some 200 demonstrators arrived in the city centre in a double-decker bus, accompanied by a removal van loaded with the evidence the Campaign intended to produce during the hearing. Carrying banners proclaiming 'Damn the Damp!' and, with reference to Hugh Brown, the Scottish Secretary for Housing, 'We're Browned Off', they marched from George Square, past the City Chambers to the Burgh Court Hall carrying their evidence. This included a filing cabinet full of documentation, a basket of written submissions, a damaged, musty sofa, ruined clothes, and even two bottles of water beetles. These objects were clearly intended to attract attention by their incongruity in a city-centre setting. The tension they created was twofold – first that objects from the private realm such as a couch and clothes should appear in the city's public space and, second, that these intimate domestic objects, associated with the home, hygiene and comfort, should be ruined by an invasive enemy. The presence of the water beetles in the bottles served to confirmed the insalubrity of the 'slum' conditions which the tenants had to endure.[145]

---

142 'Housing Chief Snubs Tenants', *The Glasgow Herald* (13 September 1977), p. 3.

143 Ibid., p. 13.

144 'Gorbals Dampness', *The View* (September 1977), p. 10. ML. Capitalized in original.

145 Jim Friel had already used the juxtaposition of 'home' with the outside or the alien when he commented, with reference to experts' visits to the flats: 'We've had all sorts of experts here – including mycologists and botanists.' 'Ministers Back Tenants in Damp Row', *The Glasgow Herald* (21 December 1976), p. 4a.

The collective nature of the issue was emphasized by Jim Friel's assertion that, if necessary, he could call 200 tenants to give evidence to corroborate his case. As it turned out, only 15 were required.[146] A theme that emerged clearly from the witnesses' comments was one that had already become well established in the Gorbals – namely, that conditions were worse in the new Gorbals than in the old. Frank McElhone, MP for Gorbals, opened the evidence, giving what 'all the tenants in the court' agreed was 'a brilliant performance':[147]

> I have visited many of these houses and find it absolutely deplorable that the conditions that people are living under are actually worse in terms of dampness than most of the older tenement properties I have to deal with. In my opinion it would be grossly unjust for these tenants to continue to pay rates on the present valuation of their houses.[148]

Helen McVicar, treasurer of the Laurieston and Hutchesontown Tenants' Association, who had paid neither rent nor rates for 18 months, said in evidence:

> When I moved in I was quite happy. We spent every penny we had on it [the apartment] and I expected to stay there for the rest of my life.
> Now to say I am disappointed would be an understatement. I was far better off in the old tenement property.[149]

She evoked the cramped conditions and poor health once associated with the old Gorbals:

> After only three months the dampness started to creep in. Eventually we were forced to sleep in the living room with our three children. The bedrooms were just not for living in. Since then, my two daughters have contracted bronchitis and my husband has arthritis. We've had enough![150]

Describing the events in the court, the 'Dampness News' in *The View* praised the determination of the tenants who gave evidence: 'No tenants showed anything but strength and confidence in the witness box. At the end of the day the tenants were still giving evidence.'[151] On learning the result of the appeal, the Campaign presented it in the best possible light: 'any reduction in rates is very difficult to obtain. It is therefore the reduction in itself which is important and not the amount gained which must be the basis for accepting the decision as being favourable to us.'[152] Although the amount offered was small, the

[146] 'Mildewed Settee Goes to Court as Angry Tenants Seek Rates Cut', *The Glasgow Herald* (16 September 1977), p. 5.

[147] 'Dampness', *The View* (October 1977), p. 10. ML.

[148] 'Mildewed Settee Goes to Court as Angry Tenants Seek Rates Cut', *The Glasgow Herald* (16 September 1977), p. 5.

[149] Ibid.

[150] 'Rates Revolt', *The View* (October 1977), p. 1. ML.

[151] 'Dampness', *The View* (October 1977), p. 10. ML.

[152] 'Dampness', *The View* (November 1977), p. 12. ML.

Anti-Dampness Campaign could claim, tapping in to the Gorbals 'spirit', that the combined effort of 'hundreds of tenants' and 'all our political representatives', was 'A truly remarkable show of strength and solidarity'.[153]

While this chapter concentrates on Hutchesontown 'E', it is important to remember that, although damp conditions were most severe in these blocks, they were not restricted to the 'Dampies'. The 1979 report for the Scottish Council of Social Services opens by taking themes developed in Hutchesontown 'E' and applying them to the Gorbals as a whole: 'Unfortunately for the residents, who number around thirteen thousand, "New" is not synonymous with "Good". Parts of the New Gorbals hide behind a facade of concrete, a twilight world of appalling manifestations of dampness more commonly associated with dereliction and slum conditions.'[154] A little further on, the report states that 'The conditions which existed in the old slums are now *existing within the walls* of these modern flats in the Gorbals'.[155]

Cases of dampness were reported throughout the Gorbals, in low- and high-rise developments alike and, apart from the Anti-Dampness Campaign, there was also a Laurieston Anti-Dampness Action Group, a Sandiefields Action Group Dampness Campaign and a Riverside Action Group covering other areas of the new Gorbals. And the cause was not only condensation, but also, in certain cases, such as the Matthews flats in the Riverside area (Hutchesontown 'B'), water penetration due to faulty designs. As for Spence's Queen Elizabeth Square development (Hutchesontown 'C'), Frank Worsdall, in his 1979 social and architectural history of the tenement block, reports that:

> The external appearance of these giant blocks has brought much criticism, and their style has not been repeated. The dark, narrow internal passages are distinctly unpleasant and already, after about ten years, the staircases are similar in appearance to those in the so-called 'slums' they replaced, and far worse in smell.[156]

In January 1983, tenants in Spence's Hutchesontown 'C' blocks accused the Council of 'chronic maladministration' with regard to their houses, reinforcing once more the theme of Council incompetence, the tenants' leader stating that 'there is water running down these flats and it is rotting the electricity wires. The state of the blocks is deplorable.'[157] The tone is familiar, as was the local councillor's claim that the flats were so damp and dirty that they contravened the 1897 Public Health Act. The Queen Elizabeth Square flats were scheduled for demolition in 1992.

---

153 'Dampness', *The View* (October 1977), p. 10. ML.

154 Bryant, *The Dampness Monster*, p. 1.

155 Ibid., p. 10.

156 Worsdall, *The Tenement: A Way of Life*, p. 147.

157 'Commissioner Called in over Damp Houses', *The Glasgow Herald* (10 January 1983), p. 2.

A postscript to the 'Dampies'

In May 1977, following the original National Building Agency report, Glasgow District Council announced a pilot scheme in a number of flats in the Hutchesontown 'E' development in order to assess how best to proceed with a full-scale remedial programme. The report on these remedial measures was issued in March 1979, and it was estimated that a full-scale programme to treat the dampness would cost over £2 million, while additional improvements to the blocks would add another million pounds to this total. All the same, the report concluded that there was no guarantee that these measures would be successful. On receiving this news, the Anti-Dampness Campaign expressed the unequivocal position 'that demolition is the only policy it would accept'.[158] The Campaign advocated that, rather than spend money on remedial work, the Council should put it towards the cost of demolishing the 'Dampies' and building new council housing for the former tenants of the flats. This pro-demolition view became increasingly entrenched as more tenants were moved out of the scheme but, as Keating explains, Glasgow District Council simply did not have the financial resources for such an undertaking. The cost of demolishing the flats was estimated to be as high as £2 million and, as if this was not bad enough, there was still an outstanding debt of £4 million on the development, opening up a real possibility that the city's councillors would face legal penalties if they were to undertake the sort of project proposed by the Anti-Dampness Campaign.[159]

In August 1982, when all but eight of the tenants of the Hutchesontown 'E' deck-access blocks had been moved out, Glasgow District Council's Labour group narrowly decided (21 votes to 19) on a third course: rather than remedial work or demolition, they would sell the flats in the Hutchesontown 'E' development to a private developer who would undertake their rehabilitation.[160] *The Glasgow Herald* reported that the Council expected to raise £2 million from the sale of the houses and that this sum would be used to fund a sheltered housing project in the Govanhill area of the city. This decision had major implications for, while Conservative central government was promoting council house sales, the District Labour Party, which had not been consulted over the issue, had made its opposition to such a policy very clear. The District

[158] 'Demolition?', *The View* (March 1979), p. 1. ML.

[159] Keating, *The City that Refused to Die. Glasgow: The Politics of Urban Regeneration* (Aberdeen: Aberdeen University Press, 1988), p. 134.

[160] Keating states that this proposal was not without precedent, even for this Labour-led council, for schemes such as this were already going on in peripheral areas of the city. This, however, was the first time that this kind of scheme had been suggested for such a central and high-profile area of the city. Ibid.

Party announced that the decision by the Council's Labour group represented a betrayal of Labour Party policy and demanded the names of the 21 party members who had voted in favour of the sale, provoking reselection fears amongst Labour councillors. It also lent its support to a 'Stop the Sale' campaign which had been initiated by the Gorbals Anti-Dampness Campaign with the support of trade union branches and other tenants' groups. This campaign demanded the complete demolition of Hutchesontown 'E' and its replacement by 'decent council housing after full consultation by the council with the local community to ascertain the needs of the area'.[161]

Why did these groups, for whom Hutchesontown 'E' symbolized both the failure of Labour local government and the return of 'slum' conditions, mount a campaign to stop what they called (echoing the title of a popular television quiz show where consumer goods were sold to contestants at extremely low prices) 'the sale of the century'?[162] Keating suggests two principal reasons for this. The first objection was based on what he calls 'localist feeling'. This is borne out by the statements of the 'Stop the Sale' campaign, which evoke the threat posed to local residents by the arrival of 'private "enterprise"':

> Young families would be forced to move out of the area to find a home for themselves: on the one hand council houses wouldn't be available (due to them having been sold off to private 'enterprise'); and, on the other hand, purchase of a private flat in Hutchie 'E' would be out of the question (who's got £20,000 to splash out for a damp flat?).[163]

Moreover, the Campaign considered that once the private sector established a base in the area, private housing would spread at the expense of public tenants:

> And once Barratts ... get a foothold in Gorbals – where would it stop? There are any number of at present derelict sites in the area which Barratts might then start expanding into. The result would be a further loss of potential sites of decent council housing in an area which badly needs it.[164]

Keating's second explanation for the opposition to the sale was founded on the crisis of the new Gorbals 'miracle' and its rise as a public-sector 'slum': 'Above all the campaign, media involvement and the involvement of the local Labour parties in the city had presented Hutchesontown E as a great council failure.'[165] Any move by the Council to sell off these flats to the private sector was therefore construed as an attempt to duck its responsibility to set things right. Seen in this light, the initiative could only provoke bitterness and resentment.

---

161 'Gorbals. Stop the Sale!', *The View* (October 1982), p. 2. ML.

162 '756 Damp Glasgow Flats Doomed to Demolition', *The Glasgow Herald* (2 June 1984), p. 1.

163 'Gorbals. Stop the Sale!', *The View* (October 1982), p. 2. ML.

164 Ibid.

165 Keating, *The City that Refused to Die*, p. 134.

We might add a third, related reason for the local resistance to the sale; on several occasions *The View* had pointed out that the blame for the situation lay not only with the District Council, but also with 'the private sector builders who constructed these concrete caves'.[166] They considered that the private sector firms involved 'have been able to clear out with their nice profits and leave the local authority picking up the pieces'.[167] From this perspective, the Council had not only failed to provide the people with adequate housing but, in so doing, they had also compromised their principles by making the private sector the main beneficiary of this failure. The 'Stop the Sale' campaign considered that the Council's plans for Hutchesontown 'E' simply allowed the private sector yet another opportunity to profit from an unhappy situation.

The opposition to the project, and in particular the fear of a political witch hunt by the District Labour Party, caused the project to stall until the District Council elections of 1984. These elections saw a new Labour group come to power in the Council – one with a more left-wing profile – which, amongst its election manifesto commitments, had voiced its clear opposition to the sale of council housing.[168] It soon dropped any proposals to sell off the flats and decided instead that the Hutchesontown 'E' development should be demolished. The news was worthy enough to make an appearance on the front page of *The Glasgow Herald*, which announced '756 Damp Glasgow Flats Doomed to Demolition'. But there were also intimations that the Council's 'no-sale' manifesto promise might be compromised as the paper added 'it is understood the administration may try to quell Scottish Office anxiety by offering to allocate the cleared site for private housing'.[169] The Scottish Office was concerned that the Council intended to demolish a building which it had not yet fully paid for. When asked if the Labour group intended selling council land, Jean McFadden, the group leader, replied that they did not believe that there was a technical solution for the severe problem of dampness and water

---

166 'Guilty!', *The View* (April 1980), p. 1. ML. See also 'Rents Up Standards Down', *The View*, (May 1978), p. 1. ML. 'Could it be that the private builders who have constructed homes in the last 10–15 years are laughing all the way to the bank after building shoddy housing ...?' See also 'Ten Years After', *The View* (August 1982), p. 1. ML: 'The contractors' firms who produced system-built plans, who persuaded Central Government to accept them as modern family housing and laughed all the way to the bank with the profits.'

167 'Guilty!', *The View* (April 1980), p. 1. ML.

168 Keating, *The City that Refused to Die*, p. 134. Indeed, the situation was more complicated than this. When questioned during the election campaign on this key 'no-sale' manifesto clause, Jean McFadden, leader of the Labour Group, repeatedly claimed 'that it did not mean what it appeared to mean'. Robertson, 'Labour Probe into Gorbals Land Deal', *The Glasgow Herald* (29 June 1985), p. 1.

169 '756 Damp Glasgow Flats Doomed to Demolition', *The Glasgow Herald* (2 June 1984), p. 1.

penetration in the flats and suggested that 'there is a possibility of land being transferred to individual owners'.[170] The opposition groups in the Council did not miss this chance to gloat at Labour's expense, and Councillor Robert Brown, the Liberal leader, told Labour members, 'If you seriously imagine the Secretary of State is going to come up with funding for this then the hole is not in the ground but in your head.'[171]

In short, whatever option the Council chose, be it rehabilitation, sale or demolition, financial realities required the involvement of the private sector. It was ironic, given that private landlords were remembered as the scourge of the old Gorbals, that the private sector should now be presented by Glasgow District Council as the panacea for the problems associated with the new Gorbals. As Keating points out, it was unclear why the sale of the vacant site to a private developer as McFadden had hinted was ideologically more acceptable than earlier plans and, indeed, this project seemed even further from socialist principles than the original proposal to sell the flats to the private sector for refurbishment as low-cost units for owner occupation.[172]

In April 1985 a property development firm called City Link Development Ltd revealed a £20 million plan for a shopping centre and 237 houses on the site of Hutchesontown 'E', and on 26 June, the Labour group made it public that the site of the flats was to be sold to City Link for £4 million. From this return, the Council estimated that it would have to spend approximately £1 million on demolition costs, while the remaining £3 million would go towards constructing some 100 houses for rental in the area.[173] The Council's housing convenor made a point of visiting community organizations in the Gorbals, to which he showed a video produced by the Council's own public relations department explaining the advantages of the City Link offer. William Robertson, writing in *The Glasgow Herald*, suggested that the Labour group's enthusiasm to win over local objectors was due to the fact that it had been Labour activists in the Gorbals who had been responsible for the key 'no-sale' clause being included in the 1984 local election manifesto.[174] Although some left-wing Labour councillors opposed the deal, and others were concerned that there had been insufficient opportunity for other developers to submit schemes, group leader Jean McFadden was decidedly relieved to have been freed from

---

170 '£130,000 Surcharge Warning to Labour', *The Glasgow Herald* (13 June 1984), p. 3.

171 Ibid.

172 Keating, *The City that Refused to Die*, p. 135.

173 'Hutchesontown E Site is Finally Sold for £4 million', *The Glasgow Herald* (27 June 1985), p. 1.

174 W. Robertson, 'Labour Probe into Gorbals Land Deal', *The Glasgow Herald* (29 June 1985), p. 2.

the legacy of the new Gorbals: 'At long last we have a solution to the problem of Hutchesontown E, which has dogged us for years. I am delighted.'[175]

McFadden's relief proved to be premature: on 27 June, the Labour group announced a 'U-turn over £20m Gorbals Flat Plan'.[176] Councillors had been on the point of confirming the City Link deal when Steven Hamilton, the town clerk, had warned them that they might be acting illegally by failing to examine a late offer which was apparently worth twice that of the City Link deal to the city. There was little choice but to abandon the project. The circumstances surrounding the City Link deal remained – and still remain – hazy, and the press wondered why, after years of delays, the sale of the site had been rushed through just before the Council's summer recess.[177] Three weeks after the Labour group's rethink the District Council formally invited developers to submit official tenders 'for the redevelopment of a 30-acre site in the Hutchesontown area of the city for both housing and non-housing purposes'.[178] By the closing date of 15 August 1985, six companies, including City Link, had submitted tenders. Of these schemes, two seemed to offer higher returns than the City Link project, while another offered a similar return. Making public the details of the various deals, McLean, the housing convenor, was unable to explain why the Labour group had considered the City Link offer as the best possible deal.[179] McFadden, fielding criticism that the flats were to be razed before they had even been paid for,[180] remained defiant and transformed structural deficiencies in the buildings into a 'stigma' that could only be removed through demolition:

> We know there is debt on the buildings. But we also know there's a stigma attached to Hutchesontown 'E' and in our view it is better to remove the stigma completely by demolishing the buildings.
> It is not the first property we have demolished that has had debt on it, and no doubt it won't be the last.[181]

---

[175] 'Hutchesontown E Site is Finally Sold for £4 million', *The Glasgow Herald* (27 June 1985), p. 1.

[176] 'U-turn over £20m Gorbals Flat Plan', *The Glasgow Herald* (28 June 1985), p. 1.

[177] '... why did McLean, McFadden and the rest of the Labour executive not publicize the site's availability, seek tenders and ensure the city was getting the best possible financial deal?' Robertson, 'Labour Probe into Gorbals Land Deal', *The Glasgow Herald* (29 June 1985), p. 1.

[178] 'The District Council Invites ...', Advertisement placed by Glasgow District Council, *The Glasgow Herald* (17 July 1985), p. 14.

[179] 'Lafferty Leads Race for Gorbals Contract', *The Glasgow Herald* (5 September 1985), p. 4.

[180] This criticism came, rather surprisingly, from the New Glasgow Society, a prominent conservation group that had opposed the construction of the flats in the first place. They were concerned that flats designed to last 60 years were already 'candidated for demolition'. 'Group's Case for Saving Gorbals Flats', *The Glasgow Herald* (15 October 1985), p. 2.

[181] Ibid.

The Council's long struggle over Hutchesontown 'E' seemed to be drawing to an end when the contract for the redevelopment was awarded to a consortium headed by Frank Lafferty, a Glasgow developer.[182] The proposed scheme was for a mixed development including some 200 houses, a glass-covered shopping centre and various leisure facilities including a swimming pool and a ten-screen cinema. The deal included houses and building services estimated to be worth £6.4 million to the city.[183] Bailie James Mullen of the Council's Labour group made the announcement, adding that 'The whole problem of Hutchie E has been hanging over us for 10 years and I am confident we are now embarked on a programme which will revamp the area'.[184] Once again, this optimism proved to be premature; in April 1986 Strathclyde Regional Council 'called in' the Lafferty application on the grounds that it breached the guidelines for commercial developments laid down in the Region's structure plan.

Throughout this period of political wrangling and equivocation, local groups had continued to press the District Council over the need to demolish the flats, a call frequently echoed in the media. These calls grew ever louder as it became clear that the deserted blocks had become a target for vandalism and were being used as a playground by children and a shelter by the homeless. One Gorbals resident explained to the author that the blocks were thought to be haunted – in part, perhaps, an adult story to dissuade children from playing there, in part an invention of children themselves, inspired by those long, dark, deserted corridors, and in part, perhaps, a form of demonizing – a projection of the negative associations of the 'Dampies'. In any case, community anxiety and the pressure for demolition increased when, in 1987, it became known that asbestos had been used in the construction of the flats.

Although the Lafferty proposal remained blocked by Strathclyde Regional Council, Glasgow District Council, alarmed at the asbestos scare and the attention it was attracting, decided to press ahead with the demolition of the blocks regardless. The Council awarded a £1 million plus, 40-week contract to Burnthill Demolition Ltd, and *The Glasgow Herald* announced the 'End of the Line for E Blocks'.[185] Subsequently, 10.30am on 22 June 1987 marked what the paper called the 'Beginning of the End for Hutchie E', with locals jeering that demolition was 'eight years too late'.[186] The last of the 12 blocks was 'reduced to rubble' on 16 December 1987, leaving a 40-acre vacant site on the

---

182 It also included Barratts, to whom the Council had originally considered selling the flats.

183 Keating, *The City that Refused to Die*, p. 135.

184 'Long Wait Ends as Lafferty Lands Gorbals Contract', *The Glasgow Herald* (17 October 1985), p. 3.

185 'End of the Line for E Blocks', *The Glasgow Herald* (30 May 1987), p. 3.

186 'Beginning of the End for Hutchie E', *The Glasgow Herald* (23 June 1987), p. 3.

edge of the city centre.[187] It is hard not to see a painful and costly parody of the Corporation's massive slum clearance operations directed at eighteenth- and nineteenth-century tenement blocks in the demolition of these deck-access flats. This final gesture seemed to confirm that the new Gorbals had indeed become a new slum.

Less than a month after the last block was demolished, Strathclyde Regional Council planning committee unanimously refused permission to the Lafferty proposal for the site. In April 1988 the consortium, unable to balance the Region's requirement to provide more housing with the need to obtain a financial return from the shopping and leisure facilities, announced that it was pulling out of the deal, with the result that the site reverted to the District Council. Glasgow's town clerk, Steven Hamilton, could only find solace in the fact that at least the 'Dampies' had gone: 'We now have to start again from scratch. But at least this time we are starting with a clear site.'[188]

In fact, the site of Hutchesontown 'E' was to remain 'clear' until the 1990s. The Crown Street Regeneration Project was formed in 1990, 'a partnership between the Glasgow Development Agency, Glasgow City Council, Scottish Homes and the community of the Gorbals',[189] with the aim of creating a high-quality, mixed-use 'urban village' on the former site of the 'Dampies'. The Crown Street Project has become, according to its own public relations, 'a nationally acclaimed showcase for best practice in inner city regeneration'.[190]

Remembering community: the 'good people of the Gorbals'

Thanks to these events, piled upon other stories of corruption, incompetence, penny-pinching, physical degradation and social fragmentation which the press relayed to the city, the Gorbals came to be identified by activists, residents, former residents and the population of Glasgow as a whole as the city's great planning fiasco. Hutchesontown 'E' was the epitome of this failure and, in summing up the saga of the 'Dampies' as 'a tangled saga of *idées fixés*, expediency and community activism',[191] Keating succinctly encapsulates the complexity of vested interests and power relations woven around this particular public housing development.

In the course of the events in the Gorbals in the 1970s and 1980s, and particularly those concerning the Hutchesontown 'E' development, Glasgow

[187] 'Flats complex Reduced to Rubble', *The Glasgow Herald* (17 December 1987), p. 3.

[188] 'Hutchesontown Deal Collapses', *The Glasgow Herald* (27 April 1988), p. 1.

[189] 'Crown Street, Glasgow', http://www.princes-foundation.org/newpage6.htm.

[190] Ibid.

[191] Keating, *The City that Refused to Die*, p. 135.

District Council was gradually compelled to renounce its definition of the new Gorbals as a 'miracle' and accept a different definition – that of the Gorbals as the symbol of the failure of its post-war planning policy. The combined effect of tenants' activism, media coverage and the Council's own inefficiency and internal divisions ensured that the negative associations which had once formed an essential element of the Gorbals' slum past were shifted into its present. The Council's reaction was to distance itself from its own creation, seeking, as we have seen, to assign the blame to central government and 'planners'. By adopting this distance, the Council, as best it could, experienced the demolition of Hutchesontown 'E' and, subsequently, also that of Hutchesontown 'C', as the removal of a 'stigma', as an act of liberation from the problems that had 'dogged' it for so long.

For many of the residents of Gorbals, and also for many others who had had to leave the area and move to peripheral schemes, the expectation and promise invested in the new Gorbals made its failure particularly bitter. They not only felt resentment at the degradation of the physical environment of the new flats, but also at having been 'cheated' of the positive aspects of life in the old Gorbals. These aspects came to be encapsulated in the term 'community'. This 'loss' can be perceived in the statistics for the new Gorbals; in 1951 the area had a population of 68 000, but by 1988 this had dropped to only 10 946, over half of whom were living in high-rise blocks.[192] The landscape of the new Gorbals was one of bleak flats, grey concrete and barren open spaces. The report from the Scottish Council for Social Services estimated that in 1979 one in five of the local population was wholly or partially dependent on social security and welfare benefits for their main source of income.[193] In 1988, 29 per cent of men and 16 per cent of women were unemployed.[194] Moreover, drug abuse had become a serious problem and many of the residents of the area lived in daily fear of crime.

Something which might be called a 'community conscience' first began to appear in the Gorbals during the 1970s. Originating in social sciences and planning, it entered the popular discourse. In this sense, it is more accurate to say that the 'community' in the Gorbals was constructed rather than remembered, for the concept had not always existed. The material for this construction was to be found in the identification of the old Gorbals as a place of close social ties. Where people had once spoken of 'family', 'friends', 'neighbours' and 'local shops', they increasingly came to use the term

[192] City of Glasgow District Council, *Gorbals Local Plan. Draft Written Statement* (Glasgow: Glasgow District Council, 1989), p. 8.

[193] Bryant, *The Dampness Monster*, pp. 1–2.

[194] City of Glasgow District Council, *Gorbals Local Plan. Draft Written Statement*, p. 9.

'community'. These elements had always been present in the interpretation of the old Gorbals, but in the fervour of demolition and reconstruction they had been largely overlooked in favour of the 'slum' identification promoted by the Corporation and inhabitants alike. As early as 1974 the concept of 'community' was evoked as an argument against plans to construct a major section of motorway through the Govanhill area which adjoined Hutchesontown. In the words of one of the district councillors for the Hutchesontown–Govanhill area: 'Things are taking shape in Gorbals, so the next step to be taken is to make sure that the Govanhill *community* is kept together. I am strictly opposed to any Expressway cutting through *the heart of a community* and uprooting and interfering with the lives of young and old.'[195] In 1977 Mrs Jeannie O'Connor, secretary of the Gorbals–Laurieston Rehousing Association, criticized the new developments in the area because of the loss of 'community', lack of facilities and also, interestingly, because they were perceived to be dangerous – here, the myth of violence in the old Gorbals is reactivated in the new:

> I was born in Cavendish Street, only a few hundred yards from here. Then the area was a community, as this area was when I moved into the house 16 years ago. Then there were many butchers' and grocery shops and the things which go to make a community.
>
> Now people go to Shawlands to shop because new developments here have left no room for shops except general stores. I will not let my three younger children out on the street because of the rising rate of muggings and assaults.
>
> There is no place for them to play. My four older children are living away from home because there is nothing for them to do.[196]

In April 1978 the Hutchesontown Tenants' Association listed its 'community development exercises' in the previous year, including a school talent contest, a Gorbals Fair, proposals for an after-school care project, and various projects for the local community centre.[197] 'Community' was even used by the 'Stop the Sale' campaign as an argument for the speedy demolition of Hutchesontown 'E'. In 1981 the Council had stated that rehousing tenants from the development was a high priority, but that demolition or rehabilitation would not take place for 'several years'. The Campaign countered this by raising concerns over the impact of delays on the Gorbals 'community', arguing that in the interim government cutbacks would cause a further deterioration of living standards in the area and that 'A boarded-up and vandalised no-mans land between Hutchesontown and Laurieston will only lead to the gradual destruction of these

---

[195] 'Councillor's Column', *The View* (November 1974), p. 8. ML. My emphases.

[196] 'Angry Gorbals Families Call for Better Homes', *The Glasgow Herald* (3 August 1977), p. 4.

[197] 'Hutchesontown Tenants Association', *The View* (April 1979), p. 2. ML.

communities by a thousand cuts and closures'.[198] They also expressed concern about the 'knock-on effect' of the depopulation of the Gorbals, and the 'grave consequences for the local community, with local shops and a nursery closing, and a comprehensive school under threat of closure'.[199]

Moreover, in the context of the concerns about community facilities which began to emerge during the 1970s, the old public houses, once despised as a moral and economic drain on the Gorbals people, became the focus of a new wave of nostalgia. In a 1975 article from *The Glasgow Herald* appropriately entitled 'Reviving Old Spirit in New Gorbals', it was noted that while the Gorbals was now 'a concrete island' and that 'there are only about 15 of the 50 pubs of a few years ago', 'former residents now in Castlemilk and Pollok return for a "hauf and a hauf" at the weekends'.[200] More recently, the expression 'a pub at every corner' has been rehabilitated from a damning indictment of the old Gorbals (recall the local minister cited in Chapter Five asserting that, 'The days of a public house on every corner have gone forever'[201]), to a nostalgic celebration of the area. By the 1990s the Gorbals History Research Group could recall, '... in the old days ... at most corners was the public house – a pub at every corner was *the boast*'.[202]

The battle over Hutchesontown 'E' and the determination of the Anti-Dampness Campaign in its various tussles with the District Council only seemed to confirm the strength of the Gorbals' community spirit, while the flats themselves, which had started as an architectural symbol of a better future provided by the Council, came to be seen as a symbol of the destruction, or near-destruction, of that same community. In the Scottish Council of Social Services' analysis of the Gorbals Anti-Dampness Campaign, intended to serve as a form of handbook for local activists, the community was celebrated as an important element in the Campaign's success:

> The local response ... has never been a passive one. The Gorbals has a long tradition of community activism and self-organisation. This tradition provided a valuable basis for the Dampness Campaign, and, especially

---

198 'Demolition', *The View* (May 1981), p. 1. ML.

199 'Hutchesontown "E" – What Next?', *The View* (December–January 1981–82), p. 6. ML.

200 See 'Reviving Old Spirit in New Gorbals', *The Glasgow Herald* (23 January 1975), p. 7. A 'hauf and a hauf' refers to a measure of whisky followed by a half-pint of beer. The 'former residents' who return to Gorbals for this refreshment are, we may assume, mostly men. This hidden gender division serves to remind us that when we talk about the population of Gorbals, it was not homogeneous, but marked by many different interests and perspectives. Thanks to Doreen Massey for this point.

201 'Tenants to ask the Secretary of State to Meet a Deputation ...', *The Glasgow Herald* (13 June 1967), p. 20.

202 Gorbals History Research Group, *Third Time Lucky? The History and Hopes of the Gorbals* (Glasgow: ABC, nd, *c.* 1995), p. 16. My emphasis.

> during the early days, the leaders of the campaign received considerable help from the existing network of community resources.[203]

According to the report, 'It was the determination and militancy of the tenants – with only limited support from representatives of the formal political system in Gorbals which transformed a local protest into a major expose of the new slums'.[204] Similarly, ten years after the opening of the Hutchesontown 'E' flats, *The View*, the Gorbals community paper, described the Gorbals Anti-Dampness Campaign as, 'one of the strongest and most successful tenants organizations in Scotland'.[205] The Campaign represented a long, hard fight in which the people of the Gorbals, always the underdogs, always 'treated like dirt', ultimately triumphed through their reserves of strength and their ability to 'give as good as they get', sustained by that magical commodity, community spirit. Not even the bulldozer could take that away from them.

In the course of the 1970s, 'community' became one of the planning profession's watchwords. At the same time, it also came to fill the space of experience of the Gorbals' population and define its horizon of expectation. The recreation of community has thus constituted one of the defining themes of the 'new' new Gorbals. As early as 1984, the Scottish Special Housing Association had completed a small, 'self-contained community village' in the Laurieston area of the Gorbals, with a range of different sized housing and flats, as well as sheltered housing and various shops, at a cost of £1.2 million. This mix was intended to create a 'ready-made community' and was heralded as the 'Return of Village Life to Gorbals'.[206] Glasgow District Council had the task of assigning tenants to this development, and their policy was to give priority to former resident of the Gorbals who had been displaced by the post-war planning operations. There was also a Gorbals Community Development Project set up in 1988 with the aim of enabling Gorbals residents to participate in the redevelopment of their neighbourhood. Two years later the Crown Street Regeneration Project[207] was established and launched a scheme to provide 250 houses for affordable rent, 750 for private sale, and 200 units for student accommodation. The plans also included a supermarket, 20 shop units and a refurbished 'historic mill' (the Corporation's 'old-fashioned factory sticking up there'[208] in yet another guise) intended to provide employment space for

---

[203] Bryant, *The Dampness Monster*, p. 2.

[204] Ibid., pp. 68–69.

[205] 'Ten Years After', *The View* (August 1982), p. 1. ML.

[206] 'The Return of Village Life to Gorbals', *The Glasgow Herald* (16 August 1984), p. 9. ML.

[207] See Crown Street Regeneration Project, *Masterplan Report*, nd, *c*. 1991. GI.

[208] ' "That Old-Fashioned Factory" in the Gorbals', *The Glasgow Herald* (10 October 1956), p. 8.

340 local jobs. In 1999 the Regeneration Project defined itself as 'committed to involving local people in *resurrecting* a lively and mixed neighbourhood from the clear site of the demolished flats'.[209] The text adds that 'The project has a strong community input, and local residents have played a major role in influencing the design of the scheme.' A feature on the Crown Street Project in *The Herald* also confirmed the importance of the community, asserting that 'Undoubtedly, the essential ingredient in this success story has been the close involvement of the local community'.[210] The Project was understood as offering another chance to the Gorbals, prompting comments about resurrection and rebirth, and in 1994 *The Herald* announced 'Gorbals Born Again, Again!', before going on to explain that the project was intended to seek 'The spirit of the old community' but, this time, given the predominance of flats for owner-occupation, a community with a 'respectable, middle class face'.[211]

As the old Gorbals was resurrected, not as a slum, but as a community, people assured each other that it had never been that bad. In an interview with the author in January 1995, a resident of Cumberland Street Heights (the SSHA flats in the Hutchesontown area) who had been living there for 30 years, recalled that people had not wanted to leave the Gorbals to go to Castlemilk, and that the elderly in particular were 'heartbroken' over the demolition of the tenements. The main problem in Castlemilk was that there was no 'social side of life', 'no dancing, no picture halls'. The men, he explained, were used to being able to go out to work and to return home for 'dinner' at midday, something which became almost impossible in this peripheral estate, far from most people's place of work.[212] And in an article in a national newspaper, *The Guardian*, a former resident of the Gorbals who was 'exiled' to Castlemilk in 1956 recalls:

> Although we had a room and a kitchen, and a toilet, and cold running water [in their new flat in Castlemilk], I always missed the Gorbals. The buildings were irrelevant; the people were the Gorbals. If you were in need, if someone had a little bit extra, they'd give it to you without having to ask. I never found that anywhere else.
>
> In the old tenements, even if you didn't see them in the entrance or on the landings, you felt that people lived there, that there was life going on.

[209] 'Crown Street, Glasgow', http://www.princes-foundation.org/newpage6.htm. My emphasis.

[210] E. Buie, 'The Great Grooming of the Gorbals', *The Herald* (3 March 1998), p. 10.

[211] 'Gorbals Born Again, Again!', *The Herald*, Scotland's Property insert (5 February 1994), p. 1.

[212] On the other hand, and here he touched upon the ambivalence of feeling surrounding the old and new Gorbals, he recalled that when he was rehoused in the Cumberland Street Heights, he was in 'seventh heaven'. At first, he remembered, the community life of the tenements was transferred to the new flats, and in particular, the stairs were kept 'spotless'.

> It was never like that in the highrises. Gorbals people are outgoing, spontaneous people. You can spot them a mile off, without asking. It's just a feeling, an affinity.[213]

Not only do these comments confirm Gorbals people as a particular type that could be spotted 'a mile off', they also suggest that in the old Gorbals the condition of the buildings was 'irrelevant' in comparison to the social structure.

Gradually, the old Gorbals has become something to be celebrated, remembered and written about. It is no surprise to learn that from the late 1980s the Gorbals has inspired a wave of literary nostalgia, with titles such as *Growing Up in the Gorbals* (1986), *Shadows on a Gorbals Wall* (1986), *The Gorbals Heritage Trails* (1988 – published by Glasgow District Council itself), *Gorbals Voices, Siren Songs* (1990), *The Magic of the Gorbals* (1990), *Gorbals Children* (1990) and *Memories of the Gorbals* (1991).[214] The community also became a defining theme in the work of the Gorbals History Research Group (and note how the history of the Gorbals has now become something to be 'researched' rather than escaped). Introducing their booklet entitled *Third Time Lucky? The History and Hopes of the Gorbals*, the group returns to the old theme of the 'type' of people who inhabit the Gorbals, but now the identification is unequivocally positive:

> The Gorbals' greatest asset in the past and her greatest strength today is her people. Sir Walter Scott once referred to the 'good people of the Gorbals' and so they have remained. This account is largely written by local people out of a sense of pride as well as of anger. The Gorbals has a long and proud history and now it must have a great future[215]

From this perspective, the identification of these 'good people' and the space of experience which this creates also defines a horizon of expectation whereby a 'long and proud history' demands and justifies 'a great future'. The Gorbals History Research Group's assessment of the area's past is marked by the theme of tragedy – the community undone, and the people cheated by those who promised them salvation:

---

[213] C. Crewe, 'Rebirth of the Gorbals Spirit', *The Guardian* (20 December 1994), p. 13. Although the interviewee speaks of life in the 'highrises', having moved from Old Gorbals to Castlemilk it is unlikely that the he had ever lived in the multi-storey flats.

[214] R. Glasser, *Growing Up in the Gorbals* (London: Chatto & Windus, 1986); E. McAllister, *Shadows on a Gorbals Wall* (Glasgow: Gorbals Fair Society, 1986); City of Glasgow District Council, *The Gorbals Heritage Trails* (Glasgow: City of Glasgow District Council, 1988); R. Glasser, *Gorbals Voices, Siren Songs* (London: Chatto & Windus, 1990); E. Perrett, *The Magic of the Gorbals* (Glasgow: Clydeside Press, 1990); J. McKenzie, *Gorbals Children: A Study in Photographs* (Glasgow: Richard Drew Publishing, 1990); J. Caplan, *Memories of the Gorbals* (Edinburgh: Pentland Press, 1991).

[215] Gorbals History Research Group, *Third Time Lucky?*, p. 7.

> Lots of people who used to stay in the Gorbals, as well as many who reside there, have fond memories of the old place. It was a place throbbing with vitality where neighbours chatted from their windows and gossiped at street corners. Large close-knit families and good neighbours resulted in a rich community spirit. Homes were internally spick and span 'little palaces' even if the outside environment had become down at heel.[216]

The first blow to the area was private sector neglect and exploitation:

> Many of those who have a warm nostalgia for the area do not like to be reminded of the fact that the Gorbals was allowed to fall into a disgraceful state. Unscrupulous landlords failed to carry out repairs and greedily crowded more and more people into subdivided property. By the inter-war years it had deteriorated into slum conditions with some of the worst housing in the city.[217]

From the perspective of the Gorbals History Research Group, post-war planning operations were not an attempt to rectify these conditions, they were simply a *continuation* of this process of decline:

> When the area had so deteriorated the final stroke which well-nigh killed-off its social fabric as well as its crumbling built environment was the intensive blanket treatment of Comprehensive Redevelopment in the 1960s and 1970s. Some of the most renowned architects – Basil Spence and Robert Matthew – were employed to create this new utopia but the planners' schemes went awry. Utopia was stillborn – much of the Gorbals of the dreams has now been laid waste once more.[218]

The introduction to the brochure on the Crown Street Regeneration Project offers a very similar appraisal of the Gorbals' history, starting in the post-war period when 'thousands of tenement buildings were cleared and replaced by a range of new and experimental housing, much of it high rise tower blocks'.[219] Creating a clear juxtaposition with the philosophy of their own 'urban village' concept, and taking a sideways swipe at Corbusian-derived architecture, the brochure emotively sums up the logic behind post-war urban policy as 'a ruthless post war dream to sweep away almost everything associated with the past and to herald in a brave new world built around the car and a "green" city of high rise towers'.[220] In the Gorbals, the summary states, the most 'notorious' product of this approach was the Hutchesontown 'E' development. Indeed, the demolition of the 'E' blocks was singled out as the key moment when the future of the Gorbals finally changed for the better: 'The turning point for the future of

[216] Ibid., p. 15.
[217] Ibid., p. 15.
[218] Ibid., p. 16.
[219] Crown Street Regeneration Project, *Crown Street Regeneration Project: Past, Present and Future*. GI.
[220] Ibid.

the Gorbals came with the demolition of the notorious Hutchesontown "E" blocks which left a 40 acre gap in the heart of the Gorbals'.[221] The same optimism is present in the appraisal of the Gorbals History Research Group, which considers that the final chapter of this story has yet to be written, for against all odds, the Gorbals did not disappear: 'In the 1940s there was a ballet entitled "The Miracle of the Gorbals" – the real miracle was that the Gorbals survived at all. Certainly it has been battered and bruised but like a phoenix it has risen from the ashes once before and will assuredly do so again.'[222] The modernist 'miracle' of the Gorbals was discredited, but a different 'miracle' had taken place: the miracle of survival. And this miracle would, in turn, guarantee another: the area's phoenix-like resurrection (Figure 6.3).

The 'tragic' nature of the events in Gorbals became widely recognized. As the last tenants moved out of the 'E' block, *The View* explained that it had 'followed the campaign throughout its many years and is pleased to report the end of a *tragic* saga'.[223] For the New Glasgow Society, an important conservation group in the city, 'The destruction of the Gorbals in the earliest comprehensive development plans was a *tragedy* in terms of the communities and the buildings lost'.[224] For the Crown Street Regeneration Project, it was 'the ultimate *tragedy* of the Gorbals that much of the redevelopment only added the new perspective of the concrete jungle to the traditional image of the slum'.[225] The use of the word 'tragedy' is interesting in this context; as Hayden White has pointed out, an event that, at first glance, 'is apprehended as simply "disastrous"' can become, through the process of mythification, translated from a 'disaster' into a 'catastrophe' – that is, 'a scene of specifically "moral" significance'.[226] White argues that:

> This translation endowed the scene in which the event had occurred with a plot-structure by reference to which the moral importance of events could be identified, thereby permitting their classification in terms of good and evil, responsibility and negligence, nobility and baseness, guilt and innocence; in a word, in terms of their significance as a drama, specifically 'tragic' in kind.[227]

---

[221] Ibid.

[222] Gorbals History Research Group, *Third Time Lucky?*, p. 42.

[223] 'Ten Years After', *The View* (August 1982), p. 1. ML. My emphasis.

[224] 'Group's Case for Saving Gorbals Flats', *The Glasgow Herald* (15 October 1985), p. 2. My emphasis.

[225] Crown Street Regeneration Project, *Crown Street Regeneration Project: Past, Present and Future*. GI. My emphasis.

[226] H. White, 'Catastrophe, Communal Memory and Mythic Discourse: The Uses of Myth in the Reconstruction of Society', in B. Stråth (ed.), *Myth and Memory in the Construction of Community* (Brussels: PIE-Peter Lang, 2000) p. 57.

[227] Ibid.

6.3 Jacket illustration from *Third Time Lucky? The History and Hopes of the Gorbals* by local artist Samuel Thomson
Reproduced from Gorbals History Research Group, *Third Time Lucky? The History and Hopes of the Gorbals* (Glasgow: ABC, nd, *c.* 1995).

This version of the Gorbals' history is indeed imbued with 'negligence' and 'guilt', and it leaves little doubt as to who bears the moral responsibility for this tragedy: 'the authorities – politicians and planners'.[228]

The life in the old tenements was no longer a source of shame, but rather one of pride and, increasingly, poor housing came to be associated with the projects of politicians and planners in the 1950s, 1960s and 1970s rather than with private sector slum landlords, who were consigned to a more distant past in these reminiscences and histories. In all this, not only tenement life but also the tenements themselves came to be celebrated. This architectural form, which remained only as a memory in the Gorbals, became 'mentally' rehabilitated, just as the examples which had survived in other parts of the city eventually

[228] Gorbals History Research Group, *Third Time Lucky?*, p. 42.

underwent physical rehabilitation. Indeed, the Gorbals History Research Group assigns the tenement a deterministic role in the formation of community: 'The tenements ... provided homes for generations of Gorbals families. They created a community which worked and lived well together, sharing good times as well as bad and sad times.'[229] The Group adds that, when the tenements were demolished, 'A community, for all its faults and failings as well as its virtues, was simply eradicated and nothing worthwhile was put in its place'.[230] The Crown Street Redevelopment Project is described by the Group as drawing 'on the traditional tenement building forms of Glasgow',[231] while the managing director of one of the development companies involved, describing the new house styles in the project, claimed that they were 'designed to reflect the famed traditional quality and style of Glasgow architecture'[232] – a rehabilitation of the tenement form if ever there was.

The tenements thus served as 'empty monuments' in the Gorbals. They formed a symbolic structure, now existing only in the collective memory, which could be filled with meaning according to the context: from a monument to the slums and private sector exploitation, to a monument of community strength in the face of public sector inefficiency. The celebration of the tenement as an inherent element of community life brings to mind Halbwach's contention that social practices outlive the physical structures around which these practices originally developed.

Hutchesontown 'E' also became a monument: one resident of Gorbals, in her recollections written before the flats were demolished, stated, 'Today the block stands derelict and neglected – a sad monument to the hopes and dreams of the Gorbals people',[233] while McPhee chose to call his 1988 article 'Hutchie E – A Monument to Corruption, Stupidity and Bad Planning'.[234] From this perspective, the demolition of Hutchesontown 'E' represented a form of urban exorcism, casting out the ghost of the new Gorbals.

With the rediscovery of 'community' and the rehabilitation of the memory of the tenements, the other aspects of the old Gorbals did not disappear, but rather, just like the positive social dimensions some 30 years before, they have been overlooked, played down or redirected. The unemployment, violence and alcohol abuse of the old Gorbals is now a key element in the identity of those parts of the new Gorbals that still remain standing today, with the difference that

---

229 Ibid.

230 Ibid.

231 'Crown Street, Glasgow', http://www.princes-foundation.org/newpage6.htm. My emphasis.

232 S. McIntosh, 'Regeneration Gorbals-style', *The Herald*, Scotland's Homes section (30 November 1994), p. 1.

233 McAllister, *Shadows on a Gorbals Wall*, p. 34.

234 McPhee, 'Hutchie E – A Monument to Corruption, Stupidity and Bad Planning', p. 47.

6.4 A view of the Gorbals from the north
The high flats in the middle ground are Matthew's 'B' development, while the flats in the background are part of the SSHA development. By the time this photograph was taken (January 1998), Hutchesontown 'C' and 'E' had been demolished.

alcohol has been supplemented by drugs. This identity is recognized both by local residents and more widely in the city. In 1991 the Centre for Housing Research at Glasgow University carried out the *Gorbals Community Survey* based on a structured questionnaire given to a random sample of 1200 Gorbals residents (representing some 7 or 8 per cent of the Gorbals population at the time). When asked about the problems of the area, 51 per cent of respondents mentioned drugs, followed by a lack of shops (31 per cent), crime and the fear of crime (27 per cent), and a lack of facilities and a poor environment (both 18 per cent).[235] The same associations are not, however, made with the Crown Street Redevelopment Project: here, if reference is made to the area's violent past in the press or public discourse, it is almost invariably to confirm that things have changed out of all recognition. Fairly representative of this trend are the comments of the chairman of the Ballater Gardens Tenants' Association reported in *The Herald*:

> We were not keen to come, to be honest. I had always heard the reputation of the Gorbals – there are more books written about it than anywhere else ... .
> I am a train driver and I walk to work at 2am and 3am. I have a son of 15 who has never been in any bother ... . We were really worried about moving into the Gorbals, but we have seen nothing.[236]

As if to confirm that the Gorbals' bad ways are a thing of the past, *The Herald* adds that when local residents heard that a bookmaker wanted to buy a unit in the Crown Street Project and stay open until 10pm, they organized a petition against it. The message is clear – this would never have happened in *No Mean City*.

[235] A.A. McArthur and D. Donnison, *Gorbals Community Survey* (Glasgow: Centre for Housing Research, 1992), p. 13. See also A. McArthur and D. Donnison, *Gorbals Community Survey – Final Report to the Glasgow Development Agency and the Crown Street Regeneration Project, Executive Summary* (January 1992). GI.

[236] Cited in Buie, 'The Great Grooming of the Gorbals', p. 10.

CHAPTER SEVEN

Conclusions

This final chapter considers the case studies of Alma-Gare and the Gorbals in a comparative context, investigating both the significance of certain similarities between the two examples as well as some of the key differences. It then assesses the global–local relations that emerge from these two cases before, finally, offering some considerations on the idea of the city as a metaphor for history.

Comparative conclusions

The reasons for employing a comparative approach for this research have been discussed in the introduction to this book. Here may it suffice to reiterate that, while both the Alma-Gare and Gorbals cases studies can stand alone as examples of public protest against urban planning projects in their respective national contexts, and one or other would permit an investigation of the construction of local, place-based identities, the opportunity for comparison opens up other possibilities. Comparison is not simply about pointing out differences and similarities between the two examples selected. It is about organizing and interpreting these differences and similarities in a way that takes us beyond the specificity of one or other of the cases. It is about a holistic dialogue in which the two case studies are enriched in a mutual 'question and answer' process.

The significance of comparison lies in what we choose to classify as similar and what we choose to identify as different and, crucially, what interpretation we subsequently apply to these observations. Were the identification of difference an end in itself, we would find that, like a fractal landscape, an infinity of difference emerges. Indeed, we would risk becoming ensnared in a tautological trap whereby Alma-Gare and the Gorbals are different because ... they are Alma-Gare and the Gorbals.

The analytical framework chosen for this research has presented the two case studies in terms of locally organized groups challenging what I have called an institutionalized construction of place, where 'institutionalized' refers to a self-justifying identification perpetuated by powerful interests. This construction was founded on the idea of 'slum', with all its social and moral implications, and it was employed by local government and planning professionals to justify their demolition and reconstruction projects. As Douglas points out, 'an answer is only seen to be a right one if it sustains the institutional thinking that is already in the minds of the individuals as they try to decide',[1] and in the cases we have examined, the 'right answer' to the question raised by the presence of 'slums' was, unequivocally, demolition.

In this dominant discourse, informed as it was by a specific reading of history, emphasis was placed on the poor condition of the physical structure of these areas. The findings of 'objective' surveys were compounded by media stories as well as by the tangible evidence of decay and decline. Yet, when the locally-based groups responded to council initiatives, they attributed alternative interpretations to these same 'slums' – interpretations based on ideas of collective strength and solidarity. In neither of the cases examined did the actors create identities entirely *ex nihilo*. Elements of all the constructions – 'slum', '*courée*', 'miracle', '*quartier*' and so on – were already present in the identities of the two areas, but they were variously suppressed, reactivated and combined in new ways, and according to the perspective of different actors.

For Alma-Gare and Gorbals alike, I have identified a moment of crisis, a point that conveniently divides the events into a 'before' and an 'after'. The nature of the crisis in both cases was the collapse of consensus over the meaning assigned to the two places. Neither of these crises arrived as a bolt from the blue, but rather both were cumulative in nature, fed by a growing realization on the part of the local populations that the golden future they were being offered by local government was perhaps not so golden after all. In the case of Alma-Gare, the crisis reached a head with the announcement that the area was finally to be demolished, but the foundation was the years of delays that enabled the population of Alma-Gare to witness the development of Longues Haies, and later Magasins Généraux and Barbe d'Or. What they saw led them to reject a future based on modernist public housing developments and the rationalization of space according to functional criteria. In the Gorbals, the 'future' arrived faster and, given that the Gorbals was one of the earliest renewal schemes in the UK, the population had little experience concerning this form of planning. Their principal concern was to be delivered from atrocious living conditions and to be provided with healthier, more spacious housing. In this case, the consensus was constructed around the 'miracle' of the new Gorbals, and the crisis, when it came, was provoked by the flaws that had begun to appear in this miracle. The elation of tenants over their new, spacious, fully-plumbed flats began to wane in the face of maintenance problems, high costs and, critically for the case of Hutchesontown 'E', the presence of conditions of extreme

[1] M. Douglas, *How Institutions Think* (Syracuse: Syracuse University Press, 1986), p. 92.

dampness in the new flats. It was in the events surrounding these crises that the different meanings of Alma-Gare and Gorbals were constructed, confronted and negotiated.

As the consensus evaporated, locally-based organizations were provoked to construct a counter-place, drawing upon ideas of solidarity, industrial militancy, mutual support, neighbourliness and so on. Without entirely rejecting the narratives that spoke of decline and degradation, they began to promote certain positive aspects of their neighbourhoods, positing a human identity in the face of the bureaucratic one, and prioritizing a collective response over an individual one. On this basis, the *Atelier Populaire d'Urbanisme* and the Gorbals Anti-Dampness Campaign set out to challenge the logic of their respective planning systems. Of course, nobody had appointed these organizations to this task, in the sense that both lacked an official democratic mandate (as the *Municipalité de Roubaix* and Glasgow District Council took pains to point out). This meant that they relied heavily on being able to demonstrate that their initiatives were well supported by the local population. We may say, therefore, that both the APU and the Anti-Dampness Campaign were actively engaged in the construction of community, by which I mean that they sought to develop a shared identity amongst groups of people whose common feature was that they lived in the same area of a particular town. It was from this identity that the APU and Anti-Dampness Campaign claimed to draw their legitimacy.

But, despite the unity implied by the label of 'community' or '*quartier*', it is important to recall that the populations of both Gorbals and Alma-Gare were extremely heterogeneous and demonstrated subdivisions according to gender, socioeconomic status, employment, age, cultural and ethnic background and so on. Moreover, despite the rhetoric of the Alma-Gare activists, neither of the populations were homogeneous working-class communities and, for this reason, there was little scope for either movement to tap into a national class discourse.[2] Nonetheless, just as the 'official' definition of these areas imposed a 'sameness' on their residents, labelling them as tenement- or *courée*-dwellers, so too the counter-projects represented this same populations as members of a unified community, irrespective of what other divisions marked them. In Douglas's terms, this is how institutional thinking shapes perceptions to achieve its mutual corroboration, assigning a sameness to the members of the institution: 'the labels stabilize the flux of social life and even create to some extent the realities to which they apply.'[3]

For a collective identity, however, the issue of 'who we are' is also a question of 'where we come from' and 'where we want to go'. In other words, for the

[2] Perhaps it is telling that the housing model which the APU in Alma-Gare finally selected as being most appropriate for the *quartier* was derived from a middle-class residential suburb of Brussels and not from a bastion of the working-class.

[3] Douglas, *How Institutions Think*, p. 100.

success of these campaigns, a collective undertaking in the present was not enough, and it was essential that the respective communities also shared a collective memory *and* conceived of a collective future. These two cases help to illustrate that the issue of identity is not simply a key concept in national histories (especially in the phase of nation-building and, more recently, after 1989 and the fall of the Berlin Wall) but also has applications in local histories, especially in moments of crisis when something of value was perceived to be under threat.[4]

Given the emphasis on collective initiatives, it is ironic that, in both cases, the momentum necessary to achieve results in the long-term struggle was maintained by a small core of campaigners supported by a relatively restricted group made up of the more active members of the population. Due to a combination of the issues at stake (domestic), the local employment structure (male-oriented), and the informal communication networks often employed by these organizations (word of mouth), the core of support in both cases was largely made up of women. In Alma-Gare, this core was less visible, almost always crediting statements and publications to the whole *quartier*, while in the Gorbals the names of committee members were often mentioned in the *Gorbals View* and the city's press. In both cases, of course, numbers swelled for major events, and marches and important meetings were well attended. It would also appear that the APU and Anti-Dampness Campaign alike could look back and locate a *moment fort* in their own historical narrative, be it the action to rehouse *Memère* in Alma-Gare, or the Citizens' Theatre meeting in the Gorbals.

I have spoken of the construction of community in a general sense, but the Anti-Dampness Campaign was also engaged in the construction of 'community' in the more restricted, sociological meaning of the term. 'Community' had become a watchword in the planning profession in Great Britain, and the Anti-Dampness Campaign used the term to describe what had existed in the Gorbals before the tenements were emptied of their inhabitants. The activists in Alma-Gare employed the term *quartier* in a similar way, charging it with meaning and ensuring that it could no longer be used as a 'neutral' term with respect to Alma-Gare. Whether a former tight-knit community which had been swept away in an insensitive planning operation, or a *quartier* which risked meeting the same fate, the historical space of experience was one of an area of the city defined by its social characteristics rather than by its housing conditions. In turn, this space of experience stretched towards a horizon of expectation – an expectation that 'wrongs' would be 'righted' and that the 'human' would triumph over the 'technocratic'.

---

[4] For a discussion of the reasons for the rise of 'identity' as a category of intellectual thought, see B. Stråth, 'Introduction. Myth, Memory and History in the Construction of Community', in B. Stråth (ed.) *Myth and Memory in the Construction of Community* (Brussels: PIE-Peter Lang, 2000), esp. pp. 22–24.

Both organizations even went as far as to 'rehabilitate' the conception of the supposedly flawed and, at one time, despised urban fabric. By this, I mean that the old environment – the *courées* and the tenements – was assimilated in the collective memory as a factor contributing to the development of the exceptional solidarity and tight social bonds the organizations claimed characterized the two areas. This is not to say that the memory founded on the suffering provoked by poor housing conditions was consigned to oblivion, but rather that it was moderated by the idea that this very same environment also played a positive, even deterministic, role in promoting social networks, cooperation, creativity and *entraide étroite* – close mutual support.

Thus it was that the bricks and mortar of the *courées*, the sandstone of the tenements and the precast concrete of Hutchesontown 'E' became invested with different, often contradictory meanings at different historical moments and by different groups. At other moments, as we have seen, there was a widely held consensus over the 'rightness' of one particular meaning. From this perspective, the built environment is not simply a physical manifestation of socioeconomic activities; it is a culturally laden landscape in which buildings are recipients of meaning, sometimes complementary, often contradictory. They are not merely the containers of social life; they help to shape this life. These observations take us back to the assertion at the start of this research, that collective memory draws upon spatial images – the images of tight-knit communities in the *courées* or tenements, for example – and that, simultaneously, social groups define their spatial setting and insert their memories there. The tenements and *courées* were clearly not constructed as monuments, but this is effectively what they became. They assumed the role of 'empty monuments' which were filled with meaning according to the historical context, and the collective memory of the community was adjusted accordingly. Nor do the meanings contained in these buildings vanish with the removal of the physical structure – the *courées* of Alma-Gare, the tenements of the Gorbals and the deck-access development called Hutchesontown 'E' continue to occupy significant places in the collective memory of the citizens of their respective towns. Hutchesontown 'E', originally emblematic of a new start, became, and continues to be, a symbol of political incompetence and the failure of public housing, and the calls to demolish these flats reflected not only a wish to see council land put to positive use, but also a need to exorcize a deeply disturbing memory. In contrast, the tenements, and those in Gorbals in particular, now represent the positive values of all that was lost in the massive post-war slum clearance programmes.

We might add that, as the meaning of the physical structure of the Gorbals and Alma-Gare changed, so too the meaning of the mechanism that brought about these changes was reassessed: the 'bulldozer', as a generic term, was transformed from the herald of a new future to the destroyer of the community.

As for the local political administrations of Roubaix and Glasgow, the initiatives of the APU and the Anti-Dampness Campaign proved to be rather problematic. From the post-war period onwards, both towns demonstrated relatively unchanging political landscapes – Roubaix with its Socialist–centrist alliance, and Glasgow with its successive Labour Party administrations. In both cases, the municipal council was engaged in promoting housing initiatives in the interests of the 'working class', from which it drew much of its support. In part, the motivation of the *Municipalité de Roubaix* and Glasgow Corporation for pursuing renewal was a philanthropic concern for the inhabitants of the poorest areas of the city. After all, the concept of the slum was deeply rooted in municipal mentality and, even if the phenomenon was identified by 'objective', scientific techniques, its meaning was compounded by a moral dimension. This dimension, derived from nineteenth-century philanthropic discourses and interpreted through the welfare state model, allowed the councils to see themselves as having a central role in a crusade against poor housing conditions. But, in addition to this preoccupation, these administrations were responding to a modernizing desire founded on rationality, functionalism and post-war optimism to create a more efficient urban fabric that would meet contemporary economic requirements. They had not reckoned, however, on the possibility of this housing being rejected by the very people for whom it had been built. In both cases, the socialist administrations found themselves in a situation whereby the most vehement opponents of their modernizing project came from elements of the social groups who traditionally provided them with their most solid support. In opposing the APU and the Anti-Dampness Campaign, the *Municipalité de Roubaix* and Glasgow Corporation/Glasgow District Council were thus involved in a dangerous game, risking the alienation of a part of their own voting base.

The difficulty experienced by the respective municipal councils in communicating with the APU and Anti-Dampness Campaign (a difficulty frankly recognized by the *Municipalité de Roubaix*) reinforces the idea that, in both the case studies, these different camps were speaking about different places, based on different interpretations of the past, present and future. In this confrontation, the councils employed an evolving array of tactics – initially disregarding the assertions of the local organizations, and then challenging the legitimacy of their claim to speak for an entire population. They also offered minor concessions as a form of appeasement. We have seen how, for example, in Alma-Gare it was claimed that the plans for the Barbe d'Or development in fact took into account the views of the local population, while in the Gorbals, the Corporation attempted to pour oil on troubled waters by sending experts to view the damp flats and then by setting up the mobile dampness exhibition.

The political stake represented by these issues for the city administrations is clear from the increased activity and the fine promises pronounced, in Roubaix and Glasgow alike, at the time of local elections and then overlooked soon after, as economic realities made these promises unfeasible. In short, the struggle between the municipal administrations and the locally-based groups was also a struggle over the location of power in urban affairs, and neither the *Municipalité de Roubaix* nor Glasgow District Council was willing to cede its authority to an unofficial group.

With respect to the links between these local events and the national context, the city councils of Roubaix and Glasgow (both of which occupied provincial positions with respect to the national cores of economic and political power), were much more likely than the local activists to attempt to locate their position with reference to a national, political centre. In Roubaix, the Socialist–centrist council repeatedly put the blame on Gaullist central government for the early delays in the Alma-Gare operation, while Glasgow District Council blamed central government for having encouraged the use of industrial construction techniques. Moreover, as a result of Glasgow District Council dragging its feet over the implementation of Margaret Thatcher's Conservative government's programme in the 1980s to sell off council housing, central government imposed spending restrictions upon the Council. These prevented it undertaking the massive repairs required by the city's public housing stock. In contrast, the tenants' groups in both Alma-Gare and Gorbals rarely referred to national government. When, in 1980, *The Gorbals View* ran the headline, 'Free Sponge With Every Council House! 1 out of every 5 council houses suffer from dampness = is this why Maggie Thatcher calls council tenants spongers?', this was a rare example of tenant discontent finding expression with respect to Westminster.[5] Moreover, it can justifiably be pointed out that these few examples have much more to do with political partisanship than with resentment in the periphery being directed at the national centre. Perhaps we should not be surprised by these findings. By necessity, both movements fed upon their local history and experience, drawing their dynamism from the 'inside', for how else could they justify their claim to community strength?

Up to this point, I have concentrated on rather specific observations concerning the two case studies, but it is important to be able to locate these in a broader historical framework. Indeed, I would suggest that the challenges presented by the events in Alma-Gare and the Gorbals are indicative of a changing paradigm, not only in the story they tell of the decline of modernist planning, but also in the roles the protesters adopted.

The rationality and functionality of modernist planning and architecture reflected the progressive ideals of the modern project. Modernity was founded in Enlightenment thought that emphasized the totality of the individual and promoted an optimistic vision of human capacity. Yet the influence of rational thought led, paradoxically, to the systematic fragmentation of human life –

[5] 'Free Sponge with Every Council House', *The View* (April 1980), p. 1. ML.

separating the home from the workplace, the public sphere from the private, and so on. This functional division according to rational criteria found its greatest economic expression in the Fordist production line, which, with its carefully divided functions, became both the epitome of, and the metaphor for, high modernity.

The production of housing followed the same logic. In the later part of the nineteenth century, both French and British governments began to play a role in influencing the production of private housing. By the inter-war period these governments had become directly involved in housing provision. At the same time, a distinct profession of planners was emerging, and the project of directing urban development became increasingly specialized. After the Second World War, modernism as an architectural movement was embraced by central governments intent upon organizing their states for efficient economic production. The functional division of space, both local and national, became the defining paradigm, and population distribution, commercial facilities, transport systems and industrial activity were separated. A massive housing drive founded on industrial construction techniques was initiated and, through the provision of different housing types, governments were able to sift and sort inner-city populations, directing urban growth where they would (one of the most celebrated examples is, of course, the New Town programme in Great Britain). However, the logic of rationality and functionalism in the modernist model of housing provision contained the seeds of its own destruction, since it was this logic that pushed governments and construction companies to build ever more quickly and ever more cheaply, until the system folded in on itself.[6]

The crisis of modernist thinking in the city was played out in the Gorbals and Alma-Gare, where a group of residents declared their resistance to the homogenizing process of classification and subdivision and challenged the idea that populations could be categorized unambiguously as one thing or another. They argued that they did not have to be a passive entity awaiting the arrival of various specialists who would decide their fate. They claimed the right to be *both* the decision-makers *and* the objects of these decisions. This initiative demanded a *simultaneity* of roles, and the APU argued that a population had the possibility of being, at one and the same time, planners, architects, managers and residents. The Anti-Dampness Campaign also represented a population seeking to assume multiple roles, both challenging the expertise of the professionals and seeking to become experts themselves. It was this multiplicity of roles that was so alien to modernist thought about the city and that heralded a new conception of urban development. Similarly, *courées* may have been slums, but they were also, simultaneously, catalysts for sociability

[6] For a discussion of the internal contradictions of modernity see, for example, S. Toulmin, *Cosmopolis: The Hidden Agenda of Modernity* (New York: Free Press, 1990).

and symbols of defiance. Equally, the tenements assumed multiple, sometimes overlapping, sometimes contradictory meanings, and could no longer be conveniently fitted into a single, rational category.

In this way, the two case studies can be regarded as representative of a fundamental shift in the way we conceive of ourselves and our world. They illustrate the waning of the modern project as manifest in modernist urban theory, and the waxing of a new conception of the city located in a new project, but emerging from the contradictions of the old. This project may be regarded as a new phase of modernity, or it may be given the label of 'postmodernity'.

It is easy to gain the impression from the discussion thus far that one can talk about Alma-Gare and the Gorbals as if they were interchangeable. From another perspective, however, the two case studies demonstrate important and informative differences.

First and foremost, there are the inevitable differences that arise as a result of different national contexts. In Alma-Gare, for example, the comments and claims of the activists suggest that the memory of 1968 was very close and very real, and their discourse resonates with explicit and implicit references to the militancy that developed in the spring of that year. Indeed, the sources indicate that the activists in Alma-Gare were driven by an ideological motivation that was, for the most part, absent in the Anti-Dampness Campaign. Moreover, 1968, with its emphasis on inversion and subversion offered a particularly provocative and innovative model for the APF/CSCV and the APU. In the Gorbals on the other hand, popular action had never been legitimated by such a profound experience. Certainly rent strikes and Red Clydeside had contributed to radical tenant politics in the west of Scotland, but this experience was much more distant than 1968 was to the activists in Roubaix. The Gorbals experience, however, taps into a different tradition – that of the tenants' associations. These associations developed as facilitators, as mechanisms of communication between tenants and their public sector landlords. This helps to explain why the Anti-Dampness Campaign was effectively *reactive*, basing its actions on the resolution of a single issue. On the other hand, the experience of 1968 and its intellectual aftermath was certainly a factor in the more ambitious, all-encompassing, prescriptive theory developed by the APU with respect to the urban environment.

Another 'national' factor was the structure of government and the relations between local and national administrations. In France there was a pyramidal hierarchy in which central government held sway and local government enjoyed relatively little autonomy. This helps to explain, for example, the ease with which the *Municipalité de Roubaix* was persuaded to allow the participation of ABAC (sponsored by central government) in the Alma-Gare project. It also explains why central government could so easily be made the scapegoat for the seemingly interminable delays in initiating the programme. On the other hand, the structure of government in Great Britain allowed much greater autonomy at the local level. Thus, for example, Glasgow Corporation could engage in strong-arm tactics with the Scottish Office concerning post-war housing policy, while Glasgow District Council could defy central government on the issue of the sale of council houses and council land. Moreover, despite the long dominance of the local political scene by Roubaix's socialist–centrist alliance, there was never the same evidence of the machine politics that gave rise to much of Glasgow's corruption and political nepotism. The Labour Party machine in Glasgow enabled the Council to push on with low-rent and no-sale policies in the face not only of central government pressure, but also a black hole of debt which, at more than one point, threatened to swallow up the city.

Related to this point of political hierarchy is the fact that, while in Britain, the project of renewal lay in the hands of the local authority, in France, the location of power at the local level was much more diffuse. Thus, in Glasgow, while the Corporation or District Council normally tendered out the construction operation, it generally maintained unitary control over the project as a whole. In contrast, operations in France fell to various agencies charged with compulsory purchase, demolition, rehousing and construction, and this inevitably created a more complex political landscape for local organizations to navigate. At times, this complexity must have worked against a small, locally-based organization, but at other moments it allowed the APU to play one actor off against the other. For example, from the events outlined in Chapters Three and Four, it emerges that the APU was much closer to SAEN, an organization more oriented towards the political left, than to ORSUCOMN, which the *Atelier* regarded as a puppet of the textile bosses' *Comité Interprofessionnelle du Logement*. It is no coincidence that, as Alma-Gare came to be heralded as an innovative success, SAEN was assigned a central role in the new project, while ORSUCOMN became increasingly marginalized.

The differences discussed here also had a bearing on the actions and reactions of the respective local governments. The relatively powerful position of central government in local affairs in France meant that, as delays arose in the Alma-Gare project, the *Municipalité de Roubaix* was quick to shift the blame to central government for what they recognized as a serious problem. On the other hand, the relative autonomy of Glasgow District Council meant that, in short, it had 'no one to blame but itself'. For this reason, it was potentially very damaging for the District Council to recognize a serious problem and consequently it preferred to resort to a tactic of denial, challenging the Anti-Dampness Campaign's claim that a problem did, in fact, exist. As protest became more persistent, the District Council began to assign the blame to the population itself, hence the famous 'heavy breathing' statement. The *Municipalité de Roubaix*, on the other hand, simply did its best to marginalize the role of the APU in the process of urban planning and, whenever it could, to disregard this organization altogether.

Later, as the activists began to make headway with their campaigns, yet more differences emerged in the position of the two administrations. In Alma-Gare, the efforts to construct a new neighbourhood eventually came to be widely regarded as a positive initiative, and, increasingly, the *Municipalité de Roubaix* sought to capitalize on this development by presenting itself as the innovative force behind the project. In contrast, the Gorbals became a target for widespread public criticism, with the result that the District Council could only hope to distance itself as best it could from the whole affair and wait until the dust had settled following the demolition of Hutchesontown 'E'. The Council was left to try to shift the blame for the 'Dampies' on to central government in its own reinterpretation of the planning history of the post-war period – something it never managed very successfully.

An awareness of the significance of the national factor is important in a study such as this but, equally, there is a danger in overemphasizing this theme and arriving at the reductive conclusion that national factors explain all differences, or, indeed, that the 'national' exists as a category in and of itself, isolated and easily distinguishable from other categories, such a 'global' or 'local'. If the most we can conclude is that 'France is France and Britain is Britain', then the exercise has been a wasted one.

A crucial difference that transcends national borders is that the Gorbals Anti-Dampness Campaign was effectively a single-issue campaign, while the APU was characterized by a politicized ambition that went far beyond a simple call to improve living conditions. The APU had the utopian ambition to take control of all aspects of the production of urban life, from the provision of housing to decision-making, economic development and social interaction. The *Atelier*'s activists saw theirs as an ideological project to seize the initiative in the production of space (in the Lefebvrian sense) and liberate the popular classes from the thrall of the pact between the town's industrialists and its political administration. On the other hand, while the Gorbals Anti-Dampness Campaign addressed profound questions about the values of modernist planning, its scope was not to challenge the logic of the system of housing provision. In the Gorbals, the growing discontent over the quality of the new flats and the disappointment in the Gorbals 'miracle' became crystallized around a very specific theme – that of water penetration in the new flats, and in Hutchesontown 'E' in particular.

We have noted that the APU and Anti-Dampness Campaign attempted to present the populations of their areas as unified and homogeneous, but the amplitude of the aims of these organizations had an impact on that unity. In particular, the singularity of the Anti-Dampness Campaign's focus made it difficult to involve residents who were *not* experiencing damp conditions, and the Campaign had to resort to emphasizing the *potential* of the dampness to spread through the whole development. In this way, it was the possibility of damp, rather than its physical presence, that provided the unifying factor amongst the population of Hutchesontown 'E'. In Alma-Gare, the scope of the project was wide enough for all the inhabitants of the area, diverse as they were, to have, in theory, an interest in the project. At the same time, of course, the new Alma-Gare was a rather vague, utopian undertaking, while the presence of damp was a tangible phenomenon which offered a daily reminder, to activists and residents alike, of the purpose of the Campaign.

The ambition of the Alma-Gare project was both its strength and its weakness. It was a strength because the APU was able to confront the logic of the urban as a whole, tying together issues of restructuring and housing provision with the *Municipalité*'s economic ambitions. Yet, it was a weakness because the APU was compelled by its own arguments to take charge of all aspects of urban life – having won the battle over housing provision, the activists turned their attention to social links, education, the economy and so on. And it was here that the project began to run into difficulties. While the single-issue Anti-Dampness Campaign was able to maintain its distance from Glasgow District Council, the APU was eventually forced to accept a degree of collaboration with the *Municipalité* and the other organizations involved in order to advance its project. As it turned out, the socioeconomic management of Alma-Gare proved to be much more problematic than its planning and construction.

If the APU's aims were more ambitious than those of the Anti-Dampness Campaign, then its tactics were also more transgressive, in the sense that the APU did not stop short of appropriating the role of their 'opponents', embarking on rehousing, walling-up and renovation operations and, of course, drawing up their own future for the *quartier* in the form of the *carte-affiche*. The Anti-Dampness Campaign did not employ this conscious appropriation of roles and it was, moreover, thwarted in one of its most innovative actions – to take its landlord, Glasgow District Council, to court under nineteenth-century 'slum' legislation. It did, however, manage the next best thing, winning a courtroom battle with Strathclyde Regional Council to obtain a rates reduction. Another significant tactic for the Campaign was the rent strike, which proved to be one of its most effective long-term actions (and also had an important historical pedigree in the west of Scotland). Beyond these more unusual tactics, both organizations also made use of the more conventional array of protest activities, including meetings, marches, lobbying, letter-writing, petitioning and so on, and both were marked by a determination that carried them through years of uncertainty.

Another important difference between the events in Alma-Gare and the Gorbals is that, while both the APU and the Anti-Dampness Campaign rejected the modernist housing futures offered to them, the APU did so *ante facto*, while the Gorbals Anti-Dampness Campaign did so *post facto*. This influenced the two cases in various ways. It operated as a brake on the Anti-Dampness Campaign's ambitions, leading it to seek to rectify a flaw in the 'miracle' rather than overturn the miracle completely – or at least not until a later stage. The physical presence of the 'A' to 'E' of the new Gorbals limited the imaginative power of the Campaign, while in Alma-Gare the blueprint future proposed by the *Municipalité* was more easily challenged, and the APU's own alternative could remain nebulous and utopian until it took the decision to produce the *carte-affiche*. On the other hand, as the Anti-Dampness Campaign began to tap into an alternative vision of the Gorbals – one constructed on community bonds – it was able to ride, rather opportunely, a wave of nostalgia for the former community, rather than actively create this phenomenon. The APU did not have this luxury and had to inform and instruct the population of Alma-Gare concerning their collective past and their future potential. For this reason, many of the APU statements concerning participation were prescriptive in nature.

Extending this point a little further, we arrive at attitudes to the built environment itself. As discussed above, both groups assigned a deterministic role to the traditional morphology of their areas, be it the *courées* or the tenements, transforming what had once been symbols of misery into symbols of solidarity. In Glasgow, the physical removal of the tenements meant that the physical evidence of the terrible living conditions had been erased, with the result that these buildings existed as symbols of community cohesion *only* in the collective memory. Their original, negative significance was transferred to the system-built blocks provided by the Corporation, and these in turn became the new slums. In a similar transformation, the *courées* went from symbols of exploitation to symbols of resistance, with the difference that their physical presence prevented their unconditional social 'rehabilitation' and they continued, simultaneously, to have negative connotations. This was one of the principal reasons why the activists in Alma-Gare were more cautious in the assignation of positive values to the built environment than their counterparts in the Gorbals, and their justifications for limited conservation, as outlined in the *carte-affiche*, were couched in more technical terms. Indeed, members of the APU never expressed a wish to return to their *courée* houses, only to transfer the organization of space to the new context and renovate a number of the more spacious street-front properties. In the example of Alma-Gare, we find an active attempt to establish a *new* place of memory, where the tight-knit community might be perpetuated. In the Gorbals, the modernist flats appeared to have reminded their residents only of what had been lost, and the pressure to demolish Hutchesontown 'E' reflected a desire on the part of Gorbals residents to consign the spatial setting of unwelcome memories to oblivion. The quotation from Montale that opens this book states that history is not the devastating bulldozer they say; it leaves underground passages, crypts, holes and hiding places.[7] And indeed, complete oblivion is difficult, perhaps

[7] E. Montale, 'La storia', from *L'opera in versi* (Torino: Giulio Einaudi editore, 1980), p. 316.

impossible to achieve. More often, memories 'survive' – to use Montale's term –and are reassessed, recast and incorporated in a group's collective memory in new ways, in accordance with the conditions of the present. Thus, if the memory of the 'Dampies' could not be swept away completely, then at least it could be recast as a justification for a new start: 'Third Time Lucky'.

In the theoretical approach adopted in this book, the idea of collective memory is closely associated with the concept of 'myth'. Alma-Gare, more theorized, more politicized, located as it was in a post-1968 context, and informed by a Marxist sociological paradigm, was characterized by the activists' desire to tap into the discourse of the trades unions, and from there to the myth of the resistance of the *courées* in times of industrial strife. On the other hand, the Gorbals myths were much more to do with the neighbourliness and social bonds associated with the old Gorbals rather than political activism. Overall, it would appear that the mythical dimension of the Gorbals surfaces much more frequently than that of Alma-Gare. In part, this may again be explained by the absence of the tenements, but it also suggests, to use White's concept,[8] that the 'building material' was more abundant, that the Gorbals was more myth-laden than Alma-Gare, and that it occupied a more central position in Glasgow's collective memory than Alma-Gare did in Roubaix's. Certainly, Glasgow, for all its socioeconomic problems, has a large, relatively affluent middle class, and there is, therefore, a fairly eager market for the products of Glasgow's particular school of literary nostalgia. Without doubt, this is fuelled by an interest in the bad old, good old, bygone days and a search for the 'defining spirit' of Glasgow that mirrors the Anti-Dampness Campaign's search for the spirit of the Gorbals. Roubaix, on the other hand, is not only smaller in population terms, but is relatively bereft of well-off groups that might encourage the business of myth and nostalgia. Its past has not yet been glamorized as Glasgow's has. Or it may simply be that the Glasgow-born author finds more resonance in the Gorbals material, recognizing more easily its mythical position in Glasgow's collective memory.

Whatever differences we may point to between Alma-Gare and the Gorbals, the APU and the Anti-Dampness Campaign both felt that, at certain points, they could unambiguously claim victory for their efforts. Certainly, the achievements of these two organizations should not be underestimated. Both fought tenaciously to challenge a system that was founded on established interests, common-sense appraisals of the 'slum', political expediency and 'mutual corroboration' – a system, moreover, in which they had no official voice. And each succeeded in inserting its own reality through determined and innovative campaigning. That said, it is not the aim of this book to compose an

[8] H. White, 'Catastrophe, Communal Memory and Mythic Discourse: The Uses of Myth in the Reconstruction of Society', in Stråth, *Myth and Memory in the Construction of Community*, pp. 49–53.

identikit of protest movements from which to assess those that are, or are likely to be, most 'successful'. Not only is the category of 'success' problematic to apply, but such an approach also suggests that protest groups are able to interpret and assess situations effectively and are free to choose their preferred course of action. It introduces ideas of stakes and instrumental tactics in situations that are rarely unambiguous and often contain contradiction and uncertainty. This, however, does not prevent us concluding this section with an assessment of the differences that appear to have been most significant in influencing the subsequent actions, initiatives and responses of the APU and Anti-Dampness Campaign. For example, it would appear that an organization that directs its efforts at a single issue might be better able to channel its resources and direct its activities than an organization founded on more ambitious programmes. Having achieved this objective, however, the single-issue initiative tends to disappear, unless it can find a fresh focus for its energies. The fact that the Anti-Dampness Campaign succeeded in forcing Glasgow District Council to accept responsibility for the living conditions in Hutchesontown 'E' meant not only that the organization lost its *raison d'être*, but also that the organization's own support base was depleted as the residents of the damp flats were evacuated. In a sense, the disappearance of the Campaign was the ultimate confirmation of its achievements. The case of Alma-Gare, however, was much more complex, for the APU had set no limit to its aims, and had no clearly defined final goal. We may also consider that an organization such as the APU, which offers an *ante facto* challenge to a planning programme, tends towards more utopian solutions. Difficulties arise in concretizing this project, as utopia comes into contact with financial, administrative and organizational realities. The activists in Alma-Gare claimed a significant and unique victory: the experience of public participation to such a degree was never to be repeated in France, although the general principle became broadly established. This claim, however, must be qualified, since the new Alma-Gare as it emerged was not a direct translation of their future vision, but a compromise built upon financial realities, political expediency and technical limitations.

Finally, we can observe that the nature of the outcome influences the appraisal of these organizations and their actions. Actors that enjoy power in urban relations may attempt to appropriate the success of future-oriented, 'positively' directed initiatives such as that of the APU. In contrast, a reactive, 'negatively' directed initiative, such as that of the Anti-Dampness Campaign in the Gorbals, is more likely to provoke amnesia should it be successful. Paradoxically, the symbol of its success is to be escaped, knocked down, blown up or, in some other way, assigned to oblivion.

Local initiatives and global forces

It is important to recognize that the success claimed by the *Atelier Populaire d'Urbanisme* and the Gorbals Anti-Dampness Campaign emerged in the context of a crisis in the respective planning systems where the blueprint paradigm had collapsed, the economies of the two countries were stagnating, and planning for certainty was beginning to appear increasingly unfeasible. Indeed, it would not be unreasonable to suggest that the influence of the APU and the Anti-Dampness Campaign might have been considerably less had they not emerged in this particular context. National governments needed new solutions to the problems of their cities (problems increasingly seen in socio-economic terms rather than in terms of the quality of the built environment). The enthusiasm for large-scale projects, and renewal operations in particular, had run its course, and concepts of small-scale operations and flexibility were coming to the fore. And, as the two case studies help to illustrate, participation was a means by which governments hoped to contain public discontent at what were coming to be perceived as the 'failures' of the planning system.

All these developments inevitably had an impact on the local level. In Roubaix the idea of participation came increasingly to be accepted and was promoted by all the major political parties at local elections. Moreover, the ambitious urban programmes in the town were proving impossibly expensive, as well as unpopular with the electorate, and a large section of Roubaix's new housing stock lay empty. In any case, the drive towards tertiary development, to which the restructuring of Alma-Gare was considered a key, came to look less plausible in the course of the 1970s. The mid-1970s also saw a greater openness on the part of the Socialist Party towards the national council of the *Association Populaire Familiale*, especially with regard to the latter's criticisms of the process of urban renewal. In 1977, the Council of Europe held a conference in Venice on the subject of 'Environment, participation and quality of life', a development indicative of the extent to which participation was becoming an accepted part of the political landscape.

In Glasgow, in the six months from March to August 1981, 8754 cases of dampness were reported across the city,[9] many of these in 'modern' housing stock. These statistics were compounded by the public discourse against modern housing developments. There can also be little doubt that successive Labour administrations in Glasgow City Chambers contributed to the situation with their low-rent policy, which inevitably meant they did not have sufficient funds to carry out routine maintenance on their properties. In short, the atmosphere was conducive to a challenge to the post-war model of public

[9] 'Council Renege', *The View* (September 1981), p. 5. ML.

housing provision, and, if the new Gorbals epitomized all that was worst with this model, then its demolition became a cathartic act.

In this way, 'global' factors worked through the urban system and impacted on the 'local' level. Indeed, from this perspective, Hutchesontown 'E' can be regarded as an exorcism of the old, modernist, blueprint paradigm, while Alma-Gare was the experimental application of the new flexible and responsive approach. But, if political decisions reflect these general developments, they are not made in isolation from social, cultural and economic relations at the local level. On the contrary, such decisions are made according to institutional interpretations on the part of administrations, politicians and their electorate. Thus, with respect to Alma-Gare one might argue that *rénovation urbaine* never took place because neither central nor local government was prepared to make the financial commitment – a reflection of global factors. But this does not take us very far unless we recognize that urban renewal, in any form, was founded on a particular interpretation of the urban fabric in a particular historical context. It was Alma-Gare's identification as an area of nineteenth-century *courées* that brought these factors into play, mediated responses and shifted the local into the global and the global into the local. The same argument holds, for example, for the involvement of ABAC. It is not enough to point to a growing emphasis on flexibility and participation in planning theory in Western Europe – the initiative was made possible by the local developments that caused Alma-Gare to be understood as a social entity, as a *quartier* rather than a collection of *courées*.

Continuing along this line of argument, despite the APU's ambition to recreate Alma-Gare as a self-sustaining organism, the *quartier* could not isolate itself from the socioeconomic problems buffeting a declining industrial town in northern France. There was no scope to create an enclave of well-being sheltered from the ill-winds of economic recession. Innovative architecture was not enough, nor was a management council made up of residents, a local restaurant and building cooperative. The employment and self-management initiatives faltered and then failed, and the spatial organization that had been intended to encourage social interaction became transformed into a landscape of crime and vandalism.

These developments reflect very well David Harvey's points about the limitations of initiatives that seek to establish a link between place and social identity.[10] As discussed in the introduction, Harvey argues that most of these initiatives are better at organizing in place than they are at commanding space. They are, moreover, inevitably founded on nostalgia and tradition, making them reactionary rather than radical. He is more optimistic concerning more radical

[10] D. Harvey, *The Condition of Postmodernity: An Enquiry into the Origins of Cultural Change* (Oxford: Basil Blackwell, 1989), p. 302.

'social movements' which search to liberate space and time from the thrall of capitalism. These movements have as their aim an alternative society in which time and value are understood in another way. The two case studies examined here fall rather neatly into Harvey's categories. As discussed, the Anti-Dampness Campaign in the Gorbals was reactionary in as much as its aim was to correct flaws in the built environment, and much of its discourse fell back upon the construction of a collective memory of tenement life. The intention of the Campaign was not to command space nor to seek to understand time and value in a new way, but to establish a place-based identity. On the other hand, the APU's project contained a strong element of utopian thought, much of which was founded on the belief that it was indeed possible to produce a model of urban life that was not determined by capitalism: 'In Roubaix, *quartier* of ALMA, our struggle proposes an alternative renovation to that of the Capitalists'.[11] Harvey suggests, however, that even these radical social movements are unlikely to succeed in their aims, since, in attempting to establish their own organization of space and time, they open themselves up to the dissolving power of money and the definitions of time and space that are the result of capital accumulation. Again, Harvey's point is supported by the example of Alma-Gare: global economic forces had a huge impact on the local. To an extent, Alma-Gare eventually reverted to its former identity, the identity to which the *Municipalité* had adhered for so long – that of the run-down problem area inhabited by a deprived population, representing a brake on the economic development of the town.

The weakness of Harvey's analysis, however, is his emphasis on the impact of global capitalism. Founding his analysis of place-based initiatives on this factor, he ignores or marginalizes social and cultural factors, makes a reductive correlation between capital and power relations and prioritizes a single direction (global to the local) in what should be conceived of as a two-way process. Massey and Jess overcome these limits by suggesting that, rather than seeing local initiatives as a battle against global capital, these disputes should be regarded as being about the very definitions of the characteristics of place, about the efforts of groups to establish, 'a different set of relations to place and to the power relations which construct social space'.[12] Alma-Gare was not just, or even primarily, a challenge to capitalism. It was an attempt to give a voice to a marginalized population, to challenge the lack of transparency in a

---

[11] 'A Roubaix, quartier de l'ALMA, notre lutte propose une autre rénovation que celle de Capitalistes'. APU, information insert re. Alma-Gare, *Combat Familial*, no. 122–3 (December 1976), p. 7.

[12] P. Jess and D. Massey, 'The Contestation of Place', in D. Massey and P. Jess (eds), *A Place in the World? Places, Culture and Globalisation* (Oxford: The Open University/ Oxford University Press, 1995) p. 150.

decision-making system, to perpetuate a particular kind of social relations, and to create an identity that evaded the categories of social classes.

In this way, the explanations for Alma-Gare and the Gorbals are not about *either* local initiatives *or* global forces, but about how global–local relations interact to produce unique outcomes.[13] Certainly, both studies can be located in the crisis of the welfare state phase of modernity experienced in the 1970s, but, just as global, or quasi-global developments contributed to influencing the events at Alma-Gare and the Gorbals, so too these events had, in a modest way, their own wider impact, informing political, professional and public opinion alike. The Anti-Dampness Campaign became a cornerstone of a city-wide, and then a national network of tenants' associations concerned with living conditions in public housing, while the APU provided the impetus for the formation of AIR, the *Association Inter-quartiers de Roubaix*. As Jess and Massey argue, while the global entered the local, so too the local entered the global. Each case was not only a product of, but also a catalyst for, a changing paradigm, either confirming the end of industrially produced public housing or the beginning of public participation in the planning process. The APU activists were explicit in their hope that the events at Alma-Gare would have an educational impact on the inhabitants of other *quartiers*, the organizations involved in redeveloping areas of the city, students who would become active in the field of planning and, finally, the planning profession itself.[14] Both initiatives attracted sociologists, students and the odd PhD researcher and, to this day, Hutchesontown 'E' and Alma-Gare continue to enjoy a particular resonance, not only in their respective towns but also in their national contexts.

The city as history; history as the city

As discussed in the opening chapter, Bernard Lepetit used the city as a metaphor for understanding history,[15] and in so doing, simultaneously made history a metaphor for understanding the city. The final section of this book explores the potential of the present work to be seen as an extended metaphor for the *métier* of the historian.

In the preceding pages we have examined how two different groups, in two western European cities, attempted to gain control over the decision-making process around their urban environment. They did this by challenging the

[13] Ibid., p. 138.

[14] CSCV/APU, 'Gare Alma: Une expérience d'intervention de la population dans la création de son habitat' (4 April 1977), p. 1. AIR.

[15] B. Lepetit, 'Une herméneutique urbaine est-elle possible?' in B. Lepetit and D. Pumain, *Temperalités Urbaines* (Paris: Anthropos, 1993), p. 293.

dominant, institutionalized construction of this environment and simultaneously attempting to insert an alternative reality – a reality that was consistent with their own experience. They also tapped into certain interpretations of the past and into myths that informed a collective memory. In part, these myths emerged without beckoning because they were consistent with the groups' visions, and in part they were consciously reinforced using a range of tactics that have been outlined in the preceding chapters. It is certain, however, that this material is not conjured out of nothing – for a construction to be successful, it must find cultural resonance.

In this sense, the approach of the *Atelier Populaire d'Urbanisme* and the Gorbals Anti-Dampness Campaign is no different to that of the historian. Not the historian in the Rankian sense, who pretends to cast a judicious eye from above and beyond the 'object' of study, not the historian who sets out to tell how it really was but, rather, the historian who conceives of his or her work as a translation of the past into a form we understand today, who recognizes, as Stråth argues, that, 'the image of the past is continuously reconsidered in the light of an ever-changing present'.[16]

According to Lepetit, all aspects of the city unfurl according to different chronologies, and yet the city is completely located in the present by the social actors who shoulder all the temporal responsibility.[17] As a metaphor for history, it is the historian who shoulders the temporal responsibility, locating historical analysis in the present, for it can be no other way. Events are inserted in a context that provides them with meaning (this study is one such context), and the context today is never identical to that of yesterday. For example, yesterday, the events at Alma-Gare were interpreted as a Marxist inspired social movement, like Marco Ferreri's Battle of Little Big Horn in the heart of Paris. Today, they represent conflict and negotiation over the meaning of a part of the city, and the struggle for power to control that meaning. And if one accepts that the work of historical analysis constructs the past in the present, then one must recognize that this same historical analysis is also aimed at a construction of the past that informs the present's *future*. In this sense, the stake for the historian now is no different from the stake of the activists then. Our view of the future is bound to our experiences in the present, and these experiences are different according to whether we live in a 'slum' or a 'neighbourhood', whether we are looking for 'urban social movements' or place-based initiatives.

What if we push the metaphor of the city as history a little further on the basis of the case studies in this research? The efforts of groups such as the APU and the Anti-Dampness Campaign to establish alternative places is an effort

---

[16] Stråth, 'Introduction. Myth, Memory and History in the Construction of Community', p. 19.

[17] Lepetit, 'Une herméneutique urbaine est-elle possible?', p. 293.

to break through institutionalized historical narratives and establish counter-histories. This means reactivating meanings that had been consigned to oblivion by the dominant narrative, challenging the meaning of historical 'givens', attempting to establish histories that give a voice to groups that are traditionally silent (or silenced), opening up the possibility of plurality in the face of a monolithic discourse, and challenging historical paradigms, just as the locally-based idea of 'community' or '*quartier*' challenged the dominance of the homogenizing modernist paradigm in architecture and planning. And, like the meaning of tenements and *courées*, the meaning of historical events is never fixed. New interpretations in new contexts bring new meaning to these events or reactivate old meanings. When these physical structures in the city are removed, they remain as traces in the collective memory, just like the historical myths that inform our thinking, perpetuated by their 'fit' in a particular narrative. We should not seek to test the absolute truth of these myths, but attempt to understand their relative truth in the context in which they are presented. 'Truth' as a historical category is contextual, and the work of historical analysis is aimed at establishing a construction of the past consistent with the present's truths.

Having said all this, it would be ingenuous to claim to have unpacked the constructions around Roubaix's *courées* and Glasgow's tenements without acknowledging that this deconstruction is simultaneously another construction, in the form of seven chapters of sorted, structured interpretation. In this book, the imposition of crisis moments and the identification of differences and similarities are all examples of the historian's constructions – after all, things or events do not have an inherent quality of 'difference' or 'similarity' and classifications are arbitrary.

It should not come as a surprise to find that, just as our vision of the city in Lepetit's metaphor equates to our vision of history, so too place-based identities, such as those constructed around Alma-Gare and the old Gorbals, equate to historically founded identities. If this book carries one message, it must be that the very act of thinking about place is a historical gesture, putting into play countless interpretations of the past and future, mediated by the present context. And more than this, on the basis of Massey's argument that place is made up of intersecting social relations, place is also a dynamic concept. It is not merely a container for historical events, but an inherent element in these events, shaping and being shaped by them.

In this world characterized by competing constructions, relative values and the absence of certainty presented in these pages, where 'there is nothing either good or bad, but thinking makes it so', is there still a possibility to make judgements on the 'right' or 'wrong' of actions and decisions? Certainly, we cannot claim to reach definitive 'right answers', but, as Massey has argued, this does not exclude the possibility of making political judgements, with the explicit knowledge that they are contingent upon the nature of the links made between past, present and future.[18] Seeking to interpret these links helps uncover the power geometry that underpins events such as those considered in Alma-Gare and the Gorbals. It helps locate particular interpretations of the past in the present, and so understand their implications for the future. It helps understand the weight of interests behind a term like '*courée*' and to conceive of the implication of this term for diverse groups with different locations in the local power geometry. These constructions of place are far from value-free: we have seen, for example, that 'slum' is a damaging term for those who are labelled 'slum-dwellers'. In the Gorbals, this identification enabled the Corporation/District Council to shift the blame for damp conditions in their housing stock from the physical structure of the flats to the living habits of their tenants, while in Alma-Gare, the resonance of the term *courées* was such that the demolition of the *quartier* was taken for granted, irrespective of the implications for those for whom the *courées* offered the only possibility of housing. Both groups of residents, in Gorbals and Alma-Gare alike, had little voice or influence in urban affairs. They occupied a marginal position in the power geometries of their respective towns, and their actions, therefore, may be adjudicated to be positive initiatives to obtain a degree of influence over their own futures.

The same holds true for history: historians may construct their narratives using the same building materials, but the implications of these constructions are never the same. Narratives that seek to oppress or exploit, marginalize or discriminate must not be allowed to become resonant 'right answers'.

[18] D. Massey, 'Places and their Pasts', *History Workshop Journal*, no. 39 (Spring 1995), p. 186.

Bibliography and references

Roubaix

ABAC-Paris and APU-Roubaix (1981), 'Roubaix: le quartier de l'Alma-Gare', in Jean-Luc Flamand, Michelle Perrot, Jaques Girault, Annie Fourcaut et al., *La Question du logement et le mouvement ouvrier français*, Paris: Editions de la Villette, pp. 162–222.

Agence de Développement et d'Urbanisme de la Métropole Lilloise, Ecole d'architecture de Lille-Regions Nord (1993), *Lille Métropole: un siècle d'architecture et d'urbanisme: 1890–1993*, Paris: Le Moniteur.

AGIR (1976), 'Pour un pool de gestion dans une économie généralisé de quartier', *Autrement*, no. 6, pp. 250–66.

AGIR and APU-Alma-Gare (1981), 'Pour un économie du quartier', *Esprit*, no. 51, March, pp. 65–79.

APU (1976), [information insert re Alma-Gare], *Combat Familial*, no. 122–3, December, p. 7.

APU-CSCV (1982), 'La démarche au quotidien', in *Roubaix Alma-Gare. Lutte Urbaine et Architecture*, Bruxelles: Editions de l'Atelier d'Art Urbain, pp. 17–38.

AUSI A et P (1982), 'Le nouveau quartier', in *Roubaix Alma-Gare. Lutte Urbaine et Architecture*, Bruxelles: Editions de l'Atelier d'Art Urbain, pp. 91–118.

AUSI A and P, M. Benoit and T. Verbiest (1980), 'Opération Fontenoy-Frasez, Quartier de l'Alma-Gare à Roubaix (Nord)', *Architecture Mouvement Continuité*, no. 52–3, June–September, pp. 100–105.

Battiau, M. (1984), 'Raisons et effets de la concentration spatiale de nombreux textiles dans l'agglomération Roubaix-Tourcoing', *Hommes et Terres du Nord*, **2**, pp. 73–6.

Benarab, Noureddine (1981), 'Appropriation d'une courée Roubaisienne par des communautés culturellement différentes et les rapports sociaux induits par ce type d'appropriation', unpublished thesis, *Travaux personnels de fin d'études de 3ème cycle, Architecture*, University of Lille.

Bernfeld, Dan with Michele Gantois and Alain Biton (1984), 'Le quartier de l'Alma-Gare à Roubaix', in Dan Bernfeld with Michele Gantois and Alain Biton, *Fichier de la Participation*, Lille: Ceidart, pp. 100–18.

Bruyelle, Pierre (1984), 'Roubaix face aux grandes mutations récentes', in Yves-Marie Hilaire (ed.), *Histoire de Roubaix*, Dunkerque: Editions des Beffrois, pp. 305–37.

Carton, Bernard and l'Atelier Populaire d'Urbanisme d'Alma-Gare – CSCV (1982), 'Introduction', in *Roubaix Alma-Gare. Lutte Urbaine et Architecture*, Bruxelles: Editions de l'Atelier d'Art Urbain, pp. 9–15.

Caul Futy, Louis (1976), 'Aujourd'hui la CSCV', *Combat Familial*, no. 122–3, December, pp. 3–4.

Caul-Futy, Louis (1976), 'L'efficacité d'un syndicalisme du cadre de vie', *Autrement*, no. 6, September, pp. 150–55.

Champenois, Michèle (1982), 'La belle aventure des citoyens bâtisseurs de Roubaix', *Le Monde*, 24 and 25 January, p. 14.

Codaccioni, Paul-Félix (1984), 'La vie politique à Roubaix sous l'administration de Victor Provo (1942–1977)', in Yves-Marie Hilaire (ed.), *Histoire de Roubaix*, Dunkerque: Editions des Beffrois, pp. 259–80.

Codaccioni, Paul-Félix (1984), 'Les changements politiques des dix dernières années (1973–1983)', in Yves-Marie Hilaire (ed.), *Histoire de Roubaix*, Dunkerque: Editions des Beffrois, pp. 281–304.

Communauté Urbaine de Lille: 10 ans: 1971–1980, Lille: Editions Axial, 1980.

Cornuel, Didier and Duriez, Bruno (1975), *Les courées de Roubaix: 1884–1974*, Villeneuve d'Ascq: Centre d'Analyse du Développement.

Cornuel, Didier and Duriez, Bruno (1976), 'L'Evolution de la propriété immobilière à Roubaix: 1884–1974', *Revue du Nord*, **58** (229), April–June, pp. 245–59.

Cornuel, Didier and Duriez, Bruno (1983), *Le mirage urbain: histoire de logement à Roubaix*, Paris: Editions Anthropos.

Delberghe, Michel (1977), 'L'avenir du quartier Alma-Gare, I – Un dialogue qui repose sur l'incompréhension et le rapport de force', *La Voix du Nord*, 25 June.

Delberghe, Michel, (1977), 'L'avenir du quartier Alma-Gare, III – Pour les élus, c'est l'apprentissage de la concertation', *La Voix du Nord*, 29 June.

Descamps, Jean (1976), 'La résorption des courées de la Métropole Nord', unpublished thesis, *Travaux personnels de fin d'études de 3ème cycle*, *Droit*, University of Lille.

Desreumaux, O. (1980), 'Roubaix: deux opérations à suivre: Alma-Gare et Alma-Centre', *La Gazette* **1**, 25–26 January, pp. 3–4.

Diligent, André (1986), 'Urbanisme Logement', *A Propos*, no. 2, February, p. 6.

Duriez, Bruno and Cornuel, Didier (1975), *Transformations économiques, évolution des rapports politiques et restructuration urbaine: Roubaix 1960–1975*, Villeneuve d'Ascq: Centre d'Analyse du Développement.

Duriez, Bruno and Cornuel, Didier (1979), 'La naissance de la politique urbaine: le cas de Roubaix', *Les annales de la recherche urbaine – recherches et débats*, no. 4, July, pp. 22–84.

Dussaud, Marie-José (1976), *Les ZAC: Dossier Bibliographique*, Lille: Docamenor.

Gantier, Fabienne (1986), 'L'évolution de la politique urbaine à roubaix depuis 1970: recherches sur un quartier', unpublished thesis, *Maîtrise d'Administration Economique et Sociale*, University of Lille.

Geus, Jacques (1977), 'Le nouvel Alma sera élaboré en concertation avec la population mais le schéma d'aménagement tiendra compte de la stratégie économique de la ville', *Nord Eclair*, 3 June, p. 8.

Grass, Gérard and Lemonier, Pierre (1976), 'Pour un schéma-directeur de l'organisation de la vie sociale', *Autrement*, no. 6, September, pp. 230–49.

Hilaire, Yves-Marie (ed.) (1984), *Histoire de Roubaix*, Dunkerque: Editions des Beffrois.

INSEE (1982), *Le Parc des Logement dans le Nord-Pas de Calais, Recensement 1982*, Lille: INSEE.

Lamarche-Vadel, Gaetane and Cotlenko, Ariane (1976), 'Alma-Gare – le singulier et le politique', *Autrement*, no. 6, September, pp. 62–69.

Le Blan, Martine (1981), 'Notes sur une étape dans la genèse d'un espace industriel: la construction des "forts" roubaisiens dans la première moitié du XIXe siècle', *Revue du Nord*, **63** (248), March, pp. 67–72.

Leman, Roger (1982), 'Roubaix: lier le social et l'économique', *Parole et Société*, no. 3–4, pp. 204–209.

Leman, Roger, (1989), 'L'Alma Gare n'est pas encore rasé', *Cadres CFDT*, no. 338–9, December 1989–January 1990, pp. 56–58.

Leman, Roger and Leman, Marie-Agnès (1980), 'A l'Alma-Gare à Roubaix: une organisation collective des habitants pour un meilleur urbanisme', *Sauvegarde de l'enfance*, no. 2, March–April, pp. 293–99.

Lemonier, Pierre, (1981), 'La concertation produit le nouveau quartier', in Albert Mollet (ed.), *Quand les Habitants Prennent la Parole*, Paris: Plan Construction, pp. 208–29.

Lemonier, Pierre, (1982), 'Production architecturale et maîtrise d'ouvrage collective', in *Roubaix Alma-Gare. Lutte Urbaine et Architecture*, Bruxelles: Editions de l'Atelier d'Art Urbain, pp. 39–80.

Le Livre Blanc des POS, Lille: Agence d'Urbanisme de la Communauté Urbaine de Lille, 1974.

Maillard, Cécile (1992), 'Alma-Gare, le mirage des années 70', *Urbanisme*, no. 256, September, pp. 49–52.

Malle-Grain, N. (pre-publication copy), *Répertoire des thèses, DEA, mémoires soutenus sur le Nord et le Pas-de Calais à l'époque contemporaine*, Lille: Centre d'histoire de la Région du Nord et de l'Europe du Nord-Ouest.

Mattëi, Bruno (1981), 'Urbanisme populaire et économie de quartier', *Autrement*, no. 8, March, pp. 19–21.

Mons-Dilly, Dominique (1979), 'Les mutations urbaines à Lille, 1968–1978', unpublished thesis, *UER de Géographie, Université des Sciences et Techniques*, University of Lille.

Prouvost, Jacques (1969), 'Les courées à Roubaix', *Revue du Nord*, **51** (201), June, pp. 307–16.

Prouvost, Pierre (1977), 'Vers une politique de l'urbanisme', *Le Métro*, Roubaix edition, March, p. 5.

Roubaix Alma-Gare. Lutte Urbaine et Architecture, Bruxelles: Editions de l'Atelier d'Art Urbain, 1982.

'Roubaix: L'APU. Naissance d'un mouvement populaire de résistance aux expulsions', *Place*, no. 5, special issue on 'l'Atelier', autumn 1976, pp. 14–16.

'Roubaix: L'APU 2. Stratégie du capital et stratégie populaire', *Place*, no. 6, winter 1977, pp. 11–20.

'Trois autres quartiers changent de visage', Roubaix: Périodique d'information municipale, August 1974.

Van der Meersch, Maxence (1951), *Quand les sirènes se taisent*, Paris: Albin Michel.

Van der Meersch, Maxence (1993), *Gens du Nord*, Paris: Presses de la Cité.

Vanrullen, Bernard (1978), *Proposition d'intégration urbaine d'une maison d'enfants pour cas sociaux*, unpublished thesis, *Travaux personnels de fin d'études de 3ème cycle, Architecture*, University of Lille.

Verbrackel, Eric (1980), 'L'Atelier populaire d'urbanisme de l'Alma-Gare à Roubaix', unpublished thesis, *Mémoire de maîtrise, Sociologie, Institut de Sociologie*, University of Lille.

Vincentini, Jocelyne and Vilment, Marie-Christine (1977), 'L'Evolution du cadre de vie à Roubaix de 1945 à 1977', unpublished thesis, *Mémoire de maîtrise, Histoire Contemporaine*, University of Lille.

Glasgow

Brennan, Tom (1959), *Reshaping a City*, Glasgow: The House of Grant.

Bryant, Richard (1979), *The Dampness Monster: A Report of the Gorbals Anti-Dampness Campaign*, Edinburgh: Scottish Council of Social Services.

Buie, Elizabeth (1998), 'The Great Grooming of the Gorbals', *The Herald*, 3 March, p. 10.

Caplan, Jack (1991), *Memories of the Gorbals*, Edinburgh: Pentland Press.

Census 1951: Report on the Fifteenth Census of Scotland. Vol. 1, Part 2: City of Glasgow, Edinburgh: HMSO, 1952.

Census 1961: Scotland, County Report. Vol. 1, Part 2: City of Glasgow, Edinburgh: HMSO, 1963.

Census 1971: Scotland, County Report: Glasgow City, Edinburgh: HMSO, 1973.

Centre For Housing Research, University of Glasgow (1990), *Housing Condition Survey 1985. Vol 2: People and Dwellings – The Household Survey*, Glasgow: Glasgow District Council.

City of Glasgow District Council (1981), *Gorbals Local Plan. Listed Building Survey Report*, Glasgow: Glasgow District Council.

City of Glasgow District Council (1984), *Gorbals Local Plan. Draft Survey Report*, Glasgow: Glasgow District Council.

City of Glasgow District Council (1987), *Housing Condition Survey 1985. Vol 1: The Condition of Glasgow's Housing Stock*, Glasgow: Glasgow District Council.

City of Glasgow District Council (1988), *The Gorbals Heritage Trails*, Glasgow: Glasgow District Council.

City of Glasgow District Council (1989), *Gorbals Local Plan. Draft Written Statement*, Glasgow: Glasgow District Council.

City of Glasgow District Council (1990), *Housing Condition Survey 1985. Vol 3: The District Council's Housing Stock*, Glasgow: Glasgow District Council.

Corporation of the City of Glasgow (1952), *Development Plan, 1951*, Glasgow: Corporation of the City of Glasgow.

Corporation of the City of Glasgow (1956), *Hutchesontown/Part Gorbals Comprehensive Development Area, 1956: Survey Report*, Glasgow: Corporation of the City of Glasgow.

Corporation of the City of Glasgow (1956), *Hutchesontown/Part Gorbals Comprehensive Development Area, 1956: Written Statement*, Glasgow: Corporation of the City of Glasgow.

Corporation of the City of Glasgow (1960), *The First Quinquennial Review of the Development Plan, 1960: The Survey Report*, Glasgow: Corporation of the City of Glasgow.

Corporation of the City of Glasgow (1964), *The First Quinquennial Review of the Development Plan, 1960: The Written Report*, Glasgow: Corporation of the City of Glasgow.

Corporation of the City of Glasgow (1965), *Laurieston/Gorbals Comprehensive Development Area, 1965. Report of Proceedings at Public Local Inquiry, Monday 4th October, 1965*, Glasgow: Corporation of the City of Glasgow.

Corporation of the City of Glasgow (1965), *Laurieston/Gorbals Comprehensive Development Area, 1965. Survey Report*, Glasgow: Corporation of the City of Glasgow.

Crewe, Candida (1994), 'Rebirth of the Gorbals Spirit', *The Guardian*, 20 December, pp. 12–13.

'Crown Street, Glasgow' (1999), http://www.princes-foundation.org/newpage6.htm.

Cunningham, Jennifer (1976), 'When Tenants Take on the Council', *The Glasgow Herald*, 1 April, p. 7.

Damer, Sean (1990), *Glasgow: Going for a Song*, London: Lawrence & Wishart.

Damer, Sean (1990), 'No Mean Writer? The Curious Case of Alexander McArthur', in Kevin McCara and Hamish Whyte (eds), *A Glasgow Collection: Essays in Honour of Joe Fisher*, Glasgow: Glasgow City Libraries.

Dampness: Council Tenants' Rights, Glasgow: Castlemilk Law Centre, 1983.

Glasser, Ralph (1986), *Growing Up in the Gorbals*, London: Chatto & Windus.

Glasser, Ralph (1990), *Gorbals Voices, Siren Songs*, London: Chatto and Windus.

Gorbals History Research Group (nd *c*. 1995), *Third Time Lucky? The History and Hopes of the Gorbals*, Glasgow: ABC.

Hanley, Cliff (1990), 'Foreword', in Joseph McKenzie, *Gorbals Children. A Study in Photographs*, Glasgow: Richard Drew Publishing.

Horsey, Miles (1990), *Tenements and Towers: Glasgow Working Class Housing 1890–1900*, Edinburgh: The Royal Commission on the Ancient and Historical Monuments of Scotland.

Housing in 20th Century Glasgow: A Collection of Source Material, Glasgow: Strathclyde Education – SRC, nd.

Jephcott, Pearl with Robinson, Hilary (1971), *Homes in High Flats: Some of the Human Problems Involved in Multi-storey Living*, Occasional Paper no. 13, Edinburgh: University of Glasgow Social and Economic Studies, Oliver and Boyd.

Keating, Michael (1988), *The City that Refused to Die. Glasgow: The Politics of Urban Regeneration*, Aberdeen: Aberdeen University Press.

McAllister, Ellen (1986), *Shadows on a Gorbals Wall*, Glasgow: Gorbals Fair Society.

McArthur, Andrew A. and Donnison, David (1992), *Gorbals Community Survey*, Glasgow: Centre for Housing Research.

McArthur, Alexander and Long, H. Kingsley (1957) [1935], *No Mean City*, London: Corgi Books.

McIntosh, Stewart (1994), 'Regeneration Gorbals-style', *The Herald*, Scotland's Homes section, 30 November, p. 1.

McKay, Ron (1995), *Mean City. The Shocking novel of Glasgow Gangland Life*, London: Hodder & Stoughton.

McKenzie, Joseph (1990), *Gorbals Children. A Study in Photographs*, Glasgow: Richard Drew Publishing.

McLay, Farquhar (1988), *Workers' City*, Glasgow: Clyde Press.

McNaughtan, Adam (1993) [1967], 'The Jeely Piece Song', in Hamish Whyte (ed.), *Mungo's Tongues. Glasgow Poems 1630–1990*, Edinburgh & London: Mainstream Publishing, pp. 192–3.

McPhee, Phil (1988), 'Hutchie E – A Monument to Corruption, Stupidity and Bad Planning', in Farquhar McLay, *Workers' City*, Glasgow: Clyde Press, pp. 47–48.

Markus, Thomas A. (1993), 'Comprehensive Development and Housing, 1945–75', in Peter Reed (ed.), *Glasgow: The Forming of the City*, Edinburgh: Edinburgh University Press, pp. 147–65.

Melling, Joseph (1989), 'Clydeside Rent Struggles and the Making of Labour Politics in Scotland, 1900–39', in Richard Rodger (ed.), *Scottish Housing in the Twentieth Century*, Leicester: Leicester University Press, pp. 54–88.

Perrett, Eddie (1990), *The Magic of the Gorbals*, Glasgow: Clydeside Press.

Rae, J.H. (1984), *Gorbals Local Plan. Draft Survey Report*, Glasgow: Glasgow District Council.

Reed, Peter (1993), 'The Tenement City', in Peter Reed (ed.), *Glasgow: The Forming of the City*, Edinburgh: Edinburgh University Press.

Robertson, William (1985), 'Labour Probe into Gorbals Land Deal', *The Glasgow Herald*, 29 June, p. 1.

Roy, Kenneth (1967), 'The Gorbals Still Waits for its Miracle', *The Glasgow Herald*, 27 March, p. 5.

The Gorbals 1965. A Christian Action Report on an Investigation into the Housing and Social Conditions of the Gorbals and Adjacent Slum Areas of Glasgow, London: Christian Action, nd *c*. 1966.

Watts, Stephen (1960), 'New Miracle in the Gorbals', *The Evening Times*, 11 January, p. 5. Copyright 1959, the New Yorker Magazine, Inc.

Watts, Stephen (1960), 'Bleak, Cold, Dirty', *The Evening Times*, 12 January, p. 5. Copyright 1959, the New Yorker Magazine, Inc.

Watts, Stephen (1960), 'Abject Poverty', *The Evening Times*, 13 January, p. 5. Copyright 1959, the New Yorker Magazine, Inc.

Watts, Stephen (1960), 'Fewer Pubs: The Drinking Men are None too Pleased', *The Evening Times*, 14 January, p. 5. Copyright 1959, the New Yorker Magazine, Inc.

Watts, Stephen (1960), 'Every Window is Curtained', *The Evening Times*, 20 January, p. 5. Copyright 1959, the New Yorker Magazine, Inc.

Worsdall, Frank (1979), *The Tenement: A Way of Life*, Edinburgh: Chambers.

Worsdall, Frank (1990), 'Introduction', in Joseph McKenzie, *Gorbals Children. A Study in Photographs*, Glasgow: Richard Drew Publishing, pp. 7–11.

General

Agnew, John, A. (1989), 'The Devaluation of Place in Social Science', in John A. Agnew and James S. Duncan (eds), *The Power of Place: Bringing Together Geographical and Sociological Imaginations*, Boston: Unwin Hyman, pp. 9–29.

Agnew, John A. and Duncan, James S. (eds) (1989), *The Power of Place: Bringing together geographical and sociological imaginations*, Boston: Unwin Hyman.

Allen, John, Massey, Doreen and Pryke, Michael (eds) (1999), *Unsettling Cities. Movement/Settlement*, London & New York: Routledge.

Bailly, G.H. and Desbat, J.P. (1973), *Les Ensembles Historiques dans la Reconquête Urbaine*, Paris: La Documentation française, no. 3969–3970.

Bardet, Gaston (1983), *L'Urbanisme*, 10th edn, Paris: Presses Universitaires de France.

Bass Warner Jr, Sam (1983), 'The Management of Multiple Urban Images', in Derek Fraser and Anthony Sutcliffe (eds), *The Pursuit of Urban History*, London: Edward Arnold, pp. 383–94.

Baudoui, Rémi (1990), 'Between Regionalism and Functionalism: French Reconstruction from 1940 to 1945', in Jeffrey M. Diefendorf (ed.), *Rebuilding Europe's Bombed Cities*, Basingstoke: Macmillan Press, pp. 31–47.

Bédarida, François (1983), 'The French Approach to Urban History: An Assessment of Recent Methodological Trends', in Derek Fraser and Anthony Sutcliffe (eds), *The Pursuit of Urban History*, London: Edward Arnold, pp. 395–406.

Berman, Marshall (1983), *All That is Solid Melts into Air: The Experience of Modernity*, London: Verso.

Bird, Jon, Curtis, Barry, Putman, Tim, Robertson, George and Tickner, Lisa (eds) (1993), *Mapping the Futures: Local Cultures, Global Changes*, London and New York: Routledge.

Blondel, Jean (1974), *Contemporary France: Politics, Society and Institutions*, London: Methuen.

Blowers, Andrew, Brook, Christopher, Dunleavy, Patrick and McDowell, Linda (eds) (1981), *Urban Change and Conflict: An Interdisciplinary Reader*, London: Harper and Row in association with Open University Press.

Booth, Charles (1984) [1889], *Descriptive Map of London Poverty*, London: London Topographical Society, Publication no. 130.

Bourdin, Pierre (1984), *Le Patrimoine Réinventé*, Paris: Presses Universitaires de France.

Boyer, M. Christine (1994), *The City of Collective Memory. Its Historical Imagery and Architectural Entertainments*, Cambridge, Mass: MIT Press.

Brevan, Claude (ed.) (1982), *Vivre en Ville: Éléments pour un débat*, Paris: Direction de l'Urbanisme et des Paysages, Service Technique de l'Urbanisme.

Brun, Jacques, (1985), 'Nouvelles approches', in Georges Duby (ed.), *Histoire de la France Urbaine*, Vol. 5, ed. Marcel Roncayolo, Paris: Seuil, pp. 333–91.

Brun, Jacques and Marcel Roncayolo (1985), 'Production de la ville et du bâti', in Georges Duby (ed.), *Histoire de la France Urbaine*, Vol. 5, ed. Marcel Roncayolo, Paris: Seuil, pp. 281–329.

Bruton, Michael J. (ed.) (1974), *The Spirit and Purpose of Planning*, London: Hutchison & Co.

Castells, Manuel (1983), *The City and the Grassroots – A Cross-cultural Theory of Urban Social Movements*, London: Arnold.

Castells, Manuel (1977), *The Urban Question*, London: Edward Arnold.

Castells, Manuel (1976), 'Mouvements urbains et voie démocratique vers le socialisme', *Autrement*, no. 6, September, pp. 199–203.

Castells, Manuel (1975), *Luttes Urbaines*, Paris: Maspero.

Cayton, Andrew R.L. (1997), 'On the Importance of Place, or, a Plea for Idiosyncrasy', *Journal of Urban History*, **24** (1), November, pp. 79–87.

Central Housing Advisory Committee (1961), *Homes for Today and Tomorrow* [Parker Morris Report], London: HMSO.

Chadwick, Edwin (*c.* 1965), *Housing Needs and Planning Policy. A Restatement of the problem of Housing need and 'Overspill' in England and Wales*, London: Routledge & Kegan Paul. First published London: Poor Law Commission, 1842.

Chaperon-Davidovitch, Elisabeth (1976), *Les Instruments de Planification Urbaine*, Paris: La Documentation Française, no. 4334–4335.

Chaplain, Jean-Michel (1984), *La chambre des tisseurs. Louviers: cité Drapière, 1680–1840*, Seyssel: Champ Vallon.

Cherki, Eddy and Mehl, Dominique (1976), 'Les luttes urbaines, facteurs de changement?', *Autrement*, no. 6, September, pp. 3–5.

Cherki, Eddy and Mehl, Dominique (1976), 'Quelles luttes? quels acteurs? quels résultats?', *Autrement*, no. 6, September, pp. 6–19.

Cherry, Gordon E. (1974), 'The Development of Planning Thought' in Michael J. Bruton (ed.), *The Spirit and Purpose of Planning*, London: Hutchison & Co.

Cherry, Gordon E. (1974), *The Evolution of British Town Planning: A History of Town Planning in the United Kingdom During the 20th Century and of the Royal Town Planning Institute, 1914–74*, Leighton Buzzard: Royal Town Planning Institute Edition.

Cherry, Gordon E. (1972), *Urban Change and Planning: A History of Urban Development in Britain since 1750*, Henley-on-Thames: G.T. Foulis & Co.

Choay, Françoise (1994), 'La règne de l'urbain et la morte de la ville', in Jean Dethier and Alain Guiheux (eds), *La Ville: Art et Architecture en Europe, 1870–1993*, Paris: Editions du Centre Pompidou, pp. 26–35.

Coing, Henri (1966), *Rénovation Urbaine et Changement Social: L'îlot no. 4 (Paris 13e)*, Paris: Les Editions Ouvrières.

Cosgrove, Denis (1989), 'Power and Place in the Venetian territories', in John A. Agnew and James S. Duncan (eds), *The Power of Place: Bringing*

Together Geographical and Sociological Imaginations, Boston: Unwin Hyman, pp. 104–23.

Cosgrove, Denis E. and Daniels, Stephen (eds) (1988), *The Iconography of Landscape: Essays on the Symbolic Representation, Design and Use of Past Environments*, Cambridge: Cambridge University Press.

Cosgrove, Denis E. (1984), *Social Formations and Symbolic Landscapes*, London: Croom Helm.

Coste, Michel (1985), 'Vivre en ville. Appropriation, appartenance, identité', in Georges Duby (ed.), *Histoire de la France Urbaine*, Vol. 5, ed. Marcel Roncayolo, Paris: Seuil, pp. 521–55.

Cullingworth, J.B. (1960), *Housing Needs and Planning Policy. A restatement of the problem of housing need and 'overspill' in England and Wales*, London: Routledge & Kegan Paul.

Cullingworth, J.B. (1974), *Town and Country Planning in Britain*, rev. 5th edn, London: George Allen & Unwin.

Cullingworth, J.B. (1976), *Town and Country Planning in Britain*, 6th edn, London: George Allen & Unwin.

Cullingworth, J.B. (1988), *Town and Country Planning in Britain* 10th edn, London: Unwin Hyman.

de Caumont, Robert (1976), 'Les GAM: une stratégie, des techniques pour changer le quotidien', *Autrement*, no. 6, September, pp. 156–67.

Depaule, Jean-Charles and Christian Topalov, (1998), 'Les mots de la ville', *Genèses*, no. 33, December, pp. 2–3.

Dethier, Jean and Guiheux, Alain (1994), *La Ville: Art et Architecture en Europe, 1870–1993*, Paris: Editions du Centre Pompidou.

Diefendorf, Jeffrey M. (ed.) (1990), *Rebuilding Europe's Bombed Cities*, Basingstoke: Macmillan Press.

Douglas, Mary (1986), *How Institutions Think*, Syracuse: Syracuse University Press.

Douglass, Mike and Friedmann, John (1998), *Cities for Citizens. Planning and the Rise of Civil Society in a Global Age*, Chichester: John Wiley & Sons.

Duby, Georges (ed.) (1985), *Histoire de la France Urbaine*, Vol. 5, ed. Marcel Roncayolo, Paris: Seuil.

Duc Nhuân, Nguyên (1976), 'Pièges et ambiguïtés de l'action militante', *Autrement*, no. 6, September, pp. 175–84.

Dunleavy, Patrick (1977), 'Protest and Quiescence in Urban Politics: A Critique of Some Pluralist and Structuralist Myths', *International Journal of Urban and Regional Research*, no. 1, pp. 193–215.

Dunleavy, Patrick (1980), *Urban Political Analysis*, London: MacMillan Press.

Engels, Friedrich (1984), *The Condition of the Working Class in England from Personal Observation and Authentic Sources*, London: Lawrence and Wishart. Originally published 1845 – English edn 1892.

Englander, David (1994), 'Alan Mayne, *The Imagined Slum*', *Urban History*, **21** (2), October, pp. 309–11.

Englander, David (1995), 'Urban History or Urban Historicism: Which? A Response to Alan Mayne', *Urban History*, **22** (3), December, pp. 390–91.

Esher, Lionel (1981), *A Broken Wave: The Rebuilding of England 1940–1980*, London: Allen Lane.

Fainstein, Susan S. and Norman I. Fainstein (1985), 'Economic Restructuring and the Rise of Urban Social Movements', *Urban Affairs Quarterly*, **21** (2), pp. 187–206.

Farnell, Richard (1983), *Local Planning in Four English Cities*, Aldershot: Gower.

Ferris, John (1972), *Participation in Urban Planning: The Barnsbury Case*, London: Bell, Social Administration Research Trust, Occasional Paper no. 48.

Fincher, Ruth and Jacobs, Jane M. (eds) (1998), *Cities of Difference*, New York & London: The Guilford Press.

Flamand, Jean-Luc, Perot, Michelle, Girault, Jacques, Fourcaut, Annie et al. (1981), *La Question du logement et le mouvement ouvrier français*, Paris: Les Editions de la Villette.

'Flashes from the Slums: Pictures Taken in Dark Places by the Lightning Process. Some of the Results of a Journey through the City with an Instantaneous Camera – the Poor, the Idle, and the Vicious', in Beaumont Newhall (ed.) (1980), *Photography: Essays and Images*, New York: Museum of Modern Art, pp. 155–57. From *The Sun* (New York), 12 February 1888.

Foucault, Michel (1971), *L'ordre du discours*, Paris: Editions Gallimard.

Fraser, Derek and Sutcliffe, Anthony (1983), *The Pursuit of Urban History*, London: Edward Arnold.

Gaudin, Jean-Pierre (1985), *L'Avenir en Plan: technique et politique dans la prévision urbaine 1900–1930*, Seyssel: Editions du Champ Vallon.

Garin, G. and Muret, J.P. (1981), 'Chronologie: 1958–1967', in P. Randet et al., *Trente-cinq ans d'urbanisme*, Paris: Centre de Recherche et de Recontres d'Urbanisme, p. 103.

Gibb, Andrew (1989), 'Policy and Politics in Scottish Housing since 1945', in Richard Rodger (ed.), *Scottish Housing in the Twentieth Century*, Leicester: Leicester University Press, pp. 155–83.

Gibson, Michael S. and Langstaff, Michael J. (1982), *An Introduction to Urban Renewal*, London: Hutchison.

Giddens, Anthony (1990), *The Consequences of Modernity*, Cambridge: Polity Press.

Glendinning, Miles and Muthesius, Stefan (1994), *Tower Block: Modern Public Housing in England, Scotland, Wales and Northern Ireland*, New Haven & London: Yale University Press Press/Paul Mellon Centre for Studies in British Art.

Grand Larousse de la langue française, Paris: Librairie Larousse, 1971.

Grand Robert de la langue française, 2nd edn, Paris: Le Robert, 1985.

Granlo Pires, Joao (1976), 'A Lisbonne: "Casa sim, barracas nao!"', *Autrement*, no. 6, September, pp. 104–14.

Halbwachs, Maurice (1971), *La topographie légendaire des évangiles en terre sainte*, 2nd edn, Paris: Presses Universitaires de France.

Halbwachs, Maurice (1976), *Les cadres sociaux de la mémoire*, Paris & Le Havre: Mouton.

Halbwachs, Maurice (1980), *The Collective Memory*, trans. Francis J. Ditter and Vida Yazdi Ditter, New York: Harper Colophon Books.

Harris, Richard (1987), 'The Social Movement in Urban Politics: A Reinterpretation of Urban Reform in Canada', *International Journal of Urban and Regional Research*, **11** (3), pp. 363–81.

Harvey, David (1973), *Social Justice and the City*, London: Edward Arnold.

Harvey, David (1985), *Consciousness and the Urban Experience*, Oxford: Basil Blackwell.

Harvey, David (1989), *The Conditon of Postmodernity: An Enquiry into the Origins of Cultural Change*, Oxford: Basil Blackwell.

Harvey, David (1993), 'From Space to Place and Back Again: Reflections on the Condition of Postmodernity', in Jon Bird, Barry Curtis, Tim Putnam, George Robertson and Lisa Tickner (eds), *Mapping the Futures: Local Cultures, Global Changes*, London & New York: Routledge, pp. 3–29.

Haupt, Heinz-Gerhard (1993), *Histoire Sociale de la France depuis 1789*, Paris: Editions de la Maison des Sciences de l'Homme.

Haupt, Heinz-Gerhard, with contributions from Crossick, Geoffrey and Kocka, Jürgen (1993), 'La Storia Comparata', *Passato e Presente*, **11** (28), pp. 19–51.

Huggins, Jackie, Huggins, Rita & Jacobs, Jane M. (1995), 'Kooramindanjie: Place and the Postcolonial', *History Workshop Journal*, no. 39, Spring, pp. 165–81.

Jacobs, Jane (1962), *The Death and Life of Great American Cities*, London: Jonathan Cape. First published New York: Random House, 1961.

Jess, Pat and Massey, Doreen (1995), 'The Contestation of Place', in Doreen Massey and Pat Jess (eds), *A Place in the World? Places, Cultures and Globalisation*, Oxford: The Open University/Oxford University Press, pp. 133–74.

Kaschuba, Wolfgang (2000), 'The Emergence and Transformation of Foundation Myths', in Stråth, Bo (ed.), *Myth and Memory in the Construction of Community*, Brussels: PIE-Peter Lang, pp. 217–26.

Kaye, James, 'Comparison, A Contingent Juxtaposition of Austria and Sweden', discussion paper presented at the European University Institute, Florence, 8 November 1999.

Keating, Michael and Boyle, Robin (1986), *Re-Making Urban Scotland: Strategies for Local Economic Development*, Edinburgh: Edinburgh University Press.

King, Geoff (1996), *Mapping Reality. An Explanation of Cultural Cartographies*, New York: St Martin's Press.

Kirby, D.A. (1979), *Slum Housing and Residential Renewal: The Case in Urban Britain*, London: Longman.

Kirby, Kathleen M. (1996), *Indifferent Boundaries: Spatial Concepts of Human Subjectivity*, New York: Guilford Press.

Kirk, Gwyneth (1980), *Urban Planning in a Capitalist Society*, London: Croom Helm.

Knox, Paul (1987), 'The Social Production of the Built Environment: Architects, Architecture and the Post-Modern City', *Progress in Human Geography*, **11**, pp. 354–77.

Knox, Paul (1994), *Urban Social Geography: An Introduction*, 3rd edn, Harlow: Longman Scientific and Technical.

Koselleck, Reinhart (1985), *Futures Past. On the Semantics of Historical Time*, Cambridge, Mass: MIT Press.

Lacaze, Jean-Paul (1990), *Les Méthodes de l'Urbanisme*, Paris: Presses Universitaires de France.

Lamarre, Christine (1998), 'La ville des géographes français de l'époque moderne, XVIIe–XVIIIe siècles', *Genèses*, no. 33, December, pp. 4–27.

Lawrence, Roderick (1992), 'Integrating Architectural, Social and Housing History', *Urban History*, **19** (1), April, pp. 39–63.

Le Galès, Patrick and Mawson, John (1994), *Management Innovations in Urban Policy: Lessons from France*, Working Paper, Luton: Local Government Management Board.

Lefebvre, Henri (1970), *La Révolution Urbaine*, Paris: Gallimard.

Lefebvre, Henri (1986) [1974], *La Production de l'Espace*, Paris: Anthropos.

Lefebvre, Henri (1991), *The Production of Space*, Oxford: Blackwell.

Lepetit, Bernard (1988), *Les Villes dans la France Moderne (1740–1840)*, Paris: Albin Michel.

Lepetit, Bernard (1993), 'Architecture, géographie, histoire: usages de l'échelle', *Genèses*, no. 13, Autumn, pp. 118–38.

Lepetit, Bernard (1993), 'Passé, présent et avenir des modèles urbains d'auto-organisation', in Bernard Lepetit and Denise Pumain (eds), *Temporalités Urbaines*, Paris: Anthropos, pp. 113–33.

Lepetit, Bernard (1993), 'Une herméneutique urbaine est-elle possible?', in Bernard Lepetit and Denise Pumain (eds), *Temporalités Urbaines*, Paris: Anthropos, pp. 287–99.

Lepetit, Bernard (1995), 'Le présent de l'histoire', in Bernard Lepetit (ed.), *Les Formes de l'expérience*, Paris: Albin Michel, pp. 273–97.

Lepetit, Bernard (ed.) (1995), *Les Formes de l'expérience*, Paris: Albin Michel.

Lepetit, Bernard and Pumain, Denise (eds) (1993), *Temporalités Urbaines*, Paris: Anthropos.

Lévi-Strauss, Claude (1962), *La Pensée Sauvage*, Paris: Plon.

Lévi-Strauss, Claude (1978), *Myth and Meaning*, London & Henley: Routledge & Kegan Paul.

Levy, Jean-Paul, (1990) 'Les quartiers anciens, une histoire qui finit bien?', in Jean-Paul Levy (ed.), *La réhabilitation des quartiers anciens et de l'habitat existant: Acteurs, procédures, effets et conséquences sociales*, Toulouse: Presses Universitaires du Mirail, pp. 11–18.

Lojkine, Jean (1975), 'Stratégies des grandes entreprises, politiques urbaines et mouvements sociaux urbains', *Sociologie du Travail*, no. 1, pp. 18–40.

Marcelloni, Maurizio (1976), 'L'Italie: un modèle?', *Autrement*, no. 6, September, pp. 82–92.

Marquis, Jean-Claude (1991), *L'Aménagement du Territoire et Urbanisme*, Hellemes: Ester.

Massey, Doreen (1993), 'Power-Geometry and a progressive sense of place', in Jon Bird, Barry Curtis, Tim Putnam, George Robertson and Lisa Tickner (eds), *Mapping the Futures: Local Cultures, Global Changes*, London & New York: Routledge, pp. 59–69.

Massey, Doreen (1994), *Space, Place and Gender*, Cambridge: Polity Press.

Massey, Doreen (1995), 'Places and Their Pasts', *History Workshop Journal*, no. 39, Spring, pp. 182–92.

Massey, Doreen (1995), 'The Conceptualization of Place', in Doreen Massey and Pat Jess (eds), *A Place in the World? Places, Cultures and Globalisation*, Oxford: The Open University and Oxford University Press, pp. 45–85.

Massey, Doreen and Jess, Pat (eds) (1995), *A Place in the World? Places, Cultures and Globalisation*, Oxford: The Open University and Oxford University Press.

Massey, Doreen & Jess, Pat (1995), 'Places and Cultures in an Uneven World', in Doreen Massey and Pat Jess (eds), *A Place in the World? Places, Cultures and Globalisation*, Oxford: The Open University and Oxford University Press, pp. 215–39.

Mayne, Alan (1993), *The Imagined Slum. Newspaper Representations in Three Cities, 1870–1914*, Leicester: Leicester University Press.

Mayne, Alan (1995), 'A Barefoot Childhood: So What? Imagining Slums and Reading Neighbourhoods', *Urban History*, **22** (3), December, pp. 380–389.

Mehl, Dominique (1975), 'Les luttes des résidents dans les grandes ensembles', *Sociologie du Travail*, no. 3, pp. 351–71.

Meller, Helen (1995), 'Urban Renewal and Citizenship: The Quality of Life in British Cities, 1890–1990', *Urban History*, **22** (1), May, pp. 63–84.

Merlin, Pierre (1991), *L'Urbanisme*, Paris: Presses Universitaires de France.

Merlin, Pierre and Choay, Françoise (eds) (1988), *Dictionnaire de l'Urbanisme et de l'Aménagement*, Paris: Presses Universitaires de France.

Merriman, John M. (1991), *The Margins of City Life. Explorations on the French Urban Frontier, 1815–1851*, Oxford and New York: Oxford University Press.

Middleton, Michael (1987), *Man Made the Town*, London: Bodley Head.

Midwinter, A. (1993), 'Shaping Scotland's New Local Authorities: Arguments, Options, Issues', *Local Government Studies*, **19** (3), pp. 351–67.

'Milan ou quand les travailleurs (s)'occupent des logements ...', *Place*, no. 5, autumn 1976, pp. 32–36.

Moe, Richard and Wilkie, Carter (1997), *Changing Places. Rebuilding Community in the Age of Sprawl*, New York: Henry Holt & Co.

Mollet, Albert (ed.) (1981), *Quand les habitants prennent la parole*, Paris: Plan Construction.

Montale, Eugenio (1980) *L'opera in versi*, Torino: Giulio Einaudi editore.

Morel, Martine (1987), 'Reconstruire, dirent-ils. Discours et doctrines de l'urbanisme', in Danièle Voldman (ed.), *Images, Discours et Enjeux de la Reconstruction des Villes Françaises après 1945*, Paris: Cahiers de l'Institut d'histoire du temps présent, no. 5, June, pp. 13–49.

Mullins, Patrick (1987), 'Community and Urban Movements', *Sociological Review*, **35** (2), pp. 347–69.

Newhall, Beaumont (ed.) (1980), *Photography: Essays and Images*, New York: Museum of Modern Art.

Niethammer, Lutz (2000), 'Maurice Halbwachs: Memory and the Feeling of Identity', in Bo Stråth, (ed.), *Myth and Memory in the Construction of Community*, Brussels: PIE-Peter Lang, pp. 75–93.

Nora, Pierre (1984), 'Entre Mémoire et Histoire; la problématique des lieux', in Pierre Nora (ed.), *Les Lieux de Mémoire, I, La République*, Paris: Gallimard, pp. xv–xlii.

Nora, Pierre, (ed.) (1984), *Les Lieux de Mémoire. I: La République*, Paris: Gallimard.

Oxford English Dictionary, 2nd edn, Oxford: Clarendon Press, 1989.

Pickvance, C. (1985), 'The Rise and Fall of Urban Movements and the Role of Comparative Analysis', *Environment and Planning D: Society and Space*, **3**, pp. 31–53.

Pickvance, C.G. (ed.) (1976), *Urban Sociology: Critical Essays*, New York: St Martin's Press.

Pierre, Christian (1976), 'Intégrer ces luttes dans le combat politique', *Autrement*, no. 6, September, pp. 135–39.

Pratt, Geraldine (1998), 'Grids of Difference: Place and Identity Formation', in Ruth Fincher and Jane Jacobs (eds), *Cities of Difference*, New York and London: The Guilford Press, pp. 26–48.

Randet, P., Arrou-Vignod, M., Lion, R., Garin, G. and Muret, J.P. (1981), *Trente-cinq ans d'urbanisme*, Paris: Centre de Recherche et de Recontres d'Urbanisme.

Ratcliffe, John (1974), *An Introduction to Town and Country Planning*, London: Hutchison Educational.

Ravetz, Alison (1980), *Remaking Cities*, London: Croom Helm.

Ravetz, Alison (1986), *The Government of Space: Town Planning in Modern Society*, London: Faber & Faber.

Reade, Eric (1987), *British Town and Country Planning*, Milton Keynes: Open University Press.

Reintges, Claudia, M. (1990), 'Urban Movements in South African Black Townships: A Case Study', *International Journal of Urban and Regional Research*, **14** (1), pp. 109–34.

Rodger, Richard (1989), *Housing in Urban Britain 1780–1914. Class, Capitalism and Construction*, Basingstoke and London: Macmillan.

Rodger, Richard (1989), 'Introduction', in Rodger, Richard (ed.), *Scottish Housing in the Twentieth Century*, Leicester: Leicester University Press, pp. 1–24.

Rodger, Richard (ed.) (1989), *Scottish Housing in the Twentieth Century*, Leicester: Leicester University Press.

Rodger, Richard (1993), 'Construir la historia de la vivienda: dimensiones historiográficas del paisaje urbano británico', *Historia Urbana*, no. 2, pp. 39–59.

Rodger, Richard and Al-Qaddo, Hunain (1989), 'The Scottish Special Housing Association and the Implementation of Housing Policy, 1937–87', in Richard Rodger (ed.), *Scottish Housing in the Twentieth Century*, Leicester: Leicester University Press, pp. 184–213.

Rose, Gillian (1993), 'Some Notes Towards Thinking about the Spaces of the Future', in Jon Bird, Barry Curtis, Tim Putnam, George Robertson and Lisa Tickner (eds), *Mapping the Futures: Local Cultures, Global Changes*, London and New York: Routledge, pp. 70–83.

Rousseau, Denis and Vauzeilles, Georges (1992), *L'Aménagement Urbain*, Paris: Presses Universitaires de France.

Rowntree, Lester B. and Conkey, Margaret W. (1980), 'Symbolism and the Cultural Landscape', *Annals of the Association of American Geographers*, **70** (4), December, pp. 459–74.

Samuel, Raphael (1990), 'The Philosophy of Brick', *New Formations*, no. 11, summer, pp. 45–55.

Sandweiss, Eric (1997), 'Searching for a "Sense of Place" ', *Journal of Urban History*, **24** (1), November, pp. 88–96.

Saunier, Pierre-Yves (1994), 'La ville en quartiers: découpages de la ville en histoire urbaine', *Genèses*, no. 15, March, pp. 103–14.

Savitch, H.V. (1988), *Post-Industrial Cities: Politics and Plans in New York, Paris and London*, Princeton, NJ: Princeton University Press.

Scottish Consumer Council (1983), *The Tenants' Handbook: A Guide to the Repair, Maintenance and Modernisation of Council Houses in Scotland*, Glasgow: Assist Architects.

Scottish Housing Advisory Committee (1967), *Scotland's Older Houses*, HMSO.

Shaffer, Frank (1970), *The New Town Story*, London: Palladin.

Smith, Michael Peter (1980), *The City and Social Theory*, Oxford: Basil Blackwell.

Soja, Edward W. (1989), *Postmodern Geographies: The Reassertion of Space in Critical Social Theory*, London: Verso.

Stråth, Bo (2000), 'Introduction. Myth, Memory and History in the Construction of Community', in Bo Stråth (ed.), *Myth and Memory in the Construction of Community*, Brussels: PIE-Peter Lang, pp. 19–46.

Sutcliffe, Anthony (1981), *Towards The Planned City*, Oxford: Basil Blackwell.

Sutcliffe, Anthony (1994), 'La Reconstruction en Grande-Bretagne', in Jean Dethier and Alain Guiheux, (eds), *La Ville: Art et Architecture en Europe, 1870–1993*, Paris: Editions du Centre Pompidou, pp. 410–11.

Tilly, Charles (1976), 'Major Forms of Collective Action in Western Europe 1500–1975', *Theory and Society*, **3** (3), Fall, pp. 365–75.

Topalov, Christian (1987), *Le Logement en France: histoire d'une marchandise impossible*, Paris: Presses de la Fondation nationale des sciences politiques.

Topalov, Christian (1990), 'La ville "congestionnée". Acteurs et langage de la reforme urbaine à New York au début du XXe siècle.', *Genèses*, no.1, September, pp. 86–111.

Topalov, Christian (1991), 'La ville "Terre Inconnue". L'enquête de Charles Booth et le peuple de Londres, 1886–1891', *Genèses*, no. 5, September, pp. 5–34.

Toulmin, Stephen (1990), *Cosmopolis: The Hidden Agenda of Modernity*, New York: Free Press.

Touraine, Alain (1978), *La voix et le regard*, Paris: Seuil.

Touraine, Alain (1988), *Return of the Actor: Social Theory in Postindustrial Society*, Minneapolis: University of Minnesota Press.

Touraine, Alain (1995), *Critique of Modernity*, Oxford: Blackwell.

Urban Vestero, Dick (1973), 'L'influence des citoyens sur les plans d'aménagement du milieu physique', *Espaces et Sociétés*, no. 8, February, pp. 131–34.

Vayssière, Bruno (1994), 'La Reconstruction en France', in Jean Dethier and Alain Guiheux, *La Ville: Art et Architecture en Europe, 1870–1993*, Paris: Editions du Centre Pompidou, p. 412.

Voldman, Danièle (ed.) (1987), *Images, Discours et Enjeux de la Reconstruction des Villes Françaises après 1945*, Cahiers de l'Institut d'histoire du temps présent, no. 5, Paris: Centre national de la recherche scientifique.

Ward, Stephen V. (1994), *Planning and Urban Change*, London: Paul Chapman Publishing.

Werlen, Benno (1993), *Society, Action and Space*, London: Routledge.

White, Hayden (2000), 'Catastrophe, Communal Memory and Mythic Discourse: The Uses of Myth in the Reconstruction of Society' in Bo Stråth (ed.), *Myth and Memory in the Construction of Community*, Brussels: PIE-Peter Lang, pp.49–74.

Whitehand, J.W.R. and Larkham, P.J. (eds) (1992), *Urban Landscapes: International Perspectives*, London: Routledge.

Withers, Charles W.J. (1995), 'Geography, Natural History and the Eighteenth Century Enlightenment: Putting the World in Place', *History Workshop Journal*, issue 39, spring, pp. 137–63.

Yelling, Jim (1995), 'Public Policy, Urban Renewal and Property Ownership, 1945–55', *Urban History*, **22**, May, pp. 48–62.

Young, Michael and Willmott, Peter (1957), *Family and Kinship in East London*, London: Routledge & Kegan Paul.

Zukin, Sharon (1991), *Landscapes of Power: From Detroit to Disney World*, Berkeley and Oxford: University of California Press.

Index